INSTRUMENTS OF PEACEMAKING 1918–1941

This book is a sequel to *Instruments of Peacemaking 1870–1914* in that it looks at how attempts were made to settle disputes between states without recourse to war after 'the war to end all wars'.

It considers the idealism of President Woodrow Wilson's Fourteen Points which formed the basis for the Armistice in 1918, and his scheme for a League of Nations providing for self-determination of nations and 'collective security' for European states.

It goes on to analyse the key challenges that faced statesmen and jurists in attempting to resolve disputes under the provisions of the Treaty of Versailles. It considers the consequences of the Peace Conference of 1919 as well as defects in the treaty as an instrument for resolving future disputes and tensions between the victors and the vanquished.

Cases referred to the Reparations Commission and to arbitration under the Treaty of Versailles regarding boundary, industrial property, and shipping including the Lusitania claims are considered. More importantly, it analyses the diplomatic challenges faced by statesmen after 1919. The decline and failure of Wilsonian idealism, the League of Nations, collective security, and diplomacy are traced through the various diplomatic exchanges that took place between governments from official records and contemporaneous accounts of the times as well as academic sources. Mr Chamberlain's private diplomacy to appease Hitler is critically analysed. The final chapter briefly considers aspects of America's isolationism resulting in the attack on Pearl Harbor and her peacetime state of unreadiness.

Instruments of Peacemaking 1918–1941

The Failure of Diplomacy

Michael Reynolds

• HART •
OXFORD • LONDON • NEW YORK • NEW DELHI • SYDNEY

HART PUBLISHING

Bloomsbury Publishing Plc

Kemp House, Chawley Park, Cumnor Hill, Oxford, OX2 9PH, UK

1385 Broadway, New York, NY 10018, USA

Bloomsbury Publishing Ireland Limited, 29 Earlsfort Terrace, Dublin 2, D02 AY28, Ireland

First published in Great Britain 2025

A catalogue record for this book is available from the British Library.

A catalogue record for this book is available from the LIbrary of Congress.

Library of Congress Control Number: 2025946148

ISBN: HB: 978-1-50997-628-7
ePDF: 978-1-50997-630-0
ePub: 978-1-50997-629-4

Typeset by Compuscript Ltd, Shannon

For product safety related questions contact productsafety@bloomsbury.com

To find out more about our authors and books visit www.hartpublishing.co.uk. Here you will find extracts, author information, details of forthcoming events and the option to sign up for our newsletters.

PREFACE

This book is a continuum of the earlier study *Instruments of Peacemaking 1870–1914* which considered certain legal and geopolitical disputes resolved by diplomatic means, or by enquiry, arbitration, or mediation as appropriate. This sequel adheres to that approach but focuses more on the diplomatic methods of British, French, American and German statesmen who were involved in crisis management during the interwar years. After the Great War 'a war to end all wars', statesmen attempted to formulate an international order replacing the old Concert System on an extended franchise. This was principally promoted by President Woodrow Wilson, a proponent of universalism, collective security, and self-determination, an ideal which was outstripped by practical realpolitik. Regrettably, Wilson's untimely death resulted in American abstentionism and isolationism and left Europe much to its own devices. Likewise, Aristide Briand's[1] aspirations of a United States of Europe (a dream espoused by Professor Seeley in 1871)[2] were never realised when Briand died.

This period, told by many eminent historians, statesmen and former diplomats, whose works are referred to in this monograph, was a period of aspirational beliefs in the efficacy of the League of Nations and hopes for world peace. Contrary to Wilsonian principles, these times witnessed a decline in the prestige of the western democracies and the rise of totalitarianism in Italy, Spain, Germany and Japan, juxtaposing the Bolshevik regime in Russia. Whereas the victors of 1918 disarmed, the defeated rearmed, with the victors being outwitted by the dictators in the Rhineland, Abyssinia, Austria, and the Sudetenland. The policy of appeasement, complacency in the face of aggression, and fear of war resulted in the betrayal and loss of Czechoslovakia. Such events have given rise to debate, especially over the Munich Agreement and the argument that the surrender of Czechoslovakia and a period to prepare for war justified that agreement. The evidence of the circumstances ascertained in a diplomatic and security context is examined in chapter four adding substance to the admonitions of Churchill, Eden, Macmillan, Amory, Nicolson, John Wheeler Bennett, Vansittart, Robert Bruce Lockhart and the British Military Attache in Prague, among others.

The period up to 1926 considered in chapter three draws upon Sir Austen Chamberlain's[3] reflections made at the Imperial Conference on 20 October 1926.[4] He reminded the delegates of Lord Curzon's words that we could not, even if we would, extricate ourselves from the entanglements of our duty and our destiny. 'We are in the

[1] Served 11 times as Prime Minister of France. He held 26 ministerial posts between 1906 and 1932.
[2] M Reynolds, *Instruments of Peacemaking 1870 to 1914* (Oxford, Hart Publishing, 2021) 1.
[3] The then Foreign Secretary.
[4] DBFP 919–958 Ser. 1A. Vol 2: *The Termination of Military Control in Germany. Middle Eastern and American Questions 1926–1927* Appendix. See also ch 5.

centre of a great world whirlpool, and we are affected by every movement of its waters.' This echoed what may be considered the British interest that the continent would not be dominated by a single power and that the Channel Ports would not be occupied by a hostile power. Yet in that postwar period, the victors of 1918 failed to reconcile Germany, although some attempts were made to bring her into the international community-the League of Nations. It is arguable whether 'the guilt clause' of the Versailles Treaty and reparations were a catalyst for extremism, but they were a contributory factor along with the Allies' neglect for the internal problems afflicting Germany after the Armistice.

The social effects in the interwar period were transmogrified into the national psyche and reflected in the outlook of the political class and public opinion; a public opinion that naturally rebelled against another war until it was too late to stop it. The irony of the interwar years is the contradiction in that shift of public opinion. Those who like Norman Angell[5] warned in 1932 and 1933 about the breaking of treaties, the flagrant disregard for international law norms, and the rise of dictatorships were told by conservative journalists that they were intolerant mischief makers and war-minded.[6] Yet in 1938 those same conservative journalists were presenting those same warnings somewhat too little too late. So far as foreign policy was concerned, it was led by politicians who naturally bowed to public opinion represented by a majority that refused to listen until something like a catastrophe occurred.[7] This not only reflected the British experience but also the American, where isolationists and America Firsters believed that European problems were none of their business and they could carry on regardless of any war in Europe. The light only dawned on Americans when they realised that if Britain was defeated and its fleet captured or sunk, the Americas would be at the mercy of a Nazi neighbour.

In hindsight it is easier to identify the mistakes of the past, but in the times of those events what was obvious to some was not obvious to others. Why? The reasons are not simple but a combination of social, economic and political tendencies. In this period, we can now see the inherent difficulties with the Versailles Treaty as considered in chapter one giving cause for resentment. We can see the failure by Britain and America to give France security guarantees, which might have avoided her occupation of the Saar and the Rhineland; the initial failure to admit Germany to the League of Nations; the implementation of a reparations policy that was an economic contradiction when Germany was prevented from expanding her economy to meet the debt payments; critically, the failure of the United States Congress to enable membership of the League of Nations their President having been its leading protagonist; and, in light of the rise of the dictators, failing to rearm to deter foreseeable aggression, as is discussed in chapters three and four. Underlying these failures was the failure of statesmen to exploit the advantage of a world assembly unique in world history. In the end it was national interests that overrode any internationalist approach and a desire for domination. These factors are considered in this discourse, as has been indicated, and finally, as with the prequel,

[5] Author, journalist and Labour MP (1929–31). He received the Nobel Peace Prize primarily for his book *The Great Illusion* in 1934. Member, Commission Exécutive de la Société des Nations (Executive Committee of the League of Nations Union and of National Peace Council).

[6] N Angell, *Peace with the Dictators*? (London, Hamish Hamilton, 1938) 219.

[7] ibid 220.

a tenuous Anglo-American relationship is considered pre-1941. Failure to achieve a closer understanding encouraged totalitarianism and dictatorship in the Axis countries. Had the ideals of Wilson and the concerns of Roosevelt been acknowledged, then the democracies would have been strengthened in their resolve to preserve democracy and the rule of law. That only became possible when Winston Churchill became Britain's Prime Minister and led to an Atlantic Alliance and a new world order.

ACKNOWLEDGEMENTS

This study was undertaken at the International Relations Department of the London School of Economics with its vast library resources. In addition, research was undertaken at The Royal Institute of Foreign Affairs. In the main, the study relies on biographies and diaries of British, American, French and Russian politicians, journalists, diplomats and statesmen who played leading roles in this period. I also rely on *Hansard*, Documents on British Foreign Policy, Documents of German Foreign Policy, the French Yellow Book, Foreign Relations of the United States, and numerous other works by historians on diplomacy in that period giving both contemporary and revisionist views. I found the *American Journal of International Law* an excellent reference for the unpublished Awards made under various treaties in the interwar years. I must thank the Librarian of the United States Congress for her assistance in locating information related to the defence of Hawaii before 1941, and to Hart Publications and the editorial team Chris Harrison, Verity Stuart and Kate Whetter. Two diplomats inspired my interest in this subject. The first, Mr J.C. Borkowski my former Principal in the Westminster firm of Graham Page & Co, a former member of the Polish Embassy in Berlin (1935–39) who escaped from the Gestapo then came to England and joined the Polish Armoured Brigade. He was a barrister by profession but transferred to become a solicitor. The second, Sir Brian Crowe, was introduced to me in 2016 at Chatham House. At that time Brexit was taking hold, and he and I had many discussions as to the risks of leaving Europe. Principally my concern and his was the security of Europe because Europe's security is our security. It was Brian who suggested I read a book on Munich, and I suppose it was that coupled with my reminiscences of what Borkowski had told me that has inspired this work. Underlying that, I could not forget the sacrifices my father's generation made for our survival. He fought at Arnhem.

CONTENTS

TABLE OF CASES

TABLE OF LEGAL AND RELATED INSTRUMENTS

1

A New International Order or a Precarious Armistice[1]

I. Reflections on International Law

In *Instruments of Peacemaking 1870-1914*, reference was made to the attempts at the Hague Conferences 1899 and 1907 to find a better way to settle international disputes between states. As indicated in that text, the Geneva Arbitration was a model for settling disputes between states by arbitration instead of by force. One of the pioneers of that approach was the eminent American jurist Elihu Root.[2] He made many speeches in defence of international arbitration. One particular extract is worth quoting:[3]

> … whilst it is highly important to have controversies between nations settled by arbitration rather than by war, and the growth of sentiment in favour of that peaceable method of settlement is one of the great advances in civilisation to the credit of this generation; yet the true basis of peace among men is to be found in a just and considerate spirit among the people who rule our modern democracies, in their regard for the rights of other countries, and in their desire to be fair and kindly in the treatment of the subjects which give rise to international controversies.

When Root addressed the first meeting of the American Society of International Law in 1907 on the question of the Japanese Treaty and the San Francisco School Board Resolution, which prohibited Japanese children from attending public schools in California, he argued against such discrimination:

> There was one great and serious question underlying the whole subject which made all questions of construction and of scope and effect of the treaty itself- all questions as to whether the claims of Japan were well founded or not; all questions as to whether the resolution of the school board was valid or not- seem temporary and comparatively unimportant. It was not a question of war with Japan … There never was even friction between the two governments. The question was: What state of feeling would be created between the great body of the people of Japan as a result of the treatment given to Japanese in this country?

[1] JC Strendale Bennett, *No.1 Foreign Office Memorandum respecting the Locarno Treaties* [C 797/1/18] (Central Department Foreign Office) 10 January 1926 describing the Treaty of Versailles as: 'rather a prolonged, and sometimes even a precarious, armistice.

[2] Root held various offices of state and although an exponent of arbitration he, a Republican, opposed President Wilson's League Covenant and American membership of the League of Nations.

[3] 'Addresses by Elihu Root on International Subjects' (1918) 12 *AJIL* 17. Reproduced with permission of the Licensor through PLSclear.

> What was to be the effect upon that proud, sensitive, highly civilised people across the Pacific, of the discourtesy, insult, imputations of the inferiority, and abuse aimed at them in the columns of American newspapers and from the platforms of American public meetings? What would be the effect upon our own people of the responses that natural resentment of such treatment would elicit from the Japanese?
>
> It is hard for democracy to learn the responsibilities of its power; but the people now, not governments, make friendship or dislike, sympathy or discord, peace or war, between nations … The people who permit themselves to treat the people of other countries with discourtesy and insult are surely sowing the wind to reap the whirlwind for a world of sullen and revengeful hatred can never be a world of peace.

Root was speaking 47 years after the establishment of the German Empire, which by 1890 appeared 'stable and secure' as a result of Bismarck's foreign policy,[4] but after his dismissal and the earlier expiration of Bismarck's *Dreikaiserbund*[5] in 1887 that policy and established balance was transformed into a system of two alliances by the Kaiser's approach. The mood was caught by the American minister in Vienna, Bartlett Tripp, in his dispatch to Secretary of State Richard Olney:[6]

> Europe is one armed camp, and every lighting flash from diplomatic wires is like the firing of a sentry gun -a call to arms.

According to Spring Rice writing to President Theodore Roosevelt in September 1896:[7]

> … it looks like the gathering of great forces for a struggle, not in the immediate. (that will be better) but in the far future … Owing to Alsace and Lorraine Europe is hopelessly divided …

Germany was perceived as a threat by France and Russia, who were joined by Britain in the Triple Entente of 1907 to deter Germany's aggressive intentions. According to Graebner and Bennett, this represented 'Europe's ultimate massing of power in defence of the old order'.[8] Such was the background to World War I which may have some resemblances to the period of this study.

II. The Utopian Dreams of Wilson and Briand

According to de Launay, Aristide Briand was of a mediative disposition and adopted a constructive approach to issues but had no sense of organisation. Briand considered that the solution to the Franco-German problem lay in economics: an expanded

[4] NA Graebner and EM Bennett, *The Versailles Treaty and its Legacy: The Failure of the Wilsonian Vision* (Cambridge, CUP, 2011) 2.

[5] Bismarck had persuaded the three Emperors of Prussia, Austria and Russia to form an unofficial alliance following the creation to the Second German Empire in 1872.

[6] NA Graebner and EM Bennett, *The Versailles Treaty and its Legacy: The Failure of the Wilsonian Vision* (Cambridge, CUP, 2011) 3; Tripp to Olney, dispatch no. 175, 18 January 1896, Diplomatic Dispatches, Austria, RG59.

[7] Quoted in NA Graebner and EM Bennett, *The Versailles Treaty and its Legacy: The Failure of the Wilsonian Vision* (Cambridge, CUP, 2011) 2; Spring Rice to Theodore Roosevelt, 14 September 1896 in S Gwynn (ed), *The Letters and Friendships of Sir Cecil Spring-Rice: A Record* (London, 1929) 1: 210–211.

[8] NA Graebner and EM Bennett, *The Versailles Treaty and its Legacy: The Failure of the Wilsonian Vision* (Cambridge, CUP, 2011) 4.

European economic market applying a 'horizontal method' to industrial organisation, a plan devised by his friend Loucheur.[9] His views corresponded to those of Coudenhove-Kalergi's[10] idea of 'Pan-Europe' which was supported by Beneš and Stresemann.[11] Loucheur became chairman of the Pan European Economic Council and proposed industrial European combines. He envisaged the elimination of customs barriers and a common market.[12] Unfortunately for those who advocated a United Europe or a United States of Europe, it was not until 14 January 1938 that a committee was actually set up to study 'the conditions under which economic solidarity of European nations can be best realised'.[13]

In a speech to the League of Nations on 1 September 1929, Briand made a famous appeal to the League stating that:[14]

> … I believe that among peoples who are geographically grouped as are the nations of Europe there should exist a sort of federal bond … I am also sure that from the political and social points of view this federal bond may be beneficial, without infringing upon the sovereignty of nations who become members of such an association.

On 17 May 1930 the Pan European Congress organised by Coudenhove and Loucheur opened in Berlin. Sadly, the initiative was frustrated by the Wall Street Crash of 1929 and the death of Stresemann. Interestingly, two English conservative MPs, Winston Churchill and Leo Amery who attended the conference were enthusiastic supporters of a united Europe, although Britain had reservations because of its imperial interests.[15] In Hungary and Romania, Loucheur, who was promoting the idea, was most warmly welcomed. At a meeting he had in Hungary with Horthy and Count Bethlen, it was suggested that Hungary and the Little Entente should consider elementary tariffs and work for European economic union.[16] Hungary's support, like Romania, Lithuania and Poland's was conditional, but Britain rejected the idea. Briand made a further appeal to the League of Nations on 11 September 1930, as a result of which a Committee of Investigation was established on 16 September to study the question of a United States of Europe and to make a report. Ten meetings took place until 1932 without meaningful results.[17] Briand's last appeal was surpassed by the Wall Street Crash of October 1929 and the Great Depression. That depression gave oxygen to extreme nationalist movements in Spain, Italy and Germany based on an ideology of racial superiority. Briand's idea was, as de Launay suggests, the last hurrah of the moderates of Versailles to forestall the division and dissension that was to follow.

[9] Louis Loucheur (1872–1931) was a French industrialist and politician. Having been an artillery lieutenant, he became undersecretary of state for artillery and munitions and later as an armaments minister. He supported Aristide Briand's European policy and is considered one of the spiritual fathers of the European Union.

[10] Count Richard Coudenhove-Kalergi founded the Pan-European Union, offering a vision of peaceful, democratic unity for Europe.

[11] J de Launay, *Major Controversies of Contemporary History* (Oxford, Pergamon Press, 1965) 125–127.

[12] ibid 127.

[13] ibid 128.

[14] Speech of Aristide Briand to the 10th General Assembly of the League of Nations, 1 September 1929.

[15] J. de Launay, *Major Controversies of Contemporary History* (Oxford, Pergamon Press, 1965) 129.

[16] ibid 129.

[17] ibid 130.

A. 'Unless justice be done to others it will not be done to us'[18]

In his address to Congress on 8 January 1918, President Woodrow Wilson considered how peace would be realised. The process would be open with no secret arrangements. He declared that the war had made America's position impossible. Every nation should be free to determine its own institutions and to 'be assured of justice and fair dealing by the other peoples of the world as against force and selfish aggression'. He then went on to define his Fourteen Points:

I. Open covenants of peace openly arrived at, after which there shall be no private international understandings of any kind but diplomacy shall proceed always frankly and in the public view.

II. Absolute freedom of navigation upon the seas, outside territorial waters, alike in peace and in war, except as the seas may be closed in whole or in part by international action for the enforcement of international covenants.

III. The removal, so far as possible, of all economic barriers and the establishment of an equality of trade conditions among all the nations consenting to the peace and associating themselves for its maintenance.

IV. Adequate guarantees given and taken that national armaments will be reduced to the lowest point consistent with domestic safety.

V. A free, open-minded, and absolutely impartial adjustment of all colonial claims, based upon a strict observance of the principle that in determining all such questions of sovereignty the interests of the populations concerned must have equal weight with the equitable claims of the government whose title is to be determined.

VI. The evacuation of all Russian territory and such a settlement of all questions affecting Russia as will secure the best and freest cooperation of the other nations of the world in obtaining for her an unhampered and unembarrassed opportunity for the independent determination of her own political development and national policy and assure her of a sincere welcome into the society of free nations under institutions of her own choosing; and, more than a welcome, assistance also of every kind that she may need and may herself desire. The treatment accorded Russia by her sister nations in the months to come will be the acid test of their good will, of their comprehension of her needs as distinguished from their own interests, and of their intelligent and unselfish sympathy.

VII. Belgium, the whole world will agree, must be evacuated and restored, without any attempt to limit the sovereignty which she enjoys in common with all other free nations. No other single act will serve as this will serve to restore confidence among the nations in the laws which they have themselves set and determined for the government of their relations with one another. Without this healing act the whole structure and validity of international law is forever impaired.

VIII. All French territory should be freed and the invaded portions restored, and the wrong done to France by Prussia in 1871 in the matter of Alsace-Lorraine, which has unsettled the peace of the world for nearly fifty years, should be righted, in order that peace may once more be made secure in the interest of all.

IX. A readjustment of the frontiers of Italy should be effected along clearly recognizable lines of nationality.

[18] President Woodrow Wilson Address to the Congress of the United States 8 January 1918.

X. The peoples of Austria-Hungary, whose place among the nations we wish to see safeguarded and assured, should be accorded the freest opportunity of autonomous development.

XI. Rumania, Serbia, and Montenegro should be evacuated; occupied territories restored; Serbia accorded free and secure access to the sea; and the relations of the several Balkan states to one another determined by friendly counsel along historically established lines of allegiance and nationality; and international guarantees of the political and economic independence and territorial integrity of the several Balkan states should be entered into.

XII. The Turkish portions of the present Ottoman Empire should be assured a secure sovereignty, but the other nationalities which are now under Turkish rule should be assured an undoubted security of life and an absolutely unmolested opportunity of an autonomous development, and the Dardanelles should be permanently opened as a free passage to the ships and commerce of all nations under international guarantees.

XIII. An independent Polish state should be erected which should include the territories inhabited by indisputably Polish populations, which should be assured a free and secure access to the sea, and whose political and economic independence and territorial integrity should be guaranteed by international covenant.

XIV. A general association of nations must be formed under specific covenants for the purpose of affording mutual guarantees of political independence and territorial integrity to great and small states alike.

These precepts were of common interest to those fighting the war against the Central Powers but not wishing 'to injure her [Germany] or to block in any way her legitimate influence or power', but rather to trade peacefully 'in covenants of justice and law and fair dealing'. The object was equality between nations instead of mastery.[19] The difficulty in negotiating with the *Kaiserreich* (German Empire) was whether to deal 'with the Reichstag majority, or for the military party and the men whose creed is imperial domination'.

He aspired to apply

> the principle of justice to all peoples and nationalities, and their right to live on equal terms of liberty and safety with one another, whether they be strong or weak. Unless this principle be made its foundation no part of the structure of international justice can stand.

It was a final war, he said, for human liberty.

Wilson's Fourteen Points laid the foundation for a new world order to replace the concert system that had broken down when Italy and Austria-Hungary unilaterally acted in defiance of the concert, but in their own national interest over the Balkan wars in 1913.[20] Wilson's construct comprised democracy, collective security, and self-determination. Ronald Steel opines that Wilson's solution to the war was democracy and a form of collective sovereignty.[21] Wilson's ideal was morally defensible, but in *Realpolitik* it did not preclude the national interest that drove Austria-Hungary and Italy

[19] In the context of ch 4 and the subterfuge used by Hitler in his conversations with Chamberlain he acted as Germany was the victim and never treated equally. He also placed heavy reliance on Article XIV of Wilson's Fourteen Points.

[20] MP Reynolds, *Instruments of Peacemaking 1870-1914* (Oxford, Hart Publishing, 2020) 274.

[21] R Steel, 'Prologue: 1919-1945-1989' in M Boeneke, G Feldman and E Glasser (eds), *Treaty of Versailles: Reassessment After 75 Years* (Cambridge, Cambridge University Press, 2008).

to abandon the concert in 1913. Carr[22] disdained the high-flown rhetoric of Wilson, which disguised, in his view, an imperial American ambition. Carr believed that the Wilsonian ideal of liberalism through self-determination was self-defeating to his 'bourgeois democracy' and 'international concord'.[23] Lentin suggested that Wilsonian liberalism had its roots in Jeffersonian democracy and Gladstonian liberalism with 'high minded justice subdued by national interests and resurgent imperial ambitions'.[24]

i. Self Determination: An Impractical Ideal?

Wilson's idea of self-determination (which in this case he only meant to apply to Europe)[25] was a laudable ideal in theory, but difficult to apply in practice. Wilson was very much influenced by his own domestic reforms, which he attempted to translate into a progressive foreign policy; hence his adherence to free trade, open agreements democracy and self-determination. The German government did not take part in the negotiations leading to the treaties. They were presented with the draft treaty on which to make observations, but to all intents it was a fait accompli.[26] Wilson believed in an ethical foreign policy, which was reflected in his Fourteen Points, but when applied in the practice of the Peace Conference in 1919, Harold Nicolson suggested the contrary:[27]

> It is impossible to read the German criticism without deriving the impression that the Paris Peace Conference was guilty of disguising an Imperialistic peace under the surplus of Wilsonism, that seldom in the history of man has such vindictiveness cloaked itself in such unctuous sophistry. Hypocrisy was the predominant and unescapable result.

So far as the Great Powers were concerned, Wilson's declaration rejected the balance of power doctrine and secret alliances; it also proposed constructive steps towards disarmament and adjustment of colonial claims. He concluded by saying that the moral climax of all the hostility had been a final war for human liberty. His aim now was to seek equality and not mastery. In essence, what Wilson was doing was simply articulating the effect of the war when four empires collapsed. Sharp concludes that the war radicalised nationalist sentiment for independence rather than home rule.[28] That may have been true of Czechoslovakia, but in Ireland much of the demand for independence was roused by the Easter Rising in 1916, although those who fought at the behest of John Redmond on a promise of Home Rule were attracted to independence. Wilson underestimated the reaction to his Fourteen Points and was surprised to be inundated with hundreds of petitions when he reached Paris for the Peace Conference. His idea of self-determination was used as a pretext by the Germans in promoting unrest in Egypt, India, Austria, and the Sudetenland. Germany's attempt to recruit Irish soldiers

[22] EH Carr, *From Napoleon to Stalin and Other Essays* (London, Macmillan, 1980) 7, 9.
[23] EH Carr, *The Twenty Years Crisis* (London, Palgrave Macmillan, reissued 2016) xxxvi.
[24] A Lentin, *Lloyd George, Woodrow Wilson and the Guilt of Germany* (Leicester, Leicester University Press, 1984) 7.
[25] S Marks, 'Mistakes and Myths: The Allies, Germany and the Versailles Treaty, 1918-1921' (2013) 85(3) *The Journal of Modern History* 648.
[26] A similar practice was adopted at Munich towards the Czechoslovakian representatives. See ch 4.
[27] H Nicolson, *Peacemaking 1919* (London, Faber and Faber, 2009) 154.
[28] A Sharp, *Versailles. A Centennial Perspective* (London, Haus Publishing, 2018) 78.

serving in the British Army to fight against Britain met with little success in the prisoner of war camps.[29] The British and French governments were concerned as to the reaction in their colonial empires. They could not relinquish Balfour's description of their supreme economic and political 'status', especially in respect of the Middle East.[30] Self-determination was a concept of governance gradually pronounced, but little practised. As in all matters the national interest or self-interest determined the redrawing of the map of Europe in 1919. Territory was apportioned between the allies, or, as Sharp concludes, 'as inducements to potential allies such as Italy or Romania with no thought to the wishes of the populations'.[31] In his account Nicolson reflects on his experiences as to how the boundary lines were drawn up 'in mists of exhaustion, disability, suspicion, and despair'.[32] He cites *The Papers of Colonel House*[33] who wrote:

> By arousing popular emotion during the war, an orthodox belligerent measure, they have created a Frankenstein monster which now held them helpless. They might compromise, if they possessed the skill, but they would not be permitted to yield.

Wilson spoke of an independent Poland to include territories 'inhabited by indisputably Polish populations, which should be assured of free and secure access to the sea'.[34] This was not the case since a minority of Germans would be domiciled within the Polish state. Access to the sea would only be enabled by cession of Danzig providing a further ground for grievance. Similar issues arose over the creation of Yugoslavia and Czechoslovakia. These questions are covered in chapter four.

As Sharp points out, one of the problems with Wilson's approach was that Wilson, familiar with the American notion of citizenship, may have confused that with nationality, which bore a different meaning in Europe. In eastern Europe nationality was determined by race, language, and religion. But in America, which was a 'nation of immigrants', whether you immigrated from Italy, Ireland, or England all became citizens of the US. In Europe ethnic nationalism prevailed; you were either a citizen or a foreigner.[35] The dilemma for the statesmen gathered at the Peace Conference in Versailles was how to redraw the boundaries. Despite allied declarations that all religious, racial or linguistic efforts had been carefully considered, they were knowingly aware that some of their decisions contradicted the principle of self-determination and the only common factor was consideration of linguistic, administrative, economic, military or communications priorities. These constructs in many cases were contradicted so much so that Germany argued for union with Austria and rejected the subjugation of its people to the Poles and Czechs.[36] Furthermore, the German delegation rejected the

[29] See: *R v Casement* (1916) 32 TLR 601 (K. B. Div.); (1916) 32 TLR 667 (C.C.A.).

[30] A Sharp, *Versailles. A Centennial Perspective* (London, Haus Publishing, 2018) 80.

[31] ibid.

[32] H Nicolson, *Peacemaking 1919* (London, Faber and Faber, 1945) 69.

[33] C Seymour, The *Intimate Papers of Colonel House Volume IV. The Ending of the War. June 1918 to November 1919* (London, Ernest Benn Limited, 1928). Cited in H Nicolson, *Peacemaking 1919* (London, Faber and Faber, 1945) 69.

[34] A Sharp, *Versailles. A Centennial Perspective* (London, Haus Publishing, 2018) 81.

[35] ibid.

[36] A Sharp, *Versailles. A Centennial Perspective* (London, Haus Publishing, 2018) 82. This was to rear its head again when the balance of power had shifted from the victors to the vanquished in March and September 1938. (See ch 4).

notion that Germany had lost the war in the East and did not see why the victors gained so much at their expense. There were, as will be seen, very important reasons as to why the Allies were keen to dismember Germany and neutralise its military effectiveness by a relatively limited dismemberment.

Thus, the plan to dismember parts of the German Reich without the consent of the whole population was a breach of this concept, as arguably were the partition of Ireland in 1921, the annexation of Austria, the exclusion of the Sudetenland from Czechoslovakia, and its annexation. But was self-determination a credible solution? In the case of Ireland, the partition possibly prevented a greater conflict; on the other hand, it was the casus belli for 100 years of civil unrest in Northern Ireland. Wilson's answer to the question was to refer such cases to the League of Nations,[37] albeit at the time Ulster was considered a British imperial problem.[38]

ii. Prelude to Defeat

What the architects of Versailles may have misunderstood, ignored or underestimated was the depth of humiliation Germans felt at the country's defeat and dismemberment. The German government itself failed to understand the implications of the revolution of November 1918. That government was divided, as were parties in the Reichstag: the War Party, which had encouraged the Kaiser with its Pan-German aspirations of annexation and expansionism if Germany obtained a decisive victory.[39] As against that the socialists, labour, left-wing liberals and those with commercial interests wanted an accommodation with neighbouring states.[40] Theobold von Bethmann-Hollweg,[41] the Chancellor, tried to avoid supporting the left or the right wing publicly. After Russia's capitulation and Russia's 'peace without annexations and indemnities', the Social Democrats (SPD) and the Independent Social Democrats (USPD) Matthias Erzberger became the leader of the Peace Movement after questioning the German submarine campaign. Erzberger was supported by the SPD Progressives and centre Reichstag parties, which later merged into the Weimar Coalition. On 19 July 1917, a peace resolution was adopted by the left-centre majority in the Reichstag to defend the independence and territorial integrity of the German state.[42] The resolution included support for international institutions guaranteeing peace, Freedom of the Seas, and free trade. It also included demands for a parliamentary system of government. Thus, when Wilson proclaimed his Fourteen Points on 8 January 1918, the then German Chancellor, Georg von Hartling, initiated secret discussions with American

[37] R Steel, 'Prologue: 1919-1945-1989' in M Boeneke, G Feldman and E Glasser (eds), *Treaty of Versailles: Reassessment After 75 Years* (Cambridge, Cambridge University Press, 2008) 39.

[38] The Irish delegation sent to Versailles was refused the right of representation at the Peace Conference.

[39] K Schwabe, 'Germany's Peace Aims and the Domestic and International Constraints' in M Boeneke, G Feldman and E Glasser (eds), *Treaty of Versailles: Reassessment After 75 Years* (Cambridge, Cambridge University Press, 2008) 38.

[40] K Epstein, *Mathias Erzberger and the Dilemma of German Democracy* (Princeton, NJ, Princeton University Press, 1959) 189.

[41] See: MP Reynolds, *Instruments of Peace Making* 1870-1914 (Oxford, Hart Publishing, 2021).

[42] K Schwabe, 'Germany's Peace Aims and the Domestic and International Constraints' in M Boeneke, G Feldman and E Glasser (eds), *Treaty of Versailles: Reassessment After 75 Years* (Cambridge, Cambridge University Press, 2008) 38–39.

intermediaries.[43] Eventually the Germans were forced by their military failures in Autumn 1918 to concede the independence of Belgium and sue for an armistice. Germany's adoption of the Fourteen Points would require changes to the German Constitution so that in the future the Reichstag would be responsible for foreign policy.[44]

To an extent the German government succeeded in their proposed peace plan policy. Secretary of State Robert Lansing on 5 November 1918 agreed that the western powers would negotiate for an armistice and a peace treaty based on Wilson's Fourteen points; this avoided unconditional surrender.[45] This was very much centred on the Fourteen Points or a piece of justice democratic republicanism (Rechtsfrieden) advocated by the moderate Left.[46] The responsibility for the peace negotiations with the allies was the new head of the German Foreign Office, Ulrich Graf Brockdorff-Rantzau. He strongly advocated the creation of the League of Nations and supported the right of self-determination, free trade, universal disarmament, renunciation of the absolute rule of a balance of power, and international arbitration of conflicts between nations.[47] Having declared Germany's intention, Brockdorff-Rantzau believed he could negotiate on behalf of a 'free people'. He believed the territorial questions could be settled on the basis of self-determination, save in respect of its eastern border. Germany required that at least two-thirds of the population would have to vote for any incorporation into the new Polish state if that were to be ceded to Poland.[48] In anticipation, the German government had prepared its own League Covenant in anticipation of proposing improvements in international law with provisions for the protection of national minorities and for labour legislation as well as a provision for a world Parliament.[49] The directives issued by the Peace Conference superseded Brockdorff-Rantzau's proposals about plebiscites, which meant that the eastern German territories required a plebiscite in Posen, but only in those parts of the province located to the East of the border between Germany and Poland. West Prussia and Upper Silesia remained in Germany.[50] Brockdorff-Rantzau tried to align German policy as close as possible with America, but this was rejected by Wilson. Brockdorff-Rantzau challenged the allies on reparations and war guilt, and in the latter, he reflected the old imperial Germany.[51] The linkage of responsibility for the war and 'all the loss and damage' in Articles 231 and 232 was not only exploited by Brockdorff-Rantzau in his disreputable defence of Germany responding to the Treaty, but also by Weimar and Nazi propaganda.

It is important in this context to consider the Allied reply to Wilson's note to the belligerents on 18 December 1916, to state their war aims. They replied on 10 January 1917 that Belgium and Serbia were to be restored with indemnities; the occupied territories of

[43] ibid 40.
[44] ibid 41.
[45] ibid 41–42.
[46] ibid 43.
[47] UG Brockdorff-Rantzau, *Dokumente und Gedenken um Versailles* (Berlin, 1825) 40–1, 57–58.
[48] K Schwabe, 'Germany's Peace Aims and the Domestic and International Constraints' in M Boeneke, G Feldman and E Glasser (eds), *Treaty of Versailles: Reassessment After 75 Years* (Cambridge, Cambridge University Press, 2008) 45.
[49] This was prepared by Walther Schücking and was far more radical than Woodrow Wilson's draft covenant.
[50] K Schwabe, 'Germany's Peace Aims and the Domestic and International Constraints' in M Boeneke, G Feldman and E Glasser (eds), *Treaty of Versailles: Reassessment After 75 Years* (Cambridge, Cambridge University Press, 2008) 46–47.
[51] ibid 47-48.

France, Russia and Romania should be evacuated; and just reparations paid.[52] The Allies wanted the liberation of Italians, Slavs, Romanians and Czechs from foreign domination; the removal of Turkey from Europe and the liberation of her subject peoples. They agreed with the Tsar's proclamation regarding the creation of a free Poland. On receiving this, Wilson told the Senate that there had to be a new international order which did not rest on force or on the balance of power. Such a new order would be dependent on American support. He also used the phrase: 'Peace without victory',[53] a phrase that was repeated by the Petrograd Soviet in 1917 – a pretext for the Bolsheviks signing the Treaty of Brest Litovsk on 3 March 1918.

iii. The Armistice 1918

When the German armies were forced to retreat in the autumn of 1918 after their summer offensive, negotiations were concluded by an armistice on 11 November 1918.[54] The key terms of the end of hostilities were that:

1. All occupied lands in Belgium, Luxembourg, and France – plus Alsace-Lorraine, held since 1870 by Germany – were to be evacuated within 14 days.
2. The Allies were to occupy land in Germany to the west of the River Rhine and bridgeheads on the river's east bank up to a depth of 30 kilometres.
3. German forces had to be withdrawn from Austria-Hungary, Romania, and Turkey.
4. Germany was to surrender to neutral or Allied ports 10 battleships, six battle cruisers, eight cruisers, and 160 submarines.
5. Germany was also to be stripped of heavy armaments, including 5,000 artillery pieces, 25,000 machine guns, and 2,000 airplanes.
6. The naval blockade would continue.
7. 5,000 locomotives, 150,000 railway cars, and 5,000 trucks would be confiscated from Germany.
8. Germany would be blamed for the war and reparations would be paid for all damage caused.

The document was divided into seven sections as to the Western Front, Germany's Eastern Frontiers, East Africa, General clauses, Naval matters, Duration of the Armistice.

The time for reply was 72 hours after notice of the terms conditional upon all hostilities on land and in the air had to cease within six hours of the signing.[55] If any German troops did not leave the German-occupied territories within the period agreed, they would become prisoners of war.[56] The inhabitants of the occupied countries, including hostages and persons being tried or convicted by the German occupiers, were to be

[52] In March 1917 Briand agreed in consideration for France retaking Alsace-Lorraine she should have discretion to extend its frontiers to include the Saar Coalfield and the left bank of the Rhine, that to become a separate state. Russia agreed this on the basis that it would be free to decide its western frontiers. G Ross, *The Great Powers and the Decline of the European State System 1914-1945* (London, Longman, 1983) 28.

[53] G Ross, *The Great Powers and the Decline of the European State System 1914-1945* (London, Longman, 1983) 30.

[54] This followed discussions of a pre-armistice arrangement which led to subsequent controversy.

[55] Clause 1.

[56] Clause 2.

released after 15 days by 26 November 1918.[57] The German Imperial Armies were to surrender in good condition 5,000 guns (2,500 heavy and 2,500 field), 25,000 machine guns, 3,000 minenwerfer, 1,700 aeroplanes (fighters, bombers – first all of the D 7'S and then all of the night bombing machines).[58]

The enemy forces were to evacuate the countries on the left bank of the Rhine to be taken over by Allied and United States garrisons holding the principal crossings of the Rhine and the bridgeheads at those points. A neutral zone was to be reserved on the right bank of the Rhine between the river and a line drawn parallel to the bridgeheads and to the river ten kilometres from the frontier of Holland up to the frontier of Switzerland. The evacuation was to be completed by 12 December 1918.[59]

The inhabitants of the occupied areas were to remain, and they and their property protected from harm and damage. Further prosecutions against those who undertook military operations for the Allies prior to the signing of the armistice were to cease. Destruction of any kind to property was to be prevented with food supplies left in situ for the civil population.[60] Roads and means of communication of every kind: railroads, waterways, main roads, bridges, telegraphs, and telephones, were not to be damaged or impaired. The railways of Alsace-Lorraine plus 5,000 locomotives and 150,000 waggons in good working order, were to be delivered to the associated powers[61] by 12 December 5,000 motor lorries (camion automobiles) were to be delivered by 17 December. All materials necessary for the working of railways in the countries on the left bank of the Rhine were to be left in situ. Barges taken from the Allies were to be restored to them.[62] The German command was required to assist in the discovery and destruction of all mines and any poisoning or polluting of springs and wells.[63]

The Allied and US armies maintained a right of requisition in the territories they occupied, and the costs for their upkeep (excluding Alsace-Lorraine) were to be charged to the German government.[64] Provision was made for the repatriation of prisoners of war.[65] The non-walking German war wounded and sick were to be attended by German personnel.[66]

On the question of the eastern frontiers of Germany, a subject that was to be increasingly important in the 1930s, all German troops present in the territories which before belonged to Austria-Hungary, Rumania, Turkey, and Russia were to be withdrawn to Germany as it existed on 1 August 1914.[67] German troops were to cease all requisitions and seizures in Rumania and Russia.[68] Germany was to renounce the treaties of

[57] Clause 3.
[58] Clause 4.
[59] Clause 5.
[60] Clause 6.
[61] Allies and the US forces.
[62] Clause 7. See also disputes referred to arbitration regarding compensation claims for river traffic taken during the war (ch 2).
[63] Clause 8.
[64] Clause 9.
[65] Clause 10.
[66] Clause 11.
[67] Clause 12 and 13.
[68] Clause 14.

Bucharest and Brest-Litovsk and the supplementary treaties.[69] The Allies were to have free access to the territories evacuated by the Germans on their eastern frontier, either through Danzig, or by the Vistula, in order to convey supplies to the populations of those territories and for the purpose of maintaining order.[70]

As to the German forces operating in East Africa they were to be withdrawn.

On financial restitution, while the armistice lasted, no public securities were to be removed by the Germans which could be utilised for the recovery or reparation of war losses. Germany was also required to return the cash deposit in the national bank of Belgium, and immediately return all documents, specie, stocks, shares, and paper money, together with plant for the issue thereof, regarding public or private interests in the countries they occupied. The Russian and Romanian gold appropriated by Germany was to be delivered in trust to the Allies until the signature of peace.[71]

On the immediate cessation of all hostilities at sea, the location and movements of all German ships were to be notified to the naval and mercantile marines of the allied and associated powers, all questions of neutrality being waived.[72] All allied and US naval and mercantile marine prisoners were to be returned without reciprocity.[73] Germany was to surrender all submarines in ports that would be specified by the Allies and US by 26 November 1918.[74] As to German surface warships, these were to be disarmed and interned in neutral ports or in Allied ports. This included: six battle cruisers, ten battleships, eight light cruisers (including two mine layers), and 50 destroyers of the most modern types. All other surface warships (including river craft) were to be completely disarmed and classed under the supervision of the Allies and the US.[75] The Associated Powers had the right to sweep up all minefields and obstructions laid by Germany outside German territorial waters.[76] The Associated Powers maintained freedom of access to and from the Baltic and were empowered to occupy all German forts, fortifications, batteries, and defence works of all kinds in all the entrances from the Kattegat into the Baltic, and to sweep up all mines and obstructions within and outside German territorial waters.[77] The existing blockade conditions remained in force.[78] All German naval aircraft were to be concentrated and immobilised in German bases to be specified by the Associated Powers.[79] The German forces were required to evacuate the Belgian coast and ports as well as all port and river navigation material, all merchant ships, tugs, lighters, all naval aeronautic apparatus, material and supplies, and all arms, apparatus, and supplies of every kind.[80]

As far as the Black Sea ports were concerned, these had to be evacuated, and all Russian war vessels seized by Germany in the Black Sea were to be handed over to the Associated Powers; neutral merchant vessels seized were to be released. All warlike and

[69] Clause 15.
[70] Clause 16.
[71] Clause 19.
[72] Clause 20.
[73] Clause 21.
[74] Clause 22.
[75] Clause 23.
[76] Clause 24.
[77] Clause 25.
[78] Clause 26.
[79] Clause 27.
[80] Clause 28.

other materials in those ports were to be returned, and German materials were to be abandoned.[81] All merchant vessels in German hands belonging to the allied and associated powers were to be restored in ports to be specified by the Associated Powers without reciprocity.[82] The German forces were prohibited from destroying ships or materials before evacuation, surrender, or restoration.[83] The German government would notify the neutral governments of the world, especially those of Norway, Sweden, Denmark, and Holland, that all restrictions placed on the trading of their vessels with the allied and associated countries, whether by the German government or by private German interests, and whether in return for specific concessions, such as the export of shipbuilding materials, or not, were immediately cancelled.[84] No transfers of German merchant shipping of any description to any neutral flag were to take place after the signature of the armistice.[85]

The armistice was to last for a period of 36 days with an option to renew. To assure the execution of the convention under the best conditions, the principle of a permanent international armistice commission was recognised. This commission would act under the authority of the allied military and naval Commanders in Chief.

The armistice was signed on 11 November 1918 at 5 o'clock French time by Marshall F Foch, R E Wemyss, Erzberger, A Oberndorff Winterfeldt and Von Salow.

This military convention was renewed on 12 February 1919 indefinitely without significant amendments.[86] President Ebert told the returning troops that 'no enemy has conquered you'.[87] This provided grounds for the myth that the German army had not been defeated, providing an early cause of resentment, grievance, distrust and suspicion exacerbated by the difference between the terms of the armistice and the terms of the Treaty of Versailles.[88] This grievance later provided a good excuse for Hitler to play the victim. The Armistice was concluded as a result of tripartite negotiations between the new government in Berlin, the Allied Supreme War Council in Paris, and President Wilson in Washington. The Germans wanted terms based on Wilson's Fourteen Points, but the French wanted compensation for war damage, and the British had concerns over freedom of the seas which resulted in a compromise, the first of a number of compromises to secure the peace.

iv. After the Armistice-Diverging Interests

The question for the Allies on the conclusion of the armistice in 1918 was to decide either on a negotiated peace or an imposed peace. Statesmen and delegates had President Wilson's Fourteen Points very much in their minds in designing the architecture of the settlement: open covenants of peace and transparent diplomacy, absolute freedom of the seas, the removal of economic and trade barriers, an end to arms races, and national self-determination to figure in the adjustment of colonial claims. It may be that Wilson's promotion of self-determination and universalism would enable the US to become the

[81] Clause 29.
[82] Clause 30.
[83] Clause 31.
[84] Clause 32.
[85] Clause 33.
[86] M Macmillan, *Peacemakers* (London, John Murray, 2002) 178.
[87] ibid 168.
[88] ibid 27.

peace broker.[89] This would certainly have helped ameliorate the tension between France and Britain.

In any negotiation you need agreement on what terms would be acceptable to both parties, but where allies are involved with diverse national interests, that is difficult. France had suffered great human losses as well as devastation to her northern provinces, as had Belgium. Clemenceau was especially vengeful, reflecting the great losses France had suffered and wanted revenge by way of reparations and territory, not just reinstatement of Alsace-Lorraine lost to Germany in the Franco-Prussian War of 1870–71. Undoubtedly there was a mood for revenge against Germany, but as James Headham-Morley, writing in 1930, concluded, the chief cause of the war was the existence of armaments. In his view it was the military preparations of Russia and Germany in mobilising that brought this about and that the outbreak of war and the final defeat of Germany were the logical outcome of the military system which she had herself advocated.[90] The position was a little more complicated, perhaps insofar as the immediate cause of the war was the Austro-Hungarian ultimatum to Serbia, the attack on Serbia and the consequent mobilisation by Russia, Germany and France.[91]

Britain and the US, on the other hand, were not seeking such revenge but a means to end the war and preserve the peace. This divergence of opinion was destined to become greater as time went on and tensions between Britain and France increased because of her insecurity and fear of a resurgent Germany. Time proved that the British government would only go so far, with Ramsay MacDonald placing trust in arbitration and the cabinet opposing any alliance with France in favour of a quadrilateral agreement between Britain, France, Belgium and Germany.[92] Lloyd George, who had survived the so-called Khaki Election,[93] was concerned that the peace terms would be too harsh, but General Foch took a more realistic appraisal and simply said it was an armistice for 20 years. George Keenan opined that the terms were too harsh, as did Henry Kissinger. Also, there was considerable weight of opinion that criticised the Versailles treaties and subsequently the League of Nations, but it is difficult in the context of those times to perceive of any different arrangement that might have been possible in the aftermath of 'the war to end all wars'. The British approach was more moderate than that of Clemenceau. At a meeting of an Allied Conference at St. James's Place in London on 3 March 1921, consideration was given to statements made on behalf of the German government. In Lloyd George's view, these constituted a definite challenge to the fundamental conditions of the Treaty of Versailles. He suggested that the Proposals of Paris had involved a substantial relaxation of the treaty in respect of disarmament and reparations. They were amicably intended as a concession to Germany. This was not helped when Dr Simons, a German delegate, repudiated responsibility for the war in a speech at Karlsruhe on 16 February 1921. German responsibility for the war was fundamental;

[89] L Ambrosis, *Woodrow Wilson and the American Diplomatic Tradition: The Treaty Fight in Perspective* (Cambridge, CUP, 1979).

[90] J Headham-Morley, *Studies in Diplomatic History* (London, Methuen and Co, 1930) 296, 297.

[91] M Reynolds, *Instruments of Peacemaking 1870-1914* (Oxford, Hart Publishing, 2021) 304–305.

[92] R Henig, *The Peace That Never Was* (London, Haus Publishing, 2019) 92, 95.

[93] H Nicolson, *Peacemaking 1919* (London, Faber and Faber, 1945) 14. An election that Sir Harold Nicolson described as the election '… of the most unintelligent body of public schoolboys which even the Mother of Parliaments has known.'

it was the basis on which the whole structure of the treaty had been created, and if that was in any way repudiated or abandoned, the treaty would be destroyed. He further suggested that responsibility for the war had to be treated by the allies as a chose jugée. Lloyd George went on to say that when Germany defeated France in the Franco-Prussian war, its peace treaty, the Treaty of Frankfurt 1871, was founded on the principle that those responsible for the war ought to pay the costs of the war. In this sense the Allies insisted that the verdict of the Great War had to be respected.[94]

As a result of the Great War the main empires of Europe: Austria-Hungary, Germany, Russia and the Ottoman Empire, were destroyed by the effects of the war and in the case of the Triple Alliance Powers their boundaries were redrawn, and populations distributed. Although Germany's population did not suffer the same fate as that of Austria-Hungary or the Ottoman Empire, it suffered the humiliation of the occupation of the Rhineland and the Saar. Also challenging for the allies was the fact that the empires which collapsed because of the war had no effective forms of government. Russia, whose empire fell in 1917, was in the throes of revolution and was not represented at the Peace Conference.

Applying the principles of the Fourteen Points, especially self-determination, would prove difficult in practice. Application of that principle would involve moving populations and redrawing boundaries, inevitably prejudicing the interests of minorities, especially in the former Ottoman and Austro-Hungarian empires. At the same time, it was important to neutralise German militaristic tendencies increased by the view that the German army had not been defeated. This would involve disarming Germany to the extent that her army would simply be sufficient for domestic purposes and not for aggressive tendencies.

III. The Peace Conference

A. Challenges for 'Peace without Victory'[95]

The task of the delegates who convened at Versailles on 18 January 1919 was unprecedented save for the Congress of Vienna 103 years before. In 1919, the aim of the delegates was to ensure the peace and neutralise Germany to end 'the war to end all wars'. It was hoped that armaments would be limited, reducing the risk of another arms race and another war. President Woodrow Wilson, who pronounced his Fourteen Points in January 1918, provided a basis on which the war could end. Germany acceded to his approach. This facilitated the negotiations leading to the armistice in November 1918.[96]

[94] *Documents on British Foreign Policy 1919-1939* First Series Vol. XV. 258–259.

[95] Wilson's 'Peace Without Victory' Speech, 22 January 1917.

[96] An earlier attempt had been made to broker a peace: in 1916. Colonel House, President Wilson's emissary agreed with Sir Edward Grey that at a suitable moment, Britain and France would ask Wilson to call for a peace conference. If Germany rejected that the US would support the allies. On 12 December 1916, Bethmann-Hollweg, the German Chancellor, indicated that the Central Powers were willing to negotiate. These suggestions were unattainable. G Ross, *The Great Powers In The Decline of The European State System 1914-1945* (London, Longman, 1983) 29, 30.

Given that his role was critical in leading the peace negotiations in Paris and promoting his League of Nations, the failure of the US Senate to accede to the Treaty of Versailles and America's membership of the League, followed by Wilson's untimely death, contributed to the rivalry between the imperial ambitions of Britain and France as against Wilson's principle of self-determination. Wilson undoubtedly raised expectations amongst the lesser states and those seeking independence, such as India and Ireland. Raising high populist expectations is applauded at first, as Wilson was on his arrival in Paris, but denounced when the expectation fails to become reality, as when the victors of 1918 became the vanquished of 1940.

Undoubtedly the ideals of Wilson were encouraging, but in practice self-determination was not easy to establish amongst the states that Versailles and the victors (the Big Four) would create. On the British side, the process of peacemaking had its critics, notably Maynard Keynes[97] and Harold Nicolson. Keynes because of the amount of reparations, which he felt were excessive and would cause Germany serious financial problems, and Nicolson because he experienced the undue burden of responsibility placed on junior Foreign Office staff to advise on the new state boundaries. The Council of Four (Wilson, Clemenceau, Lloyd George, and Vittorio Emanuele Orlando[98]) was the executive making body that had the final say, but in practice the advice given to them was often what they applied.

In Germany the army felt undefeated, betrayed by defeatists at home. They felt that the Versailles indemnities put Germany into a financial crisis causing high inflation and the Depression. For them it was the cause of World War Two. AJP Taylor took this view, as did George Kennan in 'The War to End War',[99] who opined that the Second World War was caused by 'the very silly and humiliating punitive peace imposed on Germany after World War One'. In the *Treaty of Versailles: Reassessment After 25 Years*, Boeneke, Feldman and Glasser argue that the treaty was workable and kept the peace between 1924 and 1931, demonstrating flexibility in adjustment to meet changing needs: reparations were generally resolved, the Rhineland occupation ended, and the US and Britain indicated they were willing to negotiate over the Danzig corridor.[100]

The challenges for the delegates were to alleviate the immediate humanitarian problems caused by the war, including the blockade of the German ports and feeding the population of the beleaguered countries. They also had to organise the demobilisation of the vast armies and provide security to Belgium and France as well as consider the longer-term relationships between the warring parties. These were somewhat diverse, if not contradictory aims and objectives.[101] So long as the allies could work together, they were able to progress, but eventually divergent national and imperial interests affected the collaboration between the US, Britain and France when complex issues arose, and

[97] Keynes and his friend Felix Frankfurter (legal adviser to President Wilson during the Paris Peace Conference; an Associate Justice of the US Supreme Court, legal scholar and law teacher) were in little doubt about the conference and the treaty which, in their view, was 'a breach of faith'.

[98] Prime Minister of Italy 1917–19.

[99] An article published in the *New York Times* 11 November 1984.

[100] M Boeneke, G Feldman and E Glasser, *Treaty of Versailles: Reassessment After 75 Years* (Cambridge, Cambridge University Press, 2008) 3.

[101] ibid 4.

delegations became overworked with the strains of a heavy bureaucratic administration. It has been suggested by David Stevenson[102] that if the alliance had continued, the settlement would have been more successful. We may go further and perhaps conjecture that if Marshal Foch's proposal[103] to invade Germany had been adopted and the Allies combined in an army of occupation in common cause, this would have given them a common interest.[104] This was the approach after World War Two and the Allies insistence on unconditional surrender.

Despite Clemenceau's demands for Anglo-American security guarantees to France, neither Britain nor America were inclined to incur such obligations. A Guarantee Pact proved immaterial when Wilson failed to secure approval in the Congress for the Versailles Treaty and membership of the League of Nations, which precipitated the termination of the alliance. Whilst self-determination was good in theory, it was questionable in practice: the Polish border provides a case in point. Poland's borders were more affected by geopolitical considerations than by self-determination because Poland required defensive frontiers to prevent attacks from the West and the East.

The rise of fascism in Germany at the end of the Weimar Republic is often attributed to the failure of Versailles. Sally Marks[105] opines that reparations of themselves did not account for Hitler's rise to power, but rather it went beyond the perception of Versailles to resentment because it caused an unfair distribution of monetary wealth to the detriment of Germany. It also caused a loss of prestige and humiliation in that the balance of power swung against Germany's interest after she was forced to sign a treaty which separated many German speakers from the Fatherland. This perception of unequal status was another matter that Hitler complained about as Chancellor, exploiting the idea that Germany had been the victim of Versailles.

i. Nationalism and Self Determination

Often the question of national sovereignty – a legal theory – is confused by a political adaptation. Legally the sovereign is the state authority and supreme law-making body, and in political terms it may be said the people are sovereign. In dictatorships, however, supreme power is exercised by the dictator. Whilst that is true of the nation-state such sovereignty is constrained by the state's relationship to other states by treaty and political, economic, historic, and cultural ties. In certain cases, as will be seen in this study, the public sometimes projects a constricted view of national sovereignty, thinking they are in a state of splendid isolation from what happens in the world. Lord Salisbury adopted such a policy but realised with the rise of imperial Germany (Kaiserreich) that

[102] Professor of International History at the Department of International History, London School of Economics.

[103] This was supported for military reasons by General Pershing US Army Commander (AEF).

[104] M Boeneke, G Feldman and E Glasser, *Treaty of Versailles: Reassessment After 25 Years* (Cambridge, Cambridge University Press, 2008) 10.

[105] S Marks, 'Smoke and Mirrors: In Smoke Filled Rooms and the Galerie des Glaces' in M Boeneke, G Feldman and E Glasser (eds), *Treaty of Versailles: Reassessment After 75 Years* (Cambridge, Cambridge University Press, 2008).

Britain needed friends and at Paul Cambon's[106] prompting Lord Lansdowne agreed the basis of the Entente Cordiale.[107]

After 1918 the Allies did not remain united. The interests of the leading players gradually diverged, as between Lloyd George and Clemenceau, and then between Lloyd George, Clemenceau and Wilson over reparations and pension claims. In Paris, the delegates approached the redrawing of European boundaries with good intentions to preserve the peace based on the Wilsonian principle of self-determination. It was impossible to carry out this high principle of giving each of the ethnic peoples their own state since the national borders did not correspond to ethnic ones whether cultural, linguistic, religious, political, economic, or historical. Forging multinational entities of semi-autonomous states like Yugoslavia assumed there would be no conflict between the ethnic peoples and the constituted state. The delegations at Paris thought that the combination of these entities would create a more harmonious international order.[108] It may be that President Wilson's ideas were born of experience in the US, where immigrants became citizens and cut their ties with their country of origin, whereas in Europe the ethnic minorities created in the new countries such as Yugoslavia and Czechoslovakia retained cultural ties with their homeland, eg, the Sudetendeutsche in the Sudetenland and Germans in Gdansk (Danzig). If the borders and frontiers could have been aligned to meet the wishes and aspirations of the majority population, which was united for the purposes of common defence, then maybe redrawing boundaries post-imperial times might have worked, giving economic security.

There was another aspect which was termed the doctrine of universal democracy, rooted in the traditions of the US which, as Steel points out, assumed that an act of aggression anywhere constitutes a threat to peace everywhere: it assumes there is such a thing as world peace, which turns every dispute into a crusade for the soul of mankind.[109] Such a doctrine could involve the Great Powers in wars everywhere. Local quarrels could become global wars, as in 1914 when Austria-Hungary attacked Serbia. It can lead to cultural war or charges of hypocrisy and empty rhetoric. Wilson's idea of self-determination was also problematic. As Steel points out, Lincoln did not apply it in the war with the seceding Confederate states, and he quotes Walter Lippmann who wrote that self-determination was 'licence to intervention and aggression', inviting majorities to be intransigent and leading to atomisation of human society.[110] Steel also quotes Charles Tilly,[111] who wrote that: the ethnic state makes war, and war makes the ethnic state.[112] This may be illustrated by the League's intervention in a dispute

[106] French Ambassador in London 1898–1920.

[107] MP Reynolds, *Instruments of Peacemaking 1870-1914* (Oxford, Hart Publishing, 2020) 245.

[108] R Steel, 'Prologue: 1919-1945-1989' in M Boeneke, G Feldman and E Glasser (eds), *Treaty of Versailles: Reassessment After 75 Years* (Cambridge, Cambridge University Press, 2008) 25.

[109] ibid 29.

[110] ibid 31.

[111] Tilly was an American sociologist, political scientist, and historian, who wrote on the nation-state. He obtained a doctorate from Harvard and taught at the Universities of Toronto, Michigan, The New School for Social Research, and Columbia University.

[112] R Steel, 'Prologue: 1919-1945-1989' in M Boeneke, G Feldman and E Glasser (eds), *Treaty of Versailles: Reassessment After 75 Years* (Cambridge University Press, 2008) 32.

between Finland and Sweden over the Aaland Islands, where the League's Commission held that:

> … international law does not recognise the right of national groups as such to separate themselves from the state of which they form a part by the simple expression of a wish any more than it recognises the right of other states to claim such a separation.[113]

This may be further illustrated by disputes between Poland and Germany as to Upper Silesia which, after a close referendum, was divided between the two states, and also by the League's intervention in 1923 in the Turkish war and the dispute between Greece and Bulgaria in 1925. If self-determination meant making such divisions on ethnic lines, it was a failure because the architects of the Versailles settlement failed to acknowledge the force of ethnicity, Germany being the leading example with wars in Yugoslavia between Catholic Croatians, Muslim Bosnians, and Orthodox Serbs.[114]

ii. The Daunting Task

The achievements of the Peace Conference have been overshadowed by the controversy over reparations and treatment of Germany. To form such an international association was remarkable for its time. Often overlooked, as Ruth Henig concluded,[115] were the benefits of its humanitarian and social improvements. Above all was its support for international law and arbitration as the means of resolving disputes between states. This enthusiasm for international law was driven partly by understandable war weariness and a resolve to never let it happen again. To some extent it was a revival of the enthusiasm for international dispute resolution at the two Hague Conferences in 1899 and 1907.[116] This did not allay the bitterness and an urge for revenge at the Versailles Peace Conference, reflected in the treaties which imposed retribution as well as a presumption of guilt on the Central Powers. This, like the presumption in the Armistice ensured German resentment and a desire for retaliation, which accelerated the rise of fascism. On the other hand, the Conference invented an innovative organisation that halved the number of nationalities in Europe, created two new states Czechoslovakia and Yugoslavia, and recognised Poland. It was an experiment in international trusteeship administered by a council with nation-state[117] members meeting once a year, but subject to unanimous vote.[118]

iii. American Abstention

Ironically, the promoter of world peace, self-determination, and a world organisation to enforce the peace through 'collective security' failed to secure the approval of the US

[113] ibid 32.
[114] ibid 32.
[115] R Henig, *The Peace That Never Was: A History of the League of Nations* (London, Haus Publishing, 2019) 167–185.
[116] As described in M Reynolds, *Instruments of Peacemaking 1870-1914* (Oxford, Hart Publishing, 2021).
[117] League of Nations Convention see below.
[118] H Dalton, *Hitlers War Before and After* (New York, Penguin Books, 1940) 15.

Congress for acceptance of the Convention and US accession to the League of Nations. Whilst Wilson was in Paris without any Republican members of Congress, the powerful influence of Senators Borah and Lodge, coupled with criticism from former President Taft and Secretary of State Elihu Root, undermined American support for the Covenant and the League.[119] The absence of the US disappointed its friends in Europe and left responsibility mainly in the hands of Britain and France. Britain was in debt to America and other countries were in debt to Britain. In addition, Britain's responsibilities to its empire placed an enormous burden on the Exchequer.

The League was designed to avoid another European conflagration, acknowledging that the 'Old Diplomacy' had failed.[120] The peace treaties cast a shadow over that ideal by the penalties imposed by means of reparations on Germany and Austria-Hungary. Was this a new diplomacy or retribution? If the latter, then the resultant effects of the humiliation of Germany and its allies, exacerbated by the occupation of the industrial heartlands of the Ruhr and the Saar, as well as the loss of Danzig and Silesia and the dislocation of German people within redrawn borders eventually backfired and undermined the peace. The dream of a multipolar approach gave way to a bipolar nationalist tendency, not as in the nineteenth century for independence, but for domination in the Napoleonic sense.

iv. *The Establishment of the League*

The idea of statesmen coming together in concert, possibly an evolution of the concert system, was a radical idea. It appeared that Lloyd George, Clemenceau and Wilson arrived in Paris with their own blueprint for peace. What faced them was an enormous problem of trying to establish and reconstitute states for millions of displaced people, not least the three empires that collapsed: Austria-Hungary, Germany and the Ottoman Empire. Harold Nicolson considered that the essential faults and errors of the Territorial Committees set up by the Peace Conference to advise on the new territorial boundaries were not a lack of knowledge but 'guidance, precision, coordination, principle and scope'.[121] To undertake such a task in the time was quite remarkable, notwithstanding the subsequent difficulties as outlined at the time by Nicolson and Maynard Keynes. Keynes took a dim view of the proceedings, commenting:

> In Paris where those connected with the Supreme Economic Council received almost hourly the reports of the misery, disorder, and decaying organisation of all Central and Eastern Europe, allied and enemy alike, and learned from the lips of the financial representatives of Germany and Austria unanswerable evidence, of the terrible exhaustion of their countries, an occasional visit to the hot, dry room in the President's house, where the Four fulfilled their destinies in empty and arid intrigue, only added to the sense of nightmare.'[122]

[119] A Lentin, *Lloyd George, Woodrow Wilson, and the Guilt of Germany* (Leicester, Leicester University Press, 1984) 118.

[120] A Zimmern, *The League of Nations and the Rule of Law* (London, Macmillan and Co, 1936) 1.

[121] H Nicolson, *Peacemaking 1919* (London, Faber and Faber, 1945) 102–107.

[122] Maynard Keynes was temporarily attached to the British Treasury during the First World War and was their official representative at the Paris Peace Conference until June 1919. He resigned from his position because of his dissatisfaction with the terms of the peace treaty. M Keynes, *The Economic Consequences of The Peace* (Oxford, Oxford City Press, 2012).

A dilemma for the delegates, which had adverse consequences, was how to redraw the boundaries of Europe following the war. There was no easy way to redraw those boundaries on the lines of religion, nationality, or language. Harold Nicolson gave a good account of the predicament he faced in being given the onerous responsibility of advising Lloyd George and Clemenceau on where the frontiers would be placed. In 1919, countries like Austria would have preferred to be united with Germany, but as time wore on, they became more nationalist and preferred independence.[123] The resentment of Germany caused by her defeat was exacerbated by reparations. This was especially onerous to a blockaded Germany and a starving population humiliated by the occupation of its industrial heartlands in the Saar and the Ruhr and exacerbated by the loss of Danzig and Silesia. Marshal Foch advised the allies that the Rhine was the bulwark against German aggression and should be occupied and held. If the Allies, he argued, controlled the Rhine crossing, then it could be defended and used to launch a counterattack.[124]

Whilst Keynes and Nicolson were amongst numerous critics of the Versailles conference, as Alan Sharp has written, it is remarkable that they achieved so much.[125] If you put into context the pressing need for the urgent reorganisation of Europe, bearing in mind the thousands of people starving in Germany and homeless persons on the continent, with revolution brewing in Germany and a revolution in Russia the planning was remarkable, although the execution in many cases was impractical if not impossible or later proved the cause of further problems, as in the Sudetenland, Danzig, and the Middle and Far East.[126] Whilst the principles of the Fourteen Points were idealistic and laudable, the idea of self-determination, which might satisfy nationalists, presented difficulties for newly created states with minorities whose national identity and culture were foreign to that state, eg, Czechoslovakia with German, Hungarian, Romanian and Polish minorities. The settlement might, even with these apparent deficiencies, have endured had it not been for rising inflation in Germany, the financial crisis of 1929, the collapse of the Brüning administration and the Great Depression which followed. The 1919 Paris Peace Conference encouraged the idea of international dispute resolution through arbitration and diplomacy and led to a further interest in employing international law to settle matters. It may be that without the Fourteen Points there would have been no Atlantic Charter and without the League of Nations no United Nations.

v. *The Victors Take the Spoils*

Under the Treaty of Versailles, Germany was forbidden to build tanks, to have a General Staff, to have an air force, and to build submarines, they being regarded as

[123] A Sharp, *Versailles. A Centennial Perspective* (London, Haus Publishing, 2018) 18.

[124] R Recouly, *Le Mémorial de Foch* (Paris, 1929) 156; J de Launay, *Major Controversies of Contemporary History* (Oxford, Pergamon Press, 1965) 79; J Néré, *Foreign Policy of France 1914-1945* (London, Routledge and Kagan Paul, 1975) 14.

[125] A Sharp, *Versailles. A Centennial Perspective* (London, Haus Publishing, 2018).

[126] Keynes described the process as a 'nightmare'. M Keynes, *The Economic Consequences of The Peace* (Oxford, Oxford City Press, 2012) 46.

offensive weapons. Opinion differed on the definition as to what was offensive and what was defensive. Thus, Germany paid a heavy price for the war with a reduction in her land area, the loss of population, and a reduction in her armed forces; no air force was permitted. It lost its Polish territory, and it is estimated that Germany lost 9.4 per cent of its pre-1914 land area and 1.8 per cent of its pre-war population.[127] On the other hand, contrasting the territorial boundaries of Germany in 1914 with those after 1919, it was clear that whereas in 1914 Germany was bordered by France and Russia, who were allies, by 1919 she was surrounded by smaller new states: Poland, Czechoslovakia, Lithuania, and also by France, Belgium, Luxembourg, Denmark, and Switzerland. The key problem was that Britain and France were left to implement Wilson's policy. This gave Germany the opportunity to exploit any Anglo-French differences.[128]

France retook Alsace-Lorraine and occupied the Rhineland and the Saar. In Russia, having suffered the trauma of the war and the Bolshevik Revolution, the Soviet government sought to proletarianise the world until Gregory Chickerin realised that peaceful co-existence was necessary. He then signed the Treaty of Tartu with Estonia, and in 1921 Soviet Russia signed the Anglo-Soviet Trade Agreement and subsequently the Treaty of Rapallo with Germany, although they were bourgeois states.[129] Although the German and Russian empires were extinguished and dismembered, weakened by war and revolution, they subsequently assumed a similar despotic and tyrannical character: Germany under Hitler and Russia under Stalin. As a result, the weaker nations which were created out of the Versailles settlement on the principle of self-determination: Finland, Latvia, Lithuania, Estonia, Romania, Poland, and Czechoslovakia, fell betwixt and between the dictatorships. What gave the dictatorships cause for concern was the enforced redistribution of their nationals.

vi. French Security

It was eventually agreed that the occupation of the Rhineland would be a 15-year occupation with partial withdrawals every five years. German opinion was not considered or sought. But according to de Launay, the people of the Rhineland considered Prussian militarism to have caused their defeat. The Rhineland was divided into four Allied zones. The British were in Cologne, Belgium held Aix la Chapelle, the Americans occupied Coblenz and the French, Mainz. Foch was in favour of an independent Rhenish Republic rejecting its inclusion within the German Reich.[130]

France was anxious to secure her border with Germany and to recover Alsace-Lorraine as well as secure economic compensation for the damage to infrastructure and the rich industrial area of northern France, which had been decimated in the war.[131] She also sought security guarantees from Britain and the US. Up to a point, Britain had similar

[127] M Angee, *The Great Inter War Crisis and The Collapse Of Globalisation* (London, Palgrave Macmillan, 2009) 42–58.
[128] A Sharp, *Versailles. A Centennial Perspective* (London, Haus Publishing, 2018) 41.
[129] ibid 14.
[130] J de Launay, *Major Controversies of Contemporary History* (Oxford, Pergamon Press, 1965) 80–81.
[131] J Néré, *Foreign Policy of France 1914-1945* (London, Routledge and Kagan Paul, 1975) 11.

interests to France in that a revived Germany would pose a threat to imperial interests just as much as it did to Europe. European security therefore became intertwined with imperial British security. There was also some concern that France's occupation of the Rhineland and other aggressive demonstrations made France a potential threat as much as Germany.[132] This inspired Paul Cambon's famous remark: 'The misfortune is that the English are not yet aware that Napoleon is dead.'[133]

vii. The Low Countries and Turkey

Belgium also was displeased with the settlement in that she lost her claims to Luxembourg and parts of Holland.[134] Italy, on the other hand, gained South Tyrol, the Brenner Pass, Dalmatia and Istria. Bulgaria lost access to the Aegean, lost Thrace to Greece, and land to Yugoslavia. Romania doubled in size, and Greece gained 50 per cent new territory.[135] The frontiers of Yugoslavia were contested as they displaced 75,000 Romanians and 65,000 Slavs on the wrong side of the border. These provisions were contained in the Treaty of Sèvres in 1922, but that treaty was never ratified. A more successful outcome was the Treaty of Lausanne which recognised Turkey and restored much of its former territory in July 1923.[136]

viii. The Middle East

In the Middle East there was confusion and disappointment. The Hashemite Kingdom expected to be rewarded for its part in the defeat of the Turks in the Arab Revolt. The arrangements made were very complicated. Emir Hussain, the Sheriff of Mecca, was refused recognition as 'King of the Arabs' by the British, who referred to him merely as King of Hijaz. Ibn Saud replaced him in 1932 and formed the Kingdom of Saudi Arabia. Faisal, the leader of the Arab Revolt, wanted Syria, but the French rejected this in July 1920. Faisal became King of Mesopotamia (now Iraq) in 1921. Abdullah Faisal's brother became Emir of Transjordan (now Jordan) in 1923.

The creation of Jordan resulted in serious friction between the Jews and the Arabs.[137] Britain was given a mandate for Palestine but found it very difficult to maintain the peace and any form of government. Jews in Europe and Germany supported the Jewish cause for a homeland, which resulted in a three-year Arab revolt in 1936. Britain sought to divide and rule Palestine between Arabs and Jews. This was just one of the national tensions that Britain had to deal with in its empire where imperial invincibility had been shattered by the reverses suffered during the war. As in Europe, nationalism was stirring in the empire, and in Ireland and Egypt there was unrest. Many Irishmen felt aggrieved having taken up Redmond's call to arms in 1914 on the promise of Home Rule and the

[132] A Sharp, *Versailles. A Centennial Perspective* (London, Haus Publishing, 2018) 20–21.
[133] ibid 21.
[134] Territory she lost in 1839.
[135] A Sharp, *Versailles. A Centennial Perspective* (London, Haus Publishing, 2018) 21–22.
[136] ibid 23.
[137] ibid 23–26.

subsequent pronouncements of Wilson on self-determination but their aspirations were disregarded and ignored at Versailles.

ix. Japan

During the First World War, Japan realised her objectives: the German possessions in the Far East and encroachment in China. Japan took the German islands north of the equator and German Leased Territories as well as Shantung in China. In January 1915, Japan made 'Twenty-One Demands' to the Chinese government. Britain objected to this and pressed Japan to retract. The demands were diluted, and China accepted them in May 1915. In July 1916, Japan signed a treaty with Russia acknowledging their respective interests in China and promising to act against any third power which might be hostile to such interests. In February 1917, Britain agreed to approve Japan's Chinese gains and its acquisitions, including the German islands north of the equator, after the war.[138] Thus, China was disappointed when the Paris Peace Conference acknowledged the Japanese acquisition of the Shandong Peninsula under the reassignment of a lease that Germany had given Japan in 1915. As a result, China refused to sign the Versailles Treaty in 1919. Japan returned the peninsula in 1922 but still gained the German Pacific colonies and territories: the Marianas, the Carolinas, and the Marshall Islands. Strategically, this gave Japan a foothold in China and the Pacific, a springboard for its subsequent southward expansion and a threat to the sea lanes.[139]

x. American Withdrawal

The US had increasing reservations about Japanese ambitions in the Pacific and its alliance with Britain. America's withdrawal from the League of Nations had serious future implications and consequences. This was a failure for Lloyd George because he counted on American support and its chairmanship in the Five Power Commission. Wilson's great dream of the League of Nations was now left to Britain and France, whilst America returned to isolationism and disengagement from Europe at a critical time. The French could now seize control of the process. France, Belgium and Italy would have a majority over Britain and Lloyd George would lament the predominance of France.

xi. Austria-Hungary

The Treaty of Saint-Germain en Laye, 19 September 1919, along with the Treaty of Neuilly, determined the dismemberment of the Austro-Hungarian Empire and the Kingdom of Bulgaria. The Dual Monarchy was divided between Italy, Romania and

[138] G Ross, *The Great Powers and the Decline of the European State System* 1914-1945 (London, Longman, 1983) 28, 29.

[139] About this time US Naval Intelligence set up monitoring stations to monitor the Japanese navy. L Farago, *The Broken Seal: The Story of Operation Magic and the Pearl Harbor Disaster* (London, Mayflower, 1969).

the new states of Czechoslovakia, Yugoslavia and Poland. In 1920 Austria became a Republic. On 25 March 1919, the Council of Four decided to delegate the question of the draft treaties for Austria-Hungary and Bulgaria (what became the Treaty of Trianon[140]) to the foreign ministers. That treaty was practically the exclusive agreement of these ministers and not the Big Four so that the emphasis was on strategic and economic considerations as against those of ethnic origin, language, and national sentiment.[141] Under the treaty, Hungary lost two-thirds of its pre-1914 territory and almost 60 per cent of its population. In 1918 Austrians were in favour of unification with Germany, but France opposed it.[142] A plebiscite was held in Klugenfurt, and although 68 per cent of the population were Slovenes only 40 per cent voted to secede from Austria.[143] Later, when the Nazis absorbed Austria in the *Anschluss*, they excused it as a mode of self-determination. Ironically, if they had not prevented a plebiscite by their incursion, then the result might have been the reverse of their 1918 view.[144]

In 1920 Hungary became a regency, appointing Archduke Joseph of Hapsburg as the Regent. Like Austria, Hungary nearly succumbed to bolshevism. This was countered by the government drafting a monarchical Constitution promoting a restoration of the Hapsburg dynasty. The allies opposed this, and the Archduke was forced to leave Hungary. Horthy[145] became regent with allied support. The French government, however, secretly intrigued with Hungarian diplomats to address Hungary's desire for the return of its former territory in Slovakia and Transylvania, and in exchange Hungary would grant France concessions in its railways and the Bank of Hungary.[146] This secret arrangement became public knowledge causing the Czechoslovak and Yugoslav governments to form a military alliance on 14 August 1920. Romania joined that alliance on 19 August, when Beneš, the Czechoslovak Minister for Foreign Affairs, described it as a Little Entente.[147]

The exiled Hapsburg Emperor Charles I, despite warnings from advisers, decided that the time was right for him to attempt a coup d'état and restore the monarchy in Hungary. He travelled as far as Szombathely, near the Austrian border, and awaited reports from France whose support was ambiguous. Horthy states that Briand never gave consent to Charles' restoration, and Charles was advised to leave.[148] As a result of Charles' intrigues with the French, Beneš took advantage by concluding a military

[140] Signed 4 June 1920.

[141] Lloyd D George, *The Truth About the Peace Treaties* (London, Victor Gallanz, 1938) 924.

[142] A Sharp, *Versailles 1919* (London, Haus Publishing, 2018) 15–18.

[143] J Hedham-Morley, *A Memoir* (London, Methuen & Company, 1972). Lord Hardinge, *Minute* c10/3/1919 FO 608/51. A Sharp, *Versailles 1919* (London, Haus Publishing, 2018) 84.

[144] A Sharp, *Versailles 1919* (London, Haus Publishing, 2018) 89.

[145] Miklós Horthy de Nagybánya regent of the Kingdom of Hungary from March 1920 until October 1944. Under him Hungary became an authoritarian nationalist democracy opposing the spread of Bolshevism. It resented the diminution of its territory and strove to restore the position before the Treaty of Trianon by its subsequent alliance with the Axis Powers.

[146] Duroselle, *De Wilson à Roosevelt* (Paris, 1960) 36 and Renouvin, *Les Relations Internationals: 1914-1945* (Paris, 1949 and 1954) also: J de Launay, *Major Controversies of Contemporary History* (Oxford, Pergamon Press, 1965) 93.

[147] Werkman (Zurich, 1923) 116; and J de Launay, *Major Controversies of Contemporary History* (Oxford, Pergamon Press, 1965) 93.

[148] M Horthy, *Ein leben für Ungarn* (Bonn, 1953) 118–121.

alliance with Romania, which was followed by an alliance between Czechoslovakia and Yugoslavia, extending the Little Entente. On 20 October 1921, despite the opposition to the restoration of the monarchy in Hungary, Charles and his wife, Empress Zita, attempted to restore the monarchy and planned to march on Budapest against the forces of the Regent Horthy.[149] They were both arrested and transported to Madeira, where on 1 April 1922, the emperor died. The consequence of French policy appears to have resulted in new treaties between Romania and Poland signed in March 1921 and between Czechoslovakia and Yugoslavia signed in August 1922. Thereafter, the Little Entente became the focus of French foreign policy in central and eastern Europe.[150] This had further adverse implications insofar as the states outside the Little Entente, Bulgaria, Austria and Hungary, were dissatisfied with the Versailles treaties such that they made common cause with Italy which was also dissatisfied with the treaties and the rejection of its territorial claims.

B. The Peace Treaty

The Treaty of Versailles was signed on 18 June 1919. It included recognition by the Allies of a single German state, the removal of administration from the hands of the military authorities, the setting up of an inter-Allied High Commission for the Rhine territories, the loss of territory to Poland, to Czechoslovakia, and to France, and limitations and restrictions on armaments and resources. Germany lost the heart of its industrial resources in the Ruhr and the Saar. The French occupation of the Saar for 15 years was some compensation for her loss of the mines in the Nord-Pas de Calais.[151] Germany had to reduce her army to 100,000 men, abolish her High Command structure, and surrender her fleet to the British. The question of reparations was addressed in principle but unquantified. It eventually amounted to £6.6 billion.[152] In essence, this was regarded by Germany as 'a stab in the back', and the myth of *Dolchstoss* prevailed as its government and people refused to believe that it lost the war.

i. War Guilt Clause and Reparations

Article 231 of the Treaty of Versailles provided that:[153]

> The allied governments and their associates declare, and Germany recognises, that Germany and her allies were responsible *for all the losses and damage*[154] sustained by the allied governments, their associates and their peoples in consequence of the war imposed upon them by the aggression of Germany and her allies.

[149] J de Launay, *Major Controversies of Contemporary History* (Oxford, Pergamon Press, 1965) 96.
[150] ibid.
[151] J Néré, *Foreign Policy of France 1914-1945* (London, Routledge and Kagan Paul, 1975) 17. Néré states that France lost 20 million tons of coal during the war.
[152] See ch 3, the Dawes Plan.
[153] This clause was drafted by Maynard Keynes and Foster Dulles. It was a clause that caused long lasting damage to the prospects for peace.
[154] Author's italics.

By inference, Article 231 provided that the unilateral responsibility for starting the war lay with the German Empire and her allies.[155] Germany had financial responsibility for the war damage. This linked responsibility for the war with payment of reparations. Full reparations by way of damages in respect of all the direct and indirect losses caused by the war were impractical, and therefore the Allies agreed that they would be limited to 'damage caused to the civil population and their property'.[156] Many wanted Germany to pay the whole cost of the war, which no doubt would have included all the direct and indirect costs of fighting the war and the consequential losses and expenses suffered by casualties. Anger against Germany was expressed by the *Daily Mail* headline 'The Huns Must Pay', a theme which Lloyd George exploited in the 1918 election, raising the public's expectations by demanding the payment of £25 billion as reparations. This was contrary to the Fourteen Points which had no indemnity provision. His cabinet colleagues FE Smith and Winston Churchill counselled against this.[157] Lloyd George came under intense pressure from the proprietor of the *Daily Mail* and *The Times*, Lord Northcliffe, who harassed Lloyd George, following him to France and causing deliberate mischief with misleading and ill-informed press reports, which incited rebellion on the backbenches and inflamed public opinion.[158] Lloyd George was forced to return to London during the conference and utterly defeated his critics in a debate on 16 April 1919.[159]

Under Article 232, Germany was to make compensation for all damage done to the civilian population of the Allied and Associated Powers and to their property during the war whether by land, sea or air, and in general all damage. This was to be determined by an Inter-Allied Commission, to be called the Reparation Commission.[160] Before that was agreed, the delegates were unable to calculate an exact sum to demand from Germany. This caused considerable tension between Wilson, Clemenceau and Lloyd George, undermining Wilson's credibility and adherence to the principles of his Fourteen Points.[161] Wilson forsook his principles in agreeing to reparations and the war guilt clause, Lloyd George using General Smuts to convince Wilson.[162] Lloyd George was under pressure to make good his promises to the electorate for the costs of the war and wanted an allowance for pension payments. Hughes, the Prime Minister of Australia, also demanded compensation of £25 billion which was rejected by Foster Dulles, who suggested £5 billion instead. It was impractical of them to apply Article 231 as it stood. Such a sum did not account for the value of territory

[155] In *Instruments of Peacemaking 1870-1914* the author opines as to the collective responsibility of the Great Powers, not only the German Empire, but also the Austro-Hungarian Empire and the Russian Empire, the latter by supporting Serbia activated the Franco-Russian alliance which in turn triggered British support for France when the security of the Channel ports and Belgium came into question. 305.

[156] J de Launay, *Major Controversies of Contemporary History* (Oxford, Pergamon Press, 1965) 84.

[157] A Lentin, *Lloyd George, Woodrow Wilson and the Guilt of Germany* (Leicester, Leicester University Press, 1984) 19, 24.

[158] ibid 50, 115.

[159] HC Deb. 16 April 1919 vol. 114 cc 2936-9 and cc 2951-3.

[160] Article 233 Treaty of Versailles.

[161] A Lentin, *Lloyd George, Woodrow Wilson, and the Guilt of Germany* (Leicester, Leicester University Press, 1984) 41–60.

[162] ibid 57.

lost by Germany or the resources extracted. Assessments were made of the cost of the war which came to a total of 720 billion (milliard[163]) Gold Deutsches Reich Marks (DM 720,000,000,000). This was unrealistic given the condition of Germany, and therefore the Powers had to be content with the actual cost of material damage.[164] This sum was much debated by the delegations and eventually the French agreed to reduce the amount claimed by 50 per cent with the English delegation suggesting payment over a period of 40 years. Maynard Keynes suggested that Germany should pay up to the limit of her capacity.[165] A temporary solution was agreed upon provided that Germany paid 20 billion gold marks by 1 May 1921. The US Army Corps of Engineers estimated the final Allied damage at $40 billion (160 milliard gold marks) excluding Czechoslovakia, Russia or Poland.[166] Apart from reparations, Germany lost 13 per cent of the Kaiserreich's territory, 10 per cent of its population, and 13.5 per cent of its economic potential.[167]

Keynes' subsequent critique of the Treaty[168] and his attacks on Wilson undoubtedly had some justification in the mind of Keynes, but in the wider context his analysis was questionable and greatly contributed to undermining American support for the League of Nations. It also contributed to undoubted sympathy for the aggressor irrespective of the damage caused by the war and supported the contentions of appeasers subsequently.[169] No doubt he, like others, was alarmed when the true intentions of Nazi Germany were exposed in 1938.

The method of payment was by circulation of several Bonds A and B of 50 billion gold marks. Bonds C were to be issued at 80 billion gold marks but would not be put into circulation until Germany could pay. By this means the amount of credit would reduce to 50 billion gold marks redeemable by means of annuities of 2 billion gold marks plus 26 per cent of the value of German exports, which amounted to approximately 3 billion marks per annum. Thus, in 40 years Germany would have paid 120 billion gold marks. Payments would terminate in 1962. This figure of 120 billion gold marks was adopted at the London conference on 1 May 1921, although Germany was in default by 12 billion gold marks at that date.[170] Despite suggestions for discharge of the reparation payments by way of a loan to redeem the A and B Bonds suggested by Léopold Dubois, a Swiss banker, the Germans and French rejected it. This might well have saved the Powers the 164 conferences on reparations between 1920 and 1934 to settle the question. The effect, according to de Launay, was to 'poison international relations between the two wars and hamper the setting up of a real German democracy'.[171] Reparations became

[163] One thousand million.

[164] J de Launay, *Major Controversies of Contemporary History* (Oxford, Pergamon Press, 1965) 85.

[165] R Skidelsky, *John Maynard Keynes, Hopes Betrayed 1883-1920* (London, Papermac, 1992) 365.

[166] S Marks, 'Mistakes and Myths: The Allies, Germany and the Versailles Treaty, 1918-1921' (2013) 85(3) *The Journal of Modern History* 643.

[167] ibid 652.

[168] JM Keynes, *The Economic Consequences of the Peace* (Oxford, Oxford City Press, 2021).

[169] Thus, many in Britain thought that taking back the Rhineland was like reclaiming your back garden and it was right to take Austria and Sudetenland, a view undoubtedly shared by Neville Chamberlain. This no doubt was chivalrous but not realpolitik.

[170] J de Launay, *Major Controversies of Contemporary History* (Oxford, Pergamon Press, 1965) 86.

[171] ibid 87.

the pretext for certain political activists in Germany to blame the Allies for the great inflation of 1923 and the Great Depression of 1929.[172]

There was obvious resentment in Germany. First, the people were told their army did not suffer a conclusive military defeat and felt betrayed by political manifestations on the Home Front. The German army surrendered and was defeated. Second, their delegates at Versailles were ignored, and any constructive negotiation was denied. Third, the presumption of the so-called 'war guilt clause', Article 231, was exaggerated but subsequently believed by the masses. Fourth, the humiliation of the dismemberment of the Kaiserreich and loss of its eastern provinces to Poland. Fifth, the occupation of the Ruhr, Silesia and the Rhineland, and finally the continuation of the Allied blockade, which led to hunger and starvation until March 1919 when American ships landed food supplies.

During the war, public opinion in the Allied countries had been outraged by the atrocities committed by German troops in Belgium and by submarine warfare, where ships such as the *RMS Lusitania* and *RMS Leinster* had been attacked without warning, with hundreds drowned. Such outrage gained credence when they learned of the extent of German atrocities and damage. At a meeting at St James's Palace in London on 3 March 1921, attended by representatives of France, Italy, Japan, and Germany, Lloyd George said that the German people had no idea how much damage their armies had caused in France in 1914. The reparations demanded were reasonable when compared to Bismarck's terms under the Treaty of Frankfurt in 1871, when Prussia demanded the costs of the Franco-Prussian War. Here Germany had damaged 20,603 factories in northern France, taking 10 years to restore, as well as all the mines, destruction of all electrical, mechanical and metallurgical factories, as well as 4,000 textile factories and 4,000 alimentary factories. 1,659 communes or townships were destroyed, 630,000 houses completely or partly destroyed, 8,000 kilometres of railway, 5,000 bridges, and 52,000 kilometres of roads with coal production reduced to 50 per cent (21 million tonnes instead of 42 million tonnes).[173] Those who felt reparations unjust took little account of the fact that French industry and its economy had suffered a calculated and deliberate blow so France would not be able to compete with Germany, which had no such material damage as its industries were unaffected.[174] Britain sought compensation for the eight million tonnes of shipping sunk by German action and the one million British Empire servicemen and women killed.[175] France lost 1.4 million men.[176] The fact was that Britain and France would have to raise three times the amount they received from Germany in reparations by increased taxation to cover their losses, whilst Germany made little effort to pay her debts through higher taxation.[177]

[172] AJP Taylor, *The Origins of the Second World War* (London, 1961) 46.
[173] BDFP Vol XV 1st Series. No 31. *British Stenographers Verbatim Note of an Allied Conference held in St James's Palace London SW on Thursday, March 9, 1921 at 12.00 noon.*
[174] BDFP Vol XV 1st Series. No 31. 260.
[175] ibid 261.
[176] ibid 262.
[177] ibid 263–264.

While the treaty had not specified the amount of reparations, the following penalty provisions were included in the Treaty of Versailles against the wishes of Wilson:

> VII. PENALTIES.
>
> ARTICLE 227.
>
> The Allied and Associated Powers publicly arraign William II of Hohenzollern, formerly German Emperor, for a supreme offence against international morality and the sanctity of treaties.
>
> A special tribunal will be constituted to try the accused, thereby assuring him the guarantees essential to the right of defence. It will be composed of five judges, one appointed by each of the following Powers: namely, the United States of America, Great Britain, France, Italy and Japan.
>
> In its decision the tribunal will be guided by the highest motives of international policy, with a view to vindicating the solemn obligations of international undertakings and the validity of international morality. It will be its duty to fix the punishment which it considers should be imposed.
>
> The Allied and Associated Powers will address a request to the Government of the Netherlands for the surrender to them of the ex-Emperor in order that he may be put on trial.

Despite a request in June 1920, the Dutch government refused to extradite the Kaiser to the Allies. Thus, he was never prosecuted for war crimes under Article 227.

As to other punitive provisions, the Treaty provided:

> ARTICLE 228.
>
> The German Government recognises the right of the Allied and Associated Powers to bring before military tribunals persons accused of having committed acts in violation of the laws and customs of war. Such persons shall, if found guilty, be sentenced to punishments laid down by law. This provision will apply notwithstanding any proceedings or prosecution before a tribunal in Germany or in the territory of her allies.
>
> The German Government shall hand over to the Allied and Associated Powers, or to such one of them as shall so request, all persons accused of having committed an act in violation of the laws and customs of war, who are specified either by name or by the rank, office or employment which they held under the German authorities.
>
> ARTICLE 229.
>
> Persons guilty of criminal acts against the nationals of one of the Allied and Associated Powers will be brought before the military tribunals of that Power.
>
> Persons guilty of criminal acts against the nationals of more than one of the Allied and Associated Powers will be brought before military tribunals composed of members of the military tribunals of the Powers concerned.
>
> In every case the accused will be entitled to name his own counsel.
>
> ARTICLE 230.
>
> The German Government undertakes to furnish all documents and information of every kind, the production of which may be considered necessary to ensure the full knowledge of the incriminating acts, the discovery of offenders and the just appreciation of responsibility.

Article 228 required the German government to surrender all war criminals for trial by allied military courts. Article 239 provided for the prosecution of those responsible for war crimes during the occupation. Article 228 established an International Criminal Court. Lloyd George thought the Kaiser should stand trial. FE Smith advised that if the Kaiser was not indicted, others could not be. Secretary Robert Lansing of the US said there was no court to try the Kaiser, although Lloyd George said he committed 'the greatest crime in history'. It was agreed that the German authorities should try offenders for war crimes but only 45 people were brought before the German courts. The German court rulings were repudiated by the Allies. The French convicted over 1,000 Germans in absentia. The British government took no part in this. Under Article 230 of the Treaty of Sèvres, signed 10 August 1920, the Ottomans were to surrender those responsible for the Armenian massacres. The British, however, chose to swap their Turkish prisoners for British prisoners held by the Turks. Attempts to prosecute the perpetrators for the massacre were abortive at Leipzig and Constantinople, yet there developed the acceptance that superior orders were no defence to war crimes and that political and military leaders were liable under international law.[178]

At the Preliminary Peace Conference plenary session on 25 January 1919 (Minute No. 2), it was decided to create a commission composed of fifteen members, two to be named by each of the Great Powers (US, British Empire, France, Italy and Japan) and five elected from among the Powers with special interests for the purpose of enquiring into the responsibilities relating to the war.[179]

The Commission held that the responsibility for the war:[180]

> … rested first on Germany and Austria, secondly on Turkey and Bulgaria. It was made all the graver by reason of the violation by Germany and Austria of the neutrality of Belgium and Luxemburg, which they themselves had guaranteed. It is increased, with regard to both France and Serbia, by the violation of their frontiers before the declaration of war.

It further concluded:[181]

> CONCLUSIONS
>
> 1. The war was premeditated by the Central Powers together with their Allies, Turkey and Bulgaria, and was the result of acts deliberately committed in order to make it unavoidable.
> 2. Germany, in agreement with Austria-Hungary, deliberately worked to defeat all the many conciliatory proposals made by the Entente Powers and their repeated efforts to avoid war.

As far as breaches of the laws and customs of war were committed by the German Empire and their allies the Commission considered a large number of documents including the Report of Lord Bryce, the French Commission presided over by M Payelle, numerous

[178] An International Criminal Court was not created until 2002.

[179] *Commission on the Responsibility of the Authors of the War and on Enforcement of Penalties*, Vol 14 No 1/2 *AJIL* (Cambridge, CUP, 1920) 95–154.

[180] ibid 98.

[181] ibid 107.

Belgium government publications, a Memorandum of the Greek Delegation, documents lodged by the Italian government, Greek submission on crimes committed against Greek populations by the Bulgars, Turks and Greeks, a Memorandum of the Serbian Delegation, the Report of the Inter-Allied Commission on the Violations of the Hague Conventions and of international law in general, committed between 1915 and 1918 by the Bulgars in occupied Serbia, a summary of the Polish Delegation, together with the Rumanian and Armenian Memoranda, all of which provided abundant evidence of outrages of every description committed on land, at sea, and in the air, against the laws and customs of war and of the laws of humanity.[182]

So far as civil and military authorities of the offending states were concerned, the Commission concluded that they could not be relieved from responsibility by the mere fact that a higher authority might have been convicted of the same offence. It would be for the court to decide whether a plea of superior orders was sufficient to acquit the person charged from responsibility. They concluded:[183]

> All persons belonging to enemy countries, however high their position may have been, without distinction of rank, including Chiefs of States, who have been guilty of offences against the laws and customs of war or the laws of humanity, are liable to criminal prosecution.

There was also a proposal for a high tribunal to be set up under the peace treaty.[184]

C. The League of Nations[185]

Professor Zimmern observed that the title 'League of Nations' was a misnomer. The correct description in his view would have been 'Society of Nations' (Société des Nations).[186] The term 'League' inferred an exclusive association, which it was not, or a band of crusaders opposed to some other party or cause. It implied 'a certain exclusiveness, derived from a common attachment to certain particular principles or doctrines'. But according to Zimmern, the essential underlying idea of the League of Nations was its inclusiveness. It was a new method or model for all states and its membership was intended to be universal and an all-embracing association.[187] The term 'nation' was inappropriate because the members of the League were not nations, but states. Membership of the League had nothing whatsoever to do with nationality or nationhood. It was simply concerned with statehood, ie, political status. Members of the League included the British Empire and the United Socialist Soviet Republics; neither of them were nations, nor indeed, as Zimmern pointed out did international law know anything of

[182] ibid 112–113.
[183] ibid 117.
[184] ibid 124.
[185] The idea of a 'League of Nations' was first suggested by Andrew Carnegie who set up the Carnegie Endowment for International peace in 1910 with Elihu Root as its first President. See: R Henig, *The Peace That Never Was: A History of the League of Nations* (London, Haus Publishing, 2019) 7.
[186] A Zimmern, *The League of Nations and the Rule of Law* (London, Macmillan and Co limited, 1936) 2.
[187] ibid.

'nations', only of states.[188] He explained that this misnomer occurred because of adherence to the political theory of western continental Europe in the late eighteenth century, deriving more from the age of revolution than any other. This he concluded caused confusion and conflict as it was incorporated into the Covenant of the League.[189]

The essential purpose of the League, despite these misconceptions, was intended to facilitate international relations by supporting and supplementing conventional methods. This was based on minority protection, disarmament and international law.

It was Sir Edward Grey's view[190] that

> great armaments lead inevitably to war. If there are armaments on one side there must be armaments on the other sides. While one nation arms, other nations cannot tempt it to aggression by remaining defenceless. … Each measure taken by one nation is noted and leads to countermeasures by others. … The enormous growth of armaments in Europe, the sense of insecurity and fear caused by them – it was these that made war inevitable.

Instruments of Peacemaking 1870-1914[191] considered the extent to which disputes could be resolved by arbitration. This depended upon whether the issue in question was legal or political, dependent upon the disputants agreeing to an arbitration treaty. This was often frustrated by concerns for the national interest and state sovereignty. The Peace Conference provided the means to create a process by which international disputes between states could be resolved through the League of Nations by its means and avoid another conflagration. It was an acknowledgement that the Old Diplomacy had failed. Wilson's espousal of self-determination was an idealistic approach to resolve European problems without appreciation for the historical, cultural, and political ties that had bound certain empires over time. Germany, in particular, had a problem with the dispersal of its population to the newly created states of Poland and Czechoslovakia following the demise of the German and Austro-Hungarian Empires. The hope was that future disputes would be resolved by diplomacy and not by war. This, in hindsight, was proved a forlorn hope when the peace treaties enacted far from securing the peace only secured a temporary truce. Whatever the shortcomings of the League of Nations, in concept it was an advance on the Concert of Europe, which broke down in 1913 with the fractured relations between the Great Powers with Italy, Austria-Hungary and the Kaiserreich pursuing policies independent of the concept.[192] Article 10 of the Covenant of the League provided that:

> The Members of the League undertake to respect and preserve as against external aggression the territorial integrity and existing political independence of all Members of the League. In case of any such aggression or in case of any threat or danger of such aggression the Council shall advise upon the means by which this obligation shall be fulfilled.

The League's innovation in the context of Article 10 would appear to abrogate the international relations theory of the balance of power as well as eliminate the system of alliances that existed before 1914. Such an objective coincided with the views of President Wilson

[188] ibid 3.
[189] ibid 4. The preamble to the Covenant referred to: just and honourable relations between nations.
[190] E Grey, *Twenty-five Years, 1892–1916* (Vol 1) (New York, Frederick A. Stokes Company, 1925).
[191] M Reynolds, *Instruments of Peacemaking 1870-1914* (Oxford, Hart Publishing, 2021).
[192] M Reynolds, *Instruments of Peacemaking 1870-1914* (Oxford, Hart Publishing, 2021) 274.

in his speech on 8 January 1918. Again, an idealistic notion and one which was incapable of preventing the subsequent extreme nationalist revival imbued with Prussian military culture, which the Permanent Under-Secretary to the Foreign Office and Chief Diplomatic Adviser to His Majesty's Government warned of continuously in the 1930s.[193]

i. Divergent Approaches

To understand the League, it is important to understand its purpose and why it was established. President Woodrow Wilson was one of the architects of the League of Nations, one of his famous Fourteen Points. Wilson's allies, Lloyd George and Clemenceau, were not so enthusiastic. Lloyd George was not sure, and Clemenceau wanted to limit it. Britain's difficulty was that the existence of the League would negate any idea of a balance of power in Europe. For Clemenceau it meant the loss of guarantees against German aggression. Importantly, the French view was that collective security, and the League of Nations would not be a substitute for an alliance.[194] Wilson disagreed with Lloyd George and felt that the concept of a balance of power was a cause of wars. When the Covenant of the League was drawn it abrogated any concept of a balance of power by virtue of Article 10:

> The Members of the League undertake to respect and preserve as against external aggression the territorial integrity and existing political independence of all Members of the League. In case of any such aggression or in case of any threat or danger of such any such aggression or in case of any threat or danger of such aggression the Council shall advise upon the means by which this obligation shall be fulfilled.

Wilson idealistically thought that the League would champion his notion of self-determination. Wilson also felt that the treaty was too strict and that the League would be able to administer the treaty more equitably.[195] Clemenceau was not altogether happy with Wilson's approach and remarked at the conference: *vox populi, vox diaboli,*[196] but he was not the only one to voice concern as to self-determination, which would undermine French interests in its colonial territories. As to Wilson, Clemenceau praised *la noble candeur de son esprit*, (the noble candour of his mind).[197]

Whilst the council was given this power under Article 10 questions were raised as to whether Article 19 was in conflict. Article 19 provided a possible contradiction to Article 10:

> The Assembly may from time to time advise the reconsideration by Members of the League of treaties which have become inapplicable and the consideration of international conditions whose continuance might endanger the peace of the world.

Nations could not, therefore, be certain that in the event of them being attacked by another state, that the members of the league would come to their assistance.

[193] JR Ferris, 'The indulged in all too little? Vansittart, Intelligence and Appeasement' (1995) 6(1) *Diplomacy and Statecraft* 122–175.
[194] W Lippmann, *US Foreign Policy* (London, Hamish Hamilton, 1943) 47.
[195] J de Launay, *Major Controversies of Contemporary History* (Oxford, Pergamon Press, 1965) 88.
[196] The voice of the people is the voice of the devil.
[197] A Sharp, *Versailles. A Centennial Perspective* (London, Haus Publishing, 2018) 58.

ii. Collective Security

Underpinning the League of Nations was the idea of collective security, but this was not effective because states, as we shall see, had competing interests. The US proclaimed the absolute right to trade with a belligerent if it was neutral, as Britain had proclaimed in 1861 when it recognised the Confederacy and the Union governments as belligerents but traded with both.[198] Collective security was not popular with the British Foreign Office, although it was inscribed in the Treaty of Mutual Assistance 1923 and the Geneva Protocol 1924. The obligation under the Covenant was vague and uncertain insofar as no state could be certain as to what commitment it might have to meet. This was reflected in a report by the Committee of Imperial Defence in November 1935.

D. The Covenant of the League

i. Arbitration: An Instrument for Peace

The means by which the peace was to be maintained were diplomacy and arbitration. The Covenant revived the dreams of those international jurists who championed arbitration before 1914. Thus, Article XII of the Covenant of the League provided that if any dispute should arise between members, they could submit the matter either to arbitration or to inquiry by the League Council. They would bind themselves to agree not to resort to war until three months after the award by the arbitrators or the report by the Council. Under Article XIII, members agreed that whenever any dispute arose between them that was suitable for submission to arbitration, which could not be satisfactorily settled by diplomacy, they would submit the matter to arbitration. Those submissible included disputes as to the interpretation of a treaty, any question of international law, the existence of any fact that, if established, would constitute a breach of any international obligation, or as to the extent and nature of the reparation to be made for any such breach. The members were free to agree on the members of the arbitral tribunal or as predetermined in any convention between them. Members of the League agreed to comply in good faith with any award and not to resort to war against a member which complied with the award. In the event of non-compliance, the Council would propose the steps to be taken.

ii. Permanent Court of International Justice

Under Article XIV, the Council of the League could formulate and submit to members plans for the establishment of a Permanent Court of International Justice. The Court would be competent to hear and determine any dispute of an international character that the parties submitted to it. The Court could also give an advisory opinion upon any dispute or question referred to it by the Council or by the Assembly.

[198] 'The Geneva Arbitration' in M Reynolds, *Instruments of Peacemaking* 1870-1914 (Oxford, Hart Publishing, 2021) 14 et seq.

iii. Reference to the Council under Article XV

If there was any dispute between members likely to lead to a rupture, which was not submitted to arbitration, the dispute could be submitted to the Council. Notice was to be given to the Secretary General, who could direct the matter to be investigated and given consideration. Upon receipt of the members' statements of the case with all the relevant facts and papers, the Council could direct their publication. The Council could then take steps to resolve the matter, making public the terms of settlement as it deemed appropriate. If not settled, a similar report to that effect would be published. If a report by the Council was unanimously agreed to by the members other than the Representatives of one or more of the parties to the dispute, the members of the League agreed that they would not go to war with any party to the dispute which complied with the recommendations of the report. If the Council failed to make a report unanimously agreed to by the members, other than the representatives of one or more of the parties to the dispute, the members of the League reserved the right to take appropriate action 'for the maintenance of right and justice'. If the dispute was solely within the domestic jurisdiction of a party. no recommendation would be made. The matter alternatively could be referred to the Assembly of the League within 14 days of the reference to the Council.

iv. Where a Member Committed an Act of War

Under Article XVI, if any member of the League resorted to war in disregard of its covenants under Articles XII, XIII or XV, it would be deemed to have committed an act of war against all other members of the League. Those members would immediately subject it to the severance of all trade or financial relations, the prohibition of all intercourse between their nationals and the nationals of the covenant-breaking state, and the prevention of all financial, commercial, or personal intercourse between the nationals of the covenant-breaking state and the nationals of any other state, whether a member of the League or not. The Council in such a case would then be obliged to recommend to the several governments concerned what effective military or naval force the members of the League would severally contribute to the armed forces to be used to protect the covenants of the League.

The members of the League agreed that they would mutually support one another in the financial and economic measures which were taken under Article XVI in order to minimise the loss and inconvenience resulting from the above measures and that they would mutually support one another in resisting any special measures aimed at one of their number by the covenant-breaking state. Interestingly, they would take the necessary steps to afford passage through their territory to the forces of any of the members of the League which were co-operating to protect the covenants of the League. This is a point that concerned Czechoslovakia in 1938 when the prospect of Russian help was being considered with transit of forces through Romania or Poland.[199]

If any member violated any covenant, it could be excluded by a vote of the Council concurred in by the Representatives of all the other members.

[199] See ch 4.

v. Dispute between a Member of the League and a Non-Member State

Under Article XVII of the Covenant, in the event of a dispute between a member of the League and a non-member state, or between non-member states, the state or states that were not members of the League could be invited to accept the obligations of membership in the League for the purposes of such dispute, on such conditions as the Council may deem just. If accepted, the provisions of Articles XII to XVI inclusive would apply with appropriate modifications by the Council. The Council would then institute an inquiry into the circumstances of the dispute and recommend such action 'as may seem best and most effectual in the circumstances'. If a state refused to accept the obligations of membership in the League for the purposes of such dispute and resorted to war against a member, the provisions of Article XVI would apply as against the state taking such action.

If both parties to the dispute, when so invited, refused to accept the obligations of membership in the League for the purposes of their dispute, the Council could take such measures and make such recommendations to prevent hostilities and would result in the settlement of the dispute.

vi. Other Disputes Processes under the Treaty of Versailles

Under paragraph 16 of Annex I, where the two Clearing Offices dealing with reparations payments and receipts were unable to agree whether a debt claimed was due, or in cases of difference between an enemy debtor and an enemy creditor or between the Clearing Offices, the dispute could be referred to arbitration if the parties agreed or referred to the Mixed Arbitral Tribunal provided for in Section VI of the Treaty. Alternatively, the matter could be submitted to the jurisdiction of the courts of the place of domicile of the debtor. Under Annex II Article 233 paragraph 13 of the Treaty of Versailles, there was provision for arbitration to be used to resolve differences of opinion among the Delegates of the Reparations Commission, whether a given case required a unanimous vote for its decision or not or be referred to arbitration.

These additional obligations of membership did not detract from existing obligations since Article 21 of the treaty provided that:

> nothing in the Covenant shall be deemed to affect the validity of international engagements, such as treaties of arbitration or regional understandings like the Monroe doctrine, for securing the maintenance of peace.

E. The Mechanics of World Peace under the Peace Treaties

The general geopolitical effect of the treaties was to increase minorities in European states, breeding resentment. To mitigate such discontent plebiscites were conducted and protection offered by the League of Nations. Thus, five plebiscites were held in Schleswig, Klagenfurt, Allenstein, Marienwerder and Oldenberg. In 1921 the plebiscite in Upper Silesia produced a German majority, although it had a 65 per cent Polish majority. In 1935 the Saar was transferred to Germany.[200] Britain and France had a backlash against

[200] A Sharp, *Versailles. A Centennial Perspective* (London, Haus Publishing, 2018) 83.

this policy of making the map fit the people, and whilst possibly good in theory, such boundary revisions included disinterested minorities. The British and French empires suffered as a result – Britain in India and Egypt, and France in Indochina and Syria. If self-determination was to be the panacea of all ills, then the experiment failed in March 1939 when German troops occupied what remained of Czechoslovakia.

i. Minority Rights

Whilst the Great Powers prescribed protection for religious minorities in the new Balkan states – Serbia, Montenegro and Romania – they did not apply these principles to themselves. After the Treaty of Berlin in 1878, these protective measures were ignored, for example, in Romania with its Jewish population. Contradicting this prescription was the principle of non-interference in domestic affairs of other sovereign states provided by the Treaty of Westphalia 1648. This was mitigated after 1919 by the League of Nations and the protection of minority rights. The movement for the establishment of minority rights was opposed by the US, faced with racial discrimination in its southern states and by Britain, with its rule in Ireland, which rejected any inclusion of any such protection in the League Covenant.[201] The solution to this dilemma was to make international recognition conditional upon the enactment of certain fundamental laws so that all inhabitants of the state became full citizens with the protection of life and liberty enjoying equal rights and in Poland's case, to use their own language.[202]

The basis of non-discrimination of minorities was incorporated in the treaties with Romania, Greece, Yugoslavia, Czechoslovakia, Austria, Hungary, Bulgaria, Turkey, Albania, Lithuania, Latvia, and Estonia, but Britain, France, Denmark, Belgium, and Germany were not required to give such guarantees. Unsurprisingly, the Great Powers were confused as to the difference between nationality and citizenship; this may have stemmed from Woodrow Wilson's misunderstanding mentioned earlier.

ii. Disarmament

The key objectives of German disarmament were accomplished by late 1922. Despite this, German security organised its forces so that they could be expanded. Secret arrangements were made with the Soviet Union for weapons testing after the Treaty of Rapallo in April 1922. German armaments manufacturers moved plant to other countries, and they ensured that they could compensate for all these reductions in one year. As Henig[203] cites, it is worthwhile bearing in mind the warning of Sir Eyre Crowe in October 1916 that:

> unless all the world's leading military and naval powers were involved in schemes of armament limitation, disarmament could prove very dangerous to those who undertook it.

[201] Somewhat curious in the case of Ireland where Unionists were in the minority in 1919 and if Britain had granted Irish independence such a minority would have had the League's protection.

[202] A Sharp, *Versailles. A Centennial Perspective* (London, Haus Publishing, 2018) 104–105.

[203] R Henig, *The League of Nations* (Edinburgh, Oliver and Boyd, 1973).

What was an offensive and what was a defensive armament was a question that haunted diplomats in those days just as much as it haunts diplomats today. At Geneva in 1932, Germany and France could not agree on what were defensive and what were offensive weapons. What increased concern was Japan's departure from the League in February 1933, followed by Nazi Germany. There were naval conferences in 1921 and 1922 in Washington, the Coolidge Naval Conference in 1927 and the Naval Conference in London in 1930.

iii. Reasons for Failure

Apart from the lack of proper organisation for the conference,[204] a critical failure was its numerous committees and deliberations behind closed doors from which the vanquished had been excluded from discussions. A Peace Congress of all Powers, including Germany was originally suggested but ignored.[205] In terms of enforcement, the articles were weak, and reparations payments were practically unenforceable. Disarmament obligations meant that in any crisis the League members would have difficulty in performing any military action against an aggressor.

Having been created with such high expectations and ideals of Wilsonian liberalism following 'the war to end all wars', why did it fail? An observer of this phenomenon was Hugh Dalton, who (like Harold Nicolson, John Buchan, Robert Bruce Lockhart and John Wheeler Bennet) reflected[206] on many reasons for its failure. The first was that the US repudiated the League of Nations and the Guarantee Treaty which underwrote French security. France had been persuaded to agree to a frontier west of the Rhineland in exchange for a joint undertaking by America and Britain that if Germany attacked France, Britain and America would give aid to France.[207] Britain's retreat from Europe further underlined French suspicions of British isolationism and fear of German revenge. With the departure of the US differences between France and Britain grew more bitter. Several international conferences led by Lloyd George were ineffective. Poincare sent French forces to occupy the Ruhr, disaffecting the Germans. Subsequently, the US facilitated the French withdrawal from the Ruhr by the Dawes Plan in 1924 and enabled readjustment of reparations in the Young Plan in 1929. In 1932 reparations ceased.[208]

The second reason for failure was the commercial value of membership in the League was limited, as Most Favoured Nation status was not exclusive to members. British membership was always half-hearted. Like the US, Britain did not give a guarantee to France. It also opposed a United Europe proposal of Briand just before Hitler became Chancellor of Germany in January 1933. Britain had an appearance of imperial supremacy and was afraid of 'entanglements' and commitments in Europe, like American isolationism. Public opinion was divided between Tory pro-German half-isolationists

[204] Meetings were held without proper documentation, rambling from topic to topic until Sir Maurice Hankey, Secretary to the British delegation, brought order to the chaos. S Marks, 'Mistakes and Myths: The Allies, Germany and the Versailles Treaty, 1918-1921' (2013) 85(3) *The Journal of Modern History* 638.
[205] Marks, ibid 637.
[206] H Dalton, *Hitler's War Before and After* (New York, Penguin Books, 1940) 16.
[207] ibid 18.
[208] ibid 17.

and Labour pacifists and Tory interventionists like Churchill, Julian Amory, Anthony Eden, Harold Macmillan, Ronald Tree, Harold Nicolson and Duff Cooper.

Third, former allies Italy and Japan felt aggrieved by not receiving any colonies. Japan ignored the mandates for the territories she gained in 1918.

Fourth, Germany was estranged by her diminished status as a Great Power and lack of colonies. Britain and France failed to treat Germany properly and support its fledgling democracy – the Weimar Republic. There was no acknowledgement of Germany's social development, and therefore the Prussian spirit remained. Industrialists and military leaders remained at their posts. There was no democratic reform in the army. It was not disarmed. The 'Little Reichswehr' had 100,000 highly armed soldiers who dominated the Republic.[209] Germany was splintered by rival private armies, Nazis, Socialists, Communists and Nationalists.[210] In November 1923, Hitler's attempted rebellion in Munich amounted to treason, but he was simply imprisoned for a short term.[211] This was inept and obviously gave Hitler and his followers encouragement.

The Weimar's gradual decline was witnessed by a series of events: the occupation of the Ruhr, followed by the Great Inflation, the Recovery and Locarno in 1925, Germany's accession to the League of Nations in 1925, Allied evacuation of the Rhineland in 1930, the Great Depression, and the financial crisis in 1931, the failure of the Disarmament Conference in 1932 and then the rise of Hitler (after the fall of Brüning, who desperately tried to resolve the financial crisis), who set Germany on the road to war.[212]

F. Critiques of the Conference and Treaty and *the Arbiter of Europe*

David Lloyd George, the British Prime Minister, was one of the architects of the Versailles settlement. Whilst this has been much criticised over the last century, revisionists have to a certain extent absolved the architects from some of the consequences of the Versailles Peace Treaties. Lloyd George's defence of the treaties written in 1938[213] must be given the weight it deserves. Apportioning blame is easy after the event when the consequences become clearer. At the time, the success of bringing peace was paramount, and that was achieved. On the other hand, Wilson abandoned his adherence to the Fourteen Points, acceding to the wiles of Lloyd George and Clemenceau. He became enmeshed in the intricacies and paradoxes of European diplomacy. The Peace Conference was disorganised and chaotic with no agreed agenda or priorities; the Allied blockade was in force, and people were starving, disease was rife (including the flu pandemic[214]), and the necessities of life were in short supply.[215] This tragic action caused statesmen like Lord Robert Cecil grave concern, as did the punitive provisions inserted in the Treaty without

[209] ibid 23.
[210] ibid 24.
[211] ibid.
[212] ibid.
[213] D Lloyd George, *The Truth About the Peace Treaties* (London, Victor Gallanz, 1938).
[214] L Spinney, *Pale Rider* (London, Vantage, 2017).
[215] S Marks, 'Mistakes and Myths: The Allies, Germany and the Versailles Treaty, 1918-1921' (2013) 85(3) *The Journal of Modern History* 636–637.

German agreement. Unfortunately, Cecil was not the man to rock the boat and failed to oppose provisions which he knew would cause problems later.[216]

The League of Nations organisation per se was not the cause of the decline in international relations between the wars; rather, it was the lack of enforcement powers under the Treaty that weakened respect for the new order. Lloyd George attributed the failure to those statesmen who succeeded the authors of the settlement. What fundamentally undermined the credibility of the League of Nations, almost from its inception, was the abandonment and the disaffection of its promoter: the US. The League of Nations had been Woodrow Wilson's dream, an idea which he supported as a result of conversations between Sir Edward Grey and former President Theodore Roosevelt.[217] This resulted in the Old World being left to its own historic cultural and national rivalries, whether between France and Germany or Britain and France. As Lloyd George wrote, it was the failure of 'a miscellaneous and unimpressive array of second-rate statesmen' who were incapable of properly operating the mechanics of the League and the treaties.[218] So, when Germany took aggressive military steps in the Rhineland and in Austria, inserted gunnery emplacements in the Pyrenees, constructed airfields and submarine bases in the Bay of Biscay, and placed heavy artillery on both sides of the Straits of Gibraltar, and the construction of Italian air and submarine bases threatened France and its communications in North Africa – nothing was done.[219] Domestic economics hindered arms production. In England, Neville Chamberlain was not only reluctant, but obstructive to expanding industry for defence purposes.[220]

In defence of Versailles and the treaties, Lloyd George made some telling arguments. The invention of the League was unique in history in that it replaced the Congress system based on the Treaty of Vienna 1815 which inaugurated a system of meetings between statesmen and conferences of ambassadors on an ad hoc basis. But the Versailles arrangements were responsible for an organised system by way of regular meetings of ambassadors and commissions, and in certain cases, referral to the Permanent Court of Arbitration. Above all, it was responsible for emancipating millions who had been subject to despotic rulers from the Vistula to the Euphrates.[221] For the first time an attempt was being made to apply a principle of government by consent where possible based on Woodrow Wilson's idea of self-determination; thus, plebiscites were held in various regions. Whilst the defeated German, Austro-Hungarian, and Ottoman empires were reconstructed, the victorious empires of Britain, France, and Russia were not.[222]

[216] A Lentin, *Lloyd George, Woodrow Wilson, and the Guilt of Germany* (Leicester, Leicester University Press, 1984) 127.

[217] It was an idea suggested by Mr Asquith to M Brand, the French Prime Minister that there be special conferences given at regular intervals and a regular organisation. He suggested there should be a standing Inter-Allied Committee composed of prime ministers with a secretariat of its own. This was not approved at first but subsequently a system was put into effect at a conference in Paris in March 1916. This was based on Mr Asquith's original suggestion in a more highly developed form and inaugurated a body known as the Supreme War Council. This was composed of two representatives from each of the countries concerned. This was a standing international conference and a prototype for the League of Nations. See: A Zimmern, *The League of Nations and the Rule of Law 1918-1935* (London, Macmillan and Co, 1936).

[218] D Lloyd George, *The Truth About the Peace Treaties* (London, Victor Gallanz, 1938) 1403.

[219] ibid 1402.

[220] See ch 4.

[221] D Lloyd George, *The Truth About the Peace Treaties* (London, Victor Gallanz, 1938) 1404.

[222] Save in Russia's case regarding alterations with the Polish border in 1924. See ch 3.

The imperial interests of France and Britain were met by their League mandates although Britain, after 1918, found its empire becoming more of a burden than a benefit.[223] Wilson's idealism and the concept of self-determination were not followed in Germany, Poland, Hungary, or Ireland.[224] Germany was aggrieved in losing much of its population and its colonies, a cause for resentment fuelling calls for rearmament and equality with other Powers. Although this experiment in international government could outlaw war and declare it to be a crime against society, these principled declarations did not stop Mussolini's ambitions in North Africa, nor Japanese incursions in Korea and China, much less Hitler's re-occupation of the Rhineland, the Anschluss and Munich.

Lloyd George's argument was that although there were later problems, there was power to revise the treaties. It was a failure of statesmanship and diplomacy not to utilise those revising powers. Diplomacy, as Sir Austin Chamberlain initially suggested, was easier in the League of Nations forum.[225] In 1938, Lloyd George took the view that: 'had the stipulations of these treaties been fully forcefully and honestly interpreted and fulfilled the … military and economic menace now hanging over Europe would have been averted'.[226] It would appear that the lack of leadership in the League of Nations was an essential element in its failure, as Lloyd George said: 'weakness and vacillation'. He admitted, however, that the 'crudities and injustices' that were revealed '… could have been removed under the revisionary provisions enacted for that purpose, provided these had been honesty applied'.[227] What destroyed Wilson's other ideal of collective security were cases where a member of the League had failed to aid wanton aggression against weak countries and failed to respect the rights of minorities. If anything, the cause was the dishonourable infraction of the treaties. It appears that it was not so much the organisation of the League or the substance of the treaties, but the failure to adapt the treaties or revise them to resolve the difficulties that were inevitable given the limits on the peace treaty conferences.[228] According to Lloyd George in March 1926, the Council of Ambassadors[229] reported that Germany had completed her disarmament obligations, but instead of other members complying with their disarmament pledges, they dishonoured their pledge.[230] He also concluded that the League became a means of French military and diplomatic supremacy. He suggested that when the allies reneged on the pledge Nazi Germany was born. When American influence disappeared the League of Nations was no longer impartial and its influence and authority seriously diminished.[231]

The peace arrangements for Austria-Hungary were more difficult than for Germany. President Wilson came with his ideals, but what the peacemakers had to do was deal

[223] The demands for independence in Ireland and India.

[224] The partition of Ireland was used by Hitler in a speech in September 1938 to justify his annexation of the Sudetenland.

[225] D Lloyd George, *The Truth About the Peace Treaties* (London, Victor Gallanz, 1938) 1406.

[226] ibid 1407.

[227] ibid 1406.

[228] ibid 1408.

[229] The Conference of Ambassadors of the Principal Allied and Associated Powers was an inter-allied organisation of the Entente formed in Paris in January 1920 succeeding the Supreme War Council and later incorporated into the League of Nations as one of its governing bodies. It ceased in importance after 1925.

[230] D Lloyd George, *The Truth About the Peace Treaties* (London, Victor Gallanz, 1938) 1409.

[231] ibid 1410.

with centuries-old hatreds, which Wilson did not appreciate.[232] Lloyd George was critical of the polyglot state of Czechoslovakia which included 'hundreds of thousands of protesting Magyars and millions of angry Germans'.[233] What created a problem for German Austrians was the severance of its fellow citizens in Bohemia. Four million Germans were forced into a state against self-determination. Austria lost its richest industrial part and highly developed agricultural area: Bohemia and the Sudetenland.[234] Czechoslovakia was certainly a polyglot: it contained 6.5 million Czechs, 3.5 million Germans, two million Slovaks, 750,000 Hungarians, 500,000 Ukrainians and 100,000 Poles.[235] As Lloyd George said, the failed Hapsburg empire had dominated and fragmented nations with endless conflicts and then the treaties created another polyglot conglomerate incorporating fragmented nations.[236] He considered this new polyglot state a portent for a similar disaster. Czechoslovakia could not conform to the Swiss model because the Swiss 'fought for liberty and not coercion of the Conqueror'.[237] M Vosnich of Serbia protested against the Klagenfelt plebiscite said that: 'Austria would in time unite with Germany and the German policy of pushing towards the sea would again recommence.'[238] Count Apponyi appearing before the Heads of the Five Principal Powers on behalf of Hungary at the Quai d'Orsay on 16 January 1919, protested at the draft treaty. Under the treaty, Hungary would lose two-thirds of its territory and lose its economic prosperity.[239] In his interview with the Austrian ambassador, Count Mensdorff,[240] General Smuts suggested that Austria-Hungary's component races should be given autonomy inside a federal constitution, but this was frustrated by the occupation of various regions by neighbouring states' forces, preventing any application of self-determination.[241] A Foreign Office Memorandum dated 1 December 1918 stated:[242]

> Austria Hungary has ceased to exist and there is no possibility of negotiating with it.

The Hapsburgs were eliminated, the joint army dissolved, the Ballplatz ceased to exist, and the state disintegrated. In his Fourteen Points President Wilson had declared:[243]

> X. The peoples of Austria-Hungary whose place among the nations we wish to see safeguarded and assured should be in accordance with the freeist opportunity of autonomous development.

Lloyd George favoured self-government 'on true democratic principles' for the 'Austro-Hungarian nationalities who have long deserved it.'[244] The representatives of these states

[232] ibid 877.
[233] ibid 942.
[234] ibid 943. Extract of speech by Secretary Bauer to the National Constituent Assembly of German Austria 7 June 1919.
[235] D Lloyd George, *The Truth About the Peace Treaties* (London, Victor Gallanz 1938) 944.
[236] ibid 945.
[237] ibid 946.
[238] ibid 957.
[239] ibid 962.
[240] ibid 90.
[241] ibid 91.
[242] ibid 904–905.
[243] Records of the US Senate 1783-2023, President Woodrow Wilson's Message to Congress. Other title: President Woodrow Wilson's Fourteen Points speech.
[244] D Lloyd George, *The Truth About the Peace Treaties* (London, Victor Gallanz, 1938) 758.

all made competing and conflicting claims driven by the immediate national ethnic, cultural, economic, and political interests, although strategic and economic interests were paramount. For example, there was a claim ethnically indefensible, but essential for natural military defence as in the case of the Sudetenland, Dr Edvard Beneš' claim for the Magyars territory because the Slovaks needed access to the Danube.[245]

But the greatest difficulty facing the peacemakers was what race predominated in the border areas where no such distinction could be drawn. Language was not determinative where certain races spoke the language of their conquerors. As the Chairman of the Boundary Commission, Mr Tardieu opined, 'ethnographic statistics cannot then be sufficient to lead to the solution of the problem'.[246]

The underlying problem at the Peace Conference was time and the threat of a resumption of the war as well as the impracticality of implementing Wilsonian principles against the determined spirit of revenge exhibited by Clemenceau and public opinion in France and Britain. Practically, it was an impossible task to apply the ideal of self-determination or government with the consent of the governed from the Rhine to the Euphrates in the time allowed. How would you define a specific area of mixed races and conflicting aspirations?[247] This was the great issue determined without due consideration and the prime cause for retribution since Member States tended to pursue their own national interests in an uncertain economic environment. But a key failing was, as Sally Marks points out, that events in Germany itself were ignored.[248] She also pointed to Wilson's vague and misleading statements such as suggesting the 'open covenants of peace openly arrived at' when, as Lentin describes, the deliberations were behind closed doors such that Lloyd George had to return to London to deny the rumours of *The Times* and *Daily Mail* on reparations.[249] However whilst Lloyd George's defence is substantive he does not answer the riposte to the Treaty delivered by Schücking.[250]

G. Wilson's Betrayal of the Fourteen Points

When it became clear to Wilson that he had to agree to Lloyd George's demand for pension claims being included in an indemnity and that he would have to accept the 'war guilt' clause drafted by Keynes and Foster Dulles, he also betrayed the key principle of the Fourteen Points, namely self-determination. He agreed that the South Tyrol should go to Italy, the Saar coal mines to France, the Sudetenland to Czechoslovakia, Hungarian Transylvania to Romania, and to the partitioning of Asia Minor into the spheres of influence, simply recreating the 'Old Diplomacy'.[251] Harold Nicolson

[245] ibid 913.
[246] ibid 914.
[247] ibid 917.
[248] S Marks, 'Mistakes and Myths: The Allies, Germany and the Versailles Treaty, 1918-1921' (2013) 85(3) *The Journal of Modern History* 632–659, 634.
[249] HC Deb. 16 April 1919 vol. 114. cc 2951-3.
[250] Walther Adrian Schücking was a German liberal politician, professor of public international law and the first German judge at the Permanent Court of International Justice in The Hague.
[251] A Lentin, *Lloyd George, Woodrow Wilson and the Guilt of Germany* (Leicester, Leicester University Press, 1984) 74.

described Wilson's decline after the impasse with Lloyd George over the Guilt Clause and pensions '... where he no longer meant what he said, but all too often he did not know what he was talking about'.[252]

In *Peacemaking 1919*[253] Nicolson went further and said that:

> Within a few days he had accepted an arrangement regarding the Brenner frontier. He allowed himself to be persuaded that war pensions could be classed as 'damage to the civilian population'. He allowed himself to believe that the mandatory system was in fact something different from annexation. He swallowed the war- guilt clause, and the grotesque clauses which arraigned perfectly innocent people among the war criminals. He allowed the whole disarmament question to be shunted off into the realm of one-sided disarmament of Germany. He surrendered in Shantung, even as he surrendered on Poland. He surrendered over the Rhineland, even as he surrendered in the Saar. On the reparation ... as he confessed 'not much interested in economic subjects'. He allowed the self-determination of Austria to be prohibited by one of the most specious phrases ever drafted by jurists. He permitted the frontiers of Germany Austria and Hungary to be drawn in a manner which was a flagrant violation of his own doctrine.

In short, Wilson betrayed his own principles in seeking compromises that contradicted his principles, the Fourteen Points and the Covenant. Whilst the overall intention was good, it was illusory in the context of European geopolitics. What may have seemed a good idea in the smoking room of the *George Washington*[254] was not *realpolitik*. However, this was not just a personal responsibility but a joint and several one. They failed to examine the effect of altering the German borders. By depriving Germany of its colonies, German chancellors tended to be more focused on Central Europe attempting to expand and reclaim its territories as well as predominate in its economy. The prospect of a revival of German militarism and domination was ignored, as was any consideration of the balance of power in Europe.

H. American Opposition to Wilson's Dream

Despite all Wilson's efforts in procuring agreement amongst the conflicting national interests of the Allies and undermining his own principles, he faced a greater challenge with his own countrymen. On 25 January 1919, the Peace Conference had decided that the Covenant of the League of Nations would form part of the peace treaties. On 28 June, it was included in the text presented for the signatories of the Peace of Versailles. A day later Wilson left for New York. On 8 July 1919, the Treaty of Versailles was put before the Senate and the vote for ratification was taken on 10 July. Ratification required two-thirds of the Senate to vote in favour. Of the 47 Democratic Senators, 4 opposed the treaty, leaving 43 in favour. Of the 49 Republicans, 14 voted against the treaty and 21 voted for ratification. Some Republicans required amendments before they could approve, and 20 others asked for more substantial modifications. Wilson was faced with the challenge of convincing

[252] ibid 75.

[253] Faber and Faber, 2009.

[254] *George Washington* was formerly a German passenger liner. It was converted into a troop carrier and brought President Woodrow Wilson to France.

about 10 Republicans to support the treaty. Wilson took upon himself far too much after the strain of the Paris Conference.[255] He failed to convince the Republicans led by Henry Cabot Lodge who had also previously opposed the arbitration treaty with Britain in 1911. Despite Wilson's strenuous campaign across the states, Lodge[256] was able to gather support from isolationists who believed that it was impractical to accept the treaty and the idea of the League of Nations. Wilson's utopian ideas did not appeal to the voters in the mid-western states. Like Parnell[257] before him, who destroyed his health through a bitter campaign for his ideals, Wilson also destroyed what remained of his health. He was bedridden for some time and unable to see visitors. In the meantime, his colleague Colonel House succeeded in agreeing to a compromise with Cabot Lodge. Unfortunately, House was refused admission to the President and consequently the great opportunity was lost. Lloyd George was concerned to get the treaty passed by the Senate and to that end sent Sir Edward Grey, who was highly respected as Britain's former Foreign Secretary, to see Wilson and advise him of the need to agree to an amendment. Unfortunately, he was also refused admission to the President.[258] Thus, when the matter was returned to the Senate it rejected the treaty on 19 March 1920 by 49 votes to 35 and voted in favour of Cabot Lodge's revised treaty, but with reservations. Consequently, the US did not join the League of Nations and signed a separate peace treaty with Germany in August 1921.[259]

In effect, this ended the direct influence of the US on the postwar settlement and opened the prospect of widening differences between the former allies. Wilson had played the mediator or honest broker to an extent with his Fourteen Points and his post-war design for a new world order safe for democracy, promoting self-determination underpinned by collective security. According to Walter Lippmann, had the US ratified the Treaty of Versailles the US and Britain would have found common cause, and possibly World War II might have been averted.[260] Such an optimistic judgement fails to account for certain Tory politicians' condescending attitude against Americans save for Winston Churchill and Harold Macmillan who had a better understanding of the divergent cultures. Times had changed since Canning gave Britain's undertaking to Madison, Jefferson and Monroe in 1823.[261] America was overtaking Britain in terms of democratic leadership, albeit isolationist at that time, but potentially the arsenal of democracy.

I. Heading for the Abyss[262]

In the final analysis, the Treaty of Versailles, unique in its time but misconstrued due to certain vagueness and contradictions in its terms, with secret, secluded discussions that

[255] J de Launay, *Major Controversies of Contemporary History* (Oxford, Pergamon Press, 1965) 89.

[256] He was a specialist in political science and held a PhD in history from Harvard. He was also a successful lawyer.

[257] Charles Stewart Parnell Leader of the Irish Nationalist Party (1846–1891) who failed to win popular support after the O'Shea Scandal in 1889 and died after an arduous campaign.

[258] J de Launay, *Major Controversies of Contemporary History* (Oxford, Pergamon Press, 1965) 91.

[259] ibid 92.

[260] W Lippmann, *US Foreign Policy* (Hamish Hamilton, London 1943) 47.

[261] ibid 9. Lippmann considered that Britian's protection of the Atlantic and Pacific in the nineteenth century ensured US independence.

[262] Heading inspired by the title of the *Reminiscences* of Prince Lichnowsky, German Ambassador to Britain 1912–1914 (Payson and Clark Ltd, New York, 1928).

bred suspicion amongst the vanquished, was doomed to fail by the misguided whims of politicians who raised expectations beyond the art of the possible. Wilson, obviously with his idealistic liberal predilections, and Lloyd George, for his exaggerated promises stirring public emotions, knowing that Germany would never pay all the Allies' consequential losses. The delegates failed to understand the Prussian spirit of Frederick the Great, Bismarck, and the Kaiser. The Prussian spirit which inspired militarism and obedience to the leader. Whilst the fundamental objective was to reduce the risk of war, it succeeded in that the armistice held and there was peace. Its instrument, the League of Nations, also contributed to that peace through its Council and references to arbitration, but eventually it failed due to misunderstandings, political divergent ideas, conflicting national interests, the fluctuations of public opinion propelled by propaganda, fear of Bolshevism, and *Dolchstoss.* As Sally Marks opined, the treaty was too mild to restrain Germany for long but enough to give cause for revenge.[263] It was a compromise between conflicting European interests which ignored the resentment of Germany. Germany rejected it and exploited the sympathetic Keynesian view of an unjust and harsh treaty, which troubled the conscience of English public opinion. This fuelled appeasement, American isolationism, disarmament and encouraged a revival of the Prussian spirit translated into a form of Nazi totalitarianism and domination.

More than any other provision in the Treaty of Versailles, the 'War Guilt' clause, Article 231, caused more damage than the House of Commons and Lord Northcliffe ever foresaw in their demands of Lloyd George to abide by his election promise. If anyone was to judge the 'guilt' of Germany, then the best indictment was drawn by the Kaiser's good friend Prince Lichnowsky, his Ambassador in London. Lichnowsky opined:[264]

> … Our leaders brought on the war; but more through their inability to reason and to judge correctly, combined with incredible obstinacy, than through any lust for the overlordship of the world. There were fools and fanatics of that kind, too, but they were not the ones possessed of power. I repeat, the ones in control were simply stupid and incompetent. They were responsible for a ridiculous provocative diplomacy, and after the wind was started, the whirlwind had to follow.

It was, he said, the fear of Pan Slavism-Russian determination to overrun the world.[265] It was Von Moltke who insisted on forcing a war, just as Ribbentrop encouraged Hitler to do the same.

[263] S Marks, 'Mistakes and Myths: The Allies, Germany and the Versailles Treaty, 1918-1921' (2013) 85(3) *The Journal of Modern History* 654.

[264] 'Lichnowsky on the Origin of the War', *New York Times Current History* (New York): 1 Aug 1919: 10, 2; Periodicals Archive Online 224.

[265] Lichnowsky referred to Von Moltke saying that in 5 or 10 years at the most Russia would be able to utilise her extended railways to attack. 'Lichnowsky on the Origin of the War', *New York Times Current History* (New York): 1 Aug 1919: 10, 2; Periodicals Archive Online 224.

2

Arbitration as an Instrument of Dispute Resolution

I. Promotion of International Law

Following the Geneva Arbitration in 1871[1] and the Washington Treaty that gave effect to the proceedings, many leading jurists concluded that there would be great benefits to the resolution of disputes between states through a codification of international law. To this end, an Institute of International Law of 60 members and 60 associate members was set up in addition to an Association for the Reform and Codification of the Law of Nations (International Law Association).[2] The series of regular law association meetings aimed at promoting the codification of international law held in The Hague led to the adoption by many Member States of the European continent of the Hague Conventions for the Codification of Private International Law.[3]

Preceding the constitution of the League of Nations, an American Committee of Jurists met in 1912 and continued its deliberations after the war in 1923. It was recognised at the Fifth Pan American Conference in Santiago and convened in 1925. On 2 January 1924, the governing board of the Pan American Union asked the American Institute of International Law to hold a special session to consider the question of codification for the use of the Committee of Jurists. The Institute accordingly gave general approval of 31 draft conventions on international peace prepared by the Executive Committee of the Institute. These drafts were described by Dr James Brown Scott, President of the American Institute for International Law, as 'an attempt to state in conventional form the principles of justice expressed in rules of law which should govern the relations of the American Republics in a neutral pacific intercourse'.[4] The subjects covered in these deliberations formed, in his view, 'the fundamental bases of international law' and 'declaration of the rights and duties of nations' to minor matters like exchange of publications and an interchange of professors and students. Mr Charles Evans Hughes, the United States Secretary of State, the Chairman of the Governing Body, emphasised its importance:

> I believe that this day with the submission of concrete proposals which take the question of the development of international law out of mere amiable aspiration, marks a definite step in the progress of civilisation and promotion of peace.

[1] See: MP Reynolds, *Instruments of Peacemaking 1870–1914* (Oxford, Hart Publishing, 2021).
[2] These associations held regular meeting save during 1914–18.
[3] CA McCarthy & others, *Survey of International Affairs 1925*, Vol II (Oxford, OUP, 1928) 116.
[4] ibid 119–120.

These Conventions and the recognition they received provided the basis for their application to a wider audience.

The further advancement of the cause of international law came with the Fifth Assembly of the League of Nations on 30 September 1924, which decided to establish an International Institute for the Unification of the Assimilation and Co-Ordination of Private Law in Rome. On 13 December 1924, the Council decided to communicate to the Committee on Intellectual Co-operation, to the technical organisations of the League, and to a subcommittee of the Committee on the Progressive Codification of International Law the final text of the draft statutes of the Institute prepared by the Italian government. The statutes were considered by various bodies at the end of 1925.

Andrew Carnegie established the Carnegie Endowment for International Peace in 1910. Eliah Root was its first president. This was followed by William Jennings Bryan's suggestion for an International Commission of Inquiry in 1913. Each party to a dispute would be pledged to a cooling-off period of 12 months to arbitrate before commencing hostilities. By 1914, 20 treaties had been signed with such a provision.[5] In light of the enormous war casualties during the First World War, Jennings, Bryan and others suggested an International Court of Justice with a Council of Conciliation. This also contained a provision that parties would not commence hostilities for a year; failing this, there would be sanctions. These ideas were presented by 60 peace groups in the US which supported a judicial process and codification of international law.[6] In 1915, 300 leading peace employers met in Philadelphia and proposed a League of all the great nations and medium powers to deal with such disputes judicially, with non-justiciable disputes being referred to a Council of Conciliation. They set up a League to Enforce Peace. President Wilson spoke at its first meeting in May 1916 and committed the US to creating a League of Nations. There was a British League of Nations Society founded in 1915, which gathered strong support in Britain.[7] A committee to study proposals for such a league was established in Britain under the chairmanship of Lord Phillimore, which reported in 1918. He proposed an international body meeting on a regular basis where members could agree not to resort to war without first submitting any dispute to arbitration or inquiry by a conference or fellow states and waiting for their report.[8] It was accepted by such committee that such proposals might not stop war, but if war did break out, economic sanctions could be imposed without waiting for any cooling-off period.

A. Permanent Court of International Justice

In 1918 Leon Bourgeois promoted a Permanent Court of Arbitration. He considered that prevention required a range of approaches: diplomatic, legal, economic and military, to compel Member States to abide by League decisions. The League would require a military organisation of joint forces. These forces could be supplied by Member States or by an international force with a permanent staff based at the League's headquarters.

[5] R Henig, *The Peace That Never Was: A History of the League of Nations* (London, Haus Publishing Limited, 2019) 7.
[6] ibid 10.
[7] ibid.
[8] ibid 15.

Bourgeois believed only armed force could act as a deterrent in stopping an outbreak of war. Wilson, on the other hand, argued that the League of Nations should be formed by 'solemn covenants of mutual guarantee of political independence and territorial integrity'.[9] Bourgeois promotion was effected on 28 April 1919, at a Plenary session of The Peace Conference when the Members States' representatives resolved to promote international co-operation and to achieve international peace and security by the acceptance of obligations in the Covenant of the League of Nations which established a Permanent Court of International Justice under Article IX which provided:

> The Council shall formulate and submit to the Members of the League for adoption plans for the establishment of a Permanent Court of International Justice. The Court shall be competent to hear and determine any dispute of an international character which the parties thereto submit to it. The Court may also give an advisory opinion upon any dispute or question referred to it by the Council or by the Assembly.

The first draft of the Statute of the Permanent Court was prepared for the Council of the League of Nations by the committee of jurists, the major recommendation being that an international conference should be held at intervals to carry on the work of the two conferences held in The Hague in 1899 and 1907.[10] This committee was to review the existing rules as to the law of nations as affected by the events of the war. This was to be composed in consultation with the Institute of International Law, the International Law Association, the American Institute of International Law, the Iberian Institute of Comparative Law, and the Union Juridique Internationale.[11] On 27 October 1920, the League Council decided that the international law associations should set an agenda for an international conference and then the views of government should be obtained. The Third Committee of the First Assembly disagreed and considered that this was a matter for the Assembly itself. As a result, nothing progressed for four years.[12] Despite this, the League enacted rules through the Covenant, the Statute of the Permanent Court of International Justice (PCIJ), the International Labour Conferences and the Barcelona and Geneva Conferences on Communications and Transit. In September 1924, the Assembly asked the Council to convene a Committee of Experts 'to prepare a provisional list of the subjects of international law, the regulation of which by international agreement would seem to be most desirable and realisable at the present moment'.[13] The Committee of Experts, comprising 16 members, was established by the Council on 12 December 1924. It held one plenary session in 1925 from 1–8 April. Eleven subcommittees were appointed. They studied questions of nationality, territorial waters, diplomatic privileges and immunities, the legal status of ships owned by the state and used for trade, extradition and the criminal jurisdiction of states regarding crimes perpetrated outside their jurisdiction, responsibility of states for damages suffered within their territory by foreigners,[14] the procedure of international conferences and

[9] ibid 16, 17.

[10] See: MP Reynolds, *Instruments of Peacemaking 1870-1914* (Oxford, Hart Publishing, 2021) as to the First and Second Hague Conferences.

[11] CA McCarthy & others, *Survey of International Affairs 1925*, Vol II (Oxford, OUP, 1928) 117.

[12] ibid 117–118.

[13] ibid 118.

[14] This question was raised in connection with the Janina murder of an Italian working on the Albanian frontiers and over the occupation of Corfu. ibid 348–356.

the conclusion and drafting of treaties, the suppression of piracy, limitation, the exploitation of the produce of the sea, and enumeration of the subjects of private international law. Many of these reports were completed by the end of 1925.[15]

Thus, progress was made in this postwar period to resolve future disputes between states through the mechanics of the League of Nations and the Covenant applying international law and acknowledging the role of arbitration. That role was subsequently enhanced by the Treaty of Locarno and underpinned by the Kellogg-Briand Pact.[16] The following are examples of some of the matters that were settled by arbitration or by a Commission under the reparations provisions of the Treaty of Versailles or otherwise by agreement between the parties.

II. Instruments of Dispute Resolution

A. France, Spain and Great Britain v Portugal (Confiscation of Religious Properties) 1920

In the Portuguese Revolution of October 1910, religious associations were dissolved and their property was confiscated. It also resulted in the abolition of the monarchy and the establishment of the first Portuguese republic with a desire to restore the greatness of Portugal in the age of discovery (1415–1550) in a *resurgimento.*[17] A number of British, French and Spanish Jesuits claimed that their property had been confiscated during the revolution and turned to their respective governments for diplomatic protection.[18]

To resolve matters. a *compromis* (arbitration agreement) was signed in Lisbon on 31 July 1913, providing that the claims be dealt with by way of an award to be rendered under Articles 3 and 4 of the *compromis*. A special tribunal was established within the framework of the Permanent Court of Arbitration at The Hague, composed of Elihu Root[19] (US) AF de Savornin Lohman[20] (the Netherlands) and CE Lardy[21] (Switzerland) who were to examine each claim separately and decide 'according to the provisions and

[15] CA McCarthy & others, *Survey of International Affairs 1925*, Vol II (Oxford, OUP, 1928) 119.

[16] See ch 3.

[17] For a fuller account of the revolution see: DL Wheeler, 'The Portuguese Revolution of 1910' (1972) 44(2) *The Journal of Modern History* 172–194.

[18] HG Kausch, 'Expropriated Properties Arbitration (France, UK, Spain v Portugal)' Max Planck Institute for Comparative Public Law and International Law, Vol 2 *Decisions of International Courts and Tribunals and International Arbitrations* (North-Holland Publishing Company, 1981) 92.

[19] He was a leading corporation lawyer, a US attorney for the Southern District of New York (1883–85) and a leader in New York Republican politics. Root concluded treaties of arbitration with more than 20 nations. He was chief counsel for the US in the North Atlantic coast fisheries case. He served on the Commission of Jurists that established the Permanent Court of International Justice (1920–21). Root worked closely with Andrew Carnegie on programs for international peace and for the advancement of science but led opposition to America joining the League of Nations.

[20] In 1902 he acted as one of five arbitrators at The Hague in the Pious Fund dispute between the US and Mexico, the first dispute between states arbitrated by the Permanent Court of Arbitration. (See Reynolds (n 1)).

[21] He was the sole Arbitrator in the last arbitration in the Permanent Court of Arbitration before the outbreak of World War I in a dispute between the Royal Netherlands government and the Portuguese Republic regarding the delimitation of a part of their respective possessions in the Island of Timor.

general principles of law and equity'.[22] This tribunal sat for the first time in the Palace of Peace at The Hague, which was facilitated by Mr Andrew Carnegie[23] and his support of international peace. The governments of France and Great Britain reached an agreement with Portugal upon the form and extent of the Award to be entered on behalf of their subjects or citizens. In effect, they settled through diplomatic channels out of court and agreed that this should be by way of an Award of the Permanent Court of Arbitration at The Hague.[24] The case was significant in that it was the first use of the court since the First World War.

They adopted for this purpose a summary written documents-only process without any oral hearings, adopting Article 86 of the 1907 Convention for the Pacific Settlement of International Disputes, which provided:[25]

> ARTICLE 86
>
> With a view to facilitating the working of the system of arbitration in disputes admitting of a summary procedure, the Contracting Powers adopt the following rules, which shall be observed in the absence of other arrangements and subject to the reservation that the provisions of Chapter III apply so far as may be.

But it was suggested that the parties had not followed the process of arbitration but simply adopted Article 90 to confirm the procedure they adopted in writing. Article 90 provided:

> ARTICLE 90
>
> The proceedings are conducted exclusively in writing. Each party, however, is entitled to ask that witnesses and experts should be called. The Tribunal has, for its part, the right to demand oral explanations from the agents of the two parties, as well as from the experts and witnesses whose appearance in Court it may consider useful

The efficacy of such a proceeding might be questioned in that the requirements of the summary arbitration procedure were not followed as prescribed in the Convention of 1907, although reference was made to the above Articles.

The claimants contended that as foreigners in Portugal, they were entitled to police and security protection and guarantees as to their property rights. As foreigners, they could not take part in public affairs of the country. The Portuguese government agreed with these legal principles relied on by the claimants 'without reserve, respectful of law and equity'. It based its defence on the argument that the properties belonged to the religious associations and not to the individual foreign claimants, even if they held title to the property.

On 13 August 1920, the governments of France and Great Britain agreed with Portugal in lieu of separate judgments, the tribunal was authorised 'to settle according to equity and by a single judgment or several judgments, the claims which form the

[22] HG Kausch, 'Expropriated Properties Arbitration (France, UK, Spain v Portugal)' Max Planck Institute for Comparative Public Law and International Law, Vol 2 *Decisions of International Courts and Tribunals and International Arbitrations* (North-Holland Publishing Company, 1981) 92.

[23] A Scottish-born American industrialist who led the enormous expansion of the American steel industry in the late 19th century. He was also one of the most important philanthropists of his era.

[24] J Brown Scott, 'Arbitration Resumed at The Hague' (1921) 15(1) *American Journal of International Law* 74.

[25] Unofficial Text, Centre for International Law,·ch IV Arbitration by Summary Procedure 18–19.

subject of the arbitration'.[26] The tribunal gave separate awards in favour of the French and British claimants. These were relatively straightforward, as the claimants all had similar fact cases.

On 2 September 1920, a special tribunal rendered separate awards in the claims of France, Great Britain and Spain regarding alleged damage to or destruction of church property belonging to the subjects or citizens of those countries situated in Portugal resulting from the revolution of October 3–5, 1910.

The claimants had the same grounds of claim, namely: that the claimants possessed the property in Portugal, and met the liabilities associated with ownership and thus benefitted Portugal by introducing capital into the country; that it was neither the purpose of Portugal to obtain profit from the seizure of the property, nor the intention of the claimants to 'violate the respect due to the laws and institutions of Portugal'; that in these circumstances, the settlement of the claims in favour of French and British claimants were just and equitable, and because of this fact, all such claims were therefore 'declared definitely settled and in future extinguished'.[27] It was held that the Portuguese government were the proprietors of the seized property but were liable to pay lump sums as compensation to the claimants for the appropriation. The awards reflected the diplomatic and amiable out of court settlements reached by way of the *compromis* in August 1920. The tribunal noted that it was not the intention of Portugal to obtain any profits from the seizure. It was acknowledged that the claimants had paid due respect to the laws and institutions of the state.[28]

None of the French claims were on behalf of the Jesuits, nor were any of the British claims as those originally presented by Great Britain were withdrawn, although the British government had been willing to accept them.[29] The Spanish government had not agreed to the settlement that France and Britain had agreed to in August 1920. On 4 September 1920, the tribunal rejected 17 claims by Spanish Jesuits as inadmissible because the claimants had failed to produce evidence required by Articles 325, 326 and 327 of the Spanish Civil Code and Article 2411 of the Portuguese Civil Code to establish the Spanish nationality of the claimants and consequently they could not enjoy diplomatic protection by the Spanish government.[30] Certification by the Spanish consulate had been accepted in a case concerning the lack of a birth certificate, but here two claims were rejected, one for failure to make out title to the property and another because satisfaction had been obtained in the meantime.[31] The tribunal could

[26] HG Kausch, 'Expropriated Properties Arbitration (France, UK, Spain v Portugal)' Max Planck Institute for Comparative Public Law and International Law, Vol 2 *Decisions of International Courts and Tribunals and International Arbitrations* (North-Holland Publishing Company, 1981) 93; J Brown Scott, 'Arbitration Resumed At The Hague' (1921) 15(1) *American Journal of International Law* 74.

[27] Brown Scott ibid 74.

[28] HG Kausch, 'Expropriated Properties Arbitration (France, UK, Spain v Portugal)' Max Planck Institute for Comparative Public Law and International Law, Vol 2 *Decisions of International Courts and Tribunals and International Arbitrations* (North-Holland Publishing Company, 1981) 93.

[29] J Brown Scott, 'Arbitration Resumed At The Hague' (1921) 15(1) *American Journal of International Law* 74.

[30] ibid 75.

[31] HG Kausch, 'Expropriated Properties Arbitration (France, UK, Spain v Portugal)' Max Planck Institute for Comparative Public Law and International Law, Vol 2 *Decisions of International Courts and Tribunals and International Arbitrations* (North-Holland Publishing Company, 1981) 93.

not consider the two claims on their merits, as it was only Spanish subjects which Spain had the right to present under the agreement with Portugal. The tribunal was naturally anxious to decide in such a way as to do justice but, in doing it, not to offend the *amour propre* of either of the litigating nations.[32]

Whether the compensation was fair in expropriation cases may be questioned. The awards represent the approach of certain European governments before and after World War I. What is interesting is the agreement to apply the principles of international law as stated by the claimant governments in their *Observations Généralis.*[33]

As James Brown Scott quoted in his Editorial Comment in the *American Journal of International Law*:[34]

> At the opening session of the Tribunal, on the morning of September 2, Mr. Root, President of the Tribunal, said on behalf of his two colleagues, Messrs. Savornin Lohman, of Holland, and Lardy, of Switzerland:
>
> > At the beginning of the labours of the Tribunal it is a real satisfaction for me to state, after the storms which have raged in the world in the course of these last years, that the Permanent Court of Arbitration still lives. We have the hope and the confidence that it will remain for the good of the world, for the advancement of the reign of public law and of the peace of justice among nations.
>
> At the closing session, on the 4 September, Mr. Root, speaking again as President of the Tribunal, and on behalf of his colleagues, said:
>
> > It remains for me to state that for the first time since the completion of the Peace Palace, an international judgment has been delivered within these walls. Our judgment is, therefore, an inauguration; it is an important day in the history of this building and we hope that this award will be followed by many another in the interest of peace, and of accord among the nations. May these be but the first of an endless series of awards between nations, decided upon respect for law between the nations of the world.'

B. The Jaffa Jerusalem Railway Arbitration 1922

In 1889 the Turkish government granted a 71-year concession to a French company to build and operate a one-meter-gauge railway from Jaffa to Jerusalem. This provided that on termination the railway would revert to Turkey. During the 1914–18 War, a part of the French meter-gauge private railway track was changed by the Turks to 1.05 meters to conform to the Turkish standard military railway gauge as well as the gauge of the extant Haifa to Damascus Railway and the connecting Hijaz Railway connecting Damascus and Medina. The Hijaz Railway was of particular strategic importance to the Turkish army. It was captured by British and Arab forces during

[32] J Brown Scott, 'Arbitration Resumed At The Hague' (1921) 15(1) *AJIL* 74. Reproduced with permission of the Licensor through PLSclear.

[33] HG Kausch, 'Expropriated Properties Arbitration (France, UK, Spain v Portugal)' Max Planck Institute for Comparative Public Law and International Law, Vol 2 *Decisions of International Courts and Tribunals and International Arbitrations* (North-Holland Publishing Company, 1981) 93.

[34] J Brown Scott, 'Arbitration Resumed At The Hague' (1921) 15(1) *AJIL* 75. Reproduced with permission of the Licensor through PLSclear.

the 1917–18 Middle Eastern offensive in which Colonel TE Lawrence[35] took a leading part. Following the military offensive, the railway system was converted to the standard British railway gauge and extended. The British government decided, by virtue of the Mandate of Palestine conferred on it by the League of Nations, to buy out the concession of the Jaffa-Jerusalem Railway enjoyed by the Société Du Chemin de Fer Ottoman de Jaffa à Jérusalem et Prolongements. They in turn claimed compensation in gold francs[36] from the British government in an arbitration under Article 311 of the Treaty of Sèvres.[37] Under the treaty, the British and French governments agreed to constitute an arbitral tribunal for the purposes of determining equitable compensation which would be due from the British government to the Société du Chemin de Fer Ottoman de Jaffa a Jerusalem et Prolongements.[38]

i. Constitution of the Tribunal

The constitution of this arbitral tribunal followed a long period of negotiation between the representative of His Majesty's High Commissioner for Palestine, Sir Herbert Samuel,[39] who had negotiated with the Comte de Vaureal in Palestine between December 1920 and March 1921 for the acquisition of the Jaffa-Jerusalem Railway by the government of Palestine. The Comte du Vaureal submitted a claim by and on behalf of the French company the Société de Chemin de Fer Ottoman de Jaffa a Jerusalem et Prolongements for compensation sometime in January 1921 of FRF 25,318,395. The Palestinian government[40] made counterproposals that were not acceptable to the French company. On 13 February 1922, Lord Curzon, the British Foreign Secretary, wrote to the Count de Saint Aulaire stating that neither France nor Britain had agreed on specific terms of reference for the arbitral tribunal, in which case it would be necessary for the tribunal to be given instructions as to the objects and limitations of the arbitration. He confirmed that Britain was prepared to accept a majority decision instead of a unanimous decision, as previously agreed. On 25 February 1921, after negotiations had broken down, Samuel received a letter from the Comte de Vaureal claiming FRF 2,090,330 on account of loss of enjoyment of the line by the French company from 1 November 1918 to 28 February 1921.[41] The dispute was referred to the tribunal

[35] This was described in his book *The Seven Pillars of Wisdom* (Ware, Wordsworth Editions; New edition, 1997) Colonel TE Lawrence was an archaeologist, scholar of Jesus College Oxford and subsequently a British Intelligence Officer in Cairo during the First World War. He inspired and led what became the Arab Revolt against the Ottoman Turks facilitating their defeat in 1918.

[36] Affidavit of Mr Norman Bentwich regarding the Preliminary Decision dated 14 September 1922 before the Vice President Court of Appeal, Government of Palestine National Archives TS 27/144. During the British military administration of Palestine, Bentwich served as the Senior Judicial Officer in the British military administration of Palestine and then as Legal Secretary in the civil administration and later as Attorney-General until 1931.

[37] MP Reynolds, 'The Jaffa Jerusalem Railway Company Arbitration 1922' (1991) 6(2) *Arab Law Quarterly* 215–23. Most of this narrative is taken from this article at 215–223 as here revised by the author.

[38] The Treaty had not been executed by the plenipotentiaries as at the date of the dispute. It was executed on 10 August 1920.

[39] Appointed, in 1920, as the first British High Commissioner of Palestine.

[40] Then controlled by Britain under a League of Nations Mandate.

[41] National Archives TS 27/144.

under the terms of the Anglo-French Agreement and in accordance with Article 311[42] of the Treaty of Sèvres. This provided that:

> Article 311.
>
> In territories detached from Turkey to be placed under the authority or tutelage of one of the Principal Allied Powers, Allied nationals and companies controlled by Allied groups or nationals holding concessions granted before October 29, 1914, by the Turkish Government or by any Turkish local authority shall continue in complete enjoyment of their duly acquired rights, and the Power concerned shall maintain the guarantees granted or shall assign equivalent ones. Nevertheless any such Power, if it considers that the maintenance of any of these concessions would be contrary to the public interest, shall be entitled, within a period of six months from the date on which the territory is placed under its authority or tutelage, to buy out such concession or to propose modifications therein; in that event it shall be bound to pay to the concessionaire equitable compensation in accordance with the following provisions.
>
> If the parties cannot agree on the amount of such compensation, it will be determined by Arbitral Tribunals composed of three members, one designated by the State of which the concessionaire or the holders of the majority of the capital in the case of a company is or are nationals, one by the Government exercising authority in the territory in question, and the third designated, failing agreement between the parties, by the Council of the League of Nations.
>
> The Tribunal shall take into account, from both the legal and equitable standpoints, all relevant matters, on the basis of the maintenance of the contract adapted as indicated in the following paragraph.
>
> The holder of a concession which is maintained in force shall have the right, within a period of six months after the expiration of the period specified in the second paragraph of this Article, to demand the adaptation of his contract to the new economic conditions, and in the absence of agreement direct with the Government concerned the decision shall be referred to the Arbitral Commission provided for above.

The tribunal was composed of Lieutenant Colonel Mance, the arbitrator nominated by the British government, M Ferdinand Meyer, Chief Engineer nominated by the French government, and MFVN Beichmann, President of the Superior Court of Trondheim and Deputy Judge of the Permanent Court of International Justice was the Chairman chosen by the two other arbitrators. The agent of the British government was Mr Orme Clarke, and the Jaffa-Jerusalem Railway was Colonel Barry.

ii. Rules Adopted by the Tribunal

The rules of procedure of the tribunal provided that the headquarters of the tribunal would be at 73 Boulevard Haussmann, Paris, where the Secretariat would be located for the purposes of communications. The rules provided that the parties could use the language of their choice, whether English or French, but the tribunal would exercise its discretion as regards having written communications translated from one language to another. Provision was made for the Awards to be published in English and French. Each

[42] Treaty of Peace Between the Allied Powers and Turkey. English text of the Draft Treaty as submitted to the Turkish Delegation. British Cabinet 16 June 1920. League of Nations 1919-1920, section 17, Doc No. 4928. Dossier No. 4715.

party was empowered to appoint an agent to represent it before the tribunal. Records of proceedings were recorded in the French language. Submissions consisted of a Memorial and an Answer. The claimants also had liberty to Reply if they thought it necessary. Rule 10 provided that the parties could request further and better particulars for the purposes of elucidating statements or figures presented in the submissions. The Memorial or request for arbitration was to contain succinct statements of facts. The Answer was to contain contentions of the claimants, which were challenged by the respondents by way of counterclaim. The Reply, if any, was to deal with allegations in the Answer. The respondents could file further documentary evidence to answer any allegations in the Reply. There were no written submissions other than the Memorial, the Answer, and the Reply except by agreement between the agents or by order of the tribunal. If either party wished to refer to voluminous reports or documents already published, then seven copies of such documents were required to be delivered with the submissions. Provisions were made for disclosure and inspection by the tribunal and by the parties' agents. The rules provided for interim applications to be decided by the tribunal unless there was some written application and objection to the tribunal proceeding without an oral hearing. As to the hearing itself, the tribunal was empowered to dispense with a hearing if the agents so requested. The parties were required to notify the tribunal of the names of witnesses one week before the hearing and to indicate the points upon which evidence would be given. There was no provision for the exchange of witness statements. So far as the Award was concerned, the tribunal was empowered to deliver the Award in public session as soon as possible after the hearing. If there was no oral hearing, the Award was to be published after the submissions. Members of the tribunal were empowered to dissent from the Award and sign dissenting reports giving reasons for their dissent.[43]

iii. Opinion of Sir John Simon

In May 1922, before any hearings took place, the government sought the opinion of Sir John Simon QC, a former Attorney General. He advised that the company's claim was incorrect and inadmissible under English law. He reasoned that Article 311 of the Treaty of Sèvres provided for the payment to the concessionaire of 'equitable compensation' in respect of the acquisition of the concession. In his view it was fundamental to observe what was to be paid by way of compensation. Compensation for the loss of a concession is a totally different matter from the cost of construction or the reproduction value of physical assets. In his view it was conceivable in some cases that compensation would be more than the reproduction cost or less. In his view, a concession to build a railway through an uninhabited region would involve heavy expense. If the concessionaire had no prospect of carrying any traffic and had to hand over the railway when the concession ended, the loss of the concession would not deprive him of any value. In that case it would be worthwhile giving it away as a gift. His view was that compensation for the loss of the concession could not be measured by asking what it would cost to reconstruct the physical railway. On the other hand, a concession might be so profitable that

[43] M Reynolds, 'The Jaffa Jerusalem Railway Company Arbitration 1922' (1991) 6(2) *Arab Law Quarterly* 216–217. *Rules of the Tribunal Working of the Tribunal* in Nat Archives TS 27/144.

the outlay necessary to construct the railway was trifling compared with the enormous profits from its working during the lifetime of the concession. In such a case, compensation for loss of the concession would be very large, but in the Jaffa-Jerusalem case it could not be measured by considering what it cost to build the line: the cost was quite irrelevant to the problems here. The concession of the Jaffa-Jerusalem Railway was not a concession in perpetuity but only to be enjoyed for a limited number of years, at the end of which physical constructions of the railway were to be handed over without payment. It was obvious to Simon that the concessionaires had to be compensated for the loss of any enjoyment of the concession. It was also obvious that the compensation was measured by the profit which the company would make in the final year, supposing that they continued to work the concession to the end of the term. It is equally obvious that the cost of making the railway or reproducing a similar railway would have nothing whatsoever to do with the question. He concluded that the reproduction value of the physical railway line and plant was a wholly irrelevant matter. The figure in respect of reproduction value given by the Jaffa-Jerusalem Railway Company treated the physical railway as though it was their own property free from restrictions and encumbrances, whereas at the determination of the concession, the title to the railway would pass from them to the Turkish government. The only value to the Jaffa-Jerusalem Railway was any possible profit. which would amount to compensation.[44]

iv. Expert Opinion

An expert opinion was obtained from the chief accountant of the Palestine Railways in Haifa in June 1922. He concluded that the French claim estimated during 1921 of LE 17,400 and an operating expenditure of LE 85,000 left a surplus of LE 89,000. The result of working the line by the Palestine Railways showed revenue receipts of LE 124,700 and operating expenses of LE 113,576, leaving only a small surplus of LE 11,124 to meet interest on capital, sinking fund resources, financial reserves for betterment, and annuity payments. The earnings on the Jerusalem line for the year ended 31 December 1921 only exceeded expenditure by less than 10 per cent. Palestine Railways, being a government department, paid no customs duties for materials imported for the purposes of maintaining the line, but the company operating the line would be required to pay duty at the rate of 11 per cent on coal and materials imported for working. The chief accountant estimated that during 1921 the duty would have been payable on coal consumed amounting to LE 4,500. He therefore concluded that the proportion of general superintendence on the whole of the Palestine Railways charged to the Jaffa Jerusalem Railway was considerably smaller than the charges for the services which would have been if the line were worked as a separate concern.

v. Preliminary Meeting and Decision

Following a period of negotiations and advice given to the British government by Simon, with the assistance of Mr R Newton Crane opining on US cases, Mâitre Edouard Clunet,

[44] Reynolds ibid.

Avocat à la Cour de Paris, Dr Siegfried Spier, and Mâitre G De Leval, the tribunal met briefly to deal with the question of reproduction costs as a preliminary issue. The British government asked for an interim Award.[45] In their Memorial the claimant demanded, amongst other items, payment for the physical value of the railway line calculated at the present cost of constructing and equipping the line. Their claim included rolling stock and stores amounting to LE 838,370. There were claims for the additional value of rights and powers under the concession, including the right to earn profits.

Mr Orme Clarke, the British agent, relied upon the terms of Article 18 of the Concession and Article 20 of the Cahier des Charge. This provided that within 71 years the railway's fixed properties would be handed over in good condition to the Turkish government without payment. Both agents agreed that the tribunal should decide the question of value as a preliminary question. The tribunal ordered the parties to make written observations before hearing submissions. Clarke contended that had the concession been maintained, the railway company would not have made profits beyond the expiry of the concession. He argued that such profits did not depend on the present value of the physical railway line and the fixed properties because they would be handed over to the Turkish government without any payment at the end of the concession. Clarke presented a series of advisory opinions which he had obtained from Simon, Maître Ed Clunet, Mr Newton, Dr Siegfiied Spier, and Maitre G De Level. Clarke desired a preliminary decision regarding the reproduction cost of the line and its fixed properties.[46]

The tribunal then heard the submissions from Lord Cozens-Hardy for the claimant, who said that the contention was in contradiction of the views expressly addressed by the British Secretary of State for Foreign Affairs to the French ambassador in London on 22 September 1920, who gave notice of Britain's intention to buy out the line. In his view, the tribunal was not bound by any applicable law but to decide on 'fair and equitable' compensation representing the reproduction cost of the line. He considered the advisory opinions to be irrelevant and quoted authority which would uphold any decision for compensation.[47] The British and French governments had agreed to the application of Article 311 of the Treaty of Sèvres, notwithstanding that the Treaty had not yet been ratified. The rights and obligations of the claimant were based on a Convention dated 10 October 1888 concluded between the Turkish government (Minister of Commerce and of Public Works) acting in the name of the Imperial Government and Mr Youssouf Navon Effendi, a Turkish subject, 'Cahier des Charges' of the same date, and a contract dated 4 August 1914.

Under Article 18 of the Convention on Termination of the Concession, the Imperial government of Turkey would be substituted for the concessionaire in all rights in the railway and its fixed property as well as any movables and personality and would have enjoyment of its benefits. The line and its fixed assets would be handed over free of any debts or encumbrances to the Imperial Turkish government who would purchase the rolling stock and stores in conformity with Article 20 of the 'Cahier de Charges'. This provided that on termination of the concession, the concessionaire should, without any payment, deliver to the Imperial Turkish government in good condition and free of all

[45] ibid. *Preliminary Decision*. Nat Archives TS 27/144,18.
[46] *Preliminary Decision*. Nat Archives TS 27/144,18.
[47] National Archives TS 27/144.

debt and encumbrances the stations, loading and unloading sidings, and also buildings necessary for operating the line used by employees, fixed machinery and all other fixed property. The engines, waggons trucks, construction or repair material, fuel and all moveable property used for operating purposes would be bought on the expert valuation of the Imperial Turkish government. They would be obliged to take over stores necessary for six months' operation. The 'Cahier de Charges' further provided that if five years before the termination of the concession the Turkish government could establish that the railway was not in a good state of repair, they would give notice to the concessionaire, and a period would be allowed for him to put the line into a proper state of repair. If the notice did not produce such a result, then the government would take over the running of the line, and the concessionaire would be liable for maintenance and repairs.[48]

The tribunal considered that the text of Article 311 of the Treaty of Sèvres left it open to the tribunal to decide matters freely as to what material matters were to be taken into consideration and not be bound by any opinions given in prior negotiations. The tribunal considered the situation that the claimant company would have found itself in if the British government had not decided to exercise its option under Article 311. There seemed no doubt that to hand over to the Turkish government, without payment on the termination of the concession, the railway line with its fixed properties as defined in Article 20 of the 'Cahier de Charges', the company would only have been entitled to the profits which could be earned by the operation of the line for the duration of the concession. If its profits had not been sufficiently high to cover the present value (reproduction costs of the line with its fixed properties), the company would not have had any right to be refunded the difference.[49] The tribunal further considered that the amount of the profits did not depend on the above values. Consequently, they concluded that such value could not be included as part of the compensation awarded to the claimant. It further decided that the Société Du Chemin de Fer Ottoman de Jaffa à Jérusalem et Prolongements could present an amended claim no later than 21 June and that the answer of the British government must be presented by 12 July.[50]

vi. The Final Award

The tribunal heard Clarke for the British government and Colonel HA Barry for the Jaffa-Jerusalem Railway. The claimant based its claim on the Convention dated 29 October 1889 establishing the concession of 'Cahier de Charges' and upon a Supplementary Convention of 4 August 1914, as well as annual reports submitted to the general meetings of the claimant company in the years 1894 to 1914. Correspondence between the Foreign Office in London and the French Ambassador in London was submitted in evidence, as well as further and better particulars pursuant to Mr Clarke's requests of April and May 1922.[51]

[48] *Preliminary Decision.* Nat Archives TS 27/144, 22.

[49] *Preliminary Decision.* Nat Archives TS 27/144, 24.

[50] *Preliminary Decision.* Nat Archives TS 27/144, 24. Paris 29 May 1922 Signed by Beichmann, HO Mance and F Mayer.

[51] National Archives TS 27/144. *Lord Curzon to Count de Saint -Aulaire* 13 February 1922; *Lancelot Oliphant to Count de Saint -Aulaire*, 21 December 1921 and *Count de Saint -Aulaire to Lord Curzon* 10 July 1921.

Barry submitted an amended Statement of Claim on 21 June 1922, claiming a total of LE 1,696,452 in respect of the Turkish occupation and loss and damage incurred during the Turkish occupation of the railway, as well as claims in respect of the British military occupation from 1917 to 1920, a claim in respect of loss of profits, and a claim in respect of rolling stock and compensation to staff. The claimant also claimed interest at the rate of 5 per cent per annum on the capital sum of LE 1,696,452. After obtaining a short extension of time, Mr Clarke produced further reports illustrating the damage caused by the Turks during their occupation of the line, other war damage and graphical expert evidence. Clarke disputed several statements and calculations made by the claimants and declared his willingness to accept a figure FRF 12,950,000 as representing the approximate value of the concession. From this he claimed that certain items should be deducted, such as the cost of repairs due to damage caused by the Turks during their occupation, and by way of compromise, the amount could be fixed at FRF 5,000,000. The British were willing to give credit for FRF 5,600,000 paid on account by the British government to the French government in November 1921. In their rejoinder submitted on 10 August 1922, the claimants generally maintained their allegation. The hearing took place between 25 and 30 September 1922. The parties requested the tribunal to settle all the compensation payable by the British government to the claimant even if Article 311 of the Treaty of Sèvres did not confer jurisdiction on the tribunal. On 3 October 1922, counsel for the parties informed the tribunal that they had agreed to the terms of settlement and submitted a draft Consent Award to the tribunal. Each side agreed to pay their own costs.[52] The essential difference between the parties was that the British argument as to compensation was based on the capitalised value of the probable net profits which the railway would earn during the concession, whereas the claimant's case was based on the value of the physical track and properties.[53]

vii. Decision

The tribunal published its Award by consent. It provided that the amount to be paid to the Société Du Chemin de Fer Ottoman de Jaffa à Jérusalem et Prolongements as compensation for the buying out of the concession in satisfaction of all claims by the claimants against the British government or by the British government against the claimants should be the sum of £565,000. The sum of £103,368 had already been paid on account by the British government, so that the British would pay the claimant the sum of £200,000 on or before 22 October 1922; £87,210 on 1 October 1923; £87,200 on 1 October 1924 and £87,210 on 1 October 1925, with interest on the last three sums at 5 per cent per annum from 1 October 1922 until payment. Interest would accrue die in diem and be payable half-yearly, the first payment to be made on 1 April 1923. The right to any claim for compensation against the Turkish government would pass from the Société Du Chemin de Fer Ottoman de Jaffa à Jérusalem et Prolongements to the British government. The claimant would execute any documents which might be necessary to effect such transfer of rights and would give all assistance that might reasonably be required by the British government for the prosecution of the claim against the

[52] *The Award.* Nat Archives TS 27/144, 2–12.
[53] *Letter unsigned to Brigadier General J Wickham.* 27 April 1922. National Archives TS27/1444.

Turkish government provided that the British government would indemnify the claimant against all expenses necessarily incurred by it in respect thereof. This award was given in Paris on 4 October 1922 and was signed by Beichmann, Mance and Meyer.

It is of interest to note how these proceedings were subject to the application of fair and equitable rules, although other comparative legal opinions were submitted. It was to all intents and purposes an ad hoc process with statements of case and countercase. It is also interesting to note the part that diplomacy played in these proceedings and the interaction between the legal and diplomatic processes, which underline the study in this chapter. It was successful so far as Britain was concerned in terms of the strategic importance of the League of Nations Mandate of Palestine given to Britain. It may be considered that if the British had not enlarged the gauge of the railway, then the railway might not have made as much profit as it did by complying with British standards. Furthermore, the geographical disposition of Jaffa was not perhaps as profitable as the port of Haifa.

C. Germany v Poland 1922–37

In early 1918, following the publication of President Wilson's Fourteen Points, Wilson accepted an appeal by the Kaiserreich to initiate peace talks. These did not commence until after an armistice had been signed on 11 November 1918. Negotiations started in 1919 were led by the Council of Ten but in effect dominated by President Wilson, Prime Minister David Lloyd George and Premier Georges Clemenceau.

The thirteenth point of Wilson's Fourteen Points called for the creation of a Polish state encompassing territory inhabited by Poles. This would accord with Wilson's concept of self-determination for defined nationalities, save that the population of Europe, especially the eastern regions, had a diversity of populations resulting from the breakup of the Austro-Hungarian, Ottoman and Russian Empires. Poland was enthusiastically supported by Clemenceau, who saw Poland as a bulwark against a resurgent Germany.

The Allies delegated the delineation of the boundaries to commissions of experts who initially considered transferring the whole of Upper Silesia to Poland. That region was clearly divided in terms of ethnic origin being half Polish and half German. In order to resolve this, it was decided to hold a plebiscite under Articles 87 and 88 of the Treaty of Versailles. These provisions had described the western boundary of Poland and the eastern boundary of Germany but were silent as to the possession of Upper Silesia which was subject to a plebiscite.

Prior to this plebiscite, Allied forces occupied Upper Silesia under French command. The result of a plebiscite held on 20 March 1921 was that over 700,000 voted to stay in Germany, whilst 433,000 voted to join Poland. This presented a dilemma for the Allies as any division of Upper Silesia would not be viable, but on the other hand, there was little option. The townspeople overall had voted in favour of Germany while the rural areas voted in favour of Poland. At this time Germany relied heavily on Silesia for coal which supported her industry.[54]

[54] This is another one of those examples where self-determination was not a straightforward matter with complications over race, religion, culture, history, language and geographical features.

In May 1921, Polish paramilitaries occupied the region led by Wojech Kokfany, who was opposed by German paramilitary forces. Allied occupation forces were not involved. Britain favoured the Upper Silesian regions joining Germany; France favoured them joining Poland. Following consultations by the League of Nations with residents, unions and industry leaders, as suggested by Lloyd George, the region was then mostly transferred to Poland, which received considerable mineral benefits of coal, iron, sulphur, and coke. Germany was given guarantees of access to these industrial benefits as well as a guarantee that there would be no discrimination. These arrangements were approved by the League Council on 19 October 1921. Germany and Poland then continued negotiations, which culminated in the Geneva Convention signed on 15 May 1922.[55]

Following the transfer of title of areas of Upper Silesia to Poland, issues arose as to the ownership of title to property, with claims by Germans as to their rights of ownership.[56]

A good example of the claims being made as a result of the transfer to Poland was the case of Bayerische Stickstaffwerke AG. In March 1915, the Kaiserreich entered into a contract with Bayerische Stickstaffwerke AG of Trosberg in Upper Bavaria for the management of a nitrate factory at Chorzów.[57] The Kaiserreich purchased the land in Upper Silesia as a registered owner. The term of the contract was for 26 years, expiring on 31 March 1941. On 24 December 1919, the factory at Chorzow was conveyed to Oberschlesische Stickstaffwerke AG, penned on 29 January 1920. Oberschlesische Stickstaffwerke AG was registered as owner of the factory. Oberschlesische Stickstaffwerke AG retained a legal relationship with Bayerische Stickstaffwerke AG. On 14 July 1920, the Polish Diet passed a liquidation law transferring all the German Reich's assets to Poland and declaring transactions effected prior to 11 November 1918 to be null and void.[58] On 1 July 1922, a court at Huta Krolewska declared the Polish state to be the owner in the land register. Oberschlesische Stickstaffwerke AG then brought an action to the German-Polish Mixed Arbitral Tribunal and the German government claimed that the liquidation of the Chorzów factory was in breach of the Geneva Convention regarding Upper Silesia.[59]

Another example of the problems created by the disposition of Upper Silesia to Poland was the case of estate owners in Ratibor who were served with notices under Article 15 of the Convention by the Polish government to expropriate their estates. The German government contested this action.[60] Under Article 23 of the Convention, the Permanent Court of International Justice had given jurisdiction to the German-Polish Mixed Arbitral Tribunal. But the German government brought an action before the Permanent Court of International Justice ignoring the German-Polish Mixed Arbitral

[55] Martens de, *Martens Nouveau Recuil Général de Fraites 3me* Série Vol 16, 645–875.

[56] See also: Judgment No. 6 PCIJ Series A, No. 6 (1925); Merits PCIJ Series A, No. 7 (1926); Jurisdiction Judgment No. 7 PCIJ Series A, No. 9 (1927); Order of 21 November 1927 PCIJ Series A, No. 12 (1927); Judgment No. 11 PCIJ Series A, No. 13. (1927); Merits Judgment No. 13 PCIJ Series A, No. 17 (1928); Order 25 May 1929 PCIJ Series A, No. 19 (1929); Certain German Interests in Upper Silesia PCIJ Series C, No. 9 (I): No. 11, Vols I-III; and Factory at Chorzów PCIJ Series C, No. 13(I); No. 13(V); No. 15(II); No.16(II).

[57] Seidl-Hohenveldern, 'German Interests in Polish Upper Silesia' in *Encyclopaedia of Public International Law, Decisions of International Courts and Tribunals*, Vol 2 (North-Holland Publishing Company, 1981) 111–114.

[58] ibid 111.

[59] ibid.

[60] ibid.

Tribunal. Poland submitted that such action was inadmissible and subject to awaiting the Mixed Tribunal's decision.[61]

The PCIJ decided it had jurisdiction on 25 May 1925. In its judgment a year later,[62] it held the German Reich had retained its right to dispose of its property in Upper Silesia until the sovereignty of the territory was transferred to Poland. Only a misuse of rights could support alienation of the factory by reason of a breach of the treaty. The liquidation law was thus held to conflict with the Convention on Upper Silesia. Thus, the liquidation of the Chorzów factory was not authorised or a valid liquidation.[63] The 1919 transfer was therefore a valid transfer of title and any question as to the validity of the transfer should be determined pursuant to German Civil Law by the German courts. As regards the legality of the expropriation of the estates, the PCIJ held that the liquidation of some of these estates was illegal and that the town of Ratibor was a 'German national' within the meaning of the Convention.[64]

Germany applied for compensation which was opposed by Poland on the ground that the PCIJ lacked jurisdiction in respect of obligations arising out of violations of the Articles of the Convention.[65] In its judgment of 26 July 1927, the PCIJ affirmed its jurisdiction awarding Germany an indemnity.[66] On 14 October 1927, the German Reich requested payment of 30 million Reichsmarks, but this was rejected on 21 November 1927 because it was regarded as a provisional claim of part and not provisional protection.[67] On 16 September 1927, there was an application for a declaration from the Katowice court in Poland that, according to German Civil Law, the title to ownership of the factory at Chorzów vested in Oberschlesische Stickstaffwerke AG. This application assumed that the PCIJ Judgment No. 7 reserved the right of Poland to bring an action before the court for such a declaration. The German Reich requested the PCIJ for an interpretation of its of judgments Nos. 7 and 8.[68]

On 16 December 1927, the PCIJ held that its judgments were not subject to any decision of a Polish court. The PCIJ held that the title and ownership had transferred to Oberschlesische Stickstaffwerke AG under German law.[69] In a further judgment on 13 September 1928, the court considered what indemnity the Polish government should pay but reserved fixing any amount.[70] This was settled by a compromise arrangement between the parties and proceedings were determined on 25 May 1929.[71]

These proceedings between Poland and Germany provide an illustration of how some disputes over the German boundaries were amicably settled by arbitration and the PCIJ. The Upper Silesian cases also raised interesting points of procedure; for example, the Polish claim of litispendence, that the same substantive action before different tribunals was misconceived because the action was before the German-Polish Mixed

[61] ibid 112.
[62] No. 7 PCIJ A 7.
[63] Seidl-Hohenveldern (n 57) 112.
[64] ibid.
[65] ibid.
[66] No. 8 PCIJ A 9.
[67] PCIJ A 12.
[68] Seidl-Hohenveldern (n 57) 112.
[69] Judgement No. 11 PCIJ A 13.
[70] PCIJ A 17.
[71] PCIJ A 19.

Arbitral Tribunal and before the PCIJ. The former case was in accord with restitution of private property, and in the latter it was a matter of interpretation of the Upper Silesia Convention.[72]

The PCIJ held that it had jurisdiction to interpret the Convention as opposed to giving an advisory opinion. The latter could only be given at the request of the Council of the League of Nations and the Assembly. A state had a right to apply for a declaration declaring the defendant's state had acted illegally under international law.[73] Where the PCIJ had jurisdiction to interpret a treaty, it also had jurisdiction to deal with indemnity claims based on treaty violations. It is significant that in its judgment No. 7, the PCIJ applied the doctrine of res judicata that the transfer of property of the Chorzów factory was valid also under municipal law.[74] The judgment entered by the Polish court against the Oberschlesische Stickstaffwerke AG did not conform to the Upper Silesian Convention. The liquidation of enemy property pursuant to the Treaty of Versailles and to the Upper Silesian Convention was that derogation of rules generally applied in regard to the treatment of foreigners on the principle of respect for vested rights and international law.[75] The derogation was limited to special circumstances as provided by the Upper Silesian Convention and this liquidation was incompatible with the Convention regime.[76]

The key point was that such liquidations pursuant to the Peace Treaties were held to constitute an exception to the general rule of international law, but these had to be considered in a restrictive manner.[77] Poland contended wrongly that the liquidations applied to foreigners and nationals alike. The abrogation of private rights of German nationals was contrary to Head III of the Convention.[78] Expropriation without indemnity was also contrary to Head III of the German Geneva Convention. The basic finding was that, in respect of vested rights, they are generally accepted as a principle of international law.[79]

D. Mixed Claims and Reparations Commission

i. *The* Lusitania *Claims*

The *RMS Lusitania* was a British luxury transatlantic liner of the Cunard Line which was torpedoed without warning by a German U-boat (U20) on 7 May 1915, whilst bound for Liverpool from New York. At the time of the attack, she was flying the American flag. She sank 12 miles off the Old Head of Kinsale on the southern coast of Ireland. U20's log recorded that one torpedo was fired, but after the initial explosion, it appears that there

[72] Seidl-Hohenveldern (n 57) 113.
[73] PCIJ A 7, 18.
[74] Seidl-Hohenveldern (n 57) 113.
[75] ibid.
[76] ibid. See also the Versailles Treaty and the Upper Silesia Convention.
[77] Seidl-Hohenveldern (n 57) 113–114.
[78] PCIJ A 7, 32–33.
[79] Seidl-Hohenveldern (n 57) 114.

was a second and massive explosion in the cargo holds in the bows.[80] The ship sank in 18 minutes. Few lifeboats could be launched because of the listing of the ship, although she had adequate lifeboats; 1,198 people were drowned, 128 of them being citizens of the US, which was at that time neutral.[81] She was torpedoed in a German-declared war zone.[82] In its declaration dated, 4 February 1915, the German government stated that Germany would endeavour 'to destroy every enemy merchant ship that is found in this area of war without it always being possible to avoid the peril that thus threatens persons and cargos'.[83] The German declaration was a retaliation for alleged violations by Britain of the London Declaration of 1909, following the London Naval Conference of 1908–09 and Britain's violation of the Paris Declaration of 1856 following Britain's declaration of a war zone on 3 November 1914. The US protested the institution of the German war zone in a Note of 10 February 1915 in which she reserved the rights of her vessels and nationals on the high seas. The German Embassy in Washington, DC, published a Notice on the day of *Lusitania's* departure, 1 May 1915, repeating their 4 February declaration.[84]

The drowning of American citizens caused public outrage in America. Protest was made that the *Lusitania* was sunk without proper provision having been made for the safety of the American citizens on board. The US protested to Germany that 'it was contending for nothing less high and sacred than the rights of humanity', and that only the 'actual resistance (of the *Lusitania*) to capture or refusal to stop when ordered to do so for the purpose of visit could have afforded the commander of the submarine any justification for so much as putting the lives of those on board the ship in jeopardy'.[85] There followed a series of bitter diplomatic exchanges and negotiations between the State Department and the Kaiserreich. On 4 February 1916, Germany admitted that: 'Retaliation must not aim at other than enemy subjects' and assumed liability for losses suffered by US citizens as a result of the sinking during the period that the United States was neutral.[86] Dr Lawrence opined that:

> The untenable excuse put forward was that these ships were carrying contraband. But this begged the question by assuming, first, that there was contraband on board without making any search, and secondly, that the exceptional circumstances existed which alone justify sinking a ship for the carriage of contraband; nor would it in the smallest degree answer the charge of killing innocent persons. We need not repeat the emphatic condemnation of such practices by the Conference of Washington.[87]

[80] According to the original ship's manifest, there were 1,271 cases of ammunition and 1,248 cases of shrapnel, (supposedly just the lead musket balls with which to fill shrapnel shells). It also referred to large consignments of lard, butter and cheese consigned to the Royal Navy's Weapons Testing Establishment at Shoeburyness, Essex. The shipping note, dated 28 April 1915, shows consignment number 23 as being 1,248 cases of three-inch calibre shrapnel shells, filled; four shells to each case consigned to the Royal Arsenal at Woolwich for use by the Royal Artillery in the 13-pounder field gun. www.lusitania.net/deadlycargo.htm.

[81] Under current international law, a neutral flagged vessel may not be attacked unless they are carrying contraband of war or war materials and it is not feasible to place passengers and crew in a place of safety, but in the latter case they should be given warning so far as circumstances permit.

[82] K Madders, '*The Lusitania*' in *Encyclopaedia of Public International Law*, Max Planck Institute for Comparative Public Law and International Law, Vol 2 *Decisions of International Courts and Tribunals and International Arbitrations* (North-Holland Publishing Company, 1981) 177.

[83] Foreign Relations of the United States (1915) Supplement, 96.

[84] Madders (n 82) 178.

[85] American Bar Association Journal, October 1941, Vol 27, No. 10 (October 1941) 596–599.

[86] Foreign Relations of the United States (1916) Supplement 157.

[87] TJ Lawrence, *International Law*, 7th edn (London, 1925) 469–470.

ii. Legal Action

As a result of the sinking, legal actions were brought nationally and internationally. The Coroner's Court at Kinsale in Ireland charged the Kaiser and his government with wilful and wholesale murder. The British Board of Inquiry held in June and July 1915 found that the *Lusitania* was unarmed and that she carried no explosive materials; that the German submarine fired more than one torpedo, and it did so with the intention of destroying the ship and those on board. There was a private admiralty action in the New York District Court against Cunard decided on 23 August 1918.[88] Cunard was found not liable, causation being attributed solely to the inexpressibly cowardly attack upon an unarmed passenger liner.

The claims for losses to US nationals were presented as claims before the US/Germany Mixed Claims Commission. The US derived its jurisdiction by reference to paragraph 4 of the Annex to Section IV of Part X of the Treaty of Versailles in the Treaty of Berlin so that this provision extended Article 232 and Part VIII, Section 1, Annex 1, paragraph 1 of the Treaty of Versailles to cover the period of US' neutrality. This enabled American citizens to make claims which were, in effect, reparations claims.

iii. Arbitration Commission

The Mixed Commission in this matter was composed of Mr Edwin B Parker, Umpire; Chandler P Anderson (American Commissioner); and Dr Wilhelm Kiesselbach (German Commissioner). The general rule applied in this Award in 1923 was to give complete pecuniary compensation for loss resulting to a claimant from the death of a human being. In doing so, the Commissioners applied the rules as to Germany's obligations under Treaty of Berlin and the rules laid down in the Commission's Administrative Decisions Nos. I[89] and II whereby Germany was financially obligated to pay to the US all losses suffered by American nationals, which losses have resulted from death or from personal injury or from loss of, or damage to, property sustained in the sinking of the *Lusitania*. This decision applied subject to the determination of nationality and the measure of damages in each case, save that the tribunal would determine the rules applicable to the measure of damages in death cases, giving weight to the basis of recovery in death cases in the jurisdictions.[90]

At common law there existed no cause of action for damages caused by the death of a human being. The right to maintain such actions had been conferred by English and American statutes. The applicable German Code and statutes expressly recognised

[88] 251 Fed.715.

[89] 'We are here dealing with a group of cases all growing out of a single catastrophe. As it is manifestly of paramount importance that the same rules of decision shall govern the disposition of each and all of them, whether disposed of by agreement between the two Commissioners or in the event of their disagreement by the Umpire, this opinion announcing such rules is, at the request of the two Commissioners, prepared by the Umpire, both Commissioners concurring in the conclusions. The principles and rules here laid down will, where applicable, govern the American and German Agents and their respective counsel in the preparation and presentation of all claims.' (Administrative Decision No. 1 for the definition of terms used).

[90] Reports of International Arbitral Awards. *Opinion in the Lusitania cases*. 1 November 1923, Vol VII, 32–44 (United Nations 2006) 33.

liability for the taking of life.[91] These legislative enactments were varied in their terms, as were the various court judgments which the tribunal took into consideration, as set out in their Administrative Decision No. II regarding the rules governing the measure of damages in death cases.[92] They reasoned that the tendency in measuring damages in such death cases of both statutes and decisions was to give such elasticity to such restrictive rules as to enable courts and juries in applying them to the facts of each particular case to award full and fair compensation for the injury suffered and the loss sustained. US statutes of several states authorised juries to award such damages as were 'fair and just' or 'proportionate to the injury'. Under such statutes, the decisions of the courts gave juries much broader latitude in assessing damages than those of other states where the statutes expressly limit them to so-called 'pecuniary injuries', which is a much misunderstood term. In most of the jurisdictions where the civil law was administered and where the right of action for injuries resulting in death had long existed, independent of any code or statute containing restrictions on rules for measuring damages, the courts were not hampered in so formulating such rules and adapting them to the facts of each case as to give complete compensation for the loss sustained. They further reasoned that it was a general rule of both the civil and the common law that every invasion of private right imports an injury and that for every such injury the law gives a remedy. Speaking generally, they held that the remedy must be commensurate with the injury received. It was variously expressed as 'compensation', 'reparation', 'indemnity', 'recompense', and was measured by pecuniary standards because, says Grotius, 'money is the common measure of valuable things'.[93] In death cases, the right of action was for the loss sustained by the claimants, not by the estate. The basis of damages was not the physical or mental suffering of the deceased or his loss or the loss to his estate, but the losses resulting to claimants from his death. The questions for the tribunal were: What amount will compensate claimants for such losses? Bearing in mind that they were not concerned with any problems involving the punishment of a wrongdoer but only with the question of the measure of compensation for the wrong done. The tribunal therefore arrived at a formula in general terms: to estimate the amounts (a) that the decedent, had he not been killed, would probably have contributed to the claimant, adding (b) the pecuniary value to such claimant of the deceased's personal services in claimant's care, education, or supervision, and (c) reasonable compensation for such mental suffering or shock, if any, caused by the violent severing of family ties, as claimant may actually have sustained by reason of such death.[94] The sum of these estimates, reduced to the current cash value, generally represented the loss sustained by the claimant.[95]

[91] Section 823. See also *Huebner's History of Germanic Private Law* (Boston, Little Brown and Company 1918) 578–579, and Schuster's *Principles of German Civil Law* (1907) ss 284–286.

[92] Reports of International Arbitral Awards. *Opinion in the Lusitania cases.* 1 November 1923, Vol VII, 32–44 (United Nations 2006) 34.

[93] H Grotius, *The Rights of War and Peace*, Whewell translation, 1853 (hereinafter cited as 'Grotius'), Book II, Ch XVII. Section XXII; *Sedgwick on the Measure of Damages*, 9th edn (1912) (hereinafter cited as 'Sedgwick') s 30.

[94] This seems revolutionary for the time bearing in mind the courts' reluctance to recognise psychiatric harm in those days for what in England is recognised as secondary victims. But here this is governed by international law in wartime as provided in the Versailles Treaty.

[95] Reports of International Arbitral Awards. *Opinion in the Lusitania cases.* 1 November 1923, Vol VII, 32–44 (United Nations 2006) 35.

Among other factors the following factors were to be applied by the American Agent, the German Agent and their respective counsel in the preparation and submission of all cases:[96]

(a) The age, sex, health, condition and station in life, occupation, habits of industry and sobriety, mental and physical capacity, frugality, earning capacity and customary earnings of the deceased and the uses made of such earnings by him.
(b) The probable duration of the life of the deceased but for the fatal injury, in arriving at which standard life-expectancy tables and all other pertinent evidence offered will be considered.
(c) The reasonable probability that the earning capacity of the deceased, had he lived, would either have increased or decreased.
(d) The age, sex, health, condition and station in life, and probable life expectancy of each of the claimants.
(e) The extent to which the deceased, had he lived, would have applied his income from his earnings or otherwise to his personal expenditures from which claimants would have derived no benefits.
(f) In reducing to their present cash value contributions which would probably have been made from time to time to claimants by the deceased, a five per cent interest rate and standard present-value tables will be used.
(g) Neither the physical pain nor the mental anguish which the deceased may have suffered will be considered as elements of damage.
(h) The amount of insurance on the life of the deceased collected by his estate or by the claimants will not be taken into account in computing the damages which claimants may be entitled to recover.
(i) No exemplary, punitive, or vindictive damages can be assessed.

The enumeration of factors to be considered in assessing damages was not considered as exclusive of all others. When either party conceives that other factors should be considered, having a tendency either to increase or decrease the quantum of damages, such factors would be called to the attention of the Commission in the presentation of the particular case.[97]

Counsel for Germany argued that the mental suffering of a claimant did not constitute a recoverable element of damage in death cases and also contended that life insurance benefits should be deducted in estimating the claimant's loss. The American counsel argued that exemplary, punitive, and vindictive damages should be assessed against Germany for the use and benefit of each private claimant. Both the life insurance and punitive damages arguments were rejected.

What may be interesting to tort lawyers will be the tribunal's approach to what they called 'mental suffering', which we would term 'psychiatric harm'. The tribunal held that legal concept of damages is judicially ascertained compensation for a wrong. The compensation must be adequate and balanced as near as may be to the injury suffered. In many tort cases, including those for personal injury and for death, it was manifestly

[96] ibid 35–36.
[97] ibid 36.

impossible to compute mathematically, or with any degree of accuracy, or by the use of any precise formula the damages sustained involving such inquiries as to how long the deceased would probably have lived *but for* the fatal injury; the amount he would have earned, and of such earnings the amount he would have contributed to each member of his, family; the pecuniary value of his supervision over the education and training of his children; the amount which will reasonably compensate an injured man for suffering excruciating and prolonged physical pain; and many other inquiries concerning elements universally recognised as constituting recoverable damages.[98] This, the tribunal decided, furnished no reason why the wrongdoer should escape redeeming his wrong or why he who has suffered should not receive reparation measured by rules as nearly approximating accuracy as human ingenuity could devise. To deny such reparation, in the Commission's view, would be to deny the fundamental principle that there exists a remedy for the direct invasion of every right. Mental suffering was regarded by the tribunal as a fact just as real as physical suffering and susceptible of measurement by the same standards.[99] In conclusion they held:[100]

> The interdependency of the mind and the body, now universally recognized, may result in a mental shock producing physical disorders. But quite apart from any such result, there can be no doubt of the reality of mental suffering, of sickness of mind as well as sickness of body, and of its detrimental and injurious effect on the individual and on his capacity to produce. Why, then, should he be remediless for this injury? The courts of France under the provisions of the Code Napoleon have always held that mental suffering or "prejudice morale' is a proper element to be considered in actions brought for injuries resulting in death. A like rule obtains in several American States, including Louisiana, South Carolina, and Florida.[101] The difficulty of measuring mental suffering or loss of mental capacity is conceded, but the law does not refuse to take notice of such injury on account of the difficulty of ascertaining its degree.

In its evaluation of the measure of damages, the Commission was aware that the courts permitted juries to award as exemplary damages what were in truth compensatory damages for mental suffering, rather than leave the plaintiff without a remedy for a real and actual injury sustained. As to the question raised by German Counsel on the deduction of life insurance payments, this was rejected because it was contrary to American and English authority.[102] The Commission therefore held that the German argument failed, as the law could not benefit a wrongdoer, as to do so would:[103]

[98] ibid.

[99] Again, this is revolutionary for those times as even today the courts tend to take a restricted approach to claims by secondary victims for fear of opening the floodgates to claims. However, this must be distinguished in the context of illegality under international and humanitarian law.

[100] Reports of International Arbitral Awards. *Opinion in the Lusitania cases.* 1 November 1923, Vol VII, 32–44 (United Nations 2006) 36–37.

[101] *Nohrden v Northeastern Railroad Co.*, 1900, 59 South Carolina Reports 87, 105–108, 37 Southeastern Reporter 228, 238–240; *Stuckey v Atlantic Coast Line Railroad Co.*, 1901, 60 South Carolina Reports 237, 253; *Bourg v Brownell-Drews Lumber Co.*, 1908. 120 Louisiana Reports 1009, 1022–1026, 45 Southern Reporter 972, 977–978; *Seaboard Air Line Railway v Moseley*, 1910, 60 Florida Reports 186, 189–190; *Underwood v Gulf Refining Co.*, 1911, 128 Louisiana Reports 869, 986, 990–1003; *Johnson v Industrial Lumber Co.*, 1912, 131 Louisiana Reports 897, 908–909.

[102] Reports of International Arbitral Awards. *Opinion in the Lusitania cases.* 1 November 1923, Vol VII, 32–44 (United Nations 2006) 37.

[103] ibid 37,38.

> enter the domain of speculation and consider the probability of probabilities in order to offset an absolute and certain contract right against the uncertain damages flowing from a wrong.

In estimating the damages, the Commission considered the law of probabilities and of averages, which must be resorted to in estimating damages, which precluded the possibility of making any precise computations or mathematical calculations. As an aid, the Commission considered the standard life expectancy and present value tables as well as other evidence, such as the condition of the health of the deceased, the risks incident to his vocation, and any other circumstances tending to throw light on the probable length of his life but for the act of Germany. The weight given to such tables was determined by the Commission in light of the facts developed in each particular case. Exemplary damages were not awarded because their soundness on principle is challenged by some of the leading American text writers.[104] Such damages, they explained, were reserved 'by way of punishing the guilty, and as an example to deter others from offending in like manner'.[105] The source of the rule, they explained, is frequently traced to a remark alleged to have been made by Lord Chief Justice Pratt (afterwards Lord Camden) in instructing a jury that:[106]

> Damages are designed not only as a satisfaction to the injured person, but likewise as a punishment to the guilty, to deter from any such proceeding for the future, and as a proof of the detestation of the jury to the action itself.

In England and America, this was quoted as authority for the award of exemplary damages where the tort complained of had been wilfully, wantonly or maliciously inflicted. In their opinion the words exemplary, vindictive, or punitive as applied to damages were misnomers. The fundamental concept of 'damages' is satisfaction, reparation for a loss suffered, a judicially ascertained compensation for wrong.[107]

The more enlightened principles of government and of law, they said, clothe the state with the sole power to punish but ensure to the individual full, adequate, and complete compensation for a wrong inflicted to his detriment.[108] They further held as a matter of international law that a person injured is entitled to be compensated for an injury inflicted resulting in mental suffering, injury to his feelings, humiliation, shame,degradation, loss of social position or injury to his credit or to his reputation. There can be no doubt, they said, that such compensation should be commensurate to the injury. But the preferred view was that these were compensatory not punitive damages or a penalty.[109] No case was cited to the Commission where exemplary, punitive,

[104] *Fay v Parker*, 1873, 53 New Hampshire Reports 342; Sedgwick, sec. 354; *Greenleaf on Evidence*, 15th edn (1892), Vol II, ss 253, 254, 266, and 267.

[105] *Lake Shore & Michigan Southern Railway Co. v Prentice*, 1893, 147 United States Reports 101, 107.

[106] *Wilkes v Wood*, 1763, 19 Howell's State Trials (1816) 1153, 1167, Lofft's Reports (1790), pages 1 and 19 of first case.

[107] Reports of International Arbitral Awards. *Opinion in the Lusitania cases.* 1 November 1923, Vol VII, 32–44 (United Nations 2006) 39.

[108] *Vattel's Law of Nations*, Chitty edition with notes by Ingraham, 1852 (1857), '… Hence arises the right of the sword, which belongs to a nation, or to its conductor. When the society use it against another nation, they make war; when they exert it in punishing an individual, they exercise vindictive justice.'

[109] In *Underwood v Gulf Refining Co.*, 1911, 128 Louisiana Reports 992, already cited, it was said: 'the idea that damages allowed for mental suffering are exemplary, punitory, or vindictive in their character has been very generally abandoned, and they are now recognized by this court and other courts as actual and compensatory'.

or vindictive damages had been assessed against one sovereign nation in favour of another presenting a claim on behalf of its nationals.[110]

iv. Powers of the Commission

There was, however, a fundamental reason why the Commission could not award exemplary damages: that it was without the power to make such awards under the terms of its charter – the Treaty of Berlin embodying much of the Treaty of Versailles restoring 'Friendly Relations' – a Treaty of Peace.[111] The tribunal found that its terms negated the concept of the imposition of a penalty by the US against Germany, save that the undertaking by Germany to make reparation to the US and its nationals as stipulated in the Treaty may partake of the nature of a penalty. They quoted Oppenheim:[112]

> There is no doubt that, if a belligerent can be made to pay compensation for all damage done by him in violating the laws of war, this will be an indirect means of securing legitimate warfare.

Part VII of the Treaty of Versailles (Articles 227 to 230, inclusive) dealt with 'Penalties', but these provisions were not incorporated in the Treaty of Berlin. In negotiating the Treaty of Peace, the US and Germany were dealing directly with each other. The tribunal held that had there been any intention on the part of the US to exact a penalty either as a punishment or as an example and a deterrent, such intention would have been clearly expressed in the Treaty itself; and, had it taken the form of a money payment, it would have been claimed by the government of the US on its own behalf and not on behalf of its nationals. As to such nationals, care was taken to provide for full and adequate 'indemnities', 'reparations', and 'satisfaction' of their claims for losses, damages, or injuries suffered by them. Under those provisions of the Treaty of Versailles expressly incorporated in the Treaty of Berlin, Germany accepted responsibility for all loss and damage to which the US and its nationals have been subjected because of the war.[113] Nevertheless, the US frankly recognises the fact 'that the resources of Germany are not adequate … to make complete reparation for all such loss and damage', but requires that Germany make 'compensation' for specified damages suffered by American nationals.[114]

v. Costs of Prosecuting the War

No such claim was made against Germany. No claims were asserted by the government of the US on account of pensions paid and compensation in pensions paid to naval and

[110] JH Ralston, *International Arbitral Law and Procedure* (Boston, Ginn & Co, 1910) s 369, where he says: 'While there is little doubt that in many cases the idea of punishment has influenced the amount of the award) yet we are not prepared to state that any commission has accepted the view that it possessed the power to grant anything save compensation.'

[111] Reports of International Arbitral Awards. *Opinion in the Lusitania cases.* 1 November 1923, Vol VII, 32–44 (United Nations 2006) 41.

[112] L Oppenheim, *International Law*, 3rd edn (Longmans Green and Co, 1920) Vol II, Sec 259a, 353.

[113] Reports of International Arbitral Awards. *Opinion in the Lusitania cases.* 1 November 1923, Vol VII, 32–44 (United Nations 2006) 42.

[114] Articles 231 and 232 and Annex I to Section I of Part VIII of the Treaty of Versailles.

military victims of the war and to their families and dependants.[115] In this case, the tribunal held that the US could not claim penalties for the use and benefit of a small group of American nationals who were fully compensated for losses sustained, adequate provision having been made.[116] What the US was doing was making one demand against Germany on some 12,500 counts. That demand was for compensation and reparation for certain losses sustained by the US and its nationals. While determining the amount that Germany was to pay, each claim had to be considered separately in relation to all others presented in this one demand. In all the claims, the parties were the same. They were determined and disposed of under the same Treaty and by the same tribunal.[117]

The Commission questioned why it would be right to impose a penalty for the use and benefit of a small group of American nationals who are awarded full compensation and, at the same time, waive reimbursement for the cost of the war which falls on all American taxpayers alike?[118] On that point they reasoned:[119]

> … The mere statement of the question is its answer. Putting the inquiry only serves to illustrate how repugnant to the fundamental principles of international law is the idea that this Commission should treat as justiciable the question as to what penalty should be assessed against Germany as a punishment for its alleged wrongdoing. It is our opinion that as between sovereign nations the question of the right and power to impose penalties, unlimited in amount, is political rather than legal in its nature, and therefore not a subject within the jurisdiction of this Commission. The Treaty is our charter. We can not look beyond its express provisions or its clear implications in assessing damages in any particular claim. We hold that its clear and unambiguous language does not authorize the imposition of penalties. Hence the fundamental maxim 'It is not allowable to interpret that which has no need of interpretation' applies.[120]'

They further reasoned that all the rules governing the interpretation of treaties would lead to the same result were it competent for them to consider them. For example: the Treaty being based upon the resolution of the Congress of the US, accepted and adopted by Germany; the language being that of the US and framed for its benefit, would be strictly construed against it;[121] that Treaty provisions must be so construed as to best conform to accepted principles of international law rather than in derogation of them;[122] and that penal clauses in treaties are odious and must be construed most strongly against those asserting them.[123]

[115] This was considered in the Commission's Administrative Decision No. II 1 November 1923.

[116] Reports of International Arbitral Awards. *Opinion in the Lusitania cases*. 1 November 1923, Vol VII, 32–44 (United Nations 2006) 42.

[117] ibid.

[118] ibid 43.

[119] ibid.

[120] *Vattel*, Book II, Ch XVII, s 263.

[121] ibid 264; *Digest of Justinian*, Book II, Title XIV, para 39, Monro translation, 1904; 'Treaties – Their Making and Enforcement' by SB Crandal, 2nd edn (1916)(hereinafter cited as 'Crandall'), s 171, 401; *Pothier on Obligations* (Evans, 1806), Vol I, 58 (7th rule, Article VII, Ch I, Part I); *Woolsey on International Law*, 6th edn (1891) s 113; opinion of Ralston, Umpire, Italian-Venezuelan Mixed Claims Commission, Sambiaggio Case, Venezuelan Arbitrations 1903, 666 and 688–689.

[122] Opinion of Plumley, Umpire, in Arao Mines (Limited) Case, British-Venezuelan Mixed Claims Commission, 344 and 386–387 Venezuelan Arbitrations 1903; reference to *Sambiaggio* case in n 27 above; *Vilas v Manila*, 1911, 220 United States 345, 358–359; *Crandall*, s 170.

[123] *Vattel*, Book II, Chr XVII, ss 301–303; *Grotius*, Book II, Ch XVI, s X and para 3 of s XII.

In conclusion, they held that the Treaty was one between two sovereign nations – a Treaty of Peace. There was no place in it for any vindictive or punitive provisions. Germany was required to make compensation and reparation for all losses falling within its terms sustained by American nationals, which should be 'full, adequate, and complete'. But the Commission had no power to impose penalties for the use and benefit of private claimants when the government of the US had exacted none.[124]

Their decision, insofar as it was applicable, was determinative of all cases growing out of the sinking of the *Lusitania*. They directed that all awards in such cases were to be made as of 1 November 1923 and bear interest from that date at the rate of five per cent per annum. The Award was published in Washington on 1 November 1923.[125]

This case laid down guidance on causation and remoteness of damages in international tort law in matters of hostile action by a belligerent state against neutral passengers on a belligerent passenger liner. Questions as to the status of the *Lusitania* were not in question since the Treaty of Berlin had settled the question of liability of the Kaiserreich and its successor government. But it did deal with the result of unrestricted submarine warfare in war zones. It may be argued that Germany was seeking reprisals, but for what? Tit for tat or proportionate? The circumstances of the sinking can hardly be regarded as proportionate. Whether the ship was disabled so quickly by reason of an undisclosed explosion in the bow while carrying explosives or not, the primary cause was its being torpedoed.

E. Mixed Claims Commission-United States and Germany

i. Decision in Life-Insurance Claims

Following the earlier claims by the US against Germany for compensation due to the German submarine attack on the *Lusitania* causing the deaths of American passengers, claims were made by the relatives of the deceased against the deceased's life insurance policies.[126]

In turn, the American life insurance companies then made claims against the German government to recover alleged losses resulting from the payments they made under the terms of policies insuring the lives of passengers lost on the *Lusitania*. The question of causation was clear; the sinking was caused primarily by the torpedo exploding on hitting the vessel, which appears to have set off a critical secondary explosion in the hold

[124] Interesting to contrast the Commissioner's view with that of the politicians who imposed the war guilt clause a reparations on Germany in this context. It was something President Wilson at first rejected but was pressured into it by Clemenceau and Lloyd George for political reasons. See ch 1.

[125] Edwin B Parker, Umpire, Concurring in The Conclusions: Chandler P Anderson, American Commissioner, W Klesselbach, German Commissioner.

[126] This was established in pursuance of the agreement between the US and Germany of 10 August 1922. Members of the Commission were Edwin B Parker, Umpire; Chandler P Anderson, American Commissioner; Wilhelm Kiesselbach, German Commissioner; Robert W Bonynge, American Agent; Karl von Lewinski, German Agent. This analysis is based on the report in 'Mixed Claims Commission-United States and Germany' (1925) 19 *AJIL* 593–609. Reproduced with permission of The Licensor through PLSclear.

containing American munitions for the British war effort.[127] In this case that was not the critical issue. The fundamental point was whether the insurers had suffered the loss. The relatives suffered the loss of family members, but what was the insurer's actual loss?

At the tribunal, the Umpire, Edwin B Parker,[128] ruled that the claims were indirect and too remote:

> The act of Germany in striking down an individual did not in legal contemplation proximately result in damage to all of those who had contract relations, direct or remote, with that individual, which may have been affected by his death. In this latter class these claims fall. They are not embraced within the terms of the Treaty of Berlin and are therefore ordered dismissed.

Judge Parker pronounced on 10 test cases based on 18 life insurance policies involving 11 passengers who were drowned when the *Lusitania* was torpedoed. It was for Parker to decide the case because the American and German Commissioners disagreed. The German Agent denied that payments were made by the insurers as claimed and that any part of such payments represented losses to them. The American Agent contended that the life insurance contracts in question were contracts for life based on mortality tables and that the American Experience Table of Mortality ('American Table') was one generally used by American companies in writing insurance contracts. This was compiled from the policy experience of the Mutual Life Insurance Company of New York based on the number dying each year at given ages out of groups of 100,000, and by applying the law of averages to this actual experience, this table was constructed. But this table was compiled in peacetime when the life risks are less than the risks of war. War risks were therefore not a part of the scheme of life insurance.[129]

It was explained that the cost of insurance, including death losses, was provided for from premiums paid by policyholders, with interest accruing with reference to the mortality table which determined the amount of the premiums charged. The key point here that Parker explained was that if a policyholder died prior to the date of the assumed mortality *and from a cause comprehended in the law of averages*, the policy would be paid from the funds contributed in premiums by other policyholders, *and the insurance company therefore actually suffered no loss*. This was the Achilles heel in the claimant's argument, but Judge Parker went on to analyse and interpret the policy wording and scope of cover and why damage was not direct and too remote to found liability. As he found:

> that in five of the policies involved the assumption of risk due to the policyholder engaging in the naval or military services was expressly excluded and in the other policies no mention was made of such service risks, which were regarded as non-existent, so that in none of these cases did the claimants receive a premium to pay for a *war service risk;* that the premiums charged in the policies which ignored war service risks were no higher in any instance than

[127] This was denied by successive British governments, but in 2015, the Foreign Office admitted that the liner was carrying munitions. See above n 80.

[128] Judge Parker was a renowned American jurist whose opinions on such questions as the measure of damages, interest, proximate cause, made a distinct contribution to international law, if not also to municipal law. In a report by Dr Ernst Prossinagg, an Austrian Agent in one of the many claims Judge Parker decided, tribute was paid to the unimpeachable objectivity and high-mindedness of Judge Parker.

[129] 'Mixed Claims Commission-United States and Germany' (1925) 19 *AJIL* 594. Reproduced with permission of The Licensor through PLSclear.

> the premiums charged in the policies which expressly excluded war-service risks; that *if an insurer is compelled to pay under a policy where death results from a war risk which was not in contemplation and for which no premium to provide for such risk had been specifically exacted the company sustains a loss;* that the sinking of the *Lusitania* was an act of war; that such sinking was in violation of the rules of international law and was not and could not have been in the contemplation of the parties when the policies were issued; that Germany's act in sinking the *Lusitania* forced the premature payment of the face of the policies here involved; that the insurers had not charged or received any premium with which to make such premature payments and therefore in each instance suffered a loss equal to the difference between the face of the policy and the reserve, which amounts are here claimed; and that losses so suffered are property losses.

In effect, the claimants did not suffer a loss.

The argument of American counsel was that if a policyholder died prior to the date of his life expectancy as evidenced by the mortality table used to determine the amount of the premium paid, and *from causes taken into account* in the compilation of such table and within the law of averages, payment on the face of the policy in excess of the reserve was made from funds contributed in premiums by other policyholders belonging to the same group, and therefore the insurer suffers no actual loss. But deaths from causes not contemplated or taken into account in the compilation of the mortality table used are not paid for in premiums received and hence result in losses to the insurer. The policyholders whose lives were lost on the *Lusitania* came to their deaths through a risk of war, and hence the insurers, while liable under the terms of the policies, have not been paid for this risk and have consequently suffered losses, which are property losses, equal to the difference between the face of the policies and the reserves.[130] But the problem here with this argument was that the payment was made out of the General Mortality Fund, the insurer suffering the loss.

The German Agent replied that the business of insurance was based upon the average expected death rate among a large group. Other reasons were given, including the fact that such expectation was based upon the previous experience of insurers and the fact that the previous experience of insurers does not furnish data from which the probability of the death rate from certain causes can be approximated was immaterial in determining whether or not it has sustained a loss. His key argument was that the true test of whether an insurer has suffered losses was whether the actual death rate among a given group exceeded the expected death rate from that group. The American Table was compiled from the actual experience of the Mutual Life Insurance Company of New York, covering a period from 1843 to 1860. Since it was compiled, society had not remained static, but the average human life had been very greatly lengthened through improved hygienic conditions despite numerous hazards causing many deaths, unknown at the time the American table was compiled.[131] The insurers continued to use the table because it provided a safe margin out of which to pay claims arising from uncertain hazards. This gave insurers a very wide margin of profit since their policies

[130] ibid 595.

[131] The death rate for 1915 was lower than in any previous year save 1913 and 1914; that in 1918, the year of the influenza pandemic and also the year when the US had its armies on the fighting front, the rate increased substantially, but beginning with 1919 it decreased steadily, falling to 0.79 in 1921 as against 1.22 in 1903. 'Mixed Claims Commission-United States and Germany' (1925) 19 *AJIL* 595, fn 2. Reproduced with permission of The Licensor through PLSclear.

excluded war risks. It was also argued by Germany that the risks of war-not only the risk of war service but also risks to noncombatants incident to war-were known to insurance actuaries and must have been taken into account by them before and at the time the policies were written. Some insurers, writing both straight life insurance and accident insurance, recognised the risks of war to noncombatants prior to the sinking of the *Lusitania*, since the accident policies on the lives of Mr Vanderbilt and Mr Hopkins, both lost on the *Lusitania*, which provided that:[132]

> Nor shall this insurance cover ... death ... resulting, directly or indirectly, wholly or partly, from ... war.

The German counsel concluded that the only way to determine whether an insurer had sustained a loss was to ascertain whether the actual death rate of the group to which the policy belonged exceeded the expected death rate for that group. No claim was made for any group loss. It could be inferred that the claimants' accounts showed profits and safe reserves applied to these groups and hence no losses had been suffered by the claimants.

Judge Parker considered that in issuing a life insurance policy without expressly excluding any risk and in insuring the life of an individual without any restrictions whatsoever, self-protection and sound business policy must have impelled the insurer to take into account every possible risk without limiting itself to those forming the basis of a mortality table used by the insurer compiled more than half a century before the *Lusitania* was sunk. The table was not the only factor taken into account by actuaries in determining what the risk really was and the premium to be paid. The American Agent made the erroneous assumption of fact that the mortality table determined the premium exacted. Parker accepted the German argument regarding changes in life expectancies as well as increased hazards of numerous transportation and industrial devices then unknown, unthought of, and unimagined.[133] As to losses and profits, he opined:

> ... Losses or profits are facts determinable without reference to the independent fact of the cause of death and whether or not such cause was in the contemplation of the insurer when the policy was issued. Profits may flow from policies or groups of policies where deaths result from causes not contemplated, in the sense they could not have been foreseen.

In respect of unforeseen and uncontemplated causes of death which cannot *eo nomine* be taken into account in computations under the law of averages, upon which all insurance is based, Parker concluded that such risks had not *eo nomine* been provided against in premiums received. There existed no relation of cause and effect between (1) the contemplation or not by the insurer at the time of issuing a policy of the risk which subsequently causes the death of the insured and (2) the loss or profit under such policy to the insurer. Parker rejected the contention of the American Agent that the insurers must necessarily have sustained losses where they were compelled to pay for the deaths of their insured resulting from a war risk not in contemplation and for which no premium was specifically exacted to cover such risk.

[132] *Vanderbilt et al. v Travelers' Insurance Company*, 1920, 184 N. Y. Supp. 54, affirmed 1922, 202 N. Y. App. Div. 738; *Hopkins v Connecticut General Life Insurance Company*, 1918, 225 N. Y. 76.

[133] 'Mixed Claims Commission-United States and Germany' (1925) 19 *AJIL* 597. Reproduced with permission of The Licensor through PLSclear.

Parker rejected the German Agent's contention that the insurers sustained no losses. But apart from the fundamental no-loss argument, the major international law question was whether, under the terms of the Treaty of Berlin, Germany was obligated to pay losses of this class.

ii. Application of Treaty of Berlin

The Commission's Administrative Decisions Nos. I and II[134] provided that Germany was not liable. Parker explained this by analysing the opinions of the National Commissioners regarding the Treaty of Berlin which formed the basis of the Administrative Decisions and the Opinion in the Lusitania Cases.[135]

The Treaty of Berlin was based upon the provisions of Sections 2 and 5 of a Joint Resolution of the Congress of the United States approved by President Woodrow Wilson on 2 July 1921 declaring with certain reservations and conditions, that the war between Germany and the US was at an end. These *ex parte* reservations were by Article I of the Treaty adopted by Germany, by which Germany accorded the US all the rights, privileges, indemnities, reparations, and advantages specified in the resolution of Congress.[136] Under Section 2 of that resolution, there was 'expressly reserved' to the US and its nationals all of the then existing rights, privileges, indemnities, reparations, or advantages with the right to enforce the same, and the US and its nationals would have all of these rights for its and their benefit under the Treaty of Versailles.[137] Under Section 5 of the Resolution, the US would retain all property of Germany or its nationals or the proceeds held by the US until such time as Germany would make 'suitable provision for the satisfaction of all claims' against Germany 'in consequence of hostilities or of any operations of war, or otherwise'.[138]

In effect, Germany was to pay the US claims under the Resolution, including those defined by such of the provisions of the Treaty of Versailles as were incorporated in the Treaty of Berlin.[139] Article I of the Agreement of 10 August 1922 establishing this Commission and defining its powers and jurisdiction provided that:

> The commission shall pass upon the following categories of claims which are more particularly defined in the Treaty of August 25, 1921, and in the Treaty of Versailles:
>
> (1) Claims of American citizens, arising since July 31, 1914, in respect of damage to, or seizure of, their property, rights and interests, including any company or association in which they are interested, within German territory as it existed on August 1, 1914;

[134] Decisions and Opinions, pp 1–15 inclusive. (1925) 18 *AJIL* 175–186. Reproduced with permission of The Licensor through PLSclear.

[135] Decisions and Opinions, pp 17–32 inclusive (1925) 18 *AJIL* 361–373. Reproduced with permission of The Licensor through PLSclear.

[136] (1925) 18 *AJIL* 599. Reproduced with permission of The Licensor through PLSclear.

[137] Incorporated in the Treaty between the US and Germany restoring friendly relations, signed at Berlin 25 August 1921. *Papers Relating to The Foreign Relations of The United States, The Paris Peace Conference*, 1919, Vol XIII.

[138] ibid.

[139] This construction of the Treaty of Berlin was expressly adopted by Germany in a formal declaration presented to this Commission by the German Agent on 15 May 1923, in which it was declared that 'Germany is primarily liable with respect to all claims and debts coming within the jurisdiction of the Mixed Claims Commission under the Agreement of August 10, 1922.' *Minutes of Commission, 15 May 1923.* (1925) 19 *AJIL* 599. Reproduced with permission of The Licensor through PLSclear.

(2) Other claims for loss or damage to which the United States or its nationals have been subjected with respect to injuries to persons, or to property, rights and interests, including any company or association in which American nationals are interested, since July 31, 1914, as a consequence of the war;
(3) Debts owing to American citizens by the German Government or by German nationals.'[140]

Germany's financial obligations were limited to claims falling within categories 1–3 above which were to be judicially ascertained and determined by the Commission.

Article 232 and Annex I provided the basis for Germany's financial obligations to the US arising under the Treaty of Berlin on claims for all damages suffered by American nationals *during the period of American belligerency.* The effect of which was to bind Germany to pay reparation 'claims' of American nationals for losses suffered by them growing out of Germany's acts during the period of American neutrality and falling within the categories defined in Article 232 and Annex I.[141] Under the provisions of Article 232 Treaty of Versailles, Germany was obligated to make compensation for damage done to American civilian nationals and to their property during the period of American belligerency. The annex supplementary to Article 232 expressly obligated Germany to make compensation (a) for damages suffered by the American surviving dependants of civilians whose deaths were caused by acts of war and (b) for damages caused by Germany or her allies in respect of all property wherever situated belonging to the US or its nationals.[142]

Under Section 5 of the Resolution of Congress, Germany was to pay all claims against Germany of American nationals who had, since 31 July 1914, 'suffered, through the acts of the Imperial German Government, or its agents, … loss, damage, or injury to their persons or property, directly or indirectly'. All these provisions constituted a part of the Treaty of Berlin. From them the Commission deduced the rules embraced in its Administrative Decision No. 1 which provided:

> The financial obligations of Germany to the United States arising under the Treaty of Berlin on claims other than excepted claims, put forward by the United States on behalf of its nationals, embrace:
>
> (A) all losses, damages, or injuries to them, including losses, damages, or injuries to their property wherever situated, suffered directly or indirectly during the war period, caused by acts of Germany or her agents in the prosecution of the war, provided, however, that during the period of belligerency damages with respect to injuries to and death of persons, other than prisoners of war, shall be limited to injuries to and death of civilians.[143]

Having established this, Parker finally considered what claims for damages arising out of losses of life on the *Lusitania* were within the Treaty of Berlin. The obligation of Germany was clear: to make compensation for damages suffered by the American *surviving*

[140] See also para (e), subdivision (2) of para (h), and para (i) of Art 297 and Art 243 of the Treaty of Versailles.

[141] The first category of this Annex I (to Section I of Part VIII, Reparation) reads: '(1) Damage to injured persons and to surviving dependents by personal injury to or death of civilians caused by acts of war, including bombardments or other attacks on land, on sea, or from the air, and all the direct consequences thereof, and of all operations of war by the two groups of belligerents wherever arising. (9) Damage in respect of all property wherever situated belonging to any of the Allied or Associated States or their nationals, with the exception of naval and military works or materials, which has been carried off, seized, injured or destroyed by the acts of Germany or her allies on land, on sea or from the air, or damage directly in consequence of hostilities or of any operations of war.'

[142] (1925) 19 *AJIL* 601. Reproduced with permission of The Licensor through PLSclear.

[143] ibid 602.

dependants of civilians whose deaths were caused by acts of war occurring at any time during the war period.[144] The Treaty of Berlin required Germany to make compensation in death cases, which was limited to damage suffered by American surviving dependants resulting from deaths to civilians caused by acts of war.[145] Under familiar rules of construction, this express mention of surviving dependants who, through their respective governments, were entitled to be compensated in death cases excludes all other classes, which included insurers of life. Parker applied the maxim '*expressio unius est exclusio alterius*' applicable to the construction of treaties as well as municipal statutes and contracts.[146] This construction was applied by the Allied Powers in their reparation claims against Germany, and all claims of life insurance companies similar to these claims which were excluded by them. The Commission held that Germany was financially obligated to compensate the US for all losses suffered by American nationals as surviving dependants resulting from deaths of civilians caused by acts of war as in Administrative Decision No. I.[147]

Parker decided that the general language of the definition of Administrative Decision No. I in connection with fundamental rules of Administrative Decision No. II and elsewhere.[148]

> The proximate *cause* of the loss must have been in legal contemplation the act of Germany. The proximate *result* or *consequence* of *that act* must have been the loss, damage, or injury suffered … This is but an application of the familiar rule of proximate cause-a rule of general application both in private and public law-which clearly the parties to the Treaty had no intention of abrogating … The simple test to be applied in all cases is: has an American national proven a loss of the suffered by him, susceptible of being measured with reasonable exactness by pecuniary standards, and is that loss attributable to Germany's act as a proximate cause?

Parker applied this test with the obvious result that the dependent members of the families of those who lost their lives on the *Lusitania*, and who were accustomed to receiving pecuniary contributions, suffered losses by the proximate cause of the German action. The usages, customs, and laws of civilised countries had long since recognised losses of this character as proximate results of injuries causing death. The Treaty of Versailles did not alter that.[149] The act of Germany was the immediate cause of maturing the contracts of insurance. Parker held that *this effect* so produced was a circumstance incidental to, but not flowing from, such an act as the normal consequence and was remote-not in time

[144] Paragraph 1 of Annex I to Section I of Part VIII read in connection with para 4 of the Annex to Section IV of Part X of the Treaty of Versailles and also in connection with the declaration of the German government. (1925) 19 *AJIL* 602. Reproduced with permission of The Licensor through PLSclear.

[145] (1925) 19 *AJIL* 602. Reproduced with permission of The Licensor through PLSclear.

[146] *Broom's Legal Maxims*, 8th American edn (1882) 650, 7th English edn (1900) 491.

[147] As pointed out in the *Opinion in the Lusitania Cases* (1925) 18 *AJIL* 361 the 'liability for losses sustained by American nationals was assumed by the Government of Germany through its note of February 4, 1916', and this assumption of liability was reiterated before this Commission by the German Agent. Reproduced with permission of The Licensor through PLSclear.

[148] Administrative Decision No. II, Decisions and Opinions, pp 12 and 13, all three members of the Commission concurring in the conclusions. (1925) 18 *AJIL* 183–184. Reproduced with permission of The Licensor through PLSclear.

[149] Paragraph 1 of Annex I to Section I of Part VIII (Reparation), Treaty of Versailles. Great Britain's reparation claims contain an item of £32,436,256 for damages suffered through the loss of life of civilians. In that case Britain applied the rules laid down in the *Opinion in the Lusitania cases.*

but in natural and normal sequence. Thus the payments made by the insurers to other American nationals were not caused by Germany but by their contract obligations.[150] This was quite a separate matter with no connection: Germany was not a party, had no notice of them, and the contract obligations formed no part of any life that was taken. They did not inhere in it. They were quite outside and apart from it. They did not operate on or affect it. Parker further held that the earlier maturity of the insurance contracts was 'not a natural and normal consequence of Germany's act in taking the lives, and hence not attributable to that act as a proximate cause'.[151]

Parker further explained that:[152]

> On the happening of [the insured's] death, the insurers are required to pay the amounts specified in the contracts of insurance to the beneficiaries entitled under such contracts to receive it, not because the latter have suffered any loss or because any loss has resulted from the death, but solely because they have bound themselves by contract to make such payments upon the occurrence of that death. Such losses as the insurers may sustain by reason of such payments are not substituted for and do not stand in the place of losses which would otherwise be suffered by the payee whose losses are reduced to the extent of the payment made, as in fire, marine, and war-risk insurance losses. The insurers through subrogation or otherwise are not entitled to stand in the shoes of the representatives of the estate of the insured or of the beneficiaries and pursue their rights, if any exist, against the author of the death of the insured.

In its *Opinion in the Lusitania* case, the Commission[153] held that the amount of losses suffered by American nationals resulting from the death of a *Lusitania* victim who during life contributed to them was not subject to any deduction on account of insurance moneys paid them as beneficiaries under policies of insurance on the life of such victim, stating: 'Such payment of insurance, far from springing from Germany's act, is entirely foreign to it.'[154] Following this, Parker considered that to the extent that the American insurers had sustained losses by being prematurely deprived of the use of funds paid by them to American beneficiaries, such American beneficiaries had been correspondingly benefited by the earlier payment. He also held that the losses claimed were not economic losses to the American nation but only losses sustained by one group of American nationals for the benefit of another group of American nationals, arising from their contractual relations and not from any economic injury inflicted by Germany's act.[155] In Parker's analysis it was simply the fact that one group of American nationals had lost to another group of American nationals and neither America as a nation nor its nationals had suffered.

The problem above all for the claimants in this case was that the Commission had repeatedly held that the terms of the Treaty of Berlin fixed and limited Germany's obligation to pay. That Treaty expressly required Germany to make compensation for damages suffered by the surviving dependants of civilians whose deaths were caused

[150] (1925) 19 *AJIL* 604. Reproduced with permission of The Licensor through PLSclear.
[151] ibid.
[152] ibid 605.
[153] Decisions and Opinions, pp 17–32, all three members concurring in the conclusions. (1925) 18 *AJIL* 361–373. Reproduced with permission of The Licensor through PLSclear.
[154] (1925) 19 *AJIL* 606. Further guidance on liability was given in Paragraph 1 of Annex I to Section I of Part VIII, Treaty of Versailles. Reproduced with permission of The Licensor through PLSclear.
[155] (1925) 19 *AJIL* 606. Reproduced with permission of The Licensor through PLSclear.

by acts of war and, by clear implication, excluded any obligation on Germany's part to make compensation in death cases to life insurers or any class other than *surviving dependants*.[156] Apart from that clear limitation of liability, the losses on which these claims were based were not in legal contemplation attributable to Germany's act as a proximate cause. It was not only Judge Parker who recognised the legal right of dependants to recover pecuniary damage; even Grotius recognised such a right.[157] Parker noted this rule had been recognised by the nations of western Europe. The German Code expressly conferred a cause of action for the taking of life. In the 1860s, the US Supreme Court held that the natural law and the usages, customs, and laws of civilized countries, quite independent of statute, permitted a recovery by surviving dependants for injuries resulting in death.[158]

This case is important as it was unprecedented. As Parker said: 'History records no instance of any payment by one nation to another based on claims of this nature.' There was nothing in the Treaty of Berlin or in the records of the cases before the Mixed Claims Commission (US and Germany) to indicate that claims of this class could have been within the contemplation of those who negotiated, drafted, and executed that treaty.[159] Indeed the American courts, rejected similar claims of insurers as remote so that the US could not assert such claims.

It had been recognised that the dependants of those who died were entitled to recover damages for their personal loss and the benefit they would have gained had the insured lived, caused by the natural and normal consequence of Germany's act and attributable to it as a proximate cause. But this did not apply to those who had contractual relations with the deceased insured. Consequently, he dismissed those claims for being outside the terms of the Treaty of Berlin.[160] His Award was published in Washington on 18 September 1924 and signed EDWIN B. PARKER, *Umpire*.

F. Reparations Commission 1924: Germany v Czechoslovakia 1924 Cessions Regarding River Elbe

This dispute was the subject of Part XII, Ports, Waterways and Railways, Section 1, Article 339, General Provisions of the Treaty of Versailles. Under Article 331, the Elbe from its confluence with the Vilna and the Vltava from Prague was declared an international river. Article 339 required Germany to cede to the Allied and Associated Powers a proportion of tugs and vessels remaining registered in the ports of the river systems referred to in Article 331 (in this case, the Elbe) as part of reparations and restitution, as well as materials necessary for the Allies to utilise the river system. The number of tugs and vessels and material that Germany would cede was to be determined by an arbitrator nominated by the US, 'due regard being had to the legitimate needs of the

[156] ibid 607. Emphasis added.
[157] *Grotius*, Book II, Ch XVII, ss 1, 12 and 13.
[158] *Kake v Horton*, 1860, 2 Hawaiian Reports 209.
[159] (1925) 19 *AJIL* 608. Reproduced with permission of The Licensor through PLSclear.
[160] ibid 609.

parties concerned'.[161] This was calculated with reference to the shipping traffic over the period 1909–14.

The Germans were to provide modern river craft in good repair to carry goods under Article 339.[162] The sum awarded by the arbitrator was limited to the value of the material ceded, which could be set off against the total of reparations due from Germany. The losses made by the owners were a matter for the German state.[163] Under Article 340, the Elbe was placed under the administration of an International Commission. This comprised four German delegates, two Czechoslovakian delegates, one British, one French, one Italian, and one Belgian delegate. Under Article 363, the ports of Hamburg and Stettin ceded certain areas to the Czechoslovakians as free zones. The question of the numbers of vessels and materials to be ceded was referred to Walker D Hines as arbitrator.[164] He gave his award on 14 June 1921 in Paris. He held numerous hearings with the delegations of the parties before making his determination.

The German case was that Czechoslovakia had no right to the cession of boats and materials.[165] Only in cases where the Versailles Treaty had changed the territorial boundaries did this apply. The treaty had made no territorial changes affecting the Elbe, and Germany argued that Article 339 could not impose on Germany the obligation to make any cessions to Czechoslovakia regarding the Elbe. They used Article 357 regarding similar cessions to France in respect of the ceded territories of Alsace-Lorraine.[166] The provisions were the same. But clearly in the case of Alsace-Lorraine, lost in 1870 to Germany, it was restored, and France's boundaries consequently changed. Since Czechoslovakia was situated on the Elbe, Article 339 specifically referred to rivers that were described in Article 331.[167] Czechoslovakia was directly involved in the navigation of the Elbe, as it had a free zone for 99 years in Hamburg at the mouth of the Elbe. Mr Hines found that Article 339 applied to 'Associated Powers' ie, new states created by the treaty, including Czechoslovakia. Heins rejected Germany's argument.

The next issue to be decided was the number of newer vessels to be transferred to Czechoslovakia. The arbitrator adopted 1913 as the year to which the needs of Czechoslovakia should be determined.[168] The parties' delegations agreed that the total Elba traffic in 1913 was 17,400,000 tonnes.[169]

The Czechoslovakian delegation submitted that the 1913 figures should be enhanced to accommodate the river traffic that in pre-war years was shipped via Trieste and Fiume. In those days, freight could be shipped more easily through the Austro-Hungarian Empire. Austria included Trieste, and Hungary included Fiume with affordable railroad rates. By 1924 these rates could not be obtained on favourable terms, so more traffic was transferred to Hamburg.[170] Mr Heine considered such submission speculative and was

[161] Article 339.
[162] ibid.
[163] ibid.
[164] WD Hines, 'In the Matter of the Cessions by Germany to Czechoslovakia Under Article 339 of the Treaty of Versailles' (1924) 18(1) *AJIL* 186–198. Reproduced with permission of The Licensor through PLSclear.
[165] ibid 187.
[166] ibid.
[167] ibid.
[168] ibid 188.
[169] ibid 197. Annex 1.
[170] ibid 188.

not inclined to make any adjustment over 800,000 tonnes.[171] Within Czechoslovakia, the Czechs could use their own boats, so no award was made.

Between the Czechoslovakian ports and the German Elbe ports (Middle Elbe), each country should have 50 per cent of the boats for their traffic.[172] As to the traffic between Czechoslovakia and Hamburg, Mr Hines decided that the Czechs should have 100 per cent control over the boats necessary for this traffic, as they had a free zone in Hamburg.[173] In other cases, each country was to have 50 per cent of the boats necessary to carry the traffic. As for Czechoslovakia to the Middle Elbe, after the two delegations had considered technical aspects and statistical calculations, Hines held that Czechoslovakia would require 261,000 tonnes of barge capacity and 17,800 horsepower tug capacity.[174]

Under the Treaty of Versailles, the requirements of Czechoslovakia were to be decided in light of the amount of shipping that would remain on the Elbe after Germany made the necessary cessions under the Treaty of Versailles.[175] The Reparations Commission certified the size of the German River Fleet as of 11 November 1918, as well as the losses suffered by the Allies requiring reparations by cession.[176] The amount of reparations for the losses suffered amounted to 187,000 tonnes of barges and no more than 330 horsepower of tugs. Hines decided that Czechoslovakia ought to have 1,890 horsepower of harbour tugs and 1,346 tonnes of freight boats.[177] The existing stock of barges in Czechoslovakian ports on the Elbe and controlled by Czechoslovakian nationals amounted to 50,200 tonnes of barges.[178]

To make up the shortfall, it was necessary for Czechoslovakia to make up the shortfall by:[179]

1. The transfer of all tugs vessels and other property of the Austrian Northwest Elbe Shipping Company (German capital controlled) and registered in Czechoslovakian ports.
2. To give Czechoslovakia complete control over the property of the German Austrian Steamship Company and the new German Bohemian Elbe Shipping Company (Czechoslovakian capital controlled) but tugs registered in German ports.

Germany accepted this as meeting the needs of Czechoslovakia because of Czechoslovakian interest, whether by registration or investment.

Hines was of the view that the vessels and tugs could be transferred to Czechoslovakia, provided the elements of ownership and interest were vested in Czechoslovakia, ie, as to capital and registration. If this did not satisfy the needs of Czechoslovakia, then

[171] ibid 189.

[172] The same conclusion was reached in the France v Germany Arbitration under Art 357.

[173] WD Hines, 'In the Matter of the Cessions by Germany to Czechoslovakia Under Article 339 of the Treaty of Versailles' (1924) 18(1) *AJIL* 189. Reproduced with permission of The Licensor through PLSclear.

[174] ibid 190.

[175] ibid 191.

[176] The arbitrator was empowered to decide the conditions of session under Annex III, Part VII Treaty of Versailles.

[177] WD Hines, 'In the Matter of the Cessions by Germany to Czechoslovakia Under Article 339 of the Treaty of Versailles' (1924) 18(1) *AJIL* 191. Reproduced with permission of The Licensor through PLSclear.

[178] ibid 192.

[179] ibid.

Germany should cede tugs and vessels from those registered in German Elbe ports. As to the Austrian Northwest Elbow Shipping Company, insofar as they did not meet Czechoslovakian needs, then Germany should cede other tugs and vessels to Czechoslovakia. Hines suggested that the registration of these vessels could be transferred to German ports.[180] He applied the same formula to Czechoslovakian claims in respect of the German-Austrian Steamship Company and the New German Bohemian Elbe Shipping Company.[181] Hines gave time to both parties until 10 am on 6 July 1921[182] to agree on the selection of the vessels and to hear points on which they were able to agree. In addition, Czechoslovakia asked for buildings, installations, and other material, for example, floating cranes, to be ceded under Article 339. The arbitrator refused to award any such items, being the property of the Austrian Northwest Elbe Shipping Company located or used in Germany.[183] Again, he refused to cede property belonging to the German-Austrian Steamship Company and the New German Bohemian Elbe Shipping Company since both were controlled by Czechoslovakian capital. They had also demanded other real property in Czechoslovakia belonging to the Austrian Northwest Elbe Shipping Company and the German-Austrian Shipping Company or the New German-Bohemian Elbe Shipping Company. Hines was of the opinion that since these facilities were in Czechoslovakia, there was no necessity for any cession.[184]

As to the buildings and harbour installations in Hamburg, under Article 363 of the Treaty of Versailles, they were leased to Czechoslovakia for 99 years. Under Article 364, the rent for the use of equipment was to be determined by a Commission.[185]

The question of what buildings could be ceded under Article 339 to Czechoslovakia in Germany was to be decided by Hines. He decided that Germany should cede two warehouses and two electric cranes to be agreed upon between the delegations.[186] It was further decided that Czechoslovakia had a legitimate need for three floating cranes of the Austrian Northwest Elbe Shipping Company used at Karlin, Teschen, and Aussig, even though they were controlled by German capital. In contemplation of a hearing for 6 July, the arbitrator put specific questions to the delegation to comment on the cranes, installation and pontoons, as well as office building requirements. Hines held that no need was shown for the cession by Germany to Czechoslovakia of materials for the utilisation of the Elbe. Hines directed that after the 6 July hearing, he would assess the value of the cessions under Article 339. If the Reparations Commission decided that the total amount of tugs to be ceded by Germany to Czechoslovakia was substantially less than 187,000 tonnes, then the arbitrator would consider an application by Czechoslovakia for additional units so that Czechoslovakia was given a fair proportion. Hines published his Award at Paris on 14 June 1921.

The case demonstrates the way in which the Treaty of Versailles was implemented and the relationship between the Reparations Commission and the arbitration process to assess fair compensation for war loss and damage. In terms of the grievance

[180] ibid.
[181] ibid 193.
[182] ibid.
[183] ibid 194.
[184] ibid.
[185] ibid.
[186] ibid 195.

Germans felt against the Czechs, this may have been one of those measures that gave rise to revenge and support for the Nazis. More interesting, perhaps, is the role that an American jurist played in resolving this matter when, to all intents, America had disengaged from European entanglements.

G. *Lithuania v Poland* (The Vilna Affair)

According to WJ Brocklebank,[187] Poland was one of the most difficult challenges for the League of Nations. The boundary between Lithuania and Poland was not defined in the Treaty of Versailles. They were left to be decided by the Principal Allied and Associated Powers. Vilna was occupied by German troops until Lithuania declared its independence on 16 February 1918. In January 1919 it was taken over by the Bolsheviks. They were driven out by Polish forces who occupied the town on 20 April 1919. They were then opposed by Lithuanian forces. The Principal Allied and Associated Powers[188] then found themselves between two rival armies. Ideally the Allied Powers would have supported an alliance between Lithuania and Poland.[189]

Between 1386 and 1795 Poland and Lithuania had been friendly neighbours. By the Act of Lublin 1569 and the 'Perpetual Organic Union' of 3 May 1791, the people became united by a common culture and their Catholic religion, the Poles being the dominant race.[190] After 1883 a popular nationalist Lithuanian movement developed, encouraged by Russia, which continued until July 1914. Poland then became a battlefield, and the economies of Poland and Lithuania were destroyed. In July 1920, the Bolsheviks once again took Vilna, forcing Lithuanians to accept peace terms on 12 July 1920 under the Treaty of Moscow.[191] By this treaty, Lithuania received the Vilna District and part of Grodno and Suwalki. The problem was that this arrangement overlapped the territory granted to Poland by the Supreme Council on 8 December 1919, known as 'the Curzon Line'. It was rumoured that under the Treaty of Moscow, Lithuania had given licence to Russia to use its territory for military operations against Poland.[192] Thus, in August 1920, Polish forces again attacked Lithuania. The Polish understanding of Lithuanian collaboration with the Bolsheviks was denied;[193] however, Lithuania suggested a conference in London or arbitration through the League of Nations. The matter was considered by the League of Nations at a meeting in Paris on 8 September 1920. The disputants were asked to accept Article 17 of the Covenant to become members of the League and assume membership obligations. Both governments acceded to their obligations as members and provisionally accepted the Curzon Line.[194] Grodno and Lida were occupied by the

[187] WJ Brocklebank, 'The Vilna Dispute' (1926) 20 *AJIL* 483. Reproduced with permission of The Licensor through PLSclear.

[188] The Versailles Peace Conference was organised by the representatives of the US, the British Empire, France, Italy, and Japan, and it was they that came to be designated as the 'Principal Allied and Associated Powers'.

[189] RH Lord, 'Lithuania and Poland' (1923) 4(4) *Foreign Affairs* 38.

[190] WJ Brocklebank, 'The Vilna Dispute' (1926) 20 *AJIL* 483, reproduced with permission of The Licensor through PLSclear; see also RH Lord, 'Lithuania and Poland' (1923) 4(4) *Foreign Affairs* 39–41.

[191] Brocklebank ibid 484.

[192] ibid 485.

[193] ibid.

[194] ibid 486.

Bolsheviks, although the Soviets offered to withdraw if Poland respected Lithuania's neutrality. A Commission was constituted and sent out to resolve matters.

Although hostilities continued, the disputants accepted the Curzon Line. As a provisional line of demarcation extending easterly to Bastouny, which was about 40 miles south of Vilna. Vilna remained in Lithuania. Two days later, Polish General Zeligowski occupied Vilna with his forces, proclaiming a 'Central Government of Lithuania'.[195] Despite denials, Zeligowski was supplied with munitions by the Polish government. Mr Balfour, speaking at the League of Nations Council, questioned the bona fides of the Polish action.[196] He questioned whether Poland had committed an act of war against another League of Nations member and should be sanctioned in breach of Articles 12 (arbitration or inquiry), 13 (disputes to be referred to arbitration and to accept the Award), 15 (dispute submitted to the Council) and 16 (member of the League resorting to war) of the Treaty of Versailles.[197] The Polish representative M Askenazy suggested that the act of General Zeligowski was not a Polish action and that the dispute was resolved by the Treaty of Riga between Poland and Russia, which had been concluded on 19 October 1920. Poland could not withdraw because it had agreed to the referral to the Council of the League of Nations.[198]

At this point the intervention of Mr Hymans, the Belgian representative, was critical, as he worked continuously for a settlement from this point. He suggested that a plebiscite should be held under League of Nations supervision. A Plebiscite Commission was appointed to whom the disputants could submit their claims to the disputed territory.[199] On 29 November 1920, the parties signed an armistice, but they could not agree on what territory should be included in the plebiscite.[200] An international force was proposed, but Switzerland refused passage. Tensions arose because the League of Nations gave de jure recognition to Latvia and Estonia, but not to Lithuania because of the dispute. Thus, Lithuania came under pressure because of her obligations under Article 4 Treaty of Moscow regarding allied troops whose governments had supported the Whites in the Russian Civil War.[201] The League of Nations Council asked the parties if the plebiscite could be carried out on 23 December 1920. Lithuania would agree provided that all Polish forces were withdrawn and would only agree to de jure recognition. Following this impasse, the parties were invited to Brussels to attempt an agreement on all matters in dispute.[202] This proved difficult, as it was clear that there remained irreconcilable differences between the parties. Despite all Hyman's efforts in initiating the conference and drafting a scheme based on the formation of a Lithuanian federal state giving guarantees for ethnic and religious minorities, constituting a common council for foreign affairs, an economic convention embodying principles of free trade, and free access by

[195] ibid.

[196] ibid 487.

[197] ibid.

[198] ibid 488.

[199] League of Nations Official Journal, Special Supplement, December 1920. *Differend entre en la Pologne et la Lithuanie*. 152, 153, 169, 181, and 194.

[200] WJ Brocklebank, 'The Vilna Dispute' (1926) 20 *AJIL* 488. Reproduced with permission of The Licensor through PLSclear.

[201] ibid 489; League of Nations Official Journal, Special supplement, December 1920. *Differend entre en la Pologne et la Lithuanie*. Letter from Lithuanian Chargé in London, 141 and letter from M Voldemar, 195.

[202] WJ Brocklebank, 'The Vilna Dispute' (1926) 20 *AJIL* 490. Reproduced with permission of The Licensor through PLSclear.

Poland to ports and territory in transporting goods and war materials. The scheme was accepted by Lithuania but blocked by Poland, as it insisted on participation by representatives of Vilna taking part in the discussions.[203] The matter reverted to the League Council on 27 July 1921, who resolved to refer any agreement to the Diets of the two countries and for General Zeligowski's forces to be replaced by police forces under the Military Commission of Control of the League of Nations. Poland this time agreed, but Lithuania rejected it.[204]

Hymans then invited the parties to send delegates to Geneva, at which Hymans presented another draft agreement. Lithuania accepted this as a basis for discussion. Poland, however, declined to give any view. At the next League Council meeting on 10 September 1921,[205] Askenazy said that there were distinct differences in the second draft. The first draft (the Brussels draft) promoted a federation of the two states; this draft incorporated Vilna in Lithuania and only required the ratification of the Vilna district assembly. The Council of the League of Nations accepted the second draft, which Hymans explained before the League Assembly. They also heard from the parties' delegates. But subsequently, after protest from the Kovno government, the Lithuanian government rejected the second draft. On 13 January 1922, the League Council decided to withdraw its Military Commission within a month.

The Warsaw Diet announced elections in the Vilna District for 28 January 1922.[206] The League of Nations announced that it could not accept such a solution without regard to its recommendations and the consent of Lithuania. What followed were a series of complaints and allegations of aggression, private property being confiscated, and seizures as well as school closures and illegal arrests.[207] With the withdrawal of the Military Commission on 17 February 1922, the neutral zone fell into anarchy.

An election on 8 January 1922 returned a Polish majority, which voted immediately 96 votes to six for the incorporation into Poland.[208] This was ratified by the Warsaw Diet on 24 March 1922. It was said that the Poles of Vilna were 'more Polish than the Polish themselves'.[209] Recriminations continued, and the League Council decided to send a Commission of Inquiry to study the possibilities of a provisional boundary line which simply resulted in more letters of recriminations addressed to the League.[210] Further protest was made by Lithuania on 2 August 1922, which was referred to the Third Assembly of the League of Nations, who then simply referred it to the Council in accordance with the Resolution of 13 January 1922.[211] The Commission of Inquiry led by M Saura[212] reported in December 1922 regarding the establishment of a provisional line. On 28 December 1922, the Allied Powers gave de jure recognition to Lithuania and pardoned what the Lithuanians claimed were all and what the Poles claimed were

[203] ibid 491.
[204] ibid.
[205] ibid 492.
[206] ibid.
[207] ibid 493.
[208] ibid 494.
[209] J Harly, Fortnightly Review (June 1923) 120: 110.
[210] WJ Brocklebank, 'The Vilna Dispute' (1926) 20 *AJIL* 495. Reproduced with permission of The Licensor through PLSclear.
[211] ibid.
[212] Pedro Saura, Spanish Consul General in Brussels. He was assisted by Dr Stoyan Lassitch member of the Secretariat of the League and a citizen of the Serb-Croat-Slovene State.

only a small part of the Polish political prisoners held in Lithuanian prisons.[213] The Council agreed a Polish Resolution regarding the treatment of minorities in the Vilna region to be in accordance with the Minorities Treaties of 28 June 1919. Lithuania also received the Memel territory to compensate for the loss of Vilna, but this was subject to French occupation until 1926. On 10 January 1923, an insurrection broke out at Memel, and a provisional Lithuanian government was installed. Belatedly, the Council of Ambassadors voted to transfer the Memel territory to Lithuania.[214]

On 3 February 1923, the Council concluded its deliberations by acknowledging the boundary line recommended in the Saura Report, giving Poland all the districts of Kolpanasziski, Uscleje, and Skobska as its final recommendation.[215] Polish forces then occupied those territories, and despite further protest from Lithuania that the action was in breach of the Covenant of the League of Nations, the Council declined the request.[216] France loaned Poland FRF 400 million for improving her financial economic situation.[217] Poland had gained 6,000 square miles of territory. Lithuania rejected this and protested against the decree of the Conference of Ambassadors meeting in Paris on 15 March 1923. The conference recognised the eastern boundary of Poland under the Treaty of Riga and the boundary of Poland-Lithuania as per the Council Resolution of 3 February 1923, in effect gaining all the territory won in the war with Soviet Russia as well as eastern Galicia and Vilna.[218] Lithuania then attempted to refer the case to the Permanent Court of International Justice (PCIJ) but the Assembly preferred to refer the matter to the first committee for an opinion, which considered this a matter for report and reference to the International Court of Justice.[219] The matter was referred to the Fourth Assembly but never submitted to the International Court of Justice. Eventually the Lithuanian government decided to withdraw the question, reserving the right to raise it subsequently.[220] In the event, Lithuania had few options. An appeal to the Conference of Ambassadors was unlikely to change the decision, negotiations with Poland were unlikely, an appeal to the PCIJ was not possible unless Poland consented, and finally, further hostilities were not likely to change the result.[221]

It is not difficult to appreciate the cultural and historical background to this dispute when considering that the original territorial extent of Lithuania before 1914 measured 117,000 square miles and it had a population of 12.5 million people. After 1918, its landmass was reduced to 24,000 square miles and a population of 2 million.[222] There was therefore no doubting the bitterness of the Lithuanians as to the considerable loss of territory and the loss of Vilna. On the other hand, much of the population regarded itself as Polish. During the war with Poland, Lithuania

[213] RH Lord, 'Lithuania and Poland' (1923) 4(4) *Foreign Affairs* 55.

[214] ibid 55–56.

[215] WJ Brocklebank, 'The Vilna Dispute' (1926) 20 *AJIL* 496. Reproduced with permission of The Licensor through PLSclear.

[216] ibid 497.

[217] 'The Polish-Lithuanian War' *The Outlook* 7 March 1923, 133–431 cited in Brocklebankibid ibid 496.

[218] Brocklebank ibid 497; RH Lord, 'Lithuania and Poland' (1923) 4(4) *Foreign Affairs* 57.

[219] WJ Brocklebank, 'The Vilna Dispute' (1926) 20 *AJIL* 498. Reproduced with permission of The Licensor through PLSclear.

[220] League of Nations Official Journal Special Supplement No. 29, 7–9.

[221] WJ Brocklebank, 'The Vilna Dispute' (1926) 20 *AJIL* 499. Reproduced with permission of The Licensor through PLSclear.

[222] RH Lord, 'Lithuania and Poland' (1923) 4(4) *Foreign Affairs* 44.

lost only 232 combatants, but it was the loss of Vilna that resounded in the political consciousness of Lithuanians during the interwar period.[223]

This marked the end of diplomatic attempts to resolve the border question. For two countries that had a very close relationship and history over several centuries, this was a sad episode and one that perhaps illustrated that only so much can be achieved by diplomacy between two disputants unless collective action is brought to bear. Without the political will of other nation-states in this case, League members, little could be accomplished.

H. The Tacna-Arica Dispute 1929

i. How the Dispute Arose

This case was a territorial dispute between Peru and Chile and involved a conflict between the concept of the Monroe Doctrine and the jurisdiction of the League of Nations. The provinces of Tacna and Arica belonged to Peru at the time of its independence from Spain, but after the War of the Pacific (1879–84), Chile appropriated Arica and Tacna. In 1929 negotiations between Peru and Chile produced a settlement that returned Tacna to Peru with an indemnity of $6 million and left Arica under Chilean control.

So far as the Monroe Doctrine was concerned, Article 21 Treaty of Versailles specifically excluded the doctrine and may be regarded as a reception of the Monroe Doctrine into international law.[224] It could also be argued, as Reeves pointed out,[225] that Article 21 as amended was so far outside the domain of international law that no matter involving it can come within the cognisance or jurisdiction of the League or of any of its instrumentalities. Reves also pointed out that there was nothing to stop states voluntarily referring a question between them to the head of a European state for an arbitral settlement as not being considered in contravention. What was not acceptable was any coercive reference to arbitration or other settlement of an American question by one or more European powers.[226]

The Treaty of Ancón to resolve the dispute was never executed, and the plebiscites which were to have decided the ultimate sovereignty over Tacna-Arica at the end of ten years were never held.[227] Peru likened it to an American Alsace-Lorraine. Bolivia wanted a sea outlet from Antofagasta,[228] involving Chile alone, to Arica. The Treaty of Ancón was heavily criticised by Professor Balunde[229] as a treaty signed by an illegitimate

[223] T Balkelis, 'A Dirty War' in *War, Revolution, and Nation-Making in Lithuania, 1914-1923* (Oxford, OUP, 2018).

[224] Article 21 provided: 'Nothing in this Covenant shall be deemed to affect the validity of international engagements, such as treaties of arbitration or regional understandings like the Monroe doctrine, for securing the maintenance of peace.'

[225] JS Reeves, 'The Tacna-Arica Dispute and the Monroe Doctrine' (1921) 15 *AJIL* 70. Reproduced with permission of the Licensor through PLSclear.

[226] ibid.

[227] ibid 71.

[228] Antofagasta, city, capital of Antofagasta región, northern Chile, and a Pacific port on Bahía (bay) Moreno. A Bolivian town until 1879.

[229] Author of 'The Treaty of Ancon in the Light of International Law.'

government and ratified by an assembly in which unoccupied Peruvian provinces were not represented which embodied the unjustifiable conquest of territories foreign to the object of the struggle and essential for the economic and political life against the expressed will of their inhabitants; it imposed an immoral and absurdly exorbitant war indemnity; it violated the indisputable principle of respecting the mortgage encumbrances which weighed upon the ceded territories; it opened up new problems to permit the victors continuing their policy of hostility and oppression against the vanquished.[230]

Contrary to the Monroe Doctrine, Peru announced that she would bring the matter of her lost provinces before the League of Nations. Bolivia made her claim for a Pacific port, and Chile rejected proposals for reference to arbitration to settle the matter.[231]

In 1907 Chile reserved all questions antedating her signature of The Hague Convention for the Pacific Settlement of International Disputes from the scope of that instrument. As to the League of Nations Covenant, Chile reserved its position in the Covenant:

> The Government of Chile reserves the right of considering modifications or reservations to that pact that may be made by nations signatory to the Treaty of Versailles and which have not ratified it up to the present.

As Reeves states, how such a reservation could have been made by an acceding state is not clear in view of the stipulations of Article I of the Covenant which provided:

> The original Members of the League of Nations shall be those of the Signatories which are named in the Annex to this Covenant and also such of those other States named in the Annex as shall accede without reservation to this Covenant.

There could be no such reservation in accession, although it was intended to prevent any encroachment on the Monroe Doctrine. This possibility of encroachment was highlighted by William Jennings Bryan in a speech made in March 1916 in Washington gave his objections to the programme proposed by the League to Enforce Peace and based them to a large extent upon the danger of such an encroachment. He proposed that the plan be

> amended so as to provide for the enforcement of the findings by the members of separate groups. All of the nations could join in the formation of a court and thus bring their united wisdom to bear upon an international dispute, leaving the enforcement of the findings to the group to which the nations belong, the American nations enforcing the decisions among themselves, if a majority of them approved of it, the European group doing the same under the same circumstances, and the Oriental group acting in like manner if the Orientals formed a group by themselves.[232]

Clearly Bryan did not want European states interfering in America. It raises a fundamental question, then, as to what extent American states could deal with questions outside the American continent as members of the League of Nations, and if they were

[230] HF Wright, 'The Treaty of Ancon in the Light of International Law' (1923) 17 *AJIL* 176. Reproduced with permission of the Licensor through PLSclear.

[231] JS Reeves, 'The Tacna-Arica Dispute and the Monroe Doctrine' (1921) 15 *AJIL* 71. Reproduced with permission of the Licensor through PLSclear.

[232] ibid 72.

restricted, then the League would be undermined.[233] The view was that this dispute should be settled solely by American instrumentalities.

The insistence of the US in recent notes to Chile and Bolivia that the matter be settled amicably was regarded by the Argentine journal *La Prensa* as 'arrogant', and by the American Chamber of Commerce at Valparaiso as 'discourteous and grossly mistaken'.

The Supreme Court of Chile held that all persons born within the disputed territory are Chilean nationals.[234]

ii. Opinion and Award of the Arbitrator[235]

Representatives of the Republic of Chile and the Republic of Peru met in Washington, DC May 1922 for the purpose of settling differences arising from the unfulfilled provisions of Article 3 Treaty of Ancón 20 October 1883.[236]

The agents and counsel who appeared in the arbitration were, for Chile: Carlos Aldunate and Ernesto Barros, Agents for the Republic of Chile; Robert Lansing, LH Woolsey, Counsel for the Republic of Chile. For Peru: MF Porras, Representative of the Government of Peru; Edwin M Borchard, Counsel for the Government of Peru; JS Cavero, Solon Polo, Joseph E Davies, Wade H Ellis, and Hoke Smith, Counsel for the Government of Peru. For the counter case of Peru: Solón Polo, President of the Peruvian Arbitration Commission; Edwin M Borchard, Joseph E Davies, Wade H Ellis, and Hoke Smith, Counsel for the Government of Peru; JS Cavero, Juridical Counsel to the Commission.

The parties reached agreement on a protocol of arbitration which was signed and provided:

> *Article 2.* The difficulties to which the preceding article refers will be submitted to the arbitration of the President of the United States of America who shall decide them finally and without appeal, hearing both parties and after due consideration of the arguments and evidence which they may adduce. The terms and procedure shall be determined by the Arbitrator.

At the same time, the following supplementary act was signed, which defined the scope and jurisdiction of the arbitration which provided for:

> 1. The following question raised by Peru in the session of the conference of the 27th of May last: 'In order to determine the manner in which the stipulations of Article 3 of the Treaty of Ancon shall be fulfilled, it is agreed to submit to arbitration the question whether, in the present circumstances, a plebiscite shall or shall not be held.'
>
>   The Government of Chile may submit to the Arbitrator such arguments in reply as may seem appropriate for its defence.

[233] ibid.

[234] ibid 73.

[235] This extract is based upon the printed text of the Award issued by the Department of State, Washington, DC in (1925) 'The Matter of The Arbitration Between The Republic of Chile And The Republic of Peru, With Respect to The Unfulfilled Provisions of The Treaty of Peace of October 20, 1883, Under The Protocol And Supplementary Act Signed At Washington July 20, 1922', 19 *AJIL* 393–432, reproduced with permission of The Licensor through PLSclear. Hereafter referred to as 'The Tacna-Arica Arbitration Award 1925.'

[236] Article 1 Treaty of Ancón 1883.

2. In case the holding of the plebiscite should be declared in order, the Arbitrator is empowered to determine the conditions thereof.
3. Should the Arbitrator decide that a plebiscite need not be held, both parties, at the request of either of them shall discuss the situation brought about by such award.

   It is understood, in the interest of peace and good order, that in such an event and pending an agreement as to the disposition of the territory, the administrative organization of the provinces shall not be disturbed.
4. In the event that no agreement should ensue, both Governments will solicit, for this purpose, the good offices of the Government of the United States of America.
5. Included in the arbitration likewise are the claims pending with regard to Tarata and Chilcaya, according to the determination of the final disposition of the territory to which Article 3 of the treaty refers.

   This agreement is an integral part of the protocol to which it refers.

Ratifications of the protocol and supplementary act were exchanged, the President of the US (President Coolidge[237]) accepted the office of Arbitrator, and the cases and countercases of the respective parties were submitted in accordance with a schedule of arbitral procedure proposed by the parties and approved by the Arbitrator. The record, comprising nearly 6,000 pages, was considered by the Arbitrator.

In his Opinion and Award, Coolidge first dealt with the Treaty of Ancon Article 3 of which provided:

> The territory of the provinces of Tacna and Arica, bounded on the north by the River Sama from its source in the Cordilleras on the frontier of Bolivia to its mouth at the sea, on the south by the ravine and River Camarones, on the east by the Republic of Bolivia and on the west by the Pacific Ocean, shall continue in the possession of Chile subject to Chilean laws and authority during a period of ten years, to be reckoned from the date of the ratification of the present treaty of peace.
>
> After the expiration of that term a plebiscite will decide by popular vote whether the territory of the above-mentioned provinces is to remain definitely under the dominion and sovereignty of Chile or is to continue to constitute a part of Peru. That country of the two, to which the provinces of Tacna and Arica remain annexed shall pay to the other ten million pesos of Chilean silver or of Peruvian soles of equal weight and fineness.
>
> A special protocol, which shall be considered an integral part of the present treaty, will prescribe the manner in which the plebiscite is to be carried out, and the terms and time for the payment of the ten millions by the nation which remains the owner of the provinces of Tacna and Arica.'[238]

iii. *The Arbitrator's Duty*

Coolidge was careful to outline his duties based on the protocol and supplementary act, which had to be read together. This provided not only for arbitration but, in a specified contingency, for the good offices of the government of the US. Such contingent good

[237] Coolidge was a lawyer, Republican politician and later president. His administration was responsible for the Dawes Plan in 1925, to alleviate Germany's war debt problems, and the Kellogg-Briand Pact in 1929.

[238] This text is the translation given in the Appendix to the Peruvian Case. The Chilean translation, which is taken from the Foreign Relations of the United States for 1883, is not materially different. (1925) 19 *AJIL* 395. Reproduced with permission of The Licensor through PLSclear.

offices had nothing to do with his duty. The questions he had to decide were, first, whether a plebiscite should be held to determine the sovereignty of the territory in question as between Chile and Peru. Second, if he decided in favour of a plebiscite, to determine the conditions of that plebiscite, including the terms and time of the payment to be made by the nation succeeding in the plebiscite. Third, whether the decision be for or against a plebiscite, to decide the pending questions with respect to Tarata and Chilcaya arising respectively on the northern and southern boundaries of the territory.[239]

iv. Questions at Issue: Whether in the Present Circumstances a Plebiscite shall or shall not be Held

Coolidge decided that the plebiscite issue had been debated between the parties for years since the War in the Pacific and fully argued in their respective cases. The territory in question concerned the provinces of Tacna and Arica, which were understood to be about 9,000 square miles in area and to have a population of between 30,000 and 40,000. It belonged to the desert region of the Pacific coast. There were some mineral resources, and the valleys proceeding from the mountains on the east gave opportunities for agriculture. In one of these valleys was the city of Tacna, which was the capital of the Peruvian province of that name. The city of Arica, the capital of the other Peruvian province mentioned in Article 3 Treaty of Ancon, was a port on the Pacific Ocean about 40 miles from Tacna, connected by railroad. Arica was the terminal of the railroad running to La Paz, Bolivia, and had commercial importance.[240] Coolidge held that at the time of the signing and ratification of the Treaty of Ancon, Chile was already in possession of the territory of the provinces of Tacna and Arica as a result of the War of the Pacific.[241] Under Article 3 it was agreed that Chile should continue in possession of this territory for a period of ten years and that during this period it should be 'subject to Chilean laws and authority'. It was further agreed that 'after the expiration of that term' a plebiscite should be held to decide whether the territory should 'remain definitely under the dominion and sovereignty of Chile' or should 'continue to constitute part of Peru', ie, whether the territory should be permanently Chilean or permanently Peruvian. The paragraph then provided 'that country of the two' to which the provinces of Tacna and Arica 'remain annexed' shall pay the other ten million Chilean pesos or Peruvian soles. Finally, the article provided for the negotiation by the two countries of 'a special protocol' which will prescribe, first, 'the manner in which the plebiscite is to be carried out' and second, 'the terms and time for the payment of the ten millions'. The question of whether a plebiscite shall or shall not be held depends upon the question of whether the second and third paragraphs of Article 3 of the Treaty of Ancon are still in effect. If the provisions had not expired by effluxion of time, the plebiscite should be held unless it were no longer binding.[242]

Coolidge had to confine himself to the meaning and efficacy of the agreement itself and not deviate as the parties had done in their respective cases on the war, the terms

[239] The Tacna-Arica Arbitration Award 1925 (1925) 19 *AJIL* 395. Reproduced with permission of The Licensor through PLSclear.
[240] ibid.
[241] ibid 396.
[242] ibid.

of peace, or the parties' relations with Bolivia, or upon the wisdom of the treaty or the economic effects of the treaty, or upon alleged general equities of the present situation.[243]

The plebiscite was to be held '*after* the expiration of that term', that is, after the ten years, but no limit was defined for a special protocol for the plebiscite to be negotiated. This raised an interesting debate as to an agreement to agree with no time specified and no forfeiture provided, which would be unsatisfactory or meaningless. Coolidge considered three points: first, that the Arbitrator is not empowered to alter the treaty or to insert provisions, however salutary they might be in his judgment, viewing the matter retrospectively, which the high contracting parties did not see fit to include. Second, that the Treaty of Ancon was a peace treaty – the parties were engaged in a devastating war. Apparently, the parties in 1883–84 thought it better to agree that they would agree at some unspecified time in the future than to agree to disagree in the present. Third, the present arbitration was the best evidence that the agreement, elastic as it was, was not without force, since the parties had continually failed to make the protocol.[244] What was clear was that the parties agreed to postpone the plebiscite long enough to make the result uncertain to be decided by popular vote.

v. Case of Peru

Peru argued that Chile wilfully prevented the timely holding of a plebiscite and that her action in the course of her administration of the territory constituted a perversion of the conditions essential to the plebiscite as contemplated by the treaty; in short, that Chile, by preventing the performance of Article 3, had discharged Peru from her obligations, and hence that a plebiscite should not now be held and that Chile should be regarded as a trespasser in the territory since the year 1894. This raised questions as to the conduct of Chile in relation to the efforts to reach an agreement for a plebiscite and with respect to her administration of the territory of the provinces of Tacna and Arica.[245]

vi. Delays in Negotiations

The nature of the obligation imposed by Article 3 was derived from its terms. Until the special agreement was made, there could be no plebiscite. As the parties agreed to enter into a special protocol but did not fix its terms, their undertaking was, in substance, to negotiate in good faith to that end, and it would follow that a wilful refusal of either party to do so would have justified the other party in claiming discharge from the provision. But, as the parties did not prescribe in the treaty the conditions of the plebiscite, they retained the rights of sovereign states acting in good faith. Neither party waived the right to propose conditions which it deemed to be reasonable and appropriate to the holding of the plebiscite or to oppose conditions proposed by the other party which it deemed to be inadvisable. As the special protocol was to be made by sovereign states under Article 3 it followed that these states should act respectively in accordance with

[243] ibid.
[244] ibid 397.
[245] ibid 398.

their constitutional methods, and bad faith was not to be predicated upon the refusal of ratification of a particular proposed protocol deemed by the ratifying authority to be unsatisfactory.[246]

The tribunal had to find evidence of an intent to frustrate the carrying out of the provisions of Article 3 with respect to the plebiscite, not simply the refusal of a particular agreement proposed because of its terms, but for the purpose of preventing any reasonable agreement for a plebiscite. A finding of the existence of bad faith had to be supported not by disputable inferences but by clear and convincing evidence which compelled such a conclusion.[247] Having considered delay, Coleridge considered the history of negotiations.

vii. Negotiations

Formal negotiations to arrive at the terms of the special protocol for a plebiscite began in 1892 and eventually resulted in the Jimenez-Solar exchanges of 26 January 1894, which left conditions of the plebiscite open. The ten-year period expired without further progress and was then interrupted by a cabinet crisis in Chile and the death of the President of Peru. In the early part of 1895, civil disturbances in Peru resulted in the establishment of a Provisional Board of Government with whom the Chilean minister opened negotiations in August 1895. Consequently, there were numerous conferences that ended with an exchange of notes in February 1896, but the parties were irreconcilable. In a Joint Memorandum of 14 August 1897, each government expressed its desire to have a definite solution. Senor Billinghurst, Vice President of Peru, was sent on a special mission to Santiago to negotiate the protocol. As a result, the so-called Billinghurst-Latorre protocol was signed on 16 April 1898. Most points were agreed upon save the qualifications of the voters at the plebiscite and whether the voting should be public or secret. These questions were left to the arbitration of the Queen of Spain. In Peru, the protocol was approved. In Chile, the Chamber of Deputies failed to give its approval.[248] On 25 March 1908 the Chilean Minister of Foreign Affairs, Senor Puga Borne, in a note addressed to the Peruvian minister at Santiago, proposed a series of five conventions relating respectively to commerce, merchant marine, a connecting railroad, the plebiscite and the indemnity, and set forth his views as to the manner of holding the plebiscite.[249] In the absence of diplomatic representation of either country at the capital of the other, there ensued a period of direct negotiations between the foreign ministers of the two countries. These negotiations began in August 1909. In October 1909, Chile presented certain definite proposals as to the conditions of a plebiscite, these being founded on the Billinghurst-Latorre protocol and the reference to arbitration. Peru replied in November 1909 with a memorandum of counter-proposals modifying in certain important respects the Chilean plan.[250] In a note of 3 March 1910, the Chilean Foreign Minister recurred to the idea that the plebiscites in international

[246] ibid.
[247] ibid 398–399.
[248] ibid 399–400.
[249] ibid 400.
[250] ibid 401.

law were but disguised formulas for annexation and applied this to the case of Tacna and Arica saying that the treaty was devised 'as the only means designated by history of satisfying the territorial demands of Chile without deeply wounding a national sentiment of Peru'.[251] He added:

> Nevertheless, [his government] has sought in the holding of the plebiscite the satisfaction of its legitimate exigencies, and it only asks that the act be essentially popular and that it be effected without violating for a single instant, by interrupting them, its rights as a sovereign in the territories of Tacna and Arica.

The Chilean Foreign Minister then set out proposed conditions for the plebiscite, providing that it should be held within six months after the exchange of ratifications of the protocol and setting forth the manner in which a Directive Board and Registration and Receiving Committees should be appointed and act, the qualification of voters and the canvass of the votes.[252] Peru did not answer these proposals. Once more, on 19 March 1910, as in 1901, diplomatic relations were severed as a protest against the course of Chile's administration in Tacna and Arica. Diplomatic relations were not resumed.[253] In September 1912, Senor Billinghurst became President of Peru. As a result of informal negotiations on 10 November 1912, an exchange of telegrams between the foreign ministers of the two countries called the Huneeus-Valera telegrams provided for the postponement of the plebiscite until 1933; for the supervision of the plebiscite by a committee of five delegates, two Chileans and two Peruvians, with the President of the Supreme Court of Justice of Chile presiding; and for the right to vote of persons born in Tacna and Arica and Chileans and Peruvians that may have resided for three years in the territory and who are literate.[254] When the Huneeus-Valera exchanges were made public, there was a violent outburst of public opinion in Peru against President Billinghurst, and the feeling thus engendered apparently contributed to the downfall of his government in 1914. In May 1914 a new government of Peru announced its succession to office and was promptly recognised by Chile. In December 1914, Peru requested Chile to expel the former President Billinghurst from Tacna and Arica, and this request was granted.[255] In 1920, the President of Chile authorised Senor Puga Borne to negotiate informally with the President of Peru with the instruction to keep within the limits of prior negotiations and to submit new propositions to the home government as he might think fit. This initiative was abortive. On 12 December 1921, the Chilean Foreign Minister made another attempt to reopen negotiations as to the plebiscitary protocol by proposing directly to the Peruvian Foreign Minister that the Huneeus-Valera plan be taken as a basis for perfecting the protocol. Peru responded by inviting Chile to 'submit jointly the entire question of the South Pacific that divides us to an arbitration, agreed to through the initiative of the Government of the United States of America'. The ensuing negotiations led up to the present arbitration.

[251] ibid.
[252] ibid.
[253] ibid.
[254] ibid 401–402.
[255] ibid 402.

From this analysis Coolidge concluded that both states had conducted themselves in good faith under the treaty, presenting their particular views, proposals, arguments and objections. He held on to the fact that the evidence failed:[256]

> to show that Chile has never arbitrarily refused to negotiate with Peru the terms of the plebiscitary protocol. On the contrary, the record shows affirmatively that Chile not only has accepted Peru's invitations to proceed with the negotiations but has herself initiated negotiations … The Arbitrator is of the opinion that so far as the negotiations for the special protocol are concerned neither party can be charged with bad faith and that there is no ground for the conclusion that Chile's action in respect to these negotiations has resulted in the abrogation of the second and third paragraphs of Article 3 of the Treaty of Ancon or absolved Peru from the obligation to proceed to their fulfilment.

viii. Chilean Administration in Tacna and Arica

Article 3 provided that the described territory of the Provinces of Tacna and Arica should 'continue in the possession of Chile subject to Chilean laws and authority during a period of ten years' and that 'after the expiration of that term' there should be a plebiscite to decide whether the territory 'is to remain definitely under the dominion and sovereignty of Chile or is to continue to constitute a part of Peru'.[257] The questions remained as to what authority was given to Chile and what was the status of the territories after 10 years? Chile argued that this continued until otherwise decided by the plebiscite. Peru insisted that it was sovereign and that after the expiration of 10 years, the territories reverted to Peru. But here Coleridge had no discretion; he could not depart from the wording of the Treaty. Article 3 was explicit. Chile had possession and was subject to Chilean laws and authority, ie, full legislative, executive, and judicial powers. Article 3 had no express qualification, although it could not impeach the requirement for a plebiscite.[258] The Article was silent as to what happened after 10 years. It was unreasonable that the territory should revert to Peru pending the plebiscite. A fair interpretation was that Chile would retain possession until the plebiscite. the Minister of Foreign Relations of Peru confirmed as much to the Minister of Chile on 9 March 1894: 'that the territory should remain during the plebiscite in the same state as that in which they are today'. Coleridge concluded that the territory continued to be subject to the laws and authority of Chile.[259]

Peru alleged that Chile had supported the immigration of Chilean citizens and the dispersal of the Peruvian population after 1900, a policy described as 'Chilenization' of the territory, embracing as alleged, (a) the subsidised introduction of Chilean citizens and (b) the dispersion of the Peruvian population after 1900 in particular: (1) the creation of the Department of Tarata; (2) the removal of the Court of Appeals from Iquique to Tacna; (3) the removal of military headquarters from Iquique to Tacna and the concentration of Chilean military forces in the Provinces; (4) founding of newspapers for pro-Chilean propaganda; (5) the subsidising of factories; (6) the granting of

[256] ibid 402–403.
[257] ibid 404.
[258] ibid.
[259] ibid 405.

railway, irrigation and other concessions; (7) colonisation; and (8) the arrangements in regard to the Arica customs.[260]

Coolidge dealt with these allegations as follows: as to the creation of the Department of Toronto, this was necessary for the purposes of the administration of Article 3. The same applied to the removal of the Court of Appeals from Iquique to Tacna and the removal of military headquarters from Iquique to Tacna and the concentration of military forces in the provinces, which were clearly within the authority conferred upon Chile by the treaty. Chile also had the right to subsidise industry. Similarly, it had a right to establish newspapers and periodicals there; likewise, the granting of railway, irrigation and other concessions was clearly within the authority of Chile. It appears that a number of Chilean labourers were employed in the construction of the Arica-La Paz Railway in accordance with the Chilean-Bolivian Treaty of 1904. This was nothing more than an incident in an enterprise which Chile was entitled to take. Peru could not object. If development meant a proportionate influx of Chilean people.[261]

Coolidge concluded that it was 'sufficient to say that the evidence failed to establish any such colonization on the part of Chile as would form any basis for a conclusion that Peru had been discharged from her plebiscitary obligation'.[262] Chile had conceded to Bolivia commercial and customs privileges in the ports of Tacna and Arica which gave rise to diplomatic protests on the part of Peru. But Chile conceded that in the event of a plebiscite in Peru's favour, then, Peru would take the 'territory free from any encumbrances resulting from such a trade agreement'.[263]

a. Schools

On 14 May 1900, the Governor of Takhar issued a decree closing Peruvian schools. Chile argued that the schools were subject to the law and required teachers to teach children Chile's geography and history.[264] Peru argued that its teachers had a sacred duty to instruct pupils with 'sentiments of love and self-denial in favour of the fatherland'. Coolidge could find little evidence of any discrimination against Peruvian pupils, nor any deliberate policy by Chile.[265]

b. Expulsion of Peruvian Priests

Both Chile and Peru were Catholic countries. Peru claimed that since the Catholic Church in Peru functioned under a system of patronage wholly controlled by the civil government territorial dioceses, including dioceses and vicarages, were a prerogative of Peru associated with its exercise of national sovereignty in Tacna and Arica. Peru denied any cession of sovereignty or control over them.[266] The Chilean Foreign Minister, in

[260] ibid 406.
[261] ibid 407.
[262] ibid.
[263] ibid.
[264] ibid 408.
[265] ibid 409.
[266] ibid as in the exchange of notes between the Peruvian minister and his counterpart the Chilean Foreign Minister in exchanges on the 14 November 1900 and the 19 January 1901.

reply, acknowledged that the Catholic Church developed under the auspices of a secular patronage regime and that the Treaty of Ancon placed Tacna and Arica under the dominion of Chile. Under the Chilean Constitution, it followed that the Chilean President under Article LXXXII, Section 13 of its Constitution had authority to exercise such patronage.[267] When the Chilean government demanded that Peruvian priests obtain a permit from the Chilean government the priests declined and consequently were banished as a result. Coolidge concluded that there was: 'No sufficient reason for concluding that the patronage did not pertain to the Territorial Authority.'[268]

c. Peruvian Newspapers

Peru alleged that Chile had suspended and suppressed Peruvian newspapers. There was evidence of mob violence and attacks on the press in 1911. Coolidge held that: 'it does appear the Peruvian newspapers have not been re-established and the situation thus existing demands consideration in fixing the conditions of a possible plebiscite.'[269]

d. Depriving Peruvians of the Right to Assemble and Display the Peruvian Flag

This was a trivial charge unsupported by evidence, and Chile was entitled to regulate such matters.[270]

e. Boycotting of Peruvian Labour

This was a difficult matter to prove. Chile denied the allegation save as to preference for public works such as the Arica-La Paz Railway. There were 27 specific cases examined in detail. Two allegations of boycotting were made but failed for lack of proof. 340 cases of expulsion were cited by Peru of Peruvians deprived of employment because of their nationality. Their *ex parte* evidence lacked proof that discrimination had attained such proportions so as to afford any ground for a decision against a plebiscite.[271]

f. Conscription

Peru charged that Chile applied her conscription laws to Peruvian citizens in Tacna and Arica as a means of forcing them out of the provinces and eliminating their votes in any plebiscite. Chile denied this because it was not an effective way to Chileanise a Peruvian recruit; second, children of Peruvian parents born in Tacna and Arica and claiming Peruvian nationality were not conscripted; and third, Peru did not submit relevant evidence of the requirements of Chilean law with respect to the military service of Peruvians.[272] Coolidge considered that such a rule would eliminate Peruvian votes, as

[267] The Tacna-Arica Arbitration Award 1925 (1925) 19 *AJIL* 409. Reproduced with permission of The Licensor through PLSclear.
[268] ibid 410.
[269] ibid 410–411.
[270] ibid 411.
[271] ibid.
[272] ibid.

the young would prefer to go to Peru. The Chilean Minister of Foreign Affairs dealt with this in his circular dated 12 February 1920.[273] Coolidge had to consider the affidavits of 200 claimants who claimed they had been forced to leave Tacna and Arica to avoid military service. On this evidence he could not conclude that a policy of administrative leniency was practiced by the Chilean government.[274] A considerable number of cases, especially in 1923, pointed to the Chilean conscription laws driving young Peruvians from the provinces. Coolidge concluded that whilst these infractions and abuses by the Chilean authorities were insufficient to discharge the plebiscitary obligations of the Treaty, the intermittent and sporadic infractions were important enough to consider in relation to the conditions of the plebiscite.[275]

g. Expulsion of Peruvian Citizens

Peru submitted that Chile had expelled Peruvians from Tacna and Arica en masse and as individuals. Chile admitted that 52 Peruvians were expelled and justified it on the grounds of 'repeated violations of the laws and attempted conspiracies against the State'. Peru submitted several hundred individual claims; these contained only 27 specific instances of direct or indirect expulsion, which were denied in the Chilean counter case.[276] Although there was no cross-examination of these witnesses, Coolidge held that the evidence produced by Chile's Minister of Foreign Relations showed there was no mass expulsion or depopulation and no serious and deliberate violation of Peru's treaty rights to justify Peru repudiating the plebiscitary obligations under Article 3 of the Treaty of Arun.[277]

h. General Persecution of Peruvians Through Mob Violence and Otherwise

Coolidge held that despite mob violence against Peruvians in 1911 and 1918–19, there was no evidence of it being caused by the Chilean government. There was no basis therefore in the absence of any credible or specific to justify Peru repudiating the plebiscitary obligations under Article 3.[278]

i. Conclusion

Coolidge held that there was no reason why the plebiscite could not be held subject to the conditions he provided in his award. The holding of the plebiscite was imperative as a means of 'amicable disposition to be determined by popular vote in accordance with democratic postulates'.[279]

[273] ibid 412.
[274] ibid.
[275] ibid.
[276] ibid 413.
[277] ibid 413–414.
[278] ibid 414.
[279] ibid 415.

j. The Conditions of the Plebiscite

The Treaty of Ancon provided no conditions for the plebiscite. Coolidge, in the absence of the parties' agreement, was empowered to determine these. He carefully reviewed the diplomatic negotiations between the parties between 1894 and 1912, during which there had been some measure of agreement, and met the following conditions, which were appended to his award.[280]

He decided that:[281]

> A. Male persons, 21 years old, able to read and write, who qualify under one of the following classifications numbered 1, 2, and 3:
>
> 1. Persons born in Tacna and Arica, that is, in the territory as hereinafter defined in this Award;
> 2. Chileans and Peruvians who (a) on July 20, 1922 had resided two years continuously in said territory; and
>   (b) continue so to reside in said territory until the date of registration; and
>   (c) reside for three months immediately preceding registration in the subdelegation in which they are resident at the time of registration; and
>   (d) make an affidavit as to residence in a form to be prescribed by the Plebiscitary Commission hereafter described.
> 3. Foreigners, i. e., persons who are neither Chileans nor Peruvians, who are eligible for naturalization in either Chile or Peru and who fulfil the qualifications described in subdivisions a, b, c and d, under paragraph A-2, and who, in addition, make affidavit in a form prescribed by the Plebiscitary Commission of their intention to apply at once for naturalization in the State winning the plebiscite.
>
> B. 1. Provided, however, that no person shall be denied the right to vote at the plebiscite solely because of inability to read and write who on July 20, 1922, and continuously from that date until the date when he applies for registration was the owner of real property in said territory.
>
> 2. Provided, further, that no person shall acquire a vote through residence in said territory under the provisions of paragraphs A-2 and 3 if during any part of such required period of residence he has been a member in any capacity of the army, navy, carbineers, government police, secret service, or gendarmerie of either Chile or Peru, or has received compensation as such; or has been a government official or civil employee in the political, judicial or fiscal service of either country, or has received compensation as such.
>
> 3. Provided, further, that military persons of all ranks and civil employees of every degree of both governments who were born in said territory shall be given the opportunity to return to their native place both to register and vote in the plebiscite.
>
> 4. Provided, further, (a) that no person serving a term of imprisonment after sentence for a non-political offense involving moral turpitude or (b) under guardianship, *non compos mentis* or insane, shall be allowed to register or vote.

The governments of Chile and Peru agreed to facilitate the entry into Tacna and Arica and the transit through Chile and Peru, respectively, for the purpose of any person claiming to be entitled to vote at the plebiscite, and the Plebiscitary Commission would

[280] ibid 415–417.
[281] ibid 418–419.

deal with any claims based on alleged violations.[282] In order to supervise the plebiscite, Coolidge ordered the setting up of a Plebiscitary Commission and Registration and Election Boards and specified their powers and duties.[283] The Plebiscitary Commission consisted of three members: one to be appointed by the government of Chile, one to be appointed by the government of Peru, and the third member, who shall act as President of the Commission, to be appointed by the President of the US.[284] Appeals regarding the plebiscite could be made to Coleridge, and the results of it were to be telegraphed to Coolidge, who would inform the Ministers for Foreign Affairs of Chile and Peru. Coolidge set time limits for the Commission to be appointed and to meet.[285]

k. Findings

What was significant and unique about this arbitration was Coolidge's command of the process and procedure, not only of the hearing but also of the arrangements for the plebiscite. He retained a degree of control in terms of constitution and timing. He also had oversight of costs and expenses by requiring both governments to submit schedules of expenses for his approval. The parties were required to pay a deposit of $15,000 to be paid by each party to the United States Secretary of State within four months of the Award to cover the costs of the plebiscite.[286] Coolidge made it clear that by imposing conditions for the plebiscite he was not deciding that matter as a substantive one.[287] As to the payment of 10 million pesos of Chilean silver or of Peruvian soles of equal weight and fineness by the remaining owner of Tacna and Arica as required by Article 3 of the Treaty of Ancon, Coolidge decided that one million pesos should be paid within 10 days of the declaration of the result of the plebiscite, that another one million should be paid the following year, and that two million in each of the following four years in the appropriate currency of the remaining owner.

ix. The Boundary Questions-Tarata and Chilcaya

Having dealt with the arrangements for the plebiscite, Coolidge considered the questions of boundaries. Regarding Tarata, Chile claimed that the boundary followed the river Sama from its source to its mouth. This would include a portion of the Peruvian province of Tarata. Peru objected as the Treaty of Ancon related to Tacna and Arica. Coolidge found it difficult to accept the arguments of Chile as to the Sama being the boundary, since the Sama did not have its source in the Cordilleras on Bolivia's frontier.[288] The Treaty simply referred to Tacna and Arica, not Tarata. No definitive geographical boundary line was otherwise described in the treaty. Coolidge concluded that the treaty negotiators did not know where the geographical boundary lay when they agreed to

[282] ibid 419.
[283] ibid.
[284] ibid.
[285] ibid 421.
[286] ibid 422.
[287] ibid 424.
[288] ibid 425.

the treaty. He therefore could not accept the description of a line which was impossible to lay down as described by Chile.[289] Thus, Coolidge held that no part of Tarata was included under Article 3. It only included Tacna and Arica as of 20 October 1883, and the northern boundary of that part of the territory was covered by Article 3, which was within the Peruvian province of Tacna, was the River Sama.[290] Coolidge also decided that the southern boundary of the territory covered by Article 3 Treaty of Ancon is the Peruvian provincial boundary between the Peruvian provinces of Arica and Tarapaca as they stood on 20 October 1883.[291]

At the end of his Award, Coolidge summarised his findings as above but reserved the power and right to appoint a Special Commission consisting of three persons, one to be nominated by Chile, another to be nominated by Peru, and the third to be designated by him, to draw the boundary lines of the territory covered by Article 3 of the Treaty of Ancon in accordance with his Award with provision for expenses and compensation.[292] Coolidge held that the holding of the plebiscite would not be delayed to await the proceedings or report of the special commission on boundaries.[293] Again, Coolidge was careful to maintain oversight and to 'reserve the power and right to pass upon, adopt, modify or reject the report of said Special Commission, or to appoint a new special commission and pass upon its report in like manner'.[294] He also reserved the power to withhold the proclamation of the result of the plebiscite until the boundaries had been fixed and the right of persons to register and vote had been determined accordingly.[295]

The Award was signed under seal by President Coolidge on 4 March 1925 and his Secretary of State Charles E Hughes.

x. Settlement

In 1928, a settlement was reached through the good offices of President Hoover[296] between Chile and Peru regarding Tacna Arica. The settlement satisfied Peru. Peru considered that the question was 'absolutely and finally settled' and Chile believed 'that the treaty will wholly and finally decide the only pending question arising from the War of the Pacific'.[297] President Hoover proposed that the territory under dispute be divided into two parts. Tacna for Peru and Arica for Chile. The dividing line was 10 kilometres north of and parallel to the Arica-La Paz Railroad. The sulphur deposits of Takura remained in Chilean territory, and the canals of Uchusuma and Mauri remained the property of Peru. Chile was to construct for Peru at Arika a wharf, a customs house and a station for the Arica-Tacna Railway, where Peru would enjoy an ample freeport facility. Chile would pay Peru $6 million. Children of Peruvian nationals born in Arica were considered as Peruvians until the attainment age of 21, when they would have a right

[289] ibid 427.
[290] ibid 429.
[291] ibid 430.
[292] ibid 431.
[293] ibid.
[294] ibid 432.
[295] ibid.
[296] *The Tacna-Arica Settlement*, Foreign Affairs: 1 Jan 1928, 7, 1 Periodical Articles Online 656.
[297] ibid.

to elect their definitive nationality; likewise Chileans born at Tacna. Bolivia remained landlocked.[298]

I. Railway Traffic between Lithuania and Poland. Advisory Opinion 1931[299]

The Landwarow-Kaisiadorys Railway sector formed a part of the railway from Vilna to Libau before 1914 but was destroyed during the war. Although repaired, the line was destroyed after the occupation of Vilna by Polish forces on 9 October 1920. The question of re-establishing the line was part of the dispute, which was submitted to the Council of the League of Nations. In 1928, the Polish and Lithuanian governments made attempts to negotiate a settlement without avail.[300] On 14 December 1928, the Council of the League of Nations requested the Advisory and Technical Committee for Communications and Transit to study the obstacles to freedom of communications and transit concerning the dispute.[301] A report by the Advisory and Technical Committee, submitted to the Council on 4 September 1930, contained recommendations for the re-establishment of a through service from Vilna to Kovno via Landwarow-Kaisiadorys.[302] This report also recommended the conclusion of administrative and technical agreements essential for establishing continuous railway service on through railways. On 18 September 1930, the Council adjourned its consideration of the subject to enable its rapporteur to obtain the views of the two governments. Their views differed as to the legal effect of international agreements regarding railway traffic. The rapporteur submitted his report to the Council on 23 January 1931, but the two governments rejected it for different reasons.[303] On the following day, 24 January 1931, the Council voted to request an advisory opinion by the Permanent Court of International Justice on the following question:[304]

> Do the international engagements in force oblige Lithuania in the present circumstances,-and if so in what manner-to take the necessary measures to open for traffic, or for certain categories of traffic, the Landwarow-Kaisiadorys railway sector?

The Lithuanian and Polish governments were represented before the Court on 16 September 1931, and M Stasinskas sat as Lithuanian national judge ad hoc, as the question related to an existing dispute. The Court heard oral statements by M Silvain Dreyfus, President of the Advisory and Technical Committee for Communications and Transit; by MM Sidzikauskas and Mandelstam, on behalf of the Lithuanian government; and by M Mrozowski, on behalf of the Polish government.

M Dreyfus expressed the view of the Advisory and Technical Committee that Lithuania's obligation derived from Article 23(e) of the Covenant of the League of

[298] ibid.
[299] MO Hudson, 'The Tenth Year of the Permanent Court of International Justice' (1932) 26 *AJIL* 18–20. Reproduced with permission of The Licensor through PLSclear.
[300] (1932) 26 *AJIL* 18. Reproduced with permission of The Licensor through PLSclear.
[301] *League of Nations Official Journal*, 1929, 45.
[302] League of Nations Document, C.386, M.170.1930. VIII.
[303] (1932) 26 *AJIL* 18. Reproduced with permission of The Licensor through PLSclear.
[304] *League of Nations Official Journal*, 1931, 239.

Nations[305] and from the Paris Convention concerning Memel of 8 May 1924.[306] The Polish government added a resolution of the Council of the League of Nations of 10 December 1927. The Court's opinion was handed down on 15 October 1931.[307] The representatives of the Lithuanian government declared to the Court that Lithuania did not intend to restore the use of the Landwarow-Kaisiadorys Railway sector. This attitude was adopted as a form of pacific reprisal in which Lithuania proposed to persist until the status of Vilna had been settled.[308]

The Court decided that Lithuania was entitled to exercise such reprisals only if international engagements in force obliged her to open the sector to traffic. As the Court interpreted the Council's resolution of 10 December 1927, it imposed upon the two governments obligations 'not only to enter into negotiations, but also to pursue them as far as possible with a view to concluding agreements'; but this does not imply that Lithuania had incurred an obligation to open the sector to traffic.[309]

The Advisory Committee had considered Lithuania bound to open the railway sector to international traffic under Article 23(e) of the Covenant,[310] but no third state had intervened to claim that Article 23(e) had been violated by Lithuania. The Court observed that Article 23(e) did not imply any specific obligations for any state to open a particular line of communication. Such specific obligations depended upon some 'international convention existing or hereafter to be agreed upon'. It was therefore concluded that under Article 23(e) of the Covenant, Lithuania had no obligation to open the sector for international traffic.[311]

The Court then considered the application of the Convention concerning Memel, signed at Paris on 8 May 1924, between the British Empire, France, Italy, and Japan, on the one part, and Lithuania, on the other.[312] An annex to this convention obliged Lithuania to ensure freedom of transit and traffic coming from or destined for the Memel territory and to conform in this respect to the Statute on Freedom of Transit adopted at Barcelona. Article 2 of this statute obliged a state to facilitate free transit 'on

[305] Under Article 23(e) Subject to and in accordance with the provisions of international conventions existing or hereafter to be agreed upon, the Members of the League: (e) will make provision to secure and maintain freedom of communications and of transit and equitable treatment for the commerce of all Members of the League. In this connection, the special necessities of the regions devastated during the war of 1914–18 shall be borne in mind.

[306] Under the Paris Convention the British Empire, France, Italy and Japan, signatories with the United States of America, as the Principal Allied and Associated Powers, to the Treaty of Versailles, transferred to Lithuania, subject to the conditions of the Convention, all the rights and titles ceded to them by Germany by virtue of Article 99 of the Treaty of Versailles over the territory lying between the Baltic Sea, the north-eastern frontier of East Prussia (as described in Article 28 of the said Treaty and as defined in particular by the letter sent on 18 July 1921, by the President of the Conference of Ambassadors of the Allied Governments at Paris to the German Ambassador at Paris), and the former frontier between Germany and Russia, the said territory being described 'the Memel Territory'.

[307] Permanent Court of International Justice, Twenty-Second Session 15 October 1931, General List No. 39. Series A/B, Fasc. No. 42.

[308] (1932) 26 *AJIL* 19. Reproduced with permission of The Licensor through PLSclear.

[309] ibid.

[310] Advisory Opinion. Permanent Court of International Justice 108 Twenty-Second Session. 15 October 1931. General List: No. 39. Railway Traffic Between Lithuania and Poland (Railway Sector Landwarôw-Kaisiadorys) 117.

[311] (1932) 26 *AJIL* 19, reproduced with permission of The Licensor through PLSclear, but see Judge Anzilotti's dissenting opinion below, n 366.

[312] 29 League of Nations Treaty Series, 85 and Advisory Opinion, 15 October 1931, 120.

routes in use convenient for international transit'. But the section in question was not in use, nor could it be said that the railway of which it formed a part was in use as a whole. Nor was this railway sector convenient for international transit to or from Memel. The Court also noted that under the last paragraph of Article 3 of Annex III to the Memel Convention, the Lithuanian government undertook to permit and to grant all facilities for the traffic on the river to or from or in the port of Memel and not to apply, in respect of such traffic, on the ground of the present political relations between Lithuania and Poland, the stipulations of Articles 7 and 8 of the Barcelona Statute on the Freedom of Transit and Article 13 of the Barcelona Recommendations relative to Ports placed under an International Régime. These, the Court noted, were obviously circumstances calculated to promote freedom of transit via the port of Memel, in respect of which Lithuania abandoned her right to apply so as to place certain restrictions on this freedom. But it was to be observed that this clause in the Memel Convention applied solely to waterways and not to railways.[313]

The Court decided that even if the Landwarow-Kaisiadorys sector were in use and could serve Memel traffic, Lithuania would be entitled to invoke Article 7 of the Barcelona Statute 'as a ground for refusing to open this sector for traffic or for certain categories of traffic in case of an emergency affecting her safety or vital interests'. In this respect, regard was had for the political relations between Lithuania and Poland. Consequently, the Court held that, under the Memel Convention, Lithuania was not under obligation to open the sector in question for traffic. The unanimous conclusion of the Court was, therefore,[314]

> that the international engagements in force do not oblige Lithuania in the present circumstances to take the necessary steps to open for traffic or for certain categories of traffic the Landwarow-Kaisiadorys railway sector.

Judge Altamira concurred in this conclusion but declared himself unable to agree with the observations of the Court concerning the application of the Memel Convention and the articles of the Statute of Barcelona. However, M Anzilotti, whilst concurring in the conclusion of the Court, is of the opinion that the reasons adopted, particularly those relating to Article 23(e) of the Covenant, do not adequately support that conclusion. In his opinion, the real question before the Court was not whether Lithuania was bound to open for traffic a given railway line; it was rather whether Lithuania could refuse to have railway communications with Poland. It is certain that all the railway communications directly connecting Lithuania with Poland are broken and that the sole reason why the Council's question is confined to the Landwarow-Kaisiadorys line is that this line is the only one of considerable economic importance. The Advisory Opinion of the Court recorded M Anzilotti's opinion that:[315]

> nothing but the 'present circumstances' which are mentioned in the question and which, quite obviously, refer to existing political relations between the two countries, can justify an

[313] Advisory Opinion. Permanent Court of International Justice 108 Twenty-Second Session. 15 October 1931. General List: No. 39. Railway Traffic Between Lithuania and Poland (Railway Sector Landwarôw-Kaisiadorys) 121.
[314] ibid 122.
[315] ibid 123.

attitude on the part of Lithuania which in itself would be scarcely compatible with the duties of Members of the League of Nations and particularly with certain obligations which, in normal circumstances, would seem to result from Article 23 (e) of the Covenant.

J. Ethiopia v Italy Arbitration 1934 (The Walwal Arbitration)[316]

i. Background

On 5 December 1934, a clash took place between Ethiopian and Italian military forces at the Oasis of Wal Wal on the border between Ethiopia and Italian Somaliland. The respective governments protested to each other, and the Italian government demanded reparations and satisfaction. The Ethiopian government invoked its application of the Italo-Ethiopian Treaty of Amity, Conciliation and Arbitration of 2 August 1928 to refer the dispute to arbitration under Article 5.[317] This relatively minor incident was the precursor to diplomatic exchanges involving Britain and France that eventually gave the Italian dictator a free hand in Ethiopia and demonstrated the ineffectiveness of the League of Nations and appeasement of the dictators.[318]

After several meetings of the Council of the League of Nations, the parties appointed two arbitrators each. There was an exchange of notes on the 15 and 16 May 1935 between the governments in accordance with Article 5. An Arbitration Commissioner was appointed to investigate the circumstances of the incident and to determine liability. The tribunal was composed of Count Aldrovandi, Ambassador of HM the King of Italy and M Montagna, Counsellor of State of the Kingdom of Italy, and the latter MA de Geouifre de la Pradelle, Professor of International Law at the University of Paris, Director of the Institute of International Studies, and Mr Pitman B Potter, Professor of International Organisation at the Graduate Institute of International Studies of Geneva, an American citizen. The Agents attached to the Commission, were the former Professor at the University of Florence, MS Lessona, and MG Jeze, Professor at the University of Paris.

The Commission held its first procedural session in Milan on 6 and 7 June. Its next meeting was at Scheveningen (Netherlands). This was postponed until 25 June to enable its members to take cognisance of the claims, arguments, and evidence of the parties.[319] The Commission could not progress because the boundary between the two states was

[316] 'Italo-Ethiopian Commission of Conciliation and Arbitration 1 Award of 3 September 1935' (1935) 29 *AJIL* 690, reproduced with permission of The Licensor through PLSclear. League of Nations Document C.332.M.169.1935.VII.

[317] Both governments undertake to submit to a procedure of conciliation and arbitration disputes which may arise between them and which it may not have been possible to settle by ordinary diplomatic methods, without having recourse to armed force. Notes shall be exchanged by common agreement between the two governments regarding the manner of appointing arbitrators. League of Nations Treaty Series 1929 Vol 94, 419–421 as referred to in S Magiera, 'Wal Wal Arbitration' in *Encyclopaedia of Public International Law*, Max Planck Institute for Comparative Public Law and International Law, Vol 2 *Decisions of International Courts and Tribunals and International Arbitrations* (North-Holland Publishing Company, 1981) 290. The Award, however, refers to Article 5 of the Treaty of Amity between Italy and Ethiopia of 2 August 1908 as reprinted in (1935) 29 *AJIL* 690. Reproduced with permission of The Licensor through PLSclear.

[318] The diplomatic exchanges appeasing Mussolini are further referred to in ch 6: 'Mussolini's Imperial Dreams: Ethiopian Adventure.'

[319] (1935) 29 *AJIL* 690. Reproduced with permission of The Licensor through PLSclear.

disputed. Proceedings were suspended on 9 July 1935. The Ethiopian government then referred the matter back to the League of Nations. On 3 August 1935, the Council of the League declared that in the absence of any agreement between the two governments, the question was beyond the competence of the Commission. A fifth arbitrator was to be appointed, and their award reported back to the council of the League. The Commission reached a unanimous decision on 3 September 1935, finding that neither the Italian nor Ethiopian government was responsible for the incident on 5 December 1934 nor any subsequent incidents. It was therefore unnecessary to address the question of responsibility.[320]

The interlocutory question as to the extent of jurisdiction and competence was settled by the League Council. It concluded that the two governments 'did not agree that the Commission should examine frontier questions' and that consequently:[321]

> the Commission must not, by its decision on the Walwal incident, prejudge the solution of questions which do not fall within its province, and that it would be prejudging that solution if it founded its decision on the opinion that the place at which the incident occurred is under the sovereignty either of Italy or of Ethiopia … [and that] while it is always open to the Commission to take into consideration, without entering upon any discussion on the matter, the conviction that was held by the local authorities on either side as to the sovereignty over the place of the incident, the Commission has not to take into account the circumstance that Walwal is under the sovereignty of one or other of the two parties, but must concern itself solely with the other elements in the dispute relating to the Walwal incident.

Following this determination, the Commission was directed by the Council to proceed 'without delay to designate the fifth arbitrator whose appointment might be necessary for the carrying through of their work'. The parties were invited to inform it of the result not later than 4 September 1935.[322]

The Commission met in Paris on 20 August 1935 and designated the fifth arbitrator, the eminent jurist MN Politis,[323] who was requested to assist it in the event of disagreement. After hearing a statement from the Ethiopian Agent, the Commission decided to proceed to Berne to receive the depositions of witnesses called by the Italian government. These were taken on 23, 24 and 25 August, followed by the final statement of each of the two Agents.[324]

On returning to Paris on 26 August, the Committee began its discussions on the questions submitted for its consideration, but the four arbitrators were unable to agree either as to the actual circumstances of the Walwal incident or as to who was responsible for it. At this point Professor Politis intervened and considered the question with the Committee and it was unanimously concluded[325] that the Walwal district, situated in

[320] S Magiera, 'Wal Wal Arbitration' in *Encyclopaedia of Public International Law*, Max Planck Institute for Comparative Public Law and International Law, Vol 2 *Decisions of International Courts and Tribunals and International Arbitrations* (North-Holland Publishing Company, 1981) 290.

[321] Award of 3 September 1935. League of Nations Document C.332.M.169.1935.VII. p 3, para 6.

[322] ibid.

[323] Greek minister at Paris, member of the French Institute and the *Institut de Droit international*, former Minister for Foreign Affairs, ex-President of the League Assembly, Honorary Professor in the Faculty of Law of Paris University.

[324] Award of 3 September 1935. League of Nations Document C.332.M.169.1935.VII. p 4, paras 8–9.

[325] ibid pp 4–9, paras 14–37.

a desert country and frequented by nomad tribes under the authority of Britain, Italy or Ethiopia, was of special importance owing to the wells in the territory, the water of which was indispensable for the requirements of the tribes in question and their livestock. This area had been controlled since 1928 and permanently occupied since 1930 by the authorities of the Italian Somaliland Colony. The Italian occupation of the area was symbolised by the fortified post of Wal Wal, which is subordinate to that of Warder, about 12.5 km distant. This never gave rise to any official protest from that government until the Walwal incident.[326]

The Italian authorities supposed that the Walwal area was under Italian authority and was recognised by Ethiopia and the UK because the tribes continually used the Walwal wells under the supervision of the Italian authorities. On the other hand, the Ethiopian authorities were convinced that the area formed part of their national territory.[327] In recent years prior to the dispute, mutual suspicion and animosity had developed between the Italian and Ethiopian authorities. The Italian authorities became convinced that the Ethiopians had hostile intentions, and the Ethiopian authorities had the same conviction about the Italians. In such an atmosphere of suspicion and apprehension, the slightest incident could lead to a misunderstanding and degenerate into a serious conflict.[328]

On 22 November 1934, an Ethiopian force of about 600 regular and irregular troops, under the command of Fitaorari Shiferra, Governor of Jijija and Ogaden, Fitaorari Alemayehu, and Omar Samantar, an Italian deserter with a price on his head for the murder of an Italian officer, arrived in front of the Italian post at Walwal as the protective escort of an Anglo-Ethiopian commission. It had just completed the demarcation of the frontier between Ethiopia and British Somaliland and had instructions to make a grazing survey in Ogaden, due the next day at Walwal, where there was an Italian garrison consisting at that time of about 160 native soldiers *(dubats)*.[329]

The Ethiopian force considered itself to be in national territory and advanced towards the wells; its advance was opposed by an Italian force, commanded by a native NCO who asserted that the Walwal area was Italian territory. Under the pressure of greatly superior numbers, the *dubats* were obliged to fall back, leaving the Ethiopians in possession of ten or 15 wells.[330] The next morning, 23 November, the Anglo-Ethiopian commission arrived on the scene; at its head were, on the British side, Lt Col. Clifford, and on the Ethiopian side, Fitaurari Tessama Bante. The same day, they sent a letter to the officer commanding the Italian forces in the area, protesting against the opposition to the advance of the Ethiopian force on the previous day and against the forcible carrying-off of one of the commission's NCO's with his rifle. The following morning, the Italian commanding officer, Captain Cimmaruta, visited the members of the commission; he declared that he was not competent to discuss the main subject of their protest, 'a problem which concerns only the political authorities', but in explanation of the disappearance of the Ethiopian NCO he stated that the latter was an Italian deserter who had

[326] ibid p 4, paras 15–17.
[327] ibid p 4, paras 17–18.
[328] ibid p 5, paras 19–20.
[329] ibid p 5, para 21.
[330] ibid p 5, para 22.

voluntarily given himself up. He proposed to hold an inquiry into the matter and offered, in order to avoid incidents, to establish a provisional line of separation between the Italian and Ethiopian forces. This offer, which, in form, appeared to the Anglo-Ethiopian commission to be 'sincere and opportune', was not carried out. Captain Cimmaruta proposed to indicate the position of the two opposing lines by marks and signatures on tree trunks; this proposal, however, was rejected by the Ethiopian commission, lest its acceptance of a provisional de facto situation might create a precedent favourable to the Italian view. Subsequently, however, the Ethiopian commission agreed to the establishment of a provisional line of separation marked by twigs or thorns.[331]

To give the Ethiopians access to other wells in addition to the ten or 15 in their possession, the Italians were asked to withdraw a few meters; Captain Cimmaruta refused but offered to allow the Ethiopians to draw water behind the Italian lines, under his supervision. The Anglo-Ethiopian commission did not see its way to accept this offer. During the conference between Captain Cimmaruta and the commissioners, two Italian aeroplanes flew low over the Anglo-Ethiopian camp, where the British and Ethiopian flags were flying side by side, and the commissioners had the impression that the machine gun of one of these aeroplanes, which was piloted by Major Porru Locci, had been trained upon them; they regarded this as a provocation and protested indignantly. Giving evidence before the Conciliation and Arbitration Commission, however, Major Porru Locci declared on his honour as an officer and a gentleman that the machine gun of his aeroplane was not trained upon the Anglo-Ethiopian camp, though a camera was. He explained that a wrong impression might be gained because the machine gun was mounted transversely on the fuselage, and consequently, when the aeroplane banked, the machine gun would appear to be trained on the ground. He also added that his flight over the camp was in no sense a hostile demonstration: under orders from his superior officers, he was carrying out a reconnaissance in search of Captain Cimmaruta.[332]

Lt Col. Clifford felt 'great indignation' at this incident, which he regarded as a 'provocative demonstration'.[333] He decided to withdraw the British mission to Ado, some 30 kilometres from Walwal in order not to complicate the situation for the Ethiopian authorities and to guard against any regrettable international incident; accordingly, the next day, on 25 November the British and Ethiopian missions left Walwal with their respective escorts of 30 and 50 men.

In the meantime, Fitaurari Siferra's force remained, and after receiving further reinforcements, it had a strength of 1,400 to 1,600 men. Its presence and the increase in its strength naturally added to the misgivings of the Italian authorities, which they believed to have been justified in view of documents they subsequently found in the Ethiopian camp. The Italian authorities considered that the Ethiopian troops' claim to be the escort of the Anglo-Ethiopian commission was clearly false and that the reason why it did not follow the commission was that it was planning to attack the Italian garrison at the first opportunity with a view to seizing the Walwal wells. In its report dated 30 November 1934, paragraph 20, the Anglo-Ethiopian commission explained that the 'Ethiopian escort' remained in its position at Walwal in order to avoid the

[331] ibid p 5, paras 23–24.
[332] ibid p 6, paras 25–26.
[333] ibid p 6, para 27.

appearance of a retreat which might cause a rising among the population of Ogaden seriously compromising the safety of the commission; in the proceedings before the Commission it was further stated, on behalf of Ethiopia, that believing themselves to be in their own territory, the forces which had advanced as far as the wells could not retire without wounding the pride and lowering the prestige of the nation; it should lastly be noted that on being asked by Captain Cimmaruta whether the troops which remained at Walwal and which the commission continued to regard as its escort really formed part of the commission's Ethiopian escort, Lt Col. Clifford made no reply.[334]

For ten days after the commission's departure the Ethiopian and Italian troops remained in their positions, facing each other at a distance which in places was no more than two meters, their loaded rifles in their hands, challenging, insulting and provoking each other. The Governor of Italian Somaliland continued to give the commander of the Warder-Walwal sector formal written orders to refrain absolutely from any hostile act so long as the Ethiopians did not use their arms against the Italian posts; and on his side, the commander of the sector, Captain Cimmaruta, repeatedly approached the Anglo-Ethiopian commission and the Ethiopian military chiefs, urging that the necessary precautions be taken to prevent any incident. On 26 November 1934, he felt uneasy as to the intentions of the Fitaorari Shiferra and gave a warning. On 4 December, having learnt that on the previous night his men had tried to force the Italian line by removing the brushwood which marked it, Captain Cimmaruta sent him word that any act of violence on his part would be countered by force.[335]

At this juncture reinforcements arrived on both sides of the lines. On both sides, the men watched each other, and their nervousness increased because every day shots were heard – either accidental shots or shots at game. Suddenly, on 5 December, towards 3.30 p.m. according to some and towards 5.30 p.m. according to others, following a shot the origin of which is disputed, a general fight began. At the sound of the firing, Captain Cimmaruta, who was at Warder, ordered two tanks and three aeroplanes to leave for Walwal immediately, he himself also proceeding thither in a light lorry. He arrived at Walwal shortly before 6 pm, one tank and one aeroplane arriving a few minutes before him. The other tank and aeroplanes came up shortly after his own arrival. Captain Cimmaruta found his men, consisting at this time of about 500 *dubats*, having only native non-commissioned officers in command, forced back beyond the original line, with their ammunition practically exhausted. He had some cartridges found on disabled men distributed among them and called for ammunition to be sent from Warder. This ammunition arrived two hours later. Meanwhile, night was falling, the fighting became desultory, and soon ceased altogether. On 6 December, at dawn, fighting began again and soon the Ethiopians were routed and fled in the direction of Ado, leaving on the ground and in the neighbourhood 130 dead and many wounded. The Italian *dubats* lost 30 dead and 100 wounded.[336]

As to who fired the first shot, controversy reigned. There were two diametrically opposite accounts given. According to one version, this shot was fired from the Italian line after two orders clearly heard in the Ethiopian ranks had been given, namely, first 'A

[334] ibid p 6, para 28.
[335] ibid p 7, paras 29–30.
[336] ibid p 7, paras 31–32.

terra' and then 'fuoco'. According to the other version the shot was fired by an Ethiopian soldier, standing upright, in the direction of a little tree in which was sitting, on sentinel duty, an Italian *dubat*, who, wounded slightly in the cheek, immediately fell or let himself drop down. According to both versions, the shot was the signal for firing from the same side.[337]

The Ethiopian version was based:

1. On the aggressive intentions of the Italian forces as alleged by a number of *dubat* deserters who came, before 5 December, to the headquarters of the Anglo-Ethiopian commission, which took their evidence later;
2. On the report of Fitaorari Shiferra which mentions the orders 'A terra' and 'fuoco' alleged to have been given in the ranks of the *dubats*, whereas, in the evidence given before the Commission of Conciliation and Arbitration and in particular according to Captain Cimmaruta's statement, such orders are never given to *dubats* in Italian;
3. On the evidence of an Ethiopian *sich-attendant* who was not an eyewitness of the beginning of the fight, he himself declaring that, when lying in his tent, he heard three shots one after the other and seized his rifle to proceed to the lines, during which time three bullets fell on his tent.[338]

The Italian version is based on the following:

1. The telegraphic reports, dated December 6 and 7, 1934, from Commandant Montanari, the military chief of the area, to the Government of Somaliland, conveying the evidence of the *dubats* who were the only eyewitnesses of the first events, and who state in particular that 'an attack in force, unexpectedly launched by the Ethiopians under the Fitaorari Tessamma, without any provocation on our part, compelled our *dubats* to fall back after a strenuous resistance';
2. The report dated December 14, 1934, from the Government of Somaliland to the Colonial Ministry at Rome, giving a summary of the information it had received **by** that date, according to which 'an *ascari* of the Fitaorari Shiferra stood up and fired a shot in the air, which it seems was to serve as a signal, since it was immediately followed by a sharp~fusillade on the part of the Ethiopians';
3. The evidence, taken by the Commission of Conciliation and Arbitration, in the absence of Italian officers and non-commissioned officers-since there were none on the spot at the time of the engagement-of four *dubats*, all of whom are now non-commissioned officers but only one of whom was so at the time of the incident. They were at Walwal on December 5, and state that they saw the first shot fired from the Ethiopian ranks, adding a new detail, namely, that the shot was fired at a sentry posted in a tree. These witnesses did not give their evidence until nearly nine months after the event; they did not specify whether the shot which they say they saw came from the Ethiopian ranks was fired intentionally or accidentally at the Italian sentinel or whether the latter's fall was due to a deliberate or an involuntary movement.[339]

The Commission adjudged that this incident was due to an unfortunate chain of circumstances; the first shot might have been accidental, like the numerous and frequent shots

[337] ibid p 8, para 33.
[338] ibid p 8, para 34.
[339] ibid pp 8–9, para 34–35.

that preceded it. It is quite comprehensible that, in the nervous, excited and suspicious state of mind of the opposing troops, who had for two weeks been placed in a dangerous neighbourhood, this shot led to the regrettable results which ensued. In these circumstances, the Commission, taking into account the limit of its powers under the resolution adopted by the Council of the League of Nations on 3 August found:[340]

1. That neither the Italian Government or its agents on the spot can be held responsible in any way for the actual Walwal incident; the allegations brought against them by the Ethiopian Government are disproved in particular by the many precautions taken by them to prevent any incident on the occasion of the assembling at Walwal of Ethiopian regular and irregular troops, and also by the absence of any interest on their part in provoking the engagement of December 5; and
2. That although the Ethiopian Government also had no reasonable interest in provoking that engagement, its local authorities, by their attitude and particularly by the concentration and maintenance, after the departure of the Anglo-Ethiopian commission, of numerous troops in the proximity of the Italian line at Walwal, may have given the impression that they had aggressive intentions-which would seem to render the Italian version plausible-but that nevertheless it had not been shown that they can be held responsible for the actual incident of December 5.

The tribunal briefly considered incidents after 6 December 1934 up to 25 May 1935, between the Italian and Ethiopian forces, some following upon the Walwal incident, and others unconnected with it. It held that these were of an accidental character, while the others were for the most part not serious and of very ordinary occurrence in the region in which they took place. It followed that no international responsibility need be involved.[341]

The Award was signed by Politis, Aldrovandi, A de Pradelle, and Pittman B Potter and dated 3 September 1935.

In the House of Commons, the Foreign Secretary, Sir John Simon, reported the incident to the House following events since the 23 November 1934 the date when the Anglo-Ethiopian Boundary Commission, which had completed the demarcation of the frontier between Ethiopia and British Somaliland, and investigated the watering and grazing areas which for generations had been used by nomadic British Somali tribes, arrived in the vicinity of the wells of Walwal and Wardair. He explained that the wells in the neighbourhood of the undefined border between Italian Somaliland and Ethiopia, had been in Italian occupation for some time. What he explained was in line with what the Commission found.

Simon instructed His Majesty's representatives at Rome and Addis Ababa, prior to the above incident, to recommend to the Italian and Ethiopian governments the desirability, in the interest of good relations, of proceeding to an early demarcation of the frontier. The Italian government had informed Britain of their willingness to allow Colonel Clifford and his Ethiopian colleague of the Boundary Commission to enter Walwal and Wardair to carry out their work. Once the British government learnt of the incident between Ethiopian forces and Italian troops, instructions were immediately

[340] ibid p 9, para 36–37.
[341] ibid p 10, para 38.

dispatched to Colonel Clifford to withdraw his section from the affected area, similar instructions being sent by the Emperor of Ethiopia to the Abyssinian Commissioner.

ii. Legal Difficulties

It is trite in arbitration law that the agreement to arbitrate should define the arbitral procedure. Usually in commercial cases the agreement will refer to institutional rules. In public international law cases, it follows that the treaty should indicate the process. In this case Article 5 of the Treaty of Amity 1928 did not define 'conciliation or mediation', nor did it define the nationality of the arbitrators. Worse, it did not find the terms of reference or jurisdiction of the Commission, or the location and language of proceedings. Thus, the necessity for the Council of the League's resolution of 3 August 1935, which enabled the Commission to function.[342] Its result, in the context of the larger conflict between Italy and Ethiopia, was marginal and signalled a reluctance or inability to find Italy culpable. This approach was reflected in the diplomatic exchanges subsequently.[343]

K. Radio Orient Arbitration 1940[344]

A dispute arose between the French High Commission to the States of the Levant under Mandate and the Egyptian government regarding action taken on 16 April 1935 by the Administration of Telegraphs of Egypt forbidding its telegraph offices thereafter to accept telegrams for transmission from Egypt by Radio-Orient. The issue was that the services of the French company Radio-Orient, a subsidiary of the French *Compagnie Gtnrale de Taligraphie sans Fil*, having its headquarters in Paris and principal place of business in Beirut, could not be settled by diplomatic means. The parties referred the matter under Article 15 of the Telecommunications Convention signed in Madrid on 9 December 1932,[345] enabling a submission to international arbitration.[346] The French High Commission to the States of the Levant under Mandate chose the Norwegian government as arbitrator, and the Egyptian government chose the Danish government as arbitrator. In turn, those governments jointly requested the Netherlands government to be the umpire.

[342] S Magiera, 'Wal Wal Arbitration' in *Encyclopaedia of Public International Law*, Max Planck Institute for Comparative Public Law and International Law, Vol 2 *Decisions of International Courts and Tribunals and International Arbitrations* (North-Holland Publishing Company, 1981) 290–291.

[343] See ch 6: 'Mussolini's Imperial Dreams: Ethiopian Adventure.'

[344] This is based on the original text of the Award as published in (1943) 37 *AJIL* 341–349, reproduced with permission of the Licensor through PLSclear and as translated by Eleanor H Finch from a copy of the original French text furnished through the courtesy of Mr Arnold Raestad.

[345] On 9 December 1932, the first International Telecommunication Convention was signed at Madrid. This Convention provided for the fusion of the International Telegraph Union and the International Radio-telegraph Union into a single organisation. The new organisation, the International Telecommunication Union, came into being on 1 January 1934.

[346] Article 15. Arbitration. § 1. In the case of disagreement between two or more contracting governments in respect of the execution either of the present Convention or of the Regulations provided for by Art 2, the dispute, if not settled through the diplomatic channel, is submitted to arbitration at the request of any one of the governments in disagreement (ITU Library & Archives collections, United Nations).

i. The Tribunal and Counsel

This was composed of the following appointees: by the Norwegian government: Mr AC Raestad, former Minister of Foreign Affairs, and member of the Permanent Court of Arbitration; by the Danish government: Mr CI Mondrup, Director General of Posts and Telegraphs of Denmark; and by the Netherlands government: Mr WM Van Lanschot, member of the Upper Chamber of the States General, who, as umpire, has exercised the functions of President. The French High Commission to the Levant under Mandate appointed: Mr J Paur-Boncour, member of the Bar of the Court of Appeal of Paris, as Agent; and the Egyptian government appointed: His Excellency Abdel Hamid Badawi Pacha, President of the State Claims Commission, and Mr Maurice Jacquet, Royal Counsellor, as Agents, and Mr Charles Ayoub Bey, Assistant Royal Counsellor, as Counsel.[347]

At the request of the President of the tribunal, the International Bureau of the Permanent Court of Arbitration placed its quarters and personnel at the disposition of the parties for the carrying out of the arbitral procedure, and thus the tribunal met at The Hague in the Palace of the Permanent Court of Arbitration on 11 November 1938. At its first meeting, it made procedural rules, exercising the jurisdiction conferred upon it by Article 15, paragraph 8, of the said convention.[348] These rules fixed the time limits for the presentation of the case, the countercase, the reply and the rebuttal. They extended the time limit for the rebuttal by agreement of the parties. The parties had already deposited their submissions in their respective case and countercase at the International Bureau of the Permanent Court of Arbitration, and their agents had presented their conclusions as follows:[349]

The Agent of the French High Commission asked the Tribunal:[350]

> To hold and declare that the seizure of documents by Egyptian officials, which is the basis of the disputed decision, should be held illegal and arbitrary, and consequently null and void, as a violation of the secrecy of correspondence, violation of domicile, abuse of powers, and violation of the procedure prescribed by the Capitulatory Regime then in force.
>
> To hold and declare that the decision under attack is indisputably vitiated as a violation of Article 28 of the International Convention of Madrid, and as a violation of the rights of defence during a secret and *ex parte* inquiry.
>
> To hold and declare, therefore, that the nullity of the procedure of inquiry must have the effect of the revocation, pure and simple, of the disputed decision.
>
> Also:
>
> To hold and declare that even if the errors pointed out do not nullify the contested penalty, it is the duty of the Egyptian Administration to produce the documents upon the examination of which it has based its decision.
>
> Consequently, to order the production of these documents.
>
> To state, upon examination of these documents, whether the violations set forth justify the most severe penalty in the list of sanctions in Article 33 of the Telegraph Rules.

[347] 37 *AJIL* 342. Reproduced with permission of the Licensor through PLSclear.
[348] '8. Les arbitres arretent librement la procedure a suivre.'
[349] 37 *AJIL* 342. Reproduced with permission of the Licensor through PLSclear.
[350] ibid 342–343.

> To hold and declare that in any case the word 'suspension' must be interpreted in conformity with its meaning in current juridical language, the most severe sanction consisting of a suspension for a limited time of service with private enterprises.
>
> Consequently, to order the reopening of the line which has been closed since April 16, 1935.
>
> Upon every hypothesis to deliver to the plaintiff States an official certificate of their right to claim and receive damages in case the documents produced by the Egyptian Government show, as everything seems to indicate, that the duration of the suspension is henceforth disproportionate to the gravity of the infractions set forth.

The Agent of the Egyptian government asked the tribunal:[351]

> To decide, laying aside all broader or contrary conclusions, that the penalty applied to the Radio-Orient Company by the Egyptian Administration is in conformity with the provisions of Article 33 of the Telegraph Rules annexed to the International Telecommunications Convention signed at Madrid December 9, 1932.

Once the submissions (pleadings[352]) had been concluded, the tribunal met at the Palace of the Permanent Court of Arbitration[353] on 7 February 1940. Having heard the oral arguments of the parties and their additional explanations, as well as the explanations furnished by Mr M Gredsted, Chief of the Danish Telecommunications Enterprise, who gave expert evidence, the President declared the arguments closed on 10 February 1940. They then adjourned the arbitration to consider their Award, which was given on 2 April 1940.

The French company Radio-Orient, had a share capital of FRF 6,739,000 and was a private enterprise within the meaning of the Telecommunications Convention and of the Telegraph Rules recognised by the French High Commission to the States of the Levant under Mandate. Under the terms of a concession contract concluded on 1 December 1921, it was authorised to operate wireless communications through a radiotelegraph station installed at Beirut. Under Article III of the contract, the Radio-Orient Company was to apply the international rules in force to the communications exchanged through its facilities, in conformity with Article 96, paragraph 3, of the Madrid Telegraph Rules.[354] The Radio-Orient Company had no telegraphic or radiotelegraphic stations in Egypt itself, and connection with the Egyptian services was made through telegraph lines in Egypt, across Palestine, British mandated territory, and terminating at Beirut, where the telegraph services of the States of the Levant maintained direct contact with Radio-Orient. The Radio-Orient Company had no public offices in Egypt for the transmission of telegrams, having no authority from the Egyptian government as required by the Egyptian law of 12 May 1906.[355] However, the Radio-Orient Company was able to increase its revenue by using agents who were authorised. It was the only company to operate such a service. In 1926 the Marconi Radio Telegraph Company was given authorisation, and it began to operate a radiotelegraph

[351] ibid 343.

[352] The tribunal referred to pleadings which is the English expression, but the author refers to them as submissions to distinguish from pleadings in litigation.

[353] Now known as the Peace Palace in The Hague.

[354] This was a provision binding upon the States of the Levant at the time the dispute arose, and which was retained without alteration in the Telegraph Rules of Cairo, 1938 (Art 105, para 3).

[355] 37 *AJIL* 344. Reproduced with permission of the Licensor through PLSclear.

service in Egypt, directly connecting it with foreign countries after 15 January 1928.[356] The Radio-Orient Company notified the International Telecommunications Bureau at Berne of the lines successively opened by it and its rates established for transmission by each of these lines. On 16 January 1923, the Egyptian Telegraphs Administration instructed its telegraph offices to accept telegrams via 'Beirut-Radio' ('Radio-Syria'-line identification later changed to 'Radio-Orient'), and, consequently, at no time until the prohibition in dispute did the Egyptian Administration prevent its offices from accepting telegrams for transmission via 'Radio-Orient.'[357]

On 14 April 1935, the Under-Secretary of State in the Ministry of Communications of Egypt addressed the following letter to the Director of the Radio-Orient Company in Paris:[358]

> I am instructed to notify you that the Egyptian Administration has acted under Article 33 of the International Telegraph Rules and has given instructions to the Egyptian telegraph offices not to accept telegrams for transmittal over the lines of the Radio-Orient Company.

That day a similar letter was sent to the International Telecommunications Bureau at Berne, with a copy to Mr Lucien Franc, agent of the Radio-Orient Company in Cairo. By Circular No. 162(A) of 16 April 1935, the Inspector General of the Administration of Telegraphs and Telephones of the Egyptian state notified its offices that no telegram was to be accepted for transmission via 'Radio-Orient' or via 'Radio-Syria.'[359] It stated:

> Every member of the public who sends telegrams marked for these routes must be informed that these routes are not used by Egypt. With the consent of the sender these telegrams must be sent by the most economical way. All care must be taken to avoid the least delay to the public. All requests for further information must be referred to the Head Office.

On 22 April 1935, the Inspector General sent the International Telecommunications Bureau in Berne a telegram worded as follows:[360]

> Reference letter Egyptian Administration 37-11/3 of April fourteenth please note that the information is given for registration at the Bureau. Notification to Administrations not requested now. Please acknowledge receipt.

Under Article 33 Telegraph Rules of Madrid 1932, the governments of the Union reserved the right to apply penalties to private enterprises which directly or through their agents or sub-agents, allowed senders or receivers discounts (per word, per telegram, under the form of rebates, etc) reducing the rates filed with the Bureau of the Union. These penalties could require the suspension of service with these enterprises. This article was not modified at the time of the revision of the Telegraph Rules at Cairo in 1938.[361]

The French argued, while not denying that reductions had been allowed by the agents of the Radio-Orient company in Egypt, that the suspension at issue is vitiated by defects which rendered it null in law, and at any rate a limit should have been placed upon it a

[356] ibid.
[357] ibid.
[358] ibid.
[359] ibid 345.
[360] ibid.
[361] ibid.

long time ago. The Egyptian government argued that, even aside from Article 33 of the Telegraph Rules, they, in exercise of their sovereign rights, could continue the suspension of service with Radio-Orient.[362]

ii. Competence of the Tribunal

The tribunal considered the defendant's assertion that the tribunal was incompetent because the parties had no arbitral agreement and that the competence of the tribunal extended only to the interpretation of Article 33 of the Telegraph Rules.[363] Article 15, paragraph 1, International Telecommunications Convention,[364] provided that in case of disagreement between two or several contracting governments concerning the execution either of the present Convention or of the Rules envisaged in Article 2, if the difference was not settled through diplomatic channels, it would be submitted to arbitration. Unless agreed otherwise, every international arbitral tribunal is the judge of its own competence.[365] However, in this case, Article 15 Madrid Convention stated that the competence of the tribunal was limited to the dispute concerning the execution of either the Convention or the Rules annexed thereto. The Madrid Convention did not provide for an arbitral agreement but based arbitral jurisdiction upon the sole 'demand of any one of the Governments in disagreement' and taken together, Article 15 taken together with the claimants (French) statements would cover the principal subjects normally in the arbitration agreement.[366] On the other hand, the claimant generally submitted the question of whether the suspension of service with Radio-Orient could continue despite the provisions of Article 22 of the Convention and Article 47 of the Telegraph Rules, whatever the legal basis upon which the Egyptian Administration of Telegraphs intended to rely. The tribunal declared itself competent to decide the dispute submitted to it by the claimant.[367]

iii. Questions at Issue

The tribunal considered that the Egyptian Administration of Telegraphs, at the time it informed Radio-Orient of its decision to forbid Egyptian telegraph offices to accept telegrams for transmittal via Radio-Orient, invoked Article 33 of the Telegraph Rules. The claimant argued that the nullity of the inquiry proceedings must have the effect of revoking, purely and simply, the disputed order. The answer to the question of whether, by the suspension of service with Radio-Orient, the Egyptian Administration of Telegraphs did or did not violate its obligation to execute the Convention and Telegraph Rules depended upon the nature of the action thus taken and not upon the nature of the proceedings leading up to it. Thus, the Tribunal could not declare that the suspension by the Egyptian Administration of Telegraphs should be revoked by reason of nullity.[368]

[362] ibid.
[363] ibid.
[364] Signed at Madrid 9 December 1932.
[365] Known now as the doctrine of *Kompetenz-Kompetenz*.
[366] 37 *AJIL* 346. Reproduced with permission of the Licensor through PLSclear.
[367] ibid.
[368] ibid.

A second argument of the claimant was that the Egyptian Administration of Telegraphs violated its obligations under Article 28 of the Convention, which read as follows:

> The contracting Governments undertake to inform each other in regard to violations of the provisions of the present Convention and of the Rules agreed to, in order to facilitate prosecutions to be carried out.

In the tribunal's opinion, Article 9, paragraph 2, of the Convention, in conjunction with said Article 28, constituted the principal provision in regard to penalties for violations of the Convention and Rules by private enterprises. If the prosecution of every violation of the Rules by a private enterprise constituted an obligation on the part of the government which had licensed the company, that government likewise had the right to be put in a position to carry out such prosecution. On this point the claimant stated that it presented its complaint not only by way of diplomatic protection of the private enterprise Radio-Orient but also in its own name, adding that the Administration of Telegraphs of the States of the Levant may as a result be forced to take over for its own benefit the radioelectric services of said company at Beirut.[369]

The tribunal held that the Egyptian government, when advised by its Administration of Telegraphs, should, in execution of Article 28 of the Convention, have informed without delay the government of the States of the Levant of the violations of the Telegraph Rules imputed to Radio-Orient. A telegraph administration could not apply to a foreign private enterprise the sanctions provided in the Telegraph Rules unless its government, in accordance with Article 28 of the Convention, also informed the government having jurisdiction of the company, thus enabling the latter government either to institute proceedings or, in such case, to furnish proof that the charge made against Radio-Orient was without foundation.[370]

Under these circumstances there was no reason to examine whether the suspension of service with Radio-Orient did or did not constitute a too severe penalty in proportion to the infraction imputed to Radio-Orient. The tribunal therefore decided that the decision suspending the service with Radio-Orient could not be maintained under Article 33 Telegraph Rules.[371]

The defendant invoked Article 1 of the Convention concluded in 1919 between the Administration of Telegraphs OETA (Oeust) (Occupied Enemy Territories Administration) and the Egyptian Administration of Telegraphs concerning the exchange of telegrams by lines between OETA (Oeust), on the one hand, and Egypt and the countries beyond, on the other hand, by virtue of which article each of the parties can suspend telegraphic service in whole or in part, provided it notifies the other party.[372] This convention was an agreement for the technical development of a means of telecommunication of the nature of those envisaged by Article 25 of the Convention and by Article 3 of the Telegraph Rules and could not in any way prejudice the full execution of the Telegraph Convention and Rules. The right to suspend international

[369] ibid 347.
[370] ibid.
[371] ibid.
[372] ibid.

telecommunications services, reserved to governments by Article 27 of the Convention, did not constitute a right accruing to the Egyptian government in relation to Radio-Orient, but rather a right to act, in such a case, with respect to the government of the States of the Levant.[373]

The tribunal held that Egypt invoked her sovereign right to maintain order in her own territory. Only Egypt could police her own territory, and within the framework of the Convention of Madrid and of the Rules annexed, she was obliged to do so in order to assure the carrying out of their provisions in her territory. The sovereign rights of every state are, however, limited by the obligations which it has assumed towards other states, in this case, by the Convention of Madrid and the Telegraph Rules. The situation was not changed by the fact that, according to the defendant, the Egyptian Administration of Telegraphs, in authorising the Marconi Radio Telegraph Company of Egypt to operate radiotelegraph stations in Egypt, imposed upon the latter such conditions of service that in case of equalisation of rates between the Marconi service and the Radio-Orient service, the Radio-Orient service was likely to entail financial sacrifices for Egypt. The claimant reserved the right to claim damages.[374]

The tribunal, in the face of admissions made in the diplomatic correspondence, recognised that the agents of Radio-Orient allowed discounts in violation of Article 33 Telegraph Rules, and, consequently, the Egyptian authorities had the right to make their decision. Since the tribunal was not able to ascertain the date from which a time limit should have been placed upon the suspension of service with Radio-Orient or to assess the damages suffered by the latter, the tribunal could not award the claimant damages.[375]

Consequently, the tribunal ordered that:[376]

1. the suspension of service with Radio-Orient must terminate six weeks after the date of their decision, and that,
2. the order prohibiting Egyptian telegraph offices from accepting telegrams for transmission over the lines of the Radio-Orient Company must be revoked, to take effect at once, within the said period.

The tribunal held that the Egyptian government acted contrary to Article 28 of the International Telecommunications Convention of Madrid 1932 and ordered as above. The tribunal dismissed the other contentions of the claimant.

The award was given at The Hague in the Palace of the Permanent Court of Arbitration on 2 April 1940, just weeks before France was attacked and overrun by German forces.

The case was significant insofar as it confirmed the rule that every international arbitral tribunal is the judge of its own competence[377] and that the sovereign rights of every state were limited by the obligations which it had assumed towards other states.

[373] ibid 348.
[374] ibid.
[375] ibid.
[376] ibid.
[377] 'Arbitral Decision In The Matter Of The Suspension Of The Operations At The French Company Radio Orient In Egypt' (1943) 37 *American Journal of International Law* 341–349.

3

Diplomacy as an Instrument of Prevention

I. The Tensions Resulting from the Versailles Treaty

Whilst various claims arising out of the First World War were capable of settlement by arbitration, major questions of territorial boundaries remained a potential threat to European peace. The Treaty of Versailles was a prime cause of grievance to Germany because of the 'war guilt clause' and imposition of reparations, whilst insecurity was a cause of continuing anxiety to the French, especially the Rhineland frontier. Marshal Foch, the hero of 1918, recommended occupation of the left bank of the Rhine for strategic security reasons. France had reason for its grievances due to the destruction of its northern provinces and its infrastructure. Disappointment and disgust at the termination of the tripartite agreement to guarantee France's security in the event of German aggression caused France to occupy the Rhineland.[1] Germany wanted the Danzig corridor and access to East Prussia as well as the German territories given to Belgium, Czechoslovakia and Poland. These grievances became more strident as time went on, amplified by a declining economy and the rise of fascism. In the East, Russia transformed itself from an imperial power into a Soviet Republic, from one form of autocracy to another. Against these festering differences, British foreign policy post the Armistice was to reconcile and mediate. In a Memorandum it was said that: 'The longer Europe continues in a state of economic nightmare, dominated by fluctuations of fear and revenge, the more our business suffers.'[2]

A. Economic Crisis

Following the Great War and the subsequent Peace Conference, the commercial life of Europe was transformed. Despite America's isolationism, exemplified by its rejection of membership in the League of Nations and its Covenant obligations, it was obliged by its commercial trade interests with Europe to have an indirect interest in European economic stability and security. In the 1920s a general feeling of economic uncertainty reinforced by isolationist tendencies placed limits on immigration. The period between January 1920 and October 1923 was one of increasing tension between the Allies and Germany and

[1] DBFP 1919–1939, Ser. 1 Vol XX. No. 19. *Memorandum respecting British Central Europe Policy in relation to Genoa*. [C 6875/18] Foreign Office, 9 May 1922.
[2] ibid p 32.

between the Allies themselves. Over 20 international conferences were required to deal with the effects of the Treaty of Versailles. Excessive demands were made on Germany that exacerbated relations between former enemies. Relations between former allies were undermined by the temporary occupation of Frankfurt in 1920.[3] On 3 March 1921, the Allies, in consequence of German obstruction, applied severe economic sanctions on the Rhineland and jointly occupied the Düsseldorf bridgehead, including Ruhort and Duisberg.[4]

i. The Cannes Conference

To meet the problems caused by the war the Allies and Associated Powers agreed to convene a conference in Cannes. It met from 4 to 10 January 1922. The aim was to assemble 'a great international economic conference for the reconstruction of Europe'. France, Britain, Italy, the US, and Japan were invited to the conference with Russia, Germany and former enemy states.[5] At this time there was a change of government in France, Poincaré becoming the head of the government after Aristide Briand. Lloyd George met Poincaré at Boulogne but failed to reach agreement. Despite that, Lloyd George succeeded in obtaining a general endorsement of his 'Cannes Resolutions' for economic and political relations with the Soviet Union. Delegates agreed to separate reparations from reconstruction. Securing an understanding with Russia was a difficult balancing act since capitalism and communism had little in common. Lloyd George insisted that Rathenau, the German Foreign Minister, appear before the Supreme Council. A 10-year nonreciprocal defensive pact in case of German aggression was promoted. This was rejected because the French wanted a broader agreement to include Germany's eastern frontier, but Lloyd George bullied Briand, resulting in President Millerand recalling him from Genoa. Charles Briand resigned in July 1922, and the conference closed.

ii. Paris Conference

In February 1922, a conference was held in Paris to consider the Russian debts to France, which amounted to FRF 11,000 million. British investors had invested three milliard gold francs in Russia.[6] Britain and France wished to recover their debts from Russia but did not recognise the Bolshevik regime. As far as America was concerned, it did not involve itself with the Anglo-French discussions with Russia but monitored the activities of Royal Dutch Shell Company insofar as its interests might conflict with those of Standard Oil in seeking concessions from Russia.[7]

[3] DBFP 1919–1939, Ser. 1A Vol 1. No. 1. *Foreign Office Memorandum respecting the Locarno Treaties.* [C 797/1/18] Foreign Office, 10 January 1926.
[4] GM Gathorne-Hardy, *A Short History of International Affairs* (Oxford, OUP, 1934) 34.
[5] J de Launay, *Major Controversies of Contemporary History* (Oxford, Pergamon Press, 1965) 97.
[6] ibid.
[7] ibid 98.

iii. Genoa Conference

The first plenary session of the Genoa Conference was held at the Palazzo San Giorgio on 10 April 1922, Lloyd George and Barthou, who represented France, were present. In all, 29 European nations were represented. The US was represented by their ambassador in Rome.[8] The conference was unique in that it was the first time that the Soviet Union had been represented at an international conference. Lloyd George's aim was to seek treaty revisions in favour of Germany, Austria and Hungary. He proposed a 10-year Nonaggression Pact underwritten by the US. The Versailles Treaty was impossible to enforce. But the Genoa Conference was to suffer the same fate as the Peace Conference in that it was mismanaged, lacked planning and had an overcrowded agenda.[9] Wilson's ideal to eliminate secret diplomacy was ignored. Lloyd George's aims were frustrated by the Soviets, who refused to repay the Tsarist debt to one million bondholders without loans and recognition of the Soviet Union.[10] The French ruled out discussion of reparations and disarmament and frustrated Lloyd George's desire to bring Germany into the European system on a basis of equality.[11] Lord Curzon, the Foreign Secretary, requested permission to make a statement in the House of Commons as to Britain's support for German membership in the League of Nations. He was told to postpone it.[12] Lenin, who had been invited by Lloyd George, was unable to attend the conference due to his declining health and sent Chicherin as the Soviet Head of Delegation, accompanied by Maxim Litvinov, Deputy Chief Commissar for Foreign Affairs, and Krasim.[13] Chicherin was given comprehensive instructions by Lenin and affirmed that Russia was:

> fully prepared to play her part in solving the problems before the Conference, with all the means within her power- and those are means are not inconsiderable.[14]

He confirmed that Russia would collaborate with western industrial interests by setting up a Commission for this purpose. He proposed a general reduction in armaments and a new settlement based on equality between victors and vanquished.[15] But Russia would not repay the Allied loans unless consideration was given to Russian claims for compensation for damage caused by the Allied military interventions in 1918 and 1919. Despite this, Lloyd George was able to obtain a concession for Royal Dutch Shell to exploit Russian oil deposits in the Caucasus. This did not please the Americans who had long supported the interests of Standard Oil. The US demanded equal rights with Britain. Just as America and Britain were divided by their oil interests, Germany was restoring relations with its old enemy, Russia, resulting in the Treaty of Rapallo.[16] This entailed

[8] ibid 101.

[9] Z Steiner, *The Lights That Failed* (Oxford, OUP, 2007) 211.

[10] ibid.

[11] ibid 212.

[12] DBFP 1919–1939, Ser. 1 Vol. XX. No. 66. *Lord Curzon to British Delegation at Genoa.* [C 6544/6347/66] Foreign Office, 3 May 1922.

[13] Russian Soviet diplomat, Ambassador to France,1924 and in 1925 Ambassador to Britain.

[14] J de Launay, *Major Controversies of Contemporary History* (Oxford, Pergamon Press, 1965) 102. And see: A Giannini, *Les documents de la conference de Genes* (Rome, 1922).

[15] Z Steiner, *The Lights That Failed* (Oxford, OUP, 2007) 164.

[16] This association between old enemies benefitted Germany in its rearmament avoiding Versailles inhibitions on military training whereby 18 German officers served in the All-Russian General Headquarters.

a mutual renunciation of claims and the extension of most favoured nation status in commercial relations.[17]

The outcome of the Genoa conference was an estrangement between America and Britain and between Britain, France and Belgium. There was a final impasse when Chicherin offered compensation at 18 milliard gold roubles for the Tsarist debt, provided the Allies compensated Russia for the intervention in 1919 for 30 milliard gold roubles. The Genoa Conference was continued at The Hague from 15 June–22 July 1922, but it did not resolve the reparation problem.

iv. Moratorium on Reparations and the Estrangement of Britain and France

On 24 June 1922 the German minister Rathenau was assassinated by the nationalists in Germany. On 12 July 1922 the German Chancellor Cuno confirmed that Germany was unable to pay its war debt in accordance with the 1921 agreements. Spiralling inflation was beginning to take effect in Germany, and Cuno requested a six-month moratorium. Germany could not afford two billion gold marks per year ($500,000) plus 26 per cent of the value of its exports.[18] President Poincaré did not agree; he wanted strict adherence to the letter of the legal obligations of payment. He counselled Lloyd George, and it was agreed with him that there could be a moratorium provided that the Ruhr mines were controlled by the Allies.[19] An Anglo-French conference was convened in London in August 1922 but failed to settle differences between Lloyd George and Poincaré. Lloyd George asked Poincaré to pay the French war debt to Britain, but Poincaré refused. Lloyd George's government was defeated in the October elections; he was replaced by the conservative Bonar Law. Law met Poincaré on 9 December 1922, but no agreement was reached. Poincaré held fast to his 'no moratorium without security'.

On 10 December 1922, Sir Eyre Crowe cabled Lord Curzon at the Lausanne Conference[20] confirming a meeting between the Allied Prime Ministers who met in conference on 9 December 1922 and again the following day.[21] It was generally agreed that it would be useless to send delegates to the proposed Brussels conference unless a common policy could be agreed. The Belgian Prime Minister suggested there be a connection between reparations and Allied debts; a moratorium; and finally a reduction of the total reparations debt.[22] The French were insisting on the occupation of Essen and Bochum by the Allies and suggesting a further meeting in Paris in January.[23] Bonar

German naval officers were reported in Kronstadt and German agents were identified in Poland, Romania, and Czechoslovakia. DBFP 1919–1939 Ser. 1. Vol. XX. No. 501. *Rennie (Helsingfors) to Lord Curzon.* 30 May 1922.

[17] Z Steiner, *The Lights That Failed* (Oxford, OUP, 2007) 164.

[18] G. Hodgson, *The Colonel, The Life and Times of Henry Stimson 1867-1950* (New York, Alfred A Knopf, 1990) 194.

[19] J de Launay, *Major Controversies of Contemporary History* (Oxford, Pergamon Press, 1965) 105.

[20] Lausanne Peace Conference of 1922–1923, which led to the consolidation of the Turkish Republic.

[21] DBFP 1919–39 First Series. Vol XX. 317. No. 133 *Sir Eyre Cowe to Marques Curzon* 10 December 1922.

[22] ibid Vol. XX. 317–318. No. 132 *Sir Eyre Cowe to Marques Curzon.* 10 December 1922.

[23] ibid Vol. XX. 316. No. 132 *Sir Eyre Cowe to Marques Curzon.* 10 December 1922.

Law proposed that if there was agreement on reparations, Britain would be prepared to reduce the Allied debts due to Britain even if that left Britain indebted to the US.[24] Poincaré welcomed his proposal, as the French people were subject to increased taxes because of German default. Questions arose as to reparations and inter-Allied debts, stabilisation of the Deutsche mark and a moratorium subject to guarantees and pledges. Mussolini suggested reducing German reparations to 50 milliards gold marks; a two-year moratorium; a loan of three to four million gold marks to be utilised partly to stabilise the mark and partly for payments to Allies during the period of the moratorium; revenue pledges to be taken over as security for the loan; deliveries in kind to continue; and the Reparation Commission and Committee of Guarantees to control the method of German internal reforms. The discussions unfortunately reached an impasse when Poincaré suggested that French forces would occupy Essen and Bochum if Germany insisted on a French moratorium after 15 January 1923. By such means of coercion, Poincaré promised that whatever payment was received would be placed at the disposal of the allies. The occupation was to be a guarantee that payment would be made.[25] The meeting was adjourned to 2 January 1923. The debt owed to Britain by Germany and the Allies amounted to £3,400,000,000.[26] In a note to the Secretary of State for the Colonies, the Governor General of South Africa advised that the war debts should be used as leverage against French occupation of the Rhineland 'to secure policy of real appeasement in the Empire'. Reparations, he said, should be reduced to ensure stability of the Deutsche mark.[27]

v. The Rhineland and Reparations

Poincaré wished to occupy Essen and Bochum, but he hesitated for legal reasons. The Powers reconvened on 2 January in Paris to further consider the German default. Despite objection by Britain, three French divisions, with the support of Italian, French, and Belgian engineers, took control of the mines and steelworks on 11 January 1923. In spite of vehement protests and some sabotage the trams ran and the factories produced.[28] Coercion worked in that DM 364,000,000 was paid.[29] The incursion and occupation of the Rhineland favoured the so-called Rheinist Movement, whereby the Rhineland would become independent of Germany with the support of Poincaré and a number of French senior officers, including Joffre, Foch, d'Esperey, Marchand, Weygand and Mangin. The movement was led by Dr Dorten.[30] Dorten wrote:[31]

> The birth of world peace can only take place only on the Rhine and only as guaranteed by the Rhinelanders. The disturber of peace upon the Rhine is Prussia. War is her national industry, and it is she who forces the German people, who are naturally peace loving, ever anew to

[24] ibid Vol. XX. 317. No. 132 *Sir Eyre Cowe to Marques Curzon.* 10 December 1922.
[25] ibid Vol. XX. 318. No. 132 *Sir Eyre Cowe to Marques Curzon.* 10 December 1922.
[26] ibid Vol. XX. 99 No. 45 *The Earl of Balfour to the Count de Saint-Aulaire.* 1 August 1922.
[27] ibid Vol. XX. 323. No. 140. *Governor General of South Africa to Secretary of State for the Colonies.* 13 December 1922.
[28] J de Launay, *Major Controversies of Contemporary History* (Oxford, Pergamon Press, 1965) 106.
[29] ibid 107.
[30] Jibid 108.
[31] HA Dorten, 'The Rhineland Movement' (1925) 3(3) *Foreign Affairs* 399–410.

> 'appeal to the sword.' We Rhinelanders are Germans, but we are not Prussians. Take Prussia off the Rhine and you will see that a Germany freed from Prussian leadership is quite capable of coming to a lasting understanding with France. In domestic politics the creation of a true league of German states, and in foreign politics the creation of an agreement with France-two ways to the ultimate goal of a United States of Europe-this is the ultimate goal of the Rhinelanders.

The movement gained support from Adenauer, the Burgomaster of Cologne, and Poincaré. Neither Britain nor Belgium supported this idea. They supported a united Germany and not a French corridor along the Rhine from Prüm to Coblenz.[32] The separatist Leo Deckers proclaimed Rhineland independence on 21 October 1923 at Aix la Chapelle. Dr Josef Matthes, a leader of the Rhineland Movement, took power in Coblenz. Deckers and Matthes then divided the territory. Matthes, with French collaboration, tried to take the south, but Belgian forces intervened. The British then pressed the French High Commissioner, who summoned Dr Dorten and ordered him to evacuate all occupied public buildings by Rhineland separatists. Dorten was then arrested. His followers were attacked at Pirmasens, and 40 separatists were killed.[33] The French forces stood by observing 'strict neutrality'. Elsewhere in the Reich, there were tensions between communists in Saxony and monarchists in Bavaria, with their neighbour state Thuringia appealing to Berlin for protection.[34]

Despite the obvious economic fact that without the resources Germany could not meet reparations or its debts, the currency collapsed in 1924. As a result of this, the Dawes Plan was introduced on the basis that Germany would pay a flat rate of 2.5 billion marks in gold per year after five years.[35] Under the plan, Germany was loaned £40 million ($160 million) at 7 per cent interest per annum. Even this remission was insufficient, and another plan, the Young Plan, was proposed whereby Germany would pay £5.5 billion ($22 billion) in 60 annuities by 1988 on the condition that the occupation of the Rhineland would cease and a new loan would be granted of £70 million ($280 million) at 5.5 per cent.[36] The plan was frustrated by the Wall Street Crash. Despite all this, Germany was able to pay 11 billion gold marks between 1924 and 1931 in reparations, but it received 18 billion marks in loans, whereas Britain, which had been a creditor to its allies France and Russia, lost $240 million on reparations and debts.[37]

German dissatisfaction with the Versailles Treaty was outlined by Stresemann in a letter to Crown Prince Wilhelm of Prussia on 7 September 1925, when he cited three main objectives of German foreign policy with the intention, possibly, of winning over right-wing groups to his Locarno policy. His aims were the solution of the Rhineland problem, the protection of 10 or 12 million Germans living in the Saar, Czechoslovakia and Poland; free adjustment of the existing frontiers to annex Danzig and the Polish corridor; alteration of the frontiers of Upper Silesia; and in the long term, the union of Austria and Germany.[38] This would seem somewhat disingenuous when he was at the

[32] J de Launay, *Major Controversies of Contemporary History* (Oxford, Pergamon Press, 1965) 110.
[33] ibid 113.
[34] *TIME* Magazine Report, 29 October 1923, 12:00 AM GMT-5.
[35] G Hodgson, *The Colonel, The Life and Times of Henry Stimson 1867–1950* (New York, Alfred A Knopf 1990) 194.
[36] ibid 195.
[37] ibid 197.
[38] J de Launay, *Major Controversies of Contemporary History* (Oxford, Pergamon Press, 1965) 114.

same time proposing a rapprochement with France. Stresemann succeeded in reducing the reparations burden under the Dawes Plan, altering the 1921 Payment Schedule so that Germany would pay between 1 and 2.5 billion gold marks within five years. This was facilitated by a loan of 800 million gold marks and the evacuation of the Ruhr between July 1925 and January 1926. As an inducement to France, Germany guaranteed France's eastern frontiers and recognised Alsace-Lorraine as part of France.[39]

In January 1923, France and Belgium occupied the Ruhr and parts of the right bank of the Rhine in an attempt to force the German government to pay overdue reparations as required under the Versailles treaty. 45,000 French and 2,500 Belgian troops occupied the region. The Germans reacted with passive resistance and a general strike. The occupiers retaliated by expelling 5,000 German civil servants and railwaymen who refused to work, as well as their families, plus a further 31,850 people from other zones in the Rhineland under military occupation. Altogether over half a million people were removed from the Rhineland. German saboteurs then started reprisals against the Belgian and French occupiers and Rhineland separatists. Germany was able to exploit the Allies' differences over the occupation as neither Britain nor the US supported the occupation. Occupation was counterproductive because it simply exacerbated Germany's financial problems with miners and workers leaving and production declining. It morphed into a financial crisis to the extent that one Deutsche mark was worth \$4.2 trillion. Britain deplored the offences committed by the French and Belgians in the Rhineland and the Ruhr. With the approval of the Imperial Conference, it sought the help of its old ally, the US, on the reparation question, the *causa causans* of the Ruhr occupation. This led to the setting up of the Dawes Committee.[40]

vi. The Dawes Plan

The Reparation Commission established under the Treaty of Versailles to settle the question of reparations settled the final bill at 132 billion gold marks, amounting to \$31.5 billion in reparations to be paid by Germany. As noted, Germany defaulted in January 1923. In Germany there was hyperinflation, and the value of the German currency collapsed. The US was determined to secure repayment of more than \$10 billion, which they had loaned to the Allies. Earlier in 1922, the British government (Balfour Note) declared that it would seek reparations of wartime debt repayments from its European allies equal to its debt to the US. The Congress in the US created the United States War Debt Commission to negotiate repayment terms.[41]

In late 1923 there was an impasse over reparations. Britain's Foreign Secretary, Lord Curzon, organised an international expert commission chaired by Charles Dawes[42] to recommend a new scheme. The scheme known as the Dawes Plan enabled Germany to

[39] ibid 117.

[40] DBFP 1919–1939, Ser. 1A. Vol 1. No. 1. *Foreign Office Memorandum respecting the Locarno Treaties.* [C 797/1/18] Foreign Office, 10 January 1926.

[41] The Dawes Plan, the Young Plan, German Reparations and Inter-Allied War Debts (Office of the Historian Milestones 1921–1936, Washington, DC).

[42] General Charles Dawes, an American Chicago banker and future US Vice President was chairman of the Committee of Experts appointed by the Reparation Commission on 30 November 1923 'to consider the means of balancing the budget and the measures to be taken to stabilise the currency of Germany'.

obtain American credit to pay off British and French reparations. Britain and France, in receipt of those funds, could then repay some of their debt owed to America. France agreed to evacuate the Ruhr. This in turn led to the Locarno Pact in October 1925.[43]

The Reparations Commission formed a committee to review this, headed by Charles Dawes. His committee presented its proposals on 9 April 1924, under which Germany would make reduced reparations payments, increasing when its economy improved. A draft agreement proposed by the Committee of Experts was formally adopted and signed by the Reparation Commission and the German government on 9 August 1924.[44] It was completed by the London Agreements of 30 August 1924 between the Allied governments and Germany.[45] The debt was unliquidated to be determined later. Germany's economic policy was redirected under foreign supervision. A new currency, the Reichsmark, was adopted. Belgium and France evacuated the Ruhr and foreign banks loaned $200,000,000 to encourage economic stabilisation. JP Morgan floated the loan on US market, which was oversubscribed. US banks continued to lend money to Germany to enable it to discharge its reparation debts to Britain and France. In turn, Britain and France utilised these payments to service their war debts to the US.[46]

vii. The Tribunal for the Interpretation of the Dawes Plan

To resolve disputes under the Dawes Plan, a tribunal was instituted under an agreement between the Reparation Commission and the German government, signed in London on 9 August 1924, 'for the carrying out of the Report of the First Committee of Experts'. A clause in that agreement provided that:[47]

> any dispute that might arise between the German Government and the Reparation Commission with regard to the interpretation … of the Experts' Plan should be submitted to arbitration in accordance with the methods to be fixed and subject to the conditions to be determined by the London Conference.

On 30 August 1924, the Allied governments and the German government agreed on the process for the settlement of disputes that:

> all disputes which may arise between the Reparation Commission and Germany with regard to the interpretation of … the Experts' Plan shall be submitted for decision to three arbitrators appointed for five years; one by the Reparation Commission, one by the German Government and the third, who shall act as President, by agreement between the Reparation Commission and the German Government or, failing such agreement, by the President for the time being of the Permanent Court of International Justice.[48]

The procedure was governed by the provisions of the Hague Convention of 1907 on the Pacific Settlement of International Disputes. The tribunal was originally constituted with one arbitrator from each side and a chairman. The arrangement was modified

[43] A Sharp, *Versailles. A Centennial Perspective* (London, Haus Publishing, 2018) 42.
[44] See Cmd. 2270 of 1924.
[45] See Cmd. 2259 of 1924.
[46] The Dawes Plan, the Young Plan, German Reparations and Inter-Allied War Debts (Office of the Historian Milestones 1921–1936, Washington, DC).
[47] JF Williams, 'The Tribunal for the Interpretation of the Dawes Plan' (1928) 22 *AJIL* 797. Reproduced with permission of The Licensor through PLSclear.
[48] ibid.

in June 1925 by adding two additional members, nationals of those countries which had been neutral during the war. They were to be appointed in each case by agreement between the Reparation Commission and the German government or, failing agreement, by the President of the Permanent Court. In all cases a Chairman or President was to be an American citizen.[49]

The tribunal applied its own interpretation in the three cases given in this study without prescribing any rules of interpretation or any general principles. It simply applied the Expert's Plan interpreted broadly so it would simply be interpreted as a business plan, albeit the plan placed certain interpretations on the Versailles Treaty. The plan in this case took precedence.[50]

a. Interpretation of London Agreement of 9 August 1924 (Germany, Reparation Commission)[51]

On 30 November 1923, the Committee of Experts (Dawes Committee) was invited by the Reparation Commission (conforming to Article 234 Treaty of Versailles) to consider the means of balancing the budget and the measures to be taken to stabilise the currency of Germany. On 9 April 1924, the committee presented its report to the Reparation Commission. Several of the Allied and Associated governments accepted the report as a basis for negotiations. As a result, arrangements were made between the Reparation Commission and the German government for putting the Experts' Plan into operation. Membership of the Tribunal[52] included Mr Walter P Cooke of Buffalo, US; Mr Marc Wallenberg of Stockholm; Mr AG Kröller of The Hague; Mr Rist of Paris; and Mr Mendelssohn-Bartholdy of Hamburg. The seat of the Arbitral tribunal was The Hague.

Eight questions for referral were agreed upon between the parties enquiring whether the Dawes Plan annuities (DPA) comprised certain payments to be made by Germany under the peace treaties. Questions II and VI were resolved between the parties. Arguments were made on 11 March 1926 and the following days. The Polish government was represented before the tribunal as to its interest in Questions III and V. All referral questions related to the annuities prescribed by the DPA for the discharge of reparation obligations and other pecuniary liabilities that Germany was required to pay under the Treaty of Versailles. Payments were payable to the Agent General for Reparation Payments:[53]

I. The transfers to be made by Germany to France in pursuance of Article 77 of the Treaty of Versailles, following a decision of the Council of the League of Nations dated the 21st June, 1921, in respect of social insurance funds relating to Alsace-Lorraine;
II. The transfers to be made by Germany to Belgium in pursuance of Article 312 of the Treaty of Versailles and the Agreement of the 9th July, 1920, between Germany and Belgium in respect of social insurance funds relating to territories ceded by Germany to Belgium;

[49] ibid 798.
[50] ibid 800.
[51] Vol II, 873–899 *Reports of International Arbitral Awards* 24 March 1926, 29 January 1927, 29 May 1928. United Nations.
[52] Included Annex II A, signed on 30 August 1924.
[53] Reports of International Arbitral Awards 24 March 1926, 29 January 1927, 29 May 1928 Vol II 873–899. United Nations.

III. The transfers to be made by Germany to Poland in pursuance of Article 312 of the Treaty of Versailles in respect of social insurance funds relating to Upper Silesia, the amounts of which transfers' (other than that of the miners' superannuation fund which still remains to be settled) were determined by a decision of the Council of the League of Nations dated the 9th December, 1924;
IV. Payments under Article 62 of the Treaty of Versailles in respect of civil and military pensions earned in Alsace-Lorraine on the 11th November, 1918;
V. Payments under the Agreement of the 9th January, 1920, made between the German and Polish Governments in pursuance of Article 92 of the Treaty of Versailles, in respect of civil and military pensions;
VI. Restitution of Belgian railway rolling stock effected by Germany
VII. Restitutions in specie under Article 238 of the Treaty of Versailles of objects of every nature or securities
VIII. The sum of £14,185.9.8 owing by Germany to Great Britain as payment for coal supplied in December 1918 and January 1919 to the steamship Jerusalem.

Having deliberated on these matters, the tribunal decided:[54]

A. As between the Reparation Commission representing the Allied Governments signatory to the Final Protocol of the London Conference on the one hand, and Germany on the other, the annuities prescribed by the Experts' Plan comprise:

   1. The transfers to be made by Germany to France in pursuance of Article 77 of the Treaty of Versailles, following a decision of the Council of the League of Nations dated the 21 June 1921, in respect of social insurance funds relating to Alsace-Lorraine;
   2. The Transfers to be made by Germany to Poland in pursuance of Article 312 of the Treaty of Versailles in respect of social insurance funds relating to Upper Silesia, the amounts of which transfers (other than that of the miners' superannuation fund which still remains to be settled) were determined by a decision of the Council of the League of Nations dated the 9 December 1924;
   3. Payments under Article 62 of the Treaty of Versailles in respect of civil and military pensions earned in Alsace-Lorraine on the 11 November 1918.

B. The decision stated under (2) above is also given as between the German Government and the Polish Government.

C. On the other hand, the said annuities do not comprise:

   1. Restitutions in specie under Article 238 of the Treaty of Versailles of objects of every nature or securities, and
   2. The sum of £14,185.9.8 owing by Germany to Great Britain as payment for coal supplied in December 1918 and January 1919 to the steamship *Jerusalem.*

D. The Tribunal is unable at present to give a decision on the questions whether or not, as between the Reparation Commission and the German Government, and as between the German and the Polish Governments, the said annuities comprise payments under the Agreement of the 9 January 1920 made between the German and Polish Governments in pursuance of Article 92 of the Treaty of Versailles, in respect of civil and military pensions.

[54] Reports International Arbitral Awards24 March 1926, 29 January 1927, 29 May 1928 Vol II 877–878. United Nations.

b. Second Award Delivered on January 29, 1927

In its second Award, the tribunal dealt with the question of whether the annuities prescribed by the Experts' Plan payable by Germany to the Agent General for Reparation Payments included compensation paid by the German Reich to German nationals in respect of the retention, liquidation or transfer of their property, rights or interests, such payments being made under the Treaty of Versailles.[55] This tribunal held that the annuities prescribed by the Experts' Plan did not comprise:

> Compensation paid since the 1 September 1924, or which may be paid in the future by the Germany to its nationals in respect of the retention, liquidation or transfer of their property, rights or interests, from the date on which such measures were taken.

This they held were payments made under the Treaty of Versailles as to Articles 297(i), 74, 145, and 156 (2nd paragraph) read with paragraph 2 of the Protocol signed at Versailles on 28 June 1919.[56]

c. Third Award Delivered on 29 May 1928

In this arbitration the tribunal held that Germany was not entitled to a credit against the Dawes annuities for the value of German property, rights and interests liquidated in Allied or Associated countries under Article 297 the Treaty of Versailles, or under that article combined with Article 243 taking into account: (a) the final balances that might be due to Germany regarding Alsace-Lorraine, the Economic clauses of the Treaty Sections III and IV of Part X; (b) amounts due to Germany in respect of transfers under Section IV (Saar Basin) of Part III (Political Clauses for Europe), Part IX (Financial Clauses), and Part XII (Ports, Waterways and Railways); (c) amounts which in the judgment of the Reparation Commission should be credited to Germany on account of any other transfers under the present Treaty of property, rights, concessions or other interests.

The tribunal held[57] that the experts who formulated the Dawes Plan sought means of collecting Germany's debt to the Allies under the Treaty of Versailles without allowing these questions to unbalance the German budget or render German currency unstable. The liquidation of German property, rights and interests in the territories of Allied or Associated states did not directly affect the equilibrium of the German budget. The compensation that Germany was obliged to pay to her nationals in respect of such

[55] Under Art 74, the French government reserved the right to retain and liquidate all the property, rights and interests which German nationals or societies controlled by Germany possessed in the Alsace and Lorraine. Under Art 145 the German government transferred the shares it held in the State Bank of Morocco, their value being determined by the Reparation Commission and set off against reparations payable by Germany. The German government would then indemnify the bank's German customers. Under Art 156, Germany surrendered to Japan all her rights, title and privileges particularly those concerning the territory of Kiaochow, railways, mines, and submarine cables as well as its rights in the Tsingtao-Tsinanfu Railway, as well as German state submarine cables from Tsingtao to Shanghai and from Tsingtao to Chefoo. Article 297 concerned restoration of property rights and interests for those dispossessed by the war.

[56] Arbitral Tribunal of Interpretation Created Under the Provisions Of Annex II To The London Agreement of August 9, 1924, Between The Reparation Commission And The German Government Award No. II. Delivered on 29 January 1927 (1927) 21 *AJIL* 344. Reproduced with permission of The Licensor through PLSclear.

[57] ibid (1928) 22 *AJIL* 913. Reproduced with permission of The Licensor through PLSclear.

liquidated property was considered as part of Germany's domestic needs (Award No. II, above). They explained that the indirect connection of such compensation payments to the German budget did not justify the inclusion of the liquidation proceeds in the Dawes annuities. Nor did the liquidation affect the stability of German currency, for it did not call for any conversion of German currency into any other currency or for the transfer of goods from Germany into any other country. The proceeds of such liquidated property were not included expressly or by reasonable implication in the sources of revenue provided by the Dawes Plan for raising the amount of the annuities. They were not realised in German currency, and they were not paid into the bank of issue to the credit of the Agent for Reparation Payments. Such proceeds were not, therefore, to be included in the annuities either as a contribution to the annuities or as the basis for a withdrawal from the annuities.

The fundamental point in these cases was that the experts were invited by the Reparation Commission to consider the means of balancing the German budget and the measures to be taken to stabilise the German currency. This was their underlying concern and Germany's obligation to the Allies under the Treaty of Versailles. They were concerned with the practical means of recovering this debt, the payment of which they considered Germany's primary moral obligation, without unbalancing the budget or making the German currency unstable. These cases must be seen in the light of that overriding objective so that Germany had a viable economy and was able to meet her liabilities.

d. Effect of Dawes Plan Tribunal

Over the course of its deliberations, the tribunal decided the following matters in favour of the German government: (1) the transfers of social insurance funds representing moneys earmarked under the German law of social insurance in respect of the working population of Alsace-Lorraine; (2) the transfer of the similar funds relating to Upper Silesia; and (3) the payments in respect of civil and military pensions earned in Alsace-Lorraine, which were comprised in the annuities provided for by the plan.[58]

The tribunal decided that the following did not comprise annuities and thus could not be deducted from the sum of reparations payable by the German government:

(1) the return of objects[59] belonging to Allied nationals taken out of occupied territories during the war and returned by way of restitution under Article 238 of the Treaty of Versailles;
(2) an amount owing by Germany to Great Britain for coal supplied during the armistice to a German hospital ship (these decisions were included in the first arbitration before the tribunal held in March 1926);
(3) the amounts payable by the German government to German nationals as compensation for private property sequestrated or liquidated under the Treaty of Versailles (Second decision, January 1927);

[58] JF Wiliams, 'The Tribunal for The Interpretation of The Dawes Plan' British Legal Representative on The Reparation Commission (1928) 22 *AJIL* 797. Reproduced with permission of The Licensor through PLSclear.

[59] These included under Art 238 restitution in cash of cash taken away, seized or sequestrated, and also restitution of animals, objects of every nature and securities taken away, seized or sequestrated, in the cases in which it proves possible to identify them in territory belonging to Germany or her allies.

(4) The tribunal also decided that the German government was not to set off against annuities as part of the reparations due the value of German private property liquidated or sequestrated under the Treaty of Versailles so far as such property had been brought into account under the treaty after the date when the Dawes Plan went into force (1 September 1924). (Third decision, May 1928).

In the second Award (1927), it was decided that the annuities were to be paid in full to the Allied and Associated Powers and that payments by the German government to German nationals could not be considered.

In the third Award, decided in 1928, the decision was equally based on a careful examination of the language used in the relevant passages of the Dawes Plan as well as the machinery which the plan instituted and of its general purpose and spirit.

The second Award would, had it been given in favour of Germany, have reduced the amount of the DPA by approximately £450,000,000[60] – a much larger sum, so far as was known at that time, than had ever been at issue in any lawsuit, national or international. In the case of the Alabama, the Award was $15,000,000 in gold.[61]

B. Diplomatic Assessment and Action

i. *The Nicolson Memorandum*

The Foreign Office was aware of the increasing tensions between former Allies and Germany's sense of grievance requiring a review of the Treaty of Versailles. In his Memorandum of 20 February 1925, Harold Nicolson saw the 'most menacing of all uncertainties' as Russia. Russia had disappeared from the European concert, which hung 'as a storm cloud upon the Eastern horizon of Europe impending, imponderable, but for the present detached'. Russia in his opinion and in that of Sir Eyre Crowe, Sir Austin Chamberlain and the Foreign Office at that time, was 'the most menacing of all our uncertainties', and it was because of Russia that the policy of security had to be addressed.[62]

In his Memorandum, Harold Nicolson carefully analysed the postwar position. As to potential enemies, he wrote:[63]

> All our late enemies continue full of resentment at what they have lost; all our late Allies are fearful of losing what they have won. One-half of Europe is dangerously angry; the other half is dangerously afraid. The friction between these inflamed emotions is incessant, and acts as some septic irritant, poisoning the wounds which are yet unhealed. Fear begets provocation,

[60] £100,000,000 in 1927 is equivalent in purchasing power to about £7,872,979,284.99 as in 2024, an increase of £7,772,979,284.99 over 97 years. Taking the pound at an average inflation rate of 4.60% per year between 1927 and today, producing a cumulative price increase of 7,772.98%.

[61] If the gold price in 1873 was $18.94 and in 2024 it was $2,294, (121.11 times greater) then the Alabama Award equate to $1,816,650,000 so less than the Reparations Awards. See: MP Reynolds *Instruments of Peacemaking 1870-1914* (Oxford, Hart Publishing, 2021).

[62] DBFP 1919–1939 Ser. 1. Vol 27: *Memorandum by Mr. Nicolson on British Policy considered in relation to the European Situation; prepared in pursuance of directions from the Secretary of State.* 20 February 1925.

[63] ibid 2.

> armaments, secret alliances, ill-treatment of minorities; these in their turn beget a greater hatred and stimulate a desire for revenge, whereby fear is intensified, and its consequences are enhanced. The vicious circle is thus established.

In essence he forecast what was to come: the indications were apparent, and the challenge had to be met by policy. At this time, opinion in Austria was in favour of unity with Germany; it changed later. As to Germany, it had great military and chemical potential and sooner or later would become a very powerful military factor. Germany had to re-establish its economic and financial position, and the means of doing so was the Dawes Plan and compliance with the Versailles Treaty. There were, however, two problems. The first was the Polish corridor, and the second was the partition of Silesia: issues that were to raise their head again in 1939.

ii. Poland

Under the Treaty of Versailles, Poland was restored to independence and, at the expense of Germany, given access to the sea and the use of the port of Danzig. This meant that Germany was severed from East Prussia by the 'Polish corridor'. Danzig was declared a Free City under the protection of the League of Nations. 94 per cent of the population was German. Special rights were secured for Poland, including control of foreign affairs, customs and external railway communications, and the port was separately administered for Polish trade and shipping.[64] A plebiscite was held in Upper Silesia amid turmoil and uproar. Poland polled 40 per cent of the total votes and eventually gained, by determination of the League of Nations, a considerable tract of territory containing at least 80 per cent of the developed and 95 per cent of the undeveloped mineral wealth of Silesia, as well as large enclaves inhabited by clear German majorities. Nicolson commented:[65]

> There is obviously a danger that a nation of over 60 millions will not permanently acquiesce in being thus sundered from the province which was the cradle of the Prussian State, or in being deprived of those mineral resources on which the national prosperity was largely based.

Again, Nicolson foretold the resentment that would convert to a casus belli in 1939.

iii. France

Nicolson carefully analysed the attitude of France, which was afraid of Germany. It was its neighbour; it had been twice invaded by Germany, and the birth rate of France was declining as Germany's was increasing. Marshal Foch, the victor of 1918, insisted on a Rhine boundary. A Treaty of Guarantee was discussed by Britain and the US but rejected by the latter and lapsed. French troops occupied the Rhineland, and an assurance was given under Articles 42 and 43 that any violation of the provisions for the

[64] ibid.
[65] ibid.

demilitarisation of the Rhineland would be considered an act of war.[66] The Articles provided:

> LEFT BANK OF THE RHINE.
>
> ARTICLE 42.
>
> Germany is forbidden to maintain or construct any fortifications either on the left bank of the Rhine or on the right bank to the west of a line drawn 50 kilometres to the East of the Rhine.
>
> ARTICLE 43
>
> In the area defined above the maintenance and the assembly of armed forces, either permanently or temporarily, and military manoeuvres of any kind, as well as the upkeep of all permanent works for mobilization, are in the same way forbidden.

In addition, Germany was to be disarmed by an Allied Commission as a provisional measure. France was not secure, and consequently, as Nicolson wrote, it sought alternative means due to lack of manpower by enlisting African and colonial troops. France then devised the *Little Entente*, small states neighbouring Germany: Czechoslovakia, Yugoslavia, and Romania. They were not dependable and became more of a liability to France. Such insecurity inspired the French government to press upon the Fifth Assembly of the League of Nations the acceptance of the Protocol for the Pacific Settlement of International Disputes. Britain was unlikely to support this.[67]

iv. Britain and the Dominions

Nicolson ruled out isolationism and gave a good reason to reject it as a policy:[68]

> That the policy known as 'splendid isolation' is not today a practicable policy. For America, powerful and aloof, such a course is still, perhaps, a possibility. For the British Empire no such escape is feasible. History and economics show that isolation in present conditions spells danger, vulnerability and impotence. Geography and aeronautics show that isolation is not in our case a scientific fact.

Nicolson then explained the needs for the defence of Britain and the individual Dominions, as well as the defence of the sea communications between Britain and the individual Dominions. The defence of Britain necessitated that no single Power would be able to occupy or to dominate all the Channel and the North Sea ports; that the hostility of France, Belgium, Holland, Germany and Denmark, who possessed these ports, or of any of those countries, and the hostility of any combination of them was to be avoided; that no third Power at war with France or Belgium should be allowed to invade those countries to threaten the status quo of the Channel ports, or of such French and Belgian territory as would expose Britain to aerial invasion and that it was necessary for Britain to reach some understanding with France and Belgium to guarantee that these territories would not fall into other hands.[69]

[66] ibid 3.
[67] ibid.
[68] ibid 4.
[69] ibid 5.

As to British interests as affecting European security, it was necessary to guarantee to France and Belgium the possession of their present territory. Britain should define publicly what it recognised privately as an essential condition of the future existence of the British Empire. Nicolson opined that it was 'doubtful whether even in 1914 Germany would have risked the Great War had she known for certain that the British Empire would come to France's assistance'. Therefore, it could be deterred by this being declared.[70] This approach would alleviate French uncertainty and concerns over the Rhineland and any need for the Little Entente, resulting in financial stabilisation and debt repayment. It would encourage the smaller countries in Europe to make peace with their neighbours as well as the eventual inclusion of Germany within security guarantees. He also believed, as did his colleagues, that if the concert of Europe could thus gradually be recreated, saner councils would prevail. It was conceivable, especially if Germany, with French goodwill, became a member of the League of Nations and obtained a permanent seat in the Council, that it might become possible to revise by European agreement the dangerous conditions involved in the Silesian settlement and the Polish corridor.[71]

The problem was that France had to be placated, without which no concert of Europe was possible; this required an alliance.

Nicolson thus concluded:[72]

> The essential interests of Imperial Defence are thus closely related to a policy of European security. The first hope of stability in Europe lies in a new entente between the British Empire and France.

Nicolson's views regarding security guarantees were the foundation for the Treaties of Mutual Guarantees at Locarno.

v. *Locarno Conference 1925 and Treaties of Mutual Guarantee*

In 1917 the French government considered detaching from Germany the territories west of the Rhine so that the Rhine could form a strategic line of defence. At the end of the war, France proposed that the Allies permanently occupy the Rhineland placing the political, military and economic systems under Allied control.[73] Britain and the US rejected the scheme first because it disregarded President Wilson's Fourteen Points, and second, it created an Alsace-Lorraine difficulty and would undermine any hope of a permanent peaceful settlement in Europe. France was persuaded to withdraw the idea.[74] In return, she obtained the following consolation in the peace settlement:[75]

> (a) Treaties of Guarantee, under which Great Britain and the United States pledged themselves, in the event of any unprovoked aggression on the part of Germany, to come immediately to France's assistance.

[70] See: ch 4, British *démarche* on 21 May 1938 warning Germany that Britain might be involved in any war over Czechoslovakia if France was involved.

[71] DBFP 1919–1939 Ser. 1. Vol 27: *Memorandum by Mr. Nicolson on British Policy.* 20 February 1925. 5–6.

[72] ibid 6.

[73] DBFP 1919–1939, Ser. 1A Vol 1. No. 1. *Foreign Office Memorandum respecting the Locarno Treaties.* [C 797/1/18] Foreign Office, 10 January 1926. 9.

[74] ibid 10.

[75] ibid.

(b) The occupation of the Rhineland for a period of fifteen years (evacuation to be in three stages subject to the faithful execution of the treaty by Germany, and, in the case of the third stage, subject also to the existence of adequate guarantees of French security).
(c) The demilitarisation of German territory on the left bank of the Rhine and of a strip on the right bank, coupled with an assurance under article 44 of the Treaty of Versailles that any violation by Germany of the demilitarisation provisions would be considered as an act of war.
(d) The disarmament of Germany under the supervision of an Allied commission.

The critical issue was the treaties of guarantee, which would give France security. Marshal Foch[76] pointed out at the time that safeguards (b) and (d) were but temporary, and (c) was of uncertain effect. The failure to ratify the guarantee treaties was a most serious blow to France, which felt betrayed. Not only had they been refused the Rhine barrier, but they had also been deprived of any serious consideration for withdrawing their scheme.[77] Britain rejected the idea of an Anglo-French alliance, unwilling to undertake further obligations. The unfortunate result was that France tried to ensure a right to occupy the Rhineland by giving extraneous arguments based on the vague terms of the Treaty of Versailles and making onerous demands on Germany, causing non-compliance followed by occupation.[78] France then created the Little Entente, a drain on French resources, which 'created added apprehension and increased liability'.[79] The basis for the Little Entente was the Treaties of Trianon and Neuilly, signed on 27 November 1919 and 4 June 1920, reinforced by the Treaties of Mutual Guarantee.[80]

Not only did France bear resentment, but also her enemy. The obvious bitterness of Germany was echoed by Stresemann, the German Chancellor, who wanted restoration of former territory excluded by the Versailles Treaty; in particular, Upper Silesia, Danzig and Eupen-Malmédy (a region of Belgium in the province of Liège ceded by Germany in 1919). Dr Franck was reported as saying that Germany wanted to seek League of Nations permission for the incorporation of Austria 'within a greater economic area'.[81] This was contrary to the policy of the Little Entente because the foreign ministers of the Little Entente agreed on a policy of financial reconstruction of Austria's finances and the need to maintain the peace treaties. They were against any union of Austria and Germany.[82]

Aristide Briand[83] wanted to maintain the status quo of Versailles, whilst Britain wanted to prevent German rearmament.[84] France, without any guarantees from Britain or America,

[76] Marshal Foch was appointed Allied Commander-in-Chief in April 1918. In January 1920, he was appointed President of the Allied Military Committee of Versailles instituted '(a) to act as advisory council to the Allied and Associated Governments in military questions arising out of the execution of the Treaty of Peace with Germany. (b) to carry into execution the orders given it by the Allied and Associated Powers in matters concerning the Commissions of Control and the Allied forces of occupation in the Rhineland and Plebiscite areas.'

[77] DBFP 1919–1939, Ser. 1A. Vol 1. No. 1. *Foreign Office Memorandum respecting the Locarno Treaties.* [C 797/1/18] Foreign Office, 10 January 1926. 11.

[78] ibid.

[79] ibid 12.

[80] *Survey of 1925*, The Royal Institute of International Affairs, Part II.D. 250.

[81] *The Times*, 22 January 1925.

[82] *Survey of 1925*, The Royal Institute of International Affairs, Part II.D. 252.

[83] Briand was a proponent of a Federal Europe which was the idea at that time of Count Coudenhove-Kalergi who founded the Pan European Union.

[84] A Sharp, *Versailles. A Centennial Perspective* (London, Haus Publishing, 2018) 43.

had no alternative other than to accept the conciliatory approach of its former allies and the Versailles revision, which would also give comfort to the fledgling Weimar democracy.[85] The common aim however of Stresemann, Austin Chamberlain, Briand, Vandervelde and Mussolini was to guarantee the frontiers of all signatories to the Versailles Treaty and replace that treaty with a negotiated peace. This resulted in a revision of the Treaty of Versailles by the Treaty of Locarno, a treaty of mutual guarantee commonly called the Security Pact. It led a year later to Germany joining the League of Nations on 4 September 1926.[86] Representatives of Germany, Belgium, France, Britain, Italy, Poland, and Czechoslovakia agreed on a process for the peaceful 'settlement of disputes of every nature which might eventually arise between them'. Discussions were held between 5 and 16 October 1925. They resulted in several treaties. A treaty between Germany, Belgium, France, Britain, and Italy; an Arbitration Convention between Germany and Belgium; an Arbitration Convention between Germany and France; an Arbitration treaty between Germany and Poland; and an Arbitration treaty between Germany and Czechoslovakia. It was intended that these treaties would relax tension in Europe, solve economic and political problems, and strengthen peace and security. It would also hasten disarmament as provided for in Article 8 of the Covenant of the League of Nations.[87]

The treaty was subject to serious discussion at the Foreign Office between the legal advisers of the German, Belgian, British, French and Italian governments from 1 September to 4 September 1925. Of special interest to Britain was the third paragraph of the Preamble and the reference to the abrogation of the Belgian treaties of 1839. This was introduced to meet the criticism that a special treaty to guarantee that part of the Versailles settlement which related to the Rhineland area and the western frontiers of Germany would necessarily weaken another part of the treaty which related to the arrangements on the eastern frontiers of Germany. A special guarantee had for 80 years covered this territory, and its abrogation constituted a suitable opportunity to introduce a new territorial guarantee. The second part of this paragraph embodied a veiled reference to the policy so long maintained by Great Britain that her security was intimately connected with the independence and the stability of the adjacent territory on the east of the narrow seas.

vi. Treaties of Mutual Guarantee

Under the Treaty of Mutual Guarantee between Germany, Belgium, France, Britain, and Italy, the parties agreed:[88]

> Article 1. … collectively and severally to guarantee the territorial status quo of the frontiers between Germany and Belgium and between Germany and France and recognise the inviolability of those frontiers under the Treaty of Versailles 28 June 1919, and to observe articles 42 and 43[89] of that treaty concerning the demilitarised zone.

[85] J Wright, 'Locarno: A Democratic Peace?' *Review of International Studies* (2010) 36, 392–393.
[86] J de Launay, *Major Controversies of Contemporary History* (Oxford, Pergamon Press, 1965) 117.
[87] United Nations. Public Documents. The Locarno Treaties (16 October 1925.) No. 1. Final Protocol of The Locarno Conference, 1925. United Nations.
[88] ibid. Note: the wording has been changed by the author to simplify where possible the language whilst retaining its legal meaning.
[89] As above Left Bank of the Rhine.

Article 2. Germany and Belgium, and Germany and France, mutually undertake that they will in no case attack or invade each other or resort to war against each other. This would not apply if:

1. The exercise of the right of legitimate [self] defence, i.e. resistance to a violation of the undertaking contained in the previous paragraph or to a flagrant breach of articles 42 or 43 of the Treaty of Versailles, if such breach constitutes an unprovoked act of aggression and by a concentration of armed forces in the demilitarised zone immediate action is necessary.
2. Action in pursuance of article 16 of the Covenant of the League of Nations.
3. Action as the result of a decision taken by the Assembly or by the Council of the League of Nations or in pursuance of article 15, paragraph 7, of the Covenant of the League of Nations,[90] provided that in this last event the action is directed against a State which was the first to attack.

Article 3. In accordance with the undertakings under Article 2 of this treaty, Germany and Belgium and Germany and France undertake to settle by peaceful means and in the manner laid down of all questions which may arise between them and not possible of settlement by diplomacy:

Any question regarding which the parties are in conflict as to their respective rights shall be submitted to judicial decision, and the parties undertake to comply with such decision.

All other questions shall be submitted to a conciliation commission.

If the proposals of the commission were not accepted by the parties, the question would be referred to the Council of the League of Nations under Article 15 of the Covenant of the League for settlement by the League or otherwise by action of the member. The detailed arrangements for effecting such peaceful settlement were the arbitration treaties and conventions signed on 16 October 1925. Under Article 4, if one of the parties alleged that a violation of Article 2 of the treaty or a breach of Articles 42 or 43 of the Treaty of Versailles had been or was being committed, it could bring the question to the Council of the League of Nations. As soon as the Council of the League of Nations was satisfied that such a violation or breach had been committed, it could notify its finding without delay to the Powers' signatory to the present treaty, who severally agreed that in such a case each of them could immediately go to the assistance of the Power attacked. Thus, in the cases of Czechoslovakia and Poland in 1939, Britain and France could have taken advantage of this provision. Article 4(3) provided that if there was a flagrant breach of Articles 42 or 43 of the Versailles Treaty against a contracting party, each of the other parties could come to its assistance if the violation constituted an unprovoked act of aggression by crossing a frontier, or an outbreak of hostilities, or forces assembled in the demilitarised zone.

Under Article 5, the provisions of Article 3 above were under the guarantee of the parties subject to the following stipulations: first if one of the Powers referred to in Article 3 refused to submit a dispute to peaceful settlement or to comply with an arbitral or judicial decision, and committed a violation of Article 2 of the treaty or a breach of Articles 42 or 43 of the Treaty of Versailles, the provisions of Article 4 applied; second, where one of the Powers referred to in Article 3 without committing a violation of Article 2 of the treaty or a breach of Articles 42 or 43 of the Treaty of Versailles, refused to submit a dispute to peaceful settlement or to comply with an arbitral or judicial

[90] Art XV, para VII provided that: 'If the Council fails to reach a report which is unanimously agreed to by the members thereof, other than the representatives of one or more of the parties to the dispute, the Members of the League reserve to themselves the right to take such action as they shall consider necessary for the maintenance of right and justice.'

decision, the other party could refer the matter to the Council of the League of Nations, and the Council would propose steps to be taken.

Under Article 6, the Locarno Treaty did not affect the rights and obligations of the parties under the Treaty of Versailles nor any supplementary arrangements. It was agreed that on the existing wording of the draft treaty, a dispute as to the interpretation of the text of the Treaty of Versailles fell within Article 3 and could be made the subject of arbitration proceedings, but wherever the Treaty of Versailles gave the Allied governments the right to decide a question, the treaty provision would be binding on the arbitrators, and they would be obliged to give effect to it.[91]

It should be noted that despite the concerns of Stresemann as to the guarantees provided by France to Czechoslovakia and Poland, Sir Austen Chamberlain, who was present at a meeting of the delegations in Locarno on 6 October 1938, was clearly of the opinion that Article 6 of the League Covenant should be supplemented by a special guarantee in the case of Germany's eastern frontier.[92] None of these provisions restricted the League of Nations from limiting its duty to take whatever action it deemed necessary. The treaty was signed by Luther, Stresemann, Emile Vandervelde, A Briand, Austen Chamberlain, and Benito Mussolini.

So far as Britain was concerned, the settlement reached at Locarno was in entire accord with the principles set out by the Foreign Secretary in the House of Commons on 24 June 1925,[93] that the best course was to carry out the programme of security, arbitration and disarmament through the League of Nations, supplementing the Covenant to meet special needs. These were to be mutual arrangements, not unilateral alliances. Such arrangements were purely defensive in character in the spirit of the Covenant. Britain's commitment was limited to Germany's western frontier, and whilst prepared to guarantee any arbitration treaties between Germany and France and Germany and Belgium, Britain could not accede to such treaties because of its global commitments. Similarly, Britain was not disposed to guarantee arbitration treaties between Germany and countries other than France and Belgium. In any event, any guarantee given by Britain should only become effective if the wrongdoer, in defiance of arbitration treaties, resorted to force. Britain's commitments were subject to Germany's membership in the League of Nations. Nothing in the new treaties affected the rights and obligations attaching to membership of the League under the Covenant.[94] Thus Britain achieved its aims at Locarno in relation to:[95]

(a) The territorial status quo resulting from the frontiers between Germany and Belgium and Germany and France;
(b) The inviolability of those frontiers; and
(c) The demilitarisation of the Rhineland.

[91] Documents on British Foreign Policy 1919–1939, Ser. 1, Vol 27, Reference: C 11425/459/18. (4 Sep 1925). Report on the proceedings of the meetings of the jurists held at the Foreign Office, Sept 1–4 in connection with the proposed Treaty of Mutual Guarantee.

[92] DBFP 1919–1939, Ser. 1, Vol 27 *British Secretary's Notes of the Second Meeting between the British, Belgian, French, German, and Italian Delegations, held at Locarno on October 6, 1925, at 4.30 p.m.* See also authors comments in footnotes below regarding the Kellogg Briand Pact and Foreign Office Comments on the Arbitration Treaties.

[93] DBFP 1919–1939, Ser. 1A. Vol. 1. No. 1. *Foreign Office Memorandum respecting the Locarno Treaties.* [C 797/1/18] Foreign Office, 10 January 1926. para 27.

[94] ibid para 27 (1–8).

[95] ibid para 28.

Whether the British government intervened or not was a matter for the government to determine whether a casus foederis arose.

vii. Locarno Arbitration Agreements

a. Arbitration Convention between Germany and Belgium and between Germany and France (Initialled at Locarno, 16 October 1925)

Germany, Belgium, France, Great Britain, and Italy agreed that all questions which could not be settled amicably between Germany and Belgium were to be settled by arbitration. The provisions of this Convention were identical with the Convention between Germany and France, the key provisions of which were as follows.

Under Article 1, all disputes between Germany and Belgium as to their respective rights which were not possible to settle amicably by diplomacy would be submitted either to an arbitral tribunal or to the Permanent Court of International Justice. Such matters included those mentioned in Article 13 of the Covenant of the League of Nations, which included disputes as to the interpretation of a treaty, as to any question of international law, as to the existence of any fact that, if established, would constitute a breach of any international obligation, or as to the extent and nature of the reparation to be made for any such breach, generally suitable for submission to arbitration.

Under Article 2, before any resort could be made to arbitral procedure or to procedure before the Permanent Court of International Justice, the dispute could, by agreement between the parties, be submitted, with a view to amicable settlement, to a permanent international commission styled the Permanent Conciliation Commission, constituted in accordance with the convention.

Under Article 3, in the case of a dispute which fell within the competence of the national courts of a party, no reference could be made under the convention until a final judgment had been pronounced, within a reasonable time, by the national court.

Article 4 provided that the Permanent Conciliation Commission would be composed of five members. They would be appointed by the German and Belgian governments, who would each nominate a commissioner chosen from among their respective nationals, and they would appoint, by common agreement, the three other commissioners from among the nationals of third Powers. The three commissioners had to be of different nationalities. The German and Belgian governments could appoint the president of the commission. Commissioners were appointed for three years, and their mandate was renewable.

Under Article 8, the task of the Permanent Conciliation Commission was to elucidate questions in dispute, to collect all necessary information by means of inquiry or otherwise, and to endeavour to bring the parties to an agreement. After a case had been examined, it was to inform the parties of the terms of settlement. The Commission would draw up a report confirming the agreement reached, the terms of the agreement, or that it was impossible to effect a settlement. The time was limited to six months from the day of referral of the dispute to the Commission completing its deliberations.

Article 9 provided that, failing any special provision to the contrary, the Permanent Conciliation Commission prescribed its own procedure, which provided that both parties must be heard. Regarding enquiries, the Commission, unless it decided unanimously to the contrary, acted in accordance with Chapter III (International Commissions of Enquiry) of the Hague Convention 18 October 1907 for the Pacific Settlement of International Disputes.[96]

Under Article 18, if the two parties did not reach agreement within a month from the termination of the work of the Permanent Conciliation Commission the question would, at the request of either party, be brought before the Council of the League of Nations, which would deal with it in accordance with Article 15 of the Covenant of the League.[97]

Under Article 19, provisional measures could be taken by the arbitral tribunal or the Permanent Court of International Justice, acting in accordance with Article 41 of its statute. The Council of the League of Nations owed a similar duty. The German and Belgian governments undertook to accept such measures and to abstain from any measures that might aggravate or extend the dispute.

This Convention, like the Convention between France and Germany,[98] was significant in the context of what occurred in 1939 and 1940, when the Convention's provisions were ignored, as were the League of Nations and the legal process of resolving any questions as to the inviolability of frontiers.

b. Arbitration Treaty between Germany and Poland and Germany and Czechoslovakia (Initialled at Locarno, 16 October 1925)

These treaties were identical mutatis mutandis with the convention between Germany and Belgium so far as the first 20 articles are concerned. Article 21 declared that the treaty conformed with the Covenant of the League of Nations and did not in any way affect the rights and obligations of the parties as members of the League of Nations was not to be interpreted as restricting the duty of the League to take whatever action may be deemed wise and effectual to safeguard the peace of the world.[99] During the conference, the German delegation requested certain explanations regarding Article 16 of the Covenant of the League of Nations.[100] The interpretation given was that members of the League

[96] See: MP Reynolds, *Instruments of Peacemaking 1870-1914* (Oxford, Hart Publishing, 2021).

[97] Article XV of the League Covenant provided: 'If there should arise between Members of the League any dispute likely to lead to a rupture, which is not submitted to arbitration … the Members of the League agree that they will submit the matter to the Council. Any party to the dispute may effect such submission by giving notice of the existence of the dispute to the Secretary General, who will make all necessary arrangements for a full investigation and consideration thereof.'

[98] Annex C to the First Protocol of the Locarno Conference, 1925.

[99] ibid. Also annexed the Arbitration Treaty between Germany and Czechoslovakia, initialled at Locarno, 16 October 1925, which was wholly identical mutatis mutandis with the Treaty between Germany and Poland.

[100] Annex F. Draft Collective Note to Germany regarding Article 16 of the Covenant of the League of Nations (Initialled at Locarno, 16 October 1925).

> must be understood to mean that each State member of the League is bound to co-operate loyally and effectively in support of the Covenant and in resistance to any act of aggression to an extent which is compatible with its military situation and takes its geographical position into account.

Annex F contained the treaty between France and Poland and that between France and Czechoslovakia, which were of critical importance in the Sudetenland crisis and the Danzig crisis in 1938 and 1939, where the honour of France was called into question.[101]

Under this treaty, the parties agreed (Article 1) that in the event of Poland or France being subject to an unprovoked attack, France and Poland, applying Article 16 of the Covenant of the League of Nations, undertook to give each other immediate aid and assistance. If the Council of the League of Nations was unable to make a report accepted by all members, then apart from the representatives of the parties to the dispute, in the event of Poland or France being attacked without provocation, France, or reciprocally Poland, acting under Article 15, paragraph 7[102] of the Covenant of the League of Nations, would immediately lend aid and assistance.

The treaty between France and Czechoslovakia was identical mutatis mutandis with that between France and Poland.

c. The Treaty of Rapallo and the Soviet German Trade Treaty 1925

Whilst former allies were at loggerheads, Germany was able to negotiate a treaty with Russia at Rapallo on 16 April 1922, by which means both countries normalised their diplomatic and commercial relations as well as renouncing any claims against each other. The German government was represented by Dr Walther Rathenau, Minister of State, and the government of the Russian Socialist Federal Soviet Republic was represented by M Chicherin, People's Commissary. The treaty dealt with questions arising between Germany and Russia since the Great War.

Under Article 1 of the treaty, both Russia and Germany agreed that neither state would claim damages from the other suffered by them or the nationals in war zones by acts of war. In addition, both states would waive their rights in respect of civilian claims as a result of war or emergency measures. Matters of public and private rights arising from the war, including the treatment of trading vessels seized by either party, would be settled on a basis of reciprocity. Claims for compensation for expenditure incurred by either party on behalf of prisoners of war would be waived, as well as expenditure incurred by Germany on behalf of members of the Red Army interned in Germany.

[101] See: ch 4 for a full consideration of how France failed to meet her obligations to Czechoslovakia and to what extent it failed to help Poland effectively with any aid or assistance on 1 September 1939 and thereafter. Britain also had obligations by that time to Poland.

[102] Article XV, para VII-Covenant of the League of Nations. 'If the Council fails to reach a report which is unanimously agreed to by the members thereof, other than the representatives of one or more of the parties to the dispute, the Members of the League reserve to themselves the right to take such action as they shall consider necessary for the maintenance of right and justice.'

The Russian government would waive any claims in respect of the value of Russian stores sold in Germany.

Under Article 2, Germany waived all claims against Russia in respect of any law or measure Russia took against German nationals. Importantly, under Article 3, both countries recognised each other so that diplomatic and consular relations between the German Reich and the Russian Socialist Federal Soviet Republic were resumed. Article 4 provided that the principle of mutual, commercial, and economic relations would be applied on the basis of the Most Favoured Nation status, but this would not apply to a Soviet Republic or to any state that in the past formed part of the former Russian Empire. Article 5 provided that the two governments would cooperate in a spirit of mutual goodwill in meeting the economic needs of both countries, and, interestingly, the German government declared its readiness to give all possible support to proposed arrangements between private firms. This was important because it facilitated certain secret arrangements between Russia and Germany, enabling Germany to circumvent the limitations on armaments by providing German factories with facilities in Russia to develop their weaponry.[103] Whilst the former Allies' interests were diverging, Germany was collaborating with the Soviet Union to rearm and improve her economy.

The Soviet-German Trade Treaty of 1925 was an economic development of the Treaty of Rapallo.[104] It contained three specific sections: general conditions in seven Special Agreements, an agreement as to legal assistance in civil cases, and a consular convention. This was a remarkable document considering the quite diverse legal and constitutional systems. In the Soviet Union, delegates were regarded as traders and state representatives. As state representatives, they enjoyed certain privileges, but in law they were merchants. Thus, if their property was seized by the courts in Weimar, certain property pertaining to their diplomatic functions was excluded under international law. The treaty gave Russia Most Favoured Nation status, but Russia did not reciprocate.[105] The Special Agreements included conventions dealing with railways, shipping, taxation, testamentary dispositions, commercial contracts, arbitration and other legal matters.

d. Concern as to Germany's Eastern Frontier

The Foreign Office considered that the most important instrument governing the question of the extent of Germany's undertaking not to attempt to disturb the territorial arrangements of her eastern frontier by forcible means was the Paris Peace Pact (or Kellogg-Briand Pact) signed on 27 August 1928. Germany, in common with all the

[103] An example of Nazi-Soviet co-operation was a secret agreement whereby, beginning in 1932, the Reichswehr's armoured divisions could perfect their skills in Russia. P Pailliole, *The Spy in Hitler's Inner Circles* (Oxford, Casemate, 2016) 31.

[104] The Rapallo Treaty was extended to Ukraine and Georgia as Associated States of the Soviet Union.

[105] *The Times*, 14 October 1925. *Survey of 1925*, The Royal Institute of International Affairs, Part II.D. 255–256.

other signatories, renounced war as an instrument of national policy.[106] In theory that was commendable, but there was some doubt despite the Arbitration Treaty between Germany and Poland.[107]

That treaty provided a model for conciliation and arbitration treaties, binding the contracting Powers to use these methods of dispute resolution, the preamble of which was regarded as of special importance as pronouncing certain general principles which bound Germany to seek a peaceful solution to an alteration of her Polish frontier. The preamble read as follows:

> (1) The President of the German Empire and the President of the Polish Republic:
> (2) Equally resolved to maintain peace between Germany and Poland by assuring the peaceful settlement of differences which might arise between the two countries:
> (3) Declaring that respect for the rights established by treaty or resulting from the law of nations is obligatory for international tribunals:
> (4) Agreeing to recognize that the rights of a State cannot be modified save with its consent:
> (5) And considering that sincere observance of the methods of peaceful settlement of international disputes permits of resolving, without recourse to force, questions which may become the cause of division between States:
> (6) Have decided to embody in a treaty their common intentions in this respect, and have named as their plenipotentiaries the following:.

Paragraph 33 of a paper entitled: 'Memorandum respecting the Locarno Treaties' (which was drawn up for use at the 1926 Imperial Conference) prepared in the Foreign Office on the 10 January 1926', reads as follows:[108]

> The next point concerned Germany's eastern frontiers. France was in a position of peculiar difficulty owing to her previous commitments to Poland and Czechoslovakia. She therefore would have liked a settlement on Germany's eastern frontier like that on the western frontier. To this Germany could not consent, for, as already shown, she was not willing to accept as final the existing territorial settlement in the east. The difficulty was eventually overcome by the signature of treaties of arbitration between Germany and Poland and Germany and Czechoslovakia, analogous to the arbitration conventions between Germany and Belgium and Germany and France. Side by side with these treaties, guarantee treaties were signed between France and Poland and France and Czechoslovakia, by which if Germany failed to observe the provisions of her arbitration treaties *and coupled such failure with resort to war*, the parties would reciprocally assist each other. These guarantee treaties were so worded that any assistance rendered under them would fall within Article 16 or Article 15, paragraph 7, of the Covenant of the League of Nations.[109] These treaties protected Czechoslovakia and Poland by providing mutual aid from France in the event of Germany's unprovoked resort to arms

[106] DBFP 1919–1939, Ser. 2, Vol 4, Reference: C 9438/300/18 (14 Nov 1932).
[107] ibid para 2.
[108] Cited from ibid para 4.
[109] DBFP 1919–1939, Ser. 1, Vol 27 *British Secretary's Notes of the Second Meeting between the British, Belgian.* It is worth noting that Sir A Chamberlain was of the opinion that the obligation that Britain assumed under the Locarno Treaty exceeded those obligations under Art 16 in using all its forces against either France or Germany if either were acting with flagrant aggression, *French, German, and Italian Delegations, held at Locarno on October 6, 1925, at 4.30 p.m.*

> and for similar support in the event of a German unprovoked attack which the Council of the League would have failed to prevent.[110]

Sir Austen Chamberlain,[111] the Foreign Secretary at the time, raised his concern in a letter to Sir William Tyrrell that the Germans at that time declared that 'it was impossible for them to say that they renounced war as a means of ultimately changing their eastern frontier':[112]

> But now I perceive another complication. The Germans say in effect that they are prepared so to tie themselves up by the treaty of arbitration that they cannot in fact make war, but they declare that it is impossible for them to say that they renounce war as a means of ultimately changing their eastern frontier. This declaration has, of course, not been made at the sittings of the conference, but it reappears continually in the conversations which I and other members of the delegation have with the Germans. I take a grave view of it, and I propose, if need be, to weigh in with all the authority that I can exercise.

He further instructed Sir Cecil Hurst that[113] he should get the French, German and Polish jurists together and the Czechoslovak jurist also so that the preamble or other part of the treaty should state the object of the treaty to be the avoidance of war. Chamberlain's objective was to make it impossible for Germany to overrun Europe, to induce France to adopt a more friendly and reasonable attitude towards Germany, and to prevent a German-Soviet combination against the rest of Europe.[114] Ominously, in 1926, Germany and the Soviet Union, finding themselves isolated, revived the Treaty of Rapallo to increase their economic and military ties.

e. Foreign Office Memorandum on Poland

The Foreign Office raised concerns about the willingness of Germany to respect its Locarno undertakings, especially regarding its eastern frontier. The Arbitration Treaty between Germany and Poland contained no guarantee regarding existing frontiers because the Germans refused to express in terms the fact that they renounced war as a means of ultimately changing their eastern frontier. On the other hand, they were prepared, in Sir Austen Chamberlain's words, 'so to tie themselves up by the treaty of arbitration that they could not in fact make war'. This was the object of the Arbitration

[110] Dr Stresemann's delegation to the meeting of delegates at Locarno on the 6 October 1925 had expressed reservations about the guarantees by France to Czechoslovakia and Poland. M Briand was at pains to explain that these guarantees were not in the character of alliances and were implied in any event by Art 6 Covenant of the League of Nations and the moral obligation in Art 16 of the Covenant regarding acting with armed force. DBFP 1919–1939, Ser. 1, Vol 27 *British Secretary's Notes of the Second Meeting between the British, Belgian, French, German, and Italian Delegations, held at Locarno on October 6, 1925, at 4.30 p.m.* Reference: LOC/114/CON. (6 Oct 1925).

[111] British Foreign Secretary from 1924 to 1929. Joint winner of the Nobel Prize for Peace in 1925 as being instrumental in the Treaty of Locarno.

[112] Letter written by Sir Austen Chamberlain on the 14 October 1925, from Locarno addressed to Sir William Tyrrell cited at para 5 DBFP 1919–1939, Ser. 2, Vol 4. Reference: C 9438/300/18. (14 Nov 1932).

[113] DBFP ibid para 5.

[114] J Jacobson, 'Locarno, Britain and the Security of Europe' in G Johnson (ed), *Locarno Revisited: European Diplomacy 1920–1929* (London and New York, Routledge, 2004) 6.

Treaty between Germany and Poland.[115] The Memorandum noted that paragraphs 2 and 5 of that arbitration envisaged the peaceful settlement of differences between the two countries and intimated that the methods provided permitted disputes to be resolved without recourse to force. It did not say that these 'differences' and 'disputes' covered the German claim to change her Polish frontier. But the preamble was so worded as to include territorial disputes. Paragraph 3, which declared that 'respect for the rights established by treaty … is obligatory for international tribunals', necessarily covered – as no exceptions are made – the eastern frontier, since the frontier represents for Poland one of the rights established by the Treaty of Versailles, while paragraph 4, in recognising 'that the rights of a State cannot be modified save with its consent', must obviously include the right of Poland to her treaty frontiers.[116] The Foreign Office Memorandum further noted that the explanation for the omission from the preamble of express provisions for the pacific settlement of territorial disputes and the absence of any guarantee for the existing frontier was to be found in the history of the Locarno Settlement.[117]

There were other concerns raised by the Foreign Office. Under Article 7, in the event of a dispute arising between Germany and Poland in consequence of a request by the former for a modification of her eastern frontier, the dispute would be referred to judicial determination (with or without a preliminary conciliation procedure) under Part I of the treaty or to conciliation under Part II. In the former event, the tribunal would have to deal with the case based on the statement in the preamble to the treaty providing that 'respect for rights established by treaties or resulting from international law is obligatory for international tribunal', and would therefore have to decide against Germany. That decision would be binding on Germany, and she could not then go to war with Poland without violating her treaty obligations. If the second procedure were adopted and the conciliation procedure failed to produce a settlement, the question would, by Article 18 of the treaty, be submitted to the Council of the League, which would decide in accordance with Article 15 of the Covenant. In that case, it seems plain that the Council would have to proceed based on the statement in the preamble that 'the rights of a State cannot be modified without its consent'. The Council would presumably try to negotiate a settlement by means of a modification of the frontier accepted by both parties, but if Poland refused to agree to any modification, it would seem to follow that the Council would have to report that no such modification could be made without Poland's consent. Such a report would be accepted by Poland, and if it were accepted by the other members of the Council other than Germany, Germany could not then go to war with Poland without violating paragraph 6 of Article 15 of the Covenant. If, however, the Council were not unanimous, it might be argued that Germany would, under paragraph 7 of Article 15 and subject to the possible effect of Article 12, be free to go to war with Poland under the 'gap in the Covenant'. That paragraph, however, did not confer any right to go to war; it merely stated the position that, so far as obligations created by the Covenant were concerned, there was nothing to prevent Germany going to war. In other words, Germany's position would be that

[115] DBFP 1919–1939, Ser. 2, Vol 4, Reference: C 9438/300/18 (14 Nov 1932) paras 6 and 7.
[116] ibid para 3.
[117] ibid para 4.

resulting from the general rules of international law, or any other treaty obligations into which she may have entered. Whether in such circumstances the effect of the recitals in the Preamble to the German-Polish Treaty was to prevent Germany from going to war was a question on which different views might be held since the conclusion of the Locarno treaties; both Germany and Poland became parties to the Pact of Paris.[118] By this it was argued Germany renounced, as against Poland, the right of making war as an instrument of national policy. Though the Pact did not forbid war in self-defence, it seems clear that a war by Germany with the object of altering a frontier acquired by Poland as the result of a treaty (a treaty right that Germany in 1925 freely recognised could not be altered without Poland's consent) could not be regarded as a war of self-defence, and therefore, in the circumstances postulated, Germany could not go to war without violating her obligations under the Pact. This did not stop the invasion of Poland in September 1939.

Article 19 of the treaty between Poland and Germany provided that the Conciliation Commission or the Council had the power to lay down provisional measures if an application was made on the ground that the dispute arose out of acts 'already committed or on the point of commission'. The Article further stated that Germany and Poland undertake to accept such measures and to abstain from any acts likely to have a repercussion prejudicial to the arrangements proposed by the Conciliation Commission or by the Council, and, in general, to refrain from any sort of action whatsoever which may aggravate or extend the dispute. It would seem, therefore, that, if the situation was threatening, Poland could take the case at once before the Commission or the Council and ask for provisional measures, and the Commission or the Council could probably order, amongst its provisional measures, that no movement of troops should take place. Germany was obliged to comply with this order. Any subsequent German invasion would, unless these provisional measures had been cancelled or had lapsed, be clearly contrary to the provisions of Article 19 of the treaty.[119] Again, in 1939, none of these provisions were operated, Hitler having complete disregard for treaties, having renounced Locarno.

Under the Pact of Paris, Germany renounced war as an instrument of national policy, and any attempt, therefore, to alter her eastern frontier by force would contravene her undertakings under it. Under the Locarno Treaties, Germany had specifically undertaken to submit her demand for the alteration of her eastern frontier to arbitration and/or conciliation. The Memorandum pointed out that it could be argued that the loophole provided for in Article 18 of that treaty did not give Germany complete liberty of action. The problem was that there was no express reference to Germany's Polish frontier in the Locarno Treaties. Germany's undertakings not to challenge Poland's 'rights' by force were stated in the Preamble of the treaty and not in the treaty itself and subject to interpretation. The concern stated in the Memorandum was that, apart from Germany's undertaking under the Pact of Paris, her commitments under the Locarno Treaties were ambiguous and unsatisfactory.[120]

[118] Kellogg-Briand Pact 1928, also known as the Paris Peace Pact.
[119] DBFP 1919–1939, Ser. 2, Vol 4, Reference: C 9438/300/18. (14 Nov 1932) para 8.
[120] ibid para 9.

f. German Emergence

As the memorandum concluded, the Germany of 1932 was not that of 1925, and it was doubtful if Von Papen[121] would be more inclined than Stresemann. Indeed, Stresemann was pleased that the French had evacuated the Ruhr, the Entente was divided, and there were possibilities in the East.[122] Whist the Soviet Union might have had anxieties as to sanctions Germany might implement, these were allayed by the fact that Germany had 'disarmed status' as a member of the League of Nations under Article 16 of the Covenant.[123] Thus, Germany took advantage of this to renew its 1922 Rapallo Treaty with the Soviet Union. By the Treaty of Berlin 1926, the Soviet Union and Germany undertook to continue their relations based on the Treaty of Rapallo[124] and promote understanding on political and economic questions. Under Article 2, if one of the parties was attacked by one or more third Powers, the other party would remain neutral during such conflict. Under Article 3, if there was any economic or financial boycott of one of the parties by third Powers, the other undertook not to join such coalition. One effect of this was to maintain pressure on Poland for frontier revision since both Germany and the Soviet Union claimed Polish territory. It was during this period, 1930 to 1932, that the Nazi party came into its own. During that time Germany was led by Chancellor Heinrich Brüning, who wanted a peaceful revision of the Versailles Treaty but would not concede Germany having any lesser status than that of any other member of the League of Nations. Brüning rejected the initiative of Aristide Briand for a European Union but sought an Austro-German Customs Union. Ominously, he wanted living space for the German people.[125] Such policies were not only a threat to Austrian independence but also undermined the spirit of Locarno, signalling a change in German foreign policy. This change resulted not only from the rise of nationalism but also because of the global economic crisis and the burden of reparations. Germany adopted a unilateral competitive approach to its neighbours, reflected in its rearmament planning for a field army of 21 divisions.[126] It also had an army in waiting with 4,000,000 non-commissioned officers and soldiers and 60,000 reserve officers in addition to the 100,000 men authorised by the Treaty of Versailles.[127]

C. American Overtures

i. The Kellogg Briand Pact

This International Treaty for the Renunciation of War as an Instrument of National Policy, known as the Kellogg-Briand Pact after its promoters, was signed in Paris

[121] Vice Chancellor under Hitler 1933–1934.
[122] J Wright, 'Locarno: A Democratic Peace?' (2010) 36 *Review of International Studies* 391–411, 397.
[123] Annex E. Draft Collective Note to Germany regarding Article 16 of the Covenant of the League of Nations. (Initialled at Locarno, 16 October 1925).
[124] Article 1 Treaty of Berlin 24 April 1926.
[125] J Wright, 'Locarno: A Democratic Peace?' (2010) 36 *Review of International Studies* 407.
[126] ibid 408.
[127] P Pailliole, *The Spy in Hitler's Inner Circle* (Oxford, Casemate, 2016) 38.

on 27 August 1928. It was described as 'a splendid opportunity for doing nothing in a flourish'.[128] Under this multilateral treaty the signatories agreed to renounce war, save in matters of self-defence, or in fulfilment of other treaty obligations. It contained three articles initially agreed by 15 countries and signed by nine plenipotentiaries. The three Articles were:

> ARTICLE I
>
> The High Contracting Parties solemnly declare in the names of their respective peoples that they condemn recourse to war for the solution of international controversies, and renounce it, as an instrument of national policy in their relations with one another.
>
> ARTICLE II
>
> The High Contracting Parties agree that the settlement or solution of all disputes or conflicts of whatever nature or of whatever origin they may be, which may arise among them, shall never be sought except by pacific means.
>
> ARTICLE III
>
> The present Treaty shall be ratified by the High Contracting Parties named in the Preamble in accordance with their respective constitutional requirements, and shall take effect as between them as soon as all their several instruments of ratification shall have been deposited at Washington.

The treaty was left open for all the other world Powers. Each signatory Power was given a certified copy of the treaty and of every instrument of ratification to be notified by the US government. By 24 October 1929, 55 countries had signed the treaty. The obligation to resolve all disputes and conflicts by pacific means did not mean there would be no more war but appeared to make conflict less likely. The fact was that governments had accepted the Pact expressly subject to definite limitations, preserving not only the right to use force in self-defence against aggression but also absolute discretion as to when such force was justified.[129] Sir Lionel Heald[130] reminded readers in his letter to *The Times* on 25 October 1956 that Mr Kellogg told the Council of Foreign Relations in New York on 15 March 1928 that the right to use force in self-defence was 'so inherent and so universal that it was not deemed necessary even to insert it expressly in the text'.[131] So far as Britain was concerned he said that there were 'certain regions of the world, the welfare and integrity of which constitute a special and vital interest of the peace and safety of Great Britain'.[132] At the time of the treaty, the British government expressly stated that the protection of these must be regarded as a measure of self-defence.[133]

[128] R Vansittart, *The Mist Procession* (London, Hutchinson & Co, 1958) 361.
[129] L Heald, Kellogg Pact. *The Times* 27 October 1956, 7.
[130] Barrister and Conservative politician, QC, PC. He was elected Member of Parliament for Chertsey in Surrey in 1950. He served as Attorney General in Winston Churchill's cabinet from 1951 to 1954 and was made a Privy Counsellor in 1954.
[131] United States Foreign Affairs Vol 6 *Myers* Paris peace Pact 1929).
[132] L Heald, Kellogg Pact. *The Times* 27 October 1956, 7 and British Note of 19 May 1928. See: Cmd.3109 and 3153.
[133] British Note of 19 May 1928. See: Cmd.3109 and 3153.

Lord Vansittart recalled in his memoir *The Mist Procession*[134] how Briand was encouraged by Professor Shotwell[135] to draft a renunciation of war with the US. Also, how the Polish delegation at the League of Nations then proposed to prohibit war, and then the Russians proposed to abolish everything – armies, navies, air forces, war material, and arms factories. Kellogg recoiled from this as America did not want any entanglements with France or Europe that might suggest an alliance. He extended the concept to the whole world. The signatories condemned those who had recourse to war, but this ironically deterred them from subsequently declaring war.[136] As Vansittart noted: 'When the Japanese took to wiping out Chinese in a big way, they spoke of 'incidents'. Half a dozen other invasions followed in a decade.'[137] Whilst Vansittart described the instrument as: 'A splendid opportunity for doing nothing in a flourish',[138] Briand having been congratulated by Stimson replied that 'the coming into force of the Pact against war is received with profound and unanimous satisfaction in France'.[139]

The fundamental problem with this multilateral treaty was that it was unenforceable, so in effect not a treaty at all but a declaration of intent. It did not define what 'self-defence' meant. It simply remains a tribute to its promoters, who had the best of intentions and the interests of international public law and opinion at heart. It added little if anything to the obligations of the Treaty of Versailles save that the US affirmed its idealistic objective. As Secretary of State Henry Stimson said:[140]

> For its effectiveness despatch depends solely upon public opinion – to public opinion of the world.

A General Act was promoted to implement the Kellogg Pact with a process for the Pacific Settlement of International Disputes by conciliation or by reference to justiciable disputes to the Permanent Court of International Justice or to an arbitral tribunal.[141] The US was careful not to commit itself to any terms resembling the Covenant of the League of Nations for joint action in the event of a member's aggression.

ii. The Young Plan

In the autumn of 1928, a committee of experts was formed to devise a final settlement of German reparations. In 1929 a committee under the chairmanship of

[134] R Vansittart, *The Mist Procession* (London, Hutchinson & Co, 1958) 361.

[135] James T. Shotwell, Bryce Professor of the History of International Relations at Columbia University.

[136] R Vansittart, *The Mist Procession* (London, Hutchinson & Co, 1958) 361.

[137] ibid 362.

[138] ibid 361.

[139] From Our Own Correspondent 'Limitation of Navies' *The Times* 26 July 1929, 14 *The Times Digital Archive.*

[140] Keynote of Secretary Stimson at State Convention, *New York Times* 26 September 1930, 2; and also 'Pact and Covenant' *The Times* 3 January 1930, 11. *The Times Digital Archive.*

[141] 1928 General Act (Pacific Settlement of International Disputes) Adopted in Geneva, Switzerland on 26 September 1928. Article 17. All disputes with regard to which the parties are in conflict as to their respective rights shall be submitted for decision to the Permanent Court of International Justice, unless the parties agree to have resort to an arbitral tribunal.

Owen D Young, head of General Electric and a member of the Dawes Committee, proposed a plan to reduce the total amount of reparations demanded of Germany to 121 billion gold marks, almost $29 billion payable over 58 years. Another loan was intended to be floated on foreign markets, totalling $300 million. Foreign supervision of German finances would cease, and the last occupying troops would leave Germany. The plan also called for the establishment of a bank for international settlements designed to facilitate the payment of reparations. The execution of the plan was frustrated by the Wall Street Crash and the onset of the Great Depression. The banks were unable to make the loans despite a one-year moratorium. At the Lausanne Conference in 1932, all German reparations were cancelled save a final payment. Britain and France then attempted to link their payments to the US to payments received from Germany. Roosevelt refused. Save for Finland, all European debtors to the US were in default. This experience undoubtedly affected public opinion and foreign policy of the US in the years to come; hence the Nye Committee investigations that inspired three congressional Neutrality Acts in the mid-1930s and isolationism against foreign entanglements. The Johnson Debt Default Act of 1934 and the Neutrality Act of 1939 prevented both the US government and private banks from arranging loans to the defaulting nations in their conflict with Nazi Germany.[142] It may also have given fuel to the America First Movement that vehemently opposed aid to Britain in 1940–41 and the draft for military conscription.

D. Rise of Protectionism, Isolationism and Fascism

Some historians consider that the Second World War commenced when Japan attacked China in 1937. The causes of war in Europe may be traced back to the outcome of the peace treaties and the fact that Germany and Italy were dissatisfied: Germany by the dismemberment of its territories, reparations and the 'war guilt clause', and Italy by anger at not recovering appropriate territorial reward for its part in the First World War.

By 1932 the architects of the postwar settlement were dead, save Barthou. Reparations were no longer a major issue since they were discontinued at the Lausanne Conference in 1932.[143] This caused consternation in the US when allies resiled from their commitments to repay US loans. Mussolini was regarded as the strongman who might stand up to Hitler. On 23 October 1932, Mussolini suggested a Four Power Pact of Germany, France, Italy and Britain, but this proved abortive. In February 1932, 62 nations were represented in Genoa at the Disarmament Conference. Germany, which had earlier withdrawn, rejoined when equality of rights was granted in December 1932 but withdrew again in October 1933.[144] Since 1930, in breach of the Versailles Treaty, Germany had been rearming. Poland was concerned that this was aimed at her. As de Launay suggests, there were

[142] A Glass, Congress Passes Johnson Debt Default Act, 13 April 1934, *Politico*, 13 April 2018.
[143] J de Launay, *Major Controversies of Contemporary History* (London, Pergamon Press, 1965) 131.
[144] ibid 132. This was after Hitler became Chancellor on 30 January 1933.

secret discussions with France as to a preventative war against Germany in April 1933, but France would not agree. Poland decided then to protect its own interests. The Polish ambassador in Berlin, Wysocki, met Hitler on 2 May 1933, who told him: 'The Reich government has no intention whatever of interfering with existing treaties.'[145] Colonel Beck met Goebbels and von Neurath at Genoa, and following that, a German-Polish Pact was signed on 26 January 1934.[146] Mussolini rightly predicted on 13 May 1934, writing in *Popolo d'Italia* that a preventable war was the only way to stop Germany from rearming; if not an option, then there would be an arms race leading to war.[147]

On 27 September 1937, William Shirer left Berlin[148] on other assignments for his boss, Edward R Murrow[149] in Rome, Munich, Brussels, and Vienna but recalled as he left the words of the Nazi marching song prophesying the war to come:

> To-day we own Germany,
>
> To-morrow the whole world.

Interestingly, he recalled seeing the Duke of Windsor in Munich during his assignment in October 1937. The Duke had been touring Germany to study 'labour conditions' and was chaperoned by Dr Ley, who abolished democratic trade unions.[150]

In October 1937, delegates from the Nine Power Treaty met at Brussels to bring about an adjustment of relations between Japan and China by peaceful means. Chinese delegates attended the meeting; Japanese did not. On 24 November 1937, the conference adopted a declaration that: 'Hostilities be suspended and resort be had to peaceful process.' Japan rejected the recommendation.

i. The Saar Plebiscite

Pierre Laval succeeded Barthou at the Quai d'Orsay on 17 October 1934. André Fribourg, Vice President of the Foreign Affairs Commission, visited Laval and told him that he had 'stopped everything: action in the Saar is at an end. I wish to make peace with Germany.'[151] The appointment of Laval marked a change of policy towards Germany and marked the beginnings of appeasement and therefore a decline in French prestige. This was a departure from the policy of Briand of 'collective security'[152] and a

[145] de Launay ibid 133 and Polish White Book Doc. No.1.

[146] de Launay ibid 134; Poland had earlier signed a non-aggression pact with the USSR in 1932.

[147] de Launay ibid 135.

[148] WL Shirer, *Berlin Diary* (London, Hamish Hamilton, 1941) 76.

[149] Then European Manager for CBS made famous by his broadcasts from London during the blitz. After the war he produced several incisive television exposes *Here It Now*, and *See It Now*, challenging the demagogic Senator Jospeh McCarthy. Later he was appointed the Director of the US Information Agency in 1961 by President John F Kennedy.

[150] Ley was head of the German workers' front designed to facilitate German war production. During World War 2, Ley supervised the mobilisation of German and foreign workers. He was captured by US forces and indicted for conspiracy, war crimes, and crimes against humanity at Nuremberg where he committed suicide.

[151] J de Launay, *Major Controversies of Contemporary History* (Oxford, Pergamon Press, 1965) 147.

[152] Woodrow Wilson saw 'collective security' as the antidote to the system of alliances that in his view was a cause of war in 1914. Articles 23, 24 and 25 were included in the Covenant of the League of Nations for that reason.

new bilateral approach to Germany. The Saar was a gift. Despite Catholic reservations (72 per cent of the population were Catholic), the bishops of Trier and Speier encouraged a vote for Germany. Saarlanders were encouraged to join the Deutsche Front.[153] On 3 December 1934, Germany paid 900 million francs in consideration of French credits and property in the Saar. Land was sold in the Saar before the plebiscite, which gave the Nazis 90 per cent of the vote.[154]

ii. The Rome Agreements 1935

Visiting Rome on 7 January 1935, Laval was able to secure an agreement with Mussolini under which the rights of Italians in Tunisia would be abolished over a 20-year period from 1945 until 1965, and in consideration of this, Italy would gain 114,000 square kilometres of desert in Eritrea and a share in the Djibouti Addis Ababa Railway.[155] Italy and France agreed to support Austria against any threats. Laval, in effect, gave licence to Mussolini to take another country, which he had no right to do. Laval later admitted as much when he addressed the Chamber of Deputies on 27 December 1935 and said that he considered France's economic claims and met Italy's demands and concessions in Ethiopia.[156] On 3 October 1935, Italian forces attacked Ethiopia. On 7 October 1935, the Council of the League of Nations condemned the Italian invasion and on 18 November, the League of Nations imposed sanctions on Italy, but at the request of Britain and France it excluded vital war materials: steel, copper and oil, making the sanctions ineffective. The failure of Britain and France and their appeasement of aggression in breach of international law demonstrated a weakness, giving comfort to the dictators.[157] Laval sought to act unilaterally, offering Italy two-thirds of Ethiopia. Ethiopia could remain independent with access to the sea through Eritrea (the so-called Camel Corridor). In the British cabinet, Eden and Duff Cooper opposed this. Baldwin, Neville Chamberlain, Runciman and Hoare supported it.[158] This plan was disclosed by the *Daily Telegraph* in its publication on 17 December 1935, forcing Hoare to resign and be replaced by Eden. The Labour Party accused the government of a breach of the Covenant of the League of Nations and betrayal of the Abyssinian people.[159] Laval was forced to resign when the terms of the Pact were also published in Paris.[160] The attempt at a Franco-Italian rapprochement was frustrated, as was the Anglo-French-Italian accord of Hoare-Laval, which was opposed furtively by Nazi Germany.[161]

[153] J de Launay, *Major Controversies of Contemporary History* (Oxford, Pergamon Press, 1965) 148.
[154] ibid 149.
[155] ibid 152.
[156] ibid 152–154.
[157] ibid 155.
[158] ibid.
[159] ibid 156–157.
[160] P Reynaud, *La France a sauvé l'Europe* (Paris, 1947) 161 et seq.
[161] J de Launay, *Major Controversies of Contemporary History* (Oxford, Pergamon Press, 1965) 157.

iii. A Temporary Peace

In March 1925, Lord Grey of Fallodon observed that security was the master key to the difficult problems of eastern Europe.[162] It was also a critical concern to France, which sought guarantees from Britain and America, neither of which were forthcoming. The challenge before the Powers, as Sir Austen Chamberlian opined,[163] was how could Britain give that sense of security to France on which alone there could be built her reconciliation with Germany? How could Germany be brought into the comity of nations and deprive her of the future will to wage a war of revenge? Unless Britain could achieve this purpose, Europe would have a new catastrophe dragging with her the misfortune of the whole world. He believed that the influence of Britain and its Empire, properly applied, could avoid what might otherwise be inevitable. He understood more, perhaps, than those who were delegates at the Versailles Peace Conference that peace in this context was not made in a railway carriage in Compiegne; it was made at Locarno in 1925. Sir Austen Chamberlain always regarded 'the spirit of Locarno as more important than the treaties themselves'. In that regard he was right, and one might go on to suggest if Britain had had such statesmen of his quality to succeed him, maybe the course of events might have been different. In his time the Dawes Plan was in operation, and one of the main obstacles to peace was removed. Locarno was another positive milestone. There was reason to hope that Germany regaining its productive capacity and improving economy might sustain its republic pledging to eliminate resort to force as a means of obtaining a modification of her eastern frontiers and securing her membership in the League of Nations. Whilst Austria, severed from the Austro-Hungarian Empire, initially favoured a union with Germany, that approach changed in time. Germany's desire for colonies was opposed by Britain, although Neville Chamberlain considered what might be given. So far as France was concerned, there was some revival of the concert of action and a renewal of Anglo-French relations in line with an Anglo-French reconciliation with Germany. Locarno forged a new link with Italy, and its jurists attended the London meeting of jurists.[164] Italy adhered to the Treaty as a guarantor 'on the same footing as Great Britain'. Thus, the four great nations of Europe linked together in a solemn covenant of amity and peace.[165] Italy's attention was mainly directed towards the Mediterranean and the Balkans. Her rapprochement with Spain, the annexation of the Dodecanese, and the strengthening of the Italian hold on the North African colonies were parts of a considered policy to create for Italy a position if not of dominance at least of authority in the Mediterranean. In the Balkans her policy was obscure. The real danger spot was Albania, a divided country with recurrent revolutions, defenceless and a tempting target for Italy.

[162] A view strongly supported by Sir Austen Chamberlain who was Foreign Secretary between 1924 to 1929 in the Baldwin administration. See: *The Times* 4 March 1925.

[163] Ser. 1A Vol 02: Series 1A – The Termination of Military Control in Germany. Middle Eastern and American Questions 1926–1927 Ch 06: Appendix 919–958.

[164] Vol. 2 Survey of International Affairs 1925, 45.

[165] Ser. 1A Vol. 02: Series 1A – The Termination of Military Control in Germany. Middle Eastern and American Questions 1926-1927 Ch. 06: Appendix 919–958.

Locarno resulted in *détente* being achieved, in which Britain played a vital part, and western Europe was not divided into two camps – the victors and vanquished.[166] The question of German disarmament was practically settled, the activities of the Allied Commission of Control would soon cease, and the evacuation of the Cologne zone was proceeding and would soon be an accomplished fact. The whole nature of the Rhineland occupation was transformed, and most disputes arising under the Treaty of Versailles were almost at an end.[167]

[166] DBFP 1919–1939, Ser. 1A Vol. 1. *No. 1. Foreign Office Memorandum respecting the Locarno Treaties.* [C 797/1/18] Foreign Office, 10 January 1926. Para 36.
[167] ibid.

4

The Crises that Led to War and Why Diplomacy Failed

In the interwar years the Allies – France, Britain, Russia, Italy, Japan and the US – dissolved. Russia was estranged because of its ideology, Japan was isolated, and the US adopted isolationist policies, whilst Britain and France adopted appeasement and France was estranged from Italy, so that by 1936 the defeated Weimar Republic, the former Kaiserreich, reinvented itself as Nazi Germany, the Third Reich. This prevented any realignment of the old Allies. In 1938 Hitler forced Britain and France to separate themselves from Russia. Hitler did not just gain Sudetenland but demolished Russia's outer defences in Czechoslovakia. Thus, Britain and France sacrificed the opportunity of alliance with Russia, while Hitler subsequently duped them to secure Russia's acquiescence and cooperation against Poland.[1] Hitler clearly intended to isolate Britain by forming his alliances with Italy and Japan and separating Russia from Britain and France.[2] It must be said that separating Britain from Russia was not difficult. Ambassador Maisky's diary gives abundant evidence of Tory appeasement of Hitler and the fascists with Chamberlain, Halifax, and Simon regarding the Soviets as an enemy and preferring propitiation of Germany.

Maisky sensed, like Churchill, whom he met on many occasions, the danger of the increasing display of cowardice and shortsightedness of Chamberlain and his 'ministerial nonentities', as Churchill described them, diminishing British prestige.[3] This was facilitated by meetings that took place, as William Shirer noted, between leading Nazis like Goering and Lord Lothian[4] to meet him in May 1937.[5] Lothian also met Hitler, Goering and Schacht. The Nazis wanted 'adjustments' in eastern Europe especially in Austria and for the German minorities in Danzig, Memel, Czechoslovakia and Poland. They also wanted economic and colonial arrangements to give German people a higher standard of living. Lothian urged the government to agree to this. But the government had limited German former colonies.[6] In the journals of AL Kennedy, more was said. Hitler threatened London with bombing and neighbouring countries with German minorities unless these minorities could be absorbed into the Reich. Kennedy noted,

[1] W Lippmann, *US Foreign Policy* (London, Hamish Hamilton 1943) 62.
[2] ibid 64.
[3] G Gorodetsky, *The Maisky Diaries* (New Haven, Yale University Press, 2015) 100, 108.
[4] British Ambassador to the US 1939–40. Wanted to explore peace with Nazis in July 1940.
[5] WL Shirer, *Berlin Diary* (London, Hamish Hamilton, 1941) 64.
[6] T Bouverie, *Appeasing Hitler* (London, Bodley Head, 2019) and Lothian Papers. German Memo, 11 May 1937, 250–260.

'Lothian: regards Hitler as a prophet, first and foremost.'[7] He was a regular guest of the Astors at Cliveden, pro German. He believed in 'full equality' for Germany to ensure peace.[8] This played into Hitler's hands, weakening relations between Britain and France, isolating Russia, and strengthening the Third Reich against its former enemies. So, when Hitler knew the balance was in his favour, his armies would march.

This background presented the key challenges to international stability affecting British security and hence diplomacy in the interwar period was caused by the assertion of expansionist designs of the totalitarian regimes: Japan, Germany and Italy. Such designs were displayed by Japan's incursion into Manchuria and a war with China, Nazi occupation of the Rhineland and annexation of Austria and subsequent occupation of Czechoslovakia and the attack on Poland, as well as the Italian adventures in Abyssinia and Mussolini's dreams of a new Roman Empire. Much of this was happening following the Wall Street crash in 1929. The pressure on statesmen and diplomats paralleled that before 1914,[9] and despite enthusiasm for the new diplomacy of the League of Nations, the international relations reverted to old rivalries and new alliances. The driving force behind Germany's revitalisation was its humiliation at the Versailles Peace Conference, the War Guilt clause, reparations and its loss of territory and population, which deprived Germany of its prestige as a great power. This gave the Nazis their pretext for ensuring territorial demands and rearmament, constituting a threat to British security and the hegemony of Europe. Without a strong military deterrent, diplomacy had little effect on a country with half a million men under arms.[10] Disarmament, adopted by many as a means of avoiding war, was an ideal but not a practical policy. Following the Treaty of Locarno in 1925, the British government adopted a policy of international arms limitation. Such a policy of disarmament facilitated the 'honest broker' approach of Austin Chamberlain, Baldwin's Foreign Secretary, as McKercher suggests in Franco-German and Sino-Japanese relations.[11] Disarmament was also driven by the economic depression and the psychological effects on families' sacrifices in the attrition rates of 1914–18. People were reluctant to further sacrifice for 'King and Country'. A March 1931 memorandum by the Chief of the Imperial General Staff (CIGS), prepared in anticipation of the Disarmament Conference, had determined that Britain could only field two divisions for expeditionary operations.[12] In 1936–37 British foreign policy was focused on the balance of power in Europe, the Mediterranean and the Far East.[13] Vansittart may have been right when he opined:[14]

[7] AL Kennedy, *The Journals of AL J Kennedy* (Cambridge, CUP, 2000) 247.

[8] I Kershaw, *Making Friends with Hitler* (London, Penguin, 2004)140, 212.

[9] See MP Reynolds, *Instruments of Peacemaking 1870-1914* (Oxford, Hart Publishing, 2021).

[10] Germany after 1935. See below: Notes on Meeting with Hitler 25 and 26 March 1935.

[11] BJC McKercher, 'The Foreign Office and British Diplomacy' (2014) 18(2) *Contemporary British History* 93. It may also have facilitated the compromise on naval units between Italy and France as indicted in BDFP Second Series. Vol 1 No. 236 *Henderson to Sir R Graham* 1 October 1930.

[12] TNA, CAB 4/21, 1046-B, CID, Chief of the Imperial General Staff (CIGS), 'Military Appreciation of the Situation in Europe', 31 March, 1931. See also: DE Delaney, 'Imperial Armies in the Period of Rearmament and Appeasement, 1933–1939' in *The Imperial Army Project: Britain and the Land Forces of the Dominions and India, 1902–1945* (Oxford, 2018; online edn, Oxford Academic, 15 Feb. 2018), doi.org/10.1093/oso/9780198704461.003.0006, accessed 15 June 2024.

[13] BJC McKercher, 'The Foreign Office and British Diplomacy' (2014) 18(2) *Contemporary British History* 102.

[14] Appendix II Memorandum by Sir R Vansittart 'The World Situation and British Rearmament' [C 8998/8998/18] Most Secret [775/1].

> Politically, however, it is always more normal for the mind to dwell in the immediate past than in its immediate successor – particularly when the past is more comfortable and leisurely – partly because accurate pictures take time to form and are not quickly supplied. It is always the case, and it has been our own case, that impressions thus not only follow events but follow too far behind.

I. Appeasement Policy

The problem for Britain with the collapse of the Disarmament Conference was a rapprochement between France and Russia and between Germany and Italy. In such a case, as McKercher points out, Britain would have three options, as Vansittart advised: first, to support either an old Triple Alliance or Triple Entente;[15] second, to remain outside any such arrangement and defend any attack on the Low Countries; or third, to increase military strength to deter Italy from aligning with Germany and encourage France.[16] Clear differences emerged between Eden and Vansittart. Whereas Eden wanted to concentrate on western Europe, Vansittart believed that security could only be obtained by balancing an Anglo-French relationship with that of eastern Europe, including Russia.[17]

Whilst the League had been more effective in resolving the Saar and Danzig disputes, the distribution of the German and Ottoman colonies, as well as disputes over the Aland Islands between Sweden and Finland and the Greek-Bulgarian dispute in 1925, it failed in relation to the Bolivia-Paraguay dispute in the 1930s, the Polish seizure of Vilna, the Italian occupation of Corfu, the Japanese seizure of Manchuria in 1931, and the Italian seizure of Abyssinia in 1935. These events were followed by the German occupation of the Rhineland, Austria, the Sudetenland and Czechoslovakia, which suggests that the Italian attack on Abyssinia and the lack of effective response from the League signalled its ineffectiveness to the aggressor. Without the effective support of League members, collective security could not be accomplished. The 'great experiment'[18] had been formed against a difficult background of political and economic uncertainty in the aftermath of a war that cost 12 million lives, a revolution in Russia, the breakup of Austria-Hungary, the Kaiserreich, and the Ottoman Empire. The result of such upheaval is not so surprising.

A. Countervailing British Diplomacy

The ineptitude of Britain and France to contain the fascist dictators has been explained in many historiographies on the subject.[19] The story of Chamberlain's

[15] BJC McKercher, 'The Foreign Office and British Diplomacy' (2014) 18(2) *Contemporary British History* 100 and B Lee, *Britain and the Sino-Japanese War 1937-1939: A Study in the Dilemmas of British Decline*. (Stanford, Stanford University Press, 1973) 23–49.

[16] FO 371/18527/5693/1, minute by Wigram 24 May 1934 and FO 371/18524/4153/1, minute by Vansittart 2 May 1934.

[17] FO 371/19898/2487/4, minute by Vansittart, 15 April 1936.

[18] As described by R Henig in *The Peace That Never Was* (Chicago, Haus Publishing, 2019) 190.

[19] British policy of appeasement being well explained in RAC Parker, *Churchill and Appeasement* (London, Macmillan, 2000) and by T Bouverie, in *Appeasing Hitler* (London, Bodley Head, 2019).

misplaced trust in Mussolini and Hitler is well known. Churchill warned of the Nazi threat, but he was a voice crying in the wilderness and lacking political influence whilst enjoying public acclaim.[20] It is questionable as to whether, even if Churchill's warnings had been properly acted upon and Britain re-armed sooner, whether Hitler would have been deterred. As to whether interference in the Foreign Office by Chamberlain[21] and his amateurs contributed to the outbreak of the Second World War is academic since the war was inevitable given the expansionist designs of Nazi Germany.[22] The failure to secure collective security by alliances with France and Russia and the Little Entente, as Vansittart advised, and better relations with the US might have given weight to deterrence. At a critical point in December 1937, Chamberlain removed Vansittart since neither the League nor multilateral conferences seemed to be achieving results. Chamberlain's new advisers believed in bilateral settlements, which could be more effective. He ignored the experienced advice of a diplomatic generation that understood the limitations of British power and influence in maintaining the balance of power and working with those powers that shared British interests.[23] There can be little argument that, as McKercher opines, Chamberlain's appeasement policy endangered both British and Imperial interests and the security of the state.[24]

When Hitler came to power, opinion in Britain was divided.[25] The violence of Nazi thugs eventually repelled public opinion, although the speed of economic recovery gained certain admirers.[26] At first, Hitler was underestimated in the press. *The Observer* dismissed him as a 'ranting fool', while the *Daily Mail* recognised his 'intense conviction',[27] the *Daily Telegraph* at the end of 1932 thought he was 'done for'. It was at this time that Churchill, who was well informed, challenged such attitudes and, on 23 November 1932, warned against any idea of parity in armaments.[28] He referred to the[29]

[20] The Foreign Office was not unaware of the threat. Numerous reports were received from British diplomats from 1923 onwards.

[21] Chamberlain was not the only Prime Minister in the inter-war years to take control of foreign policy, Lloyd George suffered the same temptation, and it was only through the contribution made by that doyen of the foreign office, Sir Eyre Crowe, that the prestige of the Foreign Office was restored with the understanding of Lloyd Georges' successors. BJC McKercher, 'The Foreign Office and British Diplomacy' (2004) 18(2) *Contemporary British History* 88 and see 'Johnson G, Curzon, Lloyd George and the Control of British Foreign Policy 1919-1922: A Reassessment' (2000) 11 *Diplomacy and Statecraft* 49–71.

[22] See: McKercher ibid 104.

[23] ibid.

[24] ibid 87.

[25] Sir Robert Bruce Lockhart's diary entry for 13 July 1933 refers to a conversation regarding the Prince of Wales as 'quite pro-Hitler' who reportedly said, 'it was no business of ours to interfere in Germany's internal affairs, either re Jews or really anything else, and added that dictators were very popular these days and that we might want one in England before long' (263). His entry for 8 August 1933 refers to Lady Cunard being 'pro-Hitler' and was going to Munich next day (267). His entry for 14 September 1934 states that Mrs Ronnie Greville, a society hostess, came back from Nuremberg 'full of enthusiasm for Hitler'. RB Lockhart, *The Diaries of Sir Robert Bruse Lockhart* (London, Macmillan, 1973) 263, 267, 305.

[26] I Kershaw, *Lord Londonderry: Making Friends with Hitler* (London, Penguin Books, 2005) 26.

[27] This newspaper was owned by Harold Harmsworth, Viscount Rothermere. He feared the Bolsheviks and Russia more than Nazi Germany. He likened Nazi Germany to Elizabethan England. T Bouverie, *Appeasing Hitler* (London, Bodley Head, 2019) 53.

[28] Bouverie ibid 23.

[29] RAC Parker, *Churchill and Appeasement* (London, Macmillan, 2000) 29.

> Teutonic Youths .... marching through the streets and roads of Germany ... looking for weapons and when they have the weapons believe me they will then ask for the return of lost territories and lost Colonies.

Earlier he had warned that the disarmament conference would have the reverse effect.[30] Popular opinion was against 'the merchants of death' and rearmament; even the Oxford Union would vote against fighting for King and Country.[31] The *Daily Herald* dismissed Hitler as 'a clown', but the *Economist* was apprehensive for Germany's future.[32] Whilst reporters like William Shirer for CBS in Berlin knew the truth, their editors were reluctant to report it. In Britain the political Left advocated disarmament, whilst the Right sought moderation and some relationship with Nazi Germany.[33] Churchill and his followers supported rearmament as a deterrent. Following elections in Germany, when Hitler's Nazi Party and the Nationalists won 51 per cent of the vote, the Reichstag building was destroyed by incendiaries. This was blamed on the Communist Party, and five men were tried for the crime before the Leipzig Supreme Court. One confessed and was later executed, but the Nazi prosecutors were unable to present any evidence that would convict the others. The Nazis convicted themselves.[34] It was not only a well-informed politician like Churchill who saw the danger signs, but also, as one would expect, the ever-suspicious French military and some better-informed French politicians.[35] France, however, was not in a position to take effective action over the threat, being preoccupied with the debilitating effects of the Great Depression.[36] At this time in January 1933, it appeared that Hitler's overriding ambition was eastward expansion into Russia. *Lebensraum* in European Russia would provide Germany with the arable land and raw materials to ensure both domination of the continent and world power status. In this context, France was an obstruction to *Ostpolitik* and thus Hitler's aim to transform Germany into a militarised national community.[37]

As early as April 1933, Sir Horace Rumbold, the British Ambassador in Berlin, reported that Hitler's approach to state power was that man was a fighting animal. He obviously had no regard for human beings having any legal rights: his state had rights, and people were servants of the state.[38] 'Pacifism', Hitler said, is the deadliest sin, 'for pacifism means the surrender of the race in the fight for its existence'. Clearly Hitler was obsessed with the power of a military state. Richard N Coudenhove-Kalergi wrote in *The Totalitarian State Against Man*[39] that such a totalitarian regime of a military state evolved from the tribe with its roots in the world of animals. As Tim Bouverie suggests,

[30] ibid 28.

[31] T Bouverie, *Appeasing Hitler* (London, Bodley Head, 2019) 24, 25.

[32] I Kershaw, *Lord Londonderry: Making Friends with Hitler* (London, Penguin Books, 2005) 28–30.

[33] ibid 35. What was alarming was that by 1935, the Nazis boasted air parity with Britain and declared their intention of increasing the army to 550,000 men.

[34] J Mackintosh, *The Paths That Lead to War Europe 1919-1939* (London and Glasgow, Blackie and Son Limited, 1940) 220, 221.

[35] P Jackson, 'Intelligence and Hitler's Rise to Power' (1998) 41(3) *The Historical Journal* 796.

[36] ibid. See also P Neville, 'The Foreign Office and Britain's Ambassadors to Berlin, 1933-39' (2004) 18(3) *Contemporary British History* 110–129.

[37] Jackson ibid 796–797.

[38] T Bouverie, *Appeasing Hitler* (London, Bodley Head, 2019) 15.

[39] London, Frederick Muller Ltd, 1938. 27.

Hitler wanted 'to convince the people that the recovery of freedom by force of arms is a possibility'.[40] 'Hitler', wrote Rumbold, 'starts with the assumption that man is a fighting animal; therefore, the nation is a fighting unit, being a community of fighters … A country or race which ceases to fight is doomed. The fighting capacity of a race depends on its purity'.[41]

In March 1933, Rumbold believed that Nazism represented the worst traits of the German character; 'a mean spirit of revenge, a tendency to brutality and a noisy and irresponsible jingoism'.[42] Rumbold was right to conclude that Hitler would simply lull the outer world into a sense of security. In his dispatch of 26 April 1933, he reported that:[43]

> The parliamentary régime has been replaced by a régime of brute force, and the political parties have, with the exception of the Nazis and Nationalists, disappeared from the arena. For that matter Parliament has ceased to have any raison d'être. The Nazi leader has only to express a wish to have it fulfilled by his followers …
>
> The plans of the Government are far-reaching, they will take several years to mature and they realise that it would be idle to embark on them if there were any danger of premature disturbance either abroad or at home. They may, therefore, be expected to repeat their protestations of peaceful intent from time to time and to have recourse to other measures, including propaganda, to lull the outer world into a sense of security.
>
> To this end it has embarked on a programme of political propaganda on a scale for which there is no analogy in history.
>
> Representative Government has been overthrown. Parliament has to all intents and purposes been abolished. A campaign of terror instituted by the authorities has not failed to have its effect on Democrats, Socialists and Communists alike.

Rumbold appreciated[44] the re-emergence of a warlike and revengeful Germany.[45] He warned that Hitler was 'an uncommonly clever and audacious demagogue'.[46] Rumbold, an outstanding diplomat, considered Hitler, Göring and Goebbels to be 'notoriously pathological cases' and Nazi leadership 'fantastic hooligans and eccentrics'.[47] Churchill was to echo this warning in the House of Commons that:[48]

[40] T Bouverie, *Appeasing Hitler* (London, Bodley Head, 2019) 16.

[41] R Vansittart, *The Mist Procession* (London, Hutchinson, 1958) 476.

[42] DBFP 1919–1939 Ser. 2. Vol 5. No. 36. *Rumbold to Simon*, 26 April 1933.

[43] ibid.

[44] Rumbold served in the British Embassy in Berlin 1913–1914 and deputised for Sir E Goschen in his absence in July 1914. The account of his service at this critical time is recorded in *The War Crisis in Berlin July–August 1914* (London, Constable & Company Ltd, 1944). Subsequently he served as the British Ambassador in Berlin from 1928–1933.

[45] Maynard Keynes, Harold Nicolson and EH Carr all criticised the Treaty of Versailles as punitive, and Germany being regarded as a pariah state. Lloyd George felt that Germany had fulfilled her treaty obligations. Labour MP George Lansbury went so far as to blame the Allies for the rise of Hitler. Noted in T Bouverie, *Appeasing Hitler* (London, Bodley Head, 2019) 46.

[46] P Neville, 'The Foreign Office and Britain's Ambassadors to Berlin, 1933-39' (2004) 18(3) *Contemporary British History* 111.

[47] ibid. Neville relates how Rumbold's dispatches had been prophetic in that five years later Sir Maurice Hankey sent a copy to Sir Horace Wilson, Neville's Chief Diplomatic Adviser demonstrating how right Rumbold's assessments were insofar as Hitler had adhered to Mein Kampf and might do so in the future. CAB21/540.

[48] RAC Parker, *Churchill and Appeasement* (London, Macmillan, 1993).

> We watch with surprise and distress the tumultuous resurgence of ferocity and war spirit, the pitiless ill-treatment of minorities, the normal protections of civilised society to large numbers of individuals solely on ground of race.

It must be the case that the Berlin embassy was the most difficult in this period, in that, as Rumbold wrote to Neville Henderson, his successor: 'You cannot compromise with evil'.[49] Henderson had impressed Vansittart when he was Ambassador in Yugoslavia dealing with the authoritarian King Alexander. Vansittart fell out with Henderson after going to Berlin.[50] It also appears that Henderson had no formal briefings before taking up post in Berlin and regarded himself as Chamberlain's agent.[51] It may be that such an extraordinary relationship between an ambassador and Prime Minister at such a time was highly controversial.[52] Henderson was against the *Little Entente* alliance between France, Czechoslovakia, Romania and Yugoslavia. He adhered to Lord Lothian's acceptance of Germany's conquest of Austria and Czechoslovakia and reconquest of Memel and Danzig[53] following an interview between Lothian and Hitler on 4 May 1937. Before that meeting, Lothian had a meeting with General Göring at which Lothian said that 'Britain would not fight for the League or hazy ideas, or for Abyssinia or anything else that did not directly concern them.'[54] When Lothian spoke to Hitler after the meeting with Göring he told him that '… England would in the last resort be prepared to take up arms … These were the defence of the Empire, of France and the Low Countries against aggression and the freedom of the Seas.'[55] It was, however, also reported by Mr Conwell Evans, who accompanied Lothian, that Lothian had also mentioned Egypt (Suez Canal) and Iraq, where Britain had military obligations.[56] More importantly Lothian is also reported by Evans as saying that 'Britain had no primary interest in Eastern Europe.'[57] As Vansittart noted, Lothian's suggestions in his memorandum of his visit to Berlin (May 1937) were 'quite incompatible with British interests'. Vansittart noted that the last war had been fought to prevent what Lothian suggested. He concluded that:[58]

> If HMG fell in with all this, they would be going dead against the democratic tide; *and the effect on the USA would be catastrophic. I doubt if we should ever recover*. R.V.

On the other hand, Henderson had very good relations with his colleague ambassadors, namely the French and Italian Ambassadors, as well as the states. Secretary in the German Foreign Ministry, Ernest Von Weizsäcker.[59] Also Ulrich von Hassell wrote

[49] F0 800/254 Rumbold to Henderson 15 April 1940.

[50] P Neville, 'The Foreign Office and Britain's Ambassadors to Berlin, 1933-39' (2004) 18(3) *Contemporary British History* 116 even though Vansittart recommended his appointment.

[51] Neville ibid 117.

[52] Henderson admitted in his book *Failure of Mission* (London, Pickle Partners Publishing, 2018) 17 that Chamberlain had advised him: 'a calculated indiscretion was sometimes a very useful form of diplomacy'.

[53] DBFP 1919–1939 Ser. 2. Vol 18 *European Affairs*. No. 480. Letter from Sir N Henderson (Berlin) to Sir R Vansittart Berlin, 10 May 1937.

[54] ibid 729.

[55] ibid 730.

[56] ibid 730 n 7.

[57] ibid.

[58] ibid 731 n 9. In 1937 Vansittart was concerned that Britain kept America informed of peace initiatives with Germany and Italy.

[59] P Neville, 'The Foreign Office and Britain's Ambassadors to Berlin, 1933-39' (2004) 18(3) *Contemporary British History* 121.

that Henderson warned him that if Germany resorted to force over Sudetenland, 'the English will march with France'.[60]

B. Intelligence Warnings

French and British intelligence services, although hampered by political restraints, gave warning of the coming threat, but many were ignored. In Britain there were problems of organisation. Each defence ministry had its own service with a lack of exchange between them. There were no joint staff estimates of German strength, and such uncoordinated efforts had little impact on decision makers. It was therefore difficult to assess and evaluate, let alone predict, what an enemy might do, since much of the intelligence was based on quantitative and not qualitative analysis. Overall, the intelligence services were unprepared for war.[61] In 1938 the estimates of German fighting strength were pessimistic, and that influenced the appeasement of Hitler at Munich. The rearmament programme was based on an underestimate of future German strength. After 1936, military advisers gave pessimistic intelligence predictions supporting appeasement, which appealed to Chamberlain's innermost convictions[62] and undoubtedly led to the betrayal of Czechoslovakia. Wark concludes that had the data on German deficiencies been available in September 1938, a more optimistic interpretation might have been given, avoiding the diplomatic debacle at Munich. Wark concludes that the intelligence services simply failed to be sufficiently thought-provoking, failed to provide challenges to a narrowly conceived and increasingly dogmatic appeasement policy, and were instrumental in delaying the exercise of deterrence until it was too late to be effective.[63]

The French intelligence services knew what was happening but tended to exaggerate the threat because they found it difficult to get attention.[64] The most effective in France was the Deuxième Bureau, supported by the *Service de Renseignement* (SR) the French Secret Intelligence Service. As Jackson opines, the assessments of Nazi rearmament reflected worst-case perspectives based on a close reading of *Mein Kampf* and on Hitler's lust for conquest and domination inherent in the Prussian mentality. The Deuxième Bureau was surely right in concluding that 'Hitler is a traditionalist who has pushed the Prussian notion of individual service to the state and the racist ideology of Pan-Germanism to their most extreme levels.' Hitler's ambitions were considered 'the expression of an innate German impulse'.[65] However exaggerated these reports were,[66] the fact is that considerable information to alarm those responsible for national security was given. As Jackson has discovered, Daladier (a partner in the Munich Agreement with Chamberlain) had such reports when Minister of War and Prime Minister from

[60] ibid 122.
[61] W Wark, *The Ultimate Enemy* (Oxford, OUP, 1986) 21–22.
[62] ibid 234, 235.
[63] ibid 236.
[64] P Jackson, 'Intelligence and Hitler's Rise to Power' (1998) 41(3) *The Historical Journal* 810.
[65] ibid.
[66] R Young, *In Command of France: French Foreign Policy and Military Planning, 1933–1940* (Cambridge, MA, Havard University Press, 1978) 48.

Spring 1933;[67] André Tardieu the Prime Minister and Foreign Minister, received thousands of reports detailing the military character of the German police and frontier security forces and their ties with the *Reichswehr* and other huge paramilitary organisations of the Reich, as well as reports of Soviet forces training Nazi forces. There were countless reports of other violations of Article 169 of the Treaty of Versailles.[68] On 5 July 1922, the Chief of the French Military Intelligence had reported on the need for a coalition to counter Germany, stating:[69]

> Without [the German menace] no other serious threat can exist and it is towards meeting this threat (and to destroying it) that all our policies must be aimed.

Despite the increasing evidence of German rearmament, the policy of Daladier following upon that of Aristide Briand after 1925 was that of disarmament and rapprochement with Germany resulting from the effects of the Great Depression and a policy of austerity.[70] In March 1933, Paul-Boncour was warned in a report by Pierre Viénot that Hitler's rise changed everything and that after a period of 'internal reconstruction', Hitler would turn to treaty revision. Daladier ignored the perceived consequences, but worse, France cut its defence spending by more than 25 per cent between 1931 and 1934.[71] Whilst Rumbold had a clear understanding of the threat Nazism posed, it appears that Francois-Poncet, the French Ambassador in Berlin, failed to recognise the danger possibly induced by his earlier support for improved commercial relations with Germany.[72] In 1933 the French objective remained an arms agreement with international control backed by the League of Nations, Britain and the US.[73] The Foreign Office in London felt that the French approach was a self-fulfilling prophecy. It was said:[74]

> … by talking obsessively of war, the possibility of war, and the probability of war, [France's leadership] is well on the way to making this nightmare prophecy come true.

The French intelligence services reported comprehensively, but they were ignored partly because of the policy of conciliation but also because of the economic crisis. As Jackson concludes, it was only after Munich that politicians of the Right and Left in France realised the inevitable.[75] Those and others who received the warnings had little excuse. In Cato's *Guilty Men* published in 1940, the authors criticised MacDonald and Baldwin for ignoring such warnings. They described this ostracism[76]

> In the House of Commons, a huge and docile majority yessed the government through every situation. A miasma of acquiescence settled upon our parliamentary institutions and over a

[67] P Jackson 'Intelligence and Hitler's Rise to Power' (1998) 41(3) *The Historical Journal* 799.

[68] ibid 800. Article 169 Treaty of Versailles provided that all German arms, munitions and war material, including anti-aircraft material, existing in Germany in excess of the quantities allowed, must be surrendered to the governments of the Principal Allied and Associated Powers to be destroyed or rendered useless.

[69] SHAT, 7N 2520, 'Rapport du Colonel Fournier sur les nécessités d'une coalition contre l'Allemagne' 5 July 1922 as cited in Jackson ibid 801.

[70] Jackson ibid 803.

[71] ibid 812–813.

[72] ibid 814.

[73] ibid 819.

[74] ibid 821. At this time Britain and the US favoured an arms agreement between France and Germany.

[75] Jackson ibid 824.

[76] *Guilty Men* (London, Faber and Faber Ltd, 2010) 18.

> considerable section of the press. Independent minded members went into individual opposition or, in disgust, out of public life'.

The authors described this legacy given to Chamberlain as:[77]

> ... a mass of urgent problems which they had fumbled or funked, a well-tested political apparatus for smudging the sharp edges of every issue and for smearing the personalities of those who raise complaints concerning it.

In a letter to Mr Leeper at the Foreign Office, Mr Cadogan enclosed a copy of a Memorandum by Brigadier Timperley regarding Germany's attitude to disarmament.[78] This was a very clear warning to the government of the emerging Nazi threat. The Brigadier concluded that:

> Germany had not been idle during these years and with great ingenuity had carried out a steady erosion of the disarmament clauses, ...
>
> Very extensive preparations have also been made to prepare German industry for industrial mobilisation.
>
> Within a few weeks of his arrival, Hitler has carried out a revolution and made himself complete master of Germany.
>
> The country has given itself up to a delirium of reawakened nationalism and of the most blatant and dangerous militarism.
>
> What then is to be our attitude? Are we to go forward as if nothing has happened? Can we afford to ignore what is going on behind the scenes in Germany?
>
> ... There is a mad dog abroad once more and we must resolutely combine either to ensure its destruction or at least its confinement until the disease has run its course.[79]

Brigadier Timperley's memorandum clearly called for action in light of the increasing threat of German rearmament and militarisation, putting it on a war footing. He was convinced that war seemed inevitable and that if steps were not taken, Britain would not be able to meet the challenge. He urged strong combined action with former allies and, if possible, the US to deter the Nazi menace. If members of the Cabinet had read Hitler's *Mein Kampf*, they could not have ignored his declared intention of annihilating France and dominating Europe. General Maxine Weygand, the Commander in Chief of the French army, was right in opining that German equality in armaments was a trick:[80]

> In reality there will be no equality but a very pronounced superiority for Germany given the military culture of this nation and the intensive efforts already undertaken to prepare the German armaments industry for rearmament.

Despite such warnings, in March 1933, the British government planned to limit the army to 200,000 men at a time when the Germans doubled the size of the Reichswehr.[81]

[77] ibid 18, 19.

[78] DBFP 1919–1939 Ser. 2. Vol 05. No. 127. *European affairs and war debts October 1933 – August 1934* 213–217. W 5158/40/98.

[79] ibid.

[80] T Bouverie, *Appeasing Hitler* (London, Bodley Head, 2019) 18.

[81] ibid 19.

Some imbibed the false narrative that the Allies were responsible for Hitler and that Germany had met her treaty obligations, so the government celebrated its appeasement in the Disarmament Conference. The Prime Minister's (Mr MacDonald) visit to Rome was directed to using Italy as a go-between Germany and France, as Eden said:[82]

> We have to appreciate that the situation is that, unless, as the result of the Disarmament Conference, we can secure a Convention which all the nations will sign, we cannot secure for Europe that period of appeasement which it needs. That is the problem, that confronts us. To secure a solution, he rightly said, we have to bring France and Germany closer together. To do that, what better step could my right hon. Friend have taken than his journey to Rome? What Power in Europe other than ourselves could more usefully and beneficially use its influence to bring about a *rapprochement* between France and Germany than Italy?

C. Foreign Office Warnings

On 28 August 1933, Sir R Vansittart[83] wrote a memorandum on the present and future position in Europe,[84] focusing on the Austrian crisis but noting the need for considering rearmament. Vansittart's astute perception of Hitler, like that of Rumbold, described Hitler's approach and methods. Vansittart was convinced that Hitler would not abandon – save under compulsion – his firm intention of destroying Austrian independence and creating a de facto 'Anschluss'.[85] It was an open secret that anything peaceful said by Hitler was merely for foreign consumption and designed to gain time. The great attraction about Austria was that Hitler would achieve a resounding success without having to strike a blow.[86] Vansittart foresaw the day 'a few years hence' when Germany would have the benefit of fighting on one front.[87] He saw the threat to Austria as a challenge to democracy by a totalitarian Hitlerite regime that[88]

> If Hitler wins this first round he will be hard to hold; he will, with increased confidence and enthusiasm, press on with rearmament so as to lose no time in following up his political success in Austria with, next time, a military success against Poland.

Vansittart's suggestion was that the Four Power Pact should be revived subject to:.[89]

> holding Italy to her self-imposed task of keeping Hitler under control … with the wider policy of promoting Franco-Italian conciliation in all spheres as a preliminary to that Anglo-French-Italian co-operation which is likely to be the only real bulwark of peace until Germany

[82] *Hansard*, House of Commons Debates, 8 March 1934, Vol 276, col 617.
[83] Sir Robert Vansittart was Principal Private Secretary to the Prime Minister from 1928 to 1930 and Permanent Under-Secretary at the Foreign Office from 1930 to 1938 then from 1938–1941 Chief Diplomatic Adviser to the British government.
[84] No. 371. Memorandum by Sir R Vansittart on the Present and Future Position in Europe [C 7736/2092/3] Foreign Office, 28 August 1933.
[85] ibid para 4.
[86] ibid para 9.
[87] This was enabled by the German-Soviet Non-Aggression Pact 1939 and the occupation of Czechoslovakia.
[88] No. 371. Memorandum by Sir R Vansittart on the Present and Future Position in Europe [C 7736/2092/3] Foreign Office, 28 August 1933. para 13.
[89] ibid para 32.

On 14 October 1933, Germany withdrew from the Disarmament Conference and from the League of Nations.[90] There was Tory apathy and self-interest, putting the party before the country and therefore unwilling to go against the perceived tide of public opinion in rearming,[91] although the *Daily Mail* in November 1933 demanded 5,000 new warplanes and then increased the demand to 20,000.[92] That same month Vansittart and other senior civil servants asked the Cabinet if they would warn Germany over rearmament and, if not, was the Cabinet prepared to contemplate German aggression against Poland or Austria. The government refused to do anything[93] even when Churchill warned of war materials pouring into Germany.[94] He spoke of Germany under Hitler having 'no parallel … since the days of barbarism'.[95]

Despite this, the government approved the sale of 118 aero engines to Germany.[96]

It is interesting to reflect on the information provided by the Defence Requirements Sub-Committee (DRC) and the Ministerial Committee on Disarmament (MCD) – Rearmament Budgets:

	DRC – February 1934	MCD – July 1934
Army	£39,990,980	£20,000,000
Navy	£21,067,660	£13,000,000
Air Force	£10,264,940	£20,000,000
Total	£71,323,580	£53,000,000

Sources: TNA CAB 16/110, CID: 'Defence Requirements Sub-Committee, Report', 28 February 1934; and TNA, CAB 4/23, C.P. 205 (34), Disarmament Conference 1932, 'Ministerial Committee: Defence Requirements Report', 31 July 1934.[97]

In a debate on 8 March 1934, Sir Philip Sassoon[98] had the unenviable task of trying to reconcile diametrically opposed views on the air estimates:[99]

> … two diametrically opposed schools of thought who differ with great earnestness and vigour upon the Fighting Services in general and upon the Royal Air Force in particular. Perhaps the divergence between these two schools is more acute at the present time than it has ever been before. On the one hand, there are those who regard the Air arm as an imminent threat to the survival of our present-day civilisation and would like to see all military

[90] T Bouverie, *Appeasing Hitler* (London, Bodley Head, 2019) 19, 21. According to R Boothby MP visiting Bayreuth that month there was war fever in Germany.

[91] Bouverie ibid 26. There was little opposition as the Tories had a landslide of 473 seats whereas Labour only had 52 and Liberals 35.

[92] Bouverie ibid 54.

[93] ibid 30, SW Roskill, *Hankey: Man of Secrets*, Vol III, 1931–963 (London, 1974) 86.

[94] T Bouverie, *Appeasing Hitler* (London, Bodley Head, 2019) 30. See *Hansard*, 7 November 1933 and 7 February 1934.

[95] RAC Parker, *Churchill and Appeasement* (London, Macmillan, 2000) 34.

[96] T Bouverie, *Appeasing Hitler* (London, Bodley Head, 2019) 31.

[97] See also: DE Delaney, 'Imperial Armies in the Period of Rearmament and Appeasement, 1933–1939' in *The Imperial Army Project: Britain and the Land Forces of the Dominions and India, 1902–1945* (Oxford, 2018; online edn, Oxford Academic, 15 Feb 2018), doi.org/10.1093/oso/9780198704461.003.0006, accessed 15 June 2024.

[98] The Under-Secretary of State for Air.

[99] *Hansard*, House of Commons Debates, 8 March 1934, Vol 286 col 2027.

> aircraft swept out of existence. On the other hand, there are those who consider that the provisions which His Majesty's Government have made for the air defences of this Island are utterly inadequate and who would like to see a large and immediate increase in the number of our service machines.

The estimates overall showed a moderate increase in expenditure, which he explained:

> … The net figure of £17,561,000 shows an increase of £135,000 only. A truer picture is provided this year by a comparison of the gross Estimates. These, at £20,165,000, show an increase of £527,000.

When Mr Attlee spoke, he said he could not believe there was any real air defence.[100]

According to Captain Guest, the estimates themselves were misleading in that the country was weaker because the government was trying to get a larger Air Force and spend less money.[101] Churchill in that debate called for 'the parity in air power … and, arising out of that parity, a sound system of home defence'[102] and of his dread of the day when the means of threatening the heart of the British Empire should pass into the hands of the present rulers of Germany.[103] Colonel Wedgwood spoke after Churchill spoke of real danger to the country and the essential need for the defence forces to be reorganised on the basis of the new knowledge. He also referred to the 'War Memoirs' of Lloyd George and the reference to the fanatical hostility shown by the Higher Command to any new ideas.[104] Although Chamberlain supported a significantly larger Air Force, he was only prepared to spend modestly on the army.[105] Between 1931 and 1934, defence budgets increased by 25 per cent.[106] In another debate on 28 November 1934, Churchill defined deterrence in terms of:[107]

> If two Powers show themselves equally capable of inflicting damage upon each other by some particular process of war, so that neither gains an advantage from its adoption and both suffer the most hideous reciprocal injuries, it is not only possible but it seems to be probable that neither will employ that means. What would they gain by it?

Harold Nicolson noted in his diary on 2 February 1934 that Germany was 'military mad', and a further warning was given by Sir Austin Chamberlain in the Commons that the Hitler regime was 'the worst of all Prussian imperialism'.[108]

II. Violations of the Treaty of Versailles

Hitler's forces occupied the Saar region on 1 March 1935, and six days later Hitler renounced the Locarno Treaty and ordered the Reichswehr to occupy the demilitarised

[100] ibid 2048.
[101] ibid 2057.
[102] ibid 2071.
[103] ibid 2072.
[104] ibid 2078.
[105] T Bouverie, *Appeasing Hitler* (London, Bodley Head, 2019) 34. Note by Chancellor of The Exchequer on The Report of the DRC, 20 June 1934, DRC CAB 16/111.
[106] T Bouverie, *Appeasing Hitler* (London Bodley Head, 2019) 35.
[107] *Hansard*, House of Commons Debates, 28 November 1934, Vol 295 col 863.
[108] T Bouverie *Appeasing Hitler* (London, Bodley Head, 2019) 44.

zone of the Rhineland. The British and French took no action.[109] On the 16 March, Goebbels[110] announced a fundamental breach of the Versailles Treaty with the increase in the German army to 36 divisions divided into 12 army corps of 500,000 men and the reintroduction of conscription. The British government announced spending £10 million on defence just as Goebbels made his announcement. The next day, General Von Blomberg, deputising for Hitler at a rally to celebrate the Great War dead, declared that 'We want peace with equal rights and security for all. We seek no more.'[111] This was obviously to appease Britain and France and distract them from the significant seizure of the Saar. Both countries failed again to act despite the clear breach of the military limitations imposed by the Versailles Treaty. William Shirer, a perceptive journalist, understood from the time of his reassignment in Berlin for the Hearst Press what was coming and could not understand the 'conciliatory' reaction of the British press. To underscore Shirer's insight, Goering's bombers flew over Berlin for the first time in defiance of the treaty on 18 March 1935.[112]

A. Appeasing Hitler

A few days later Eden and Simon had a meeting with Hitler and Neurath,[113] but according to Simon, nothing was agreed.[114] During the first meeting, Eden was intrigued to discuss a shared experience of trench warfare with Hitler but had been cautioned about not being taken in by Hitler. There was some discussion about Germany joining the League of Nations and promises to honour the Locarno Treaty.[115] Eden believed that Hitler was a 'typical Austrian'. That first meeting took place on 25 March 1935, at 10.30 am,[116] with opening statements by Simon and Hitler and discussion of a proposed Eastern European Pact. In the afternoon there was a further meeting on this, followed by the question of Austria and a proposed Central European Pact. Hitler discussed his views on the League of Nations, whilst Simon expressed a desire to have a closer association with Germany without prejudice to Britain's relations with France. Hitler expressed Germany's desire for colonies like other Powers. The next day they discussed naval armaments and agreed in principle to meet in London for exchanges in view of the naval conference to be held in 1935. They also discussed military and air armaments. Baron von Neurath, the German Foreign Secretary, handed over a draft agreement giving suggestions for an Eastern Pact. At the last meeting they discussed a proposed air pact and prohibition of bombing.[117]

[109] WL Shirer, *Berlin Diary* (London, Hamish Hamilton, 1941) 61.
[110] Hitler's Minister of Propaganda 1933–1945.
[111] WL Shirer, *Berlin Diary* (London, Hamish Hamilton, 1941) 33, 34.
[112] ibid 37.
[113] Foreign Minister of Germany between 1932 and 1938.
[114] WL Shirer, *Berlin Diary* (London, Hamish Hamilton, 1941) 37.
[115] T Bouverie, *Appeasing Hitler* (London Bodley Head, 2019) 43.
[116] DBFP 1919–1939, Ser. 2. Vol 12. *Notes of Anglo-German Conversations, held at the Chancellor's Palace, Berlin, on March 25 and 26, 1935*, Reference: C 2580/55/18.
[117] DBFP 1919–1939, Ser. 2. Vol 12. No. 651. *Notes of Anglo-German Conversations, held at the Chancellor's Palace, Berlin, on March 25 and 26, 1935* – ProQuest.

Simon outlined the British aim:

> to preserve general peace by helping to secure co-operation amongst all European countries. He wished that Germany should work with all countries for that object. They felt that the future of Europe would take one of two forms. It would either take the form of general co-operation for securing continued peace or it would take the form of a division into two camps-isolation on the one side, and combination (which might look like encirclement) on the other.[118]

The withdrawal of Germany from the League of Nations, events relating to Austria, and the recent unilateral announcement connected with rapid German rearmament made it difficult for the British ministers to fulfil their engagement to go to Berlin. He therefore went to Berlin with Eden to have a free and frank discussion with Hitler, which ensued. For his part, Hitler wanted to present a 'true picture of what the German people wanted'. He spoke of the 'immeasurable disaster' that had befallen Germany, and 'such co-operation as the German people desired was only realisable with the disappearance of a psychosis which had been inherited from the War and was a burden upon every kind of cooperation'.[119] He said that 'the German people had no interest in pursuing an imperialist policy', although it was surrounded by countries 'inhabited by intensely nationalistic peoples'. His third task was 'moral rehabilitation and reconstruction of the German people'. He also spoke of 'political reconstruction' of no interest to the outside world, and he made it quite clear that Germany could not make any concession where the 'rehabilitation of their honour was concerned'.[120] He wanted equality for Germany, and that is why Germany withdrew from the League. He questioned the regime in Austria but clearly resented its separation from fellow Germans, as he did of the German minority in Lithuania. He considered the territorial clauses of the Treaty of Versailles as 'moral defamation', which Germany could never accept. He asked them to understand the feelings of a country which, in a situation of isolation, had suffered unprecedented humiliation for twenty years. He was prepared to make concessions, except where honour was concerned.

i. British Interests

Hitler was remarkably frank in this conversation, but he obviously resented the way Germany had been treated, and his reference to 'national honour' and his apparent resentment of France and Russia were ominous signs of his approach. Although he suggested that after the Saar plebiscite. there were no further territorial differences dividing France and Germany.[121] His preoccupation with the rehabilitation of national honour was his mantra and conviction that would be echoed in his speeches and demands. The problem was that Germany wanted to be treated as an equal Power by Britain with overseas interests. That was impossible if Britain had ties to France.

[118] ibid 2.
[119] ibid 3.
[120] ibid 4. At one point Hitler referred to Prussian help at Waterloo that 'Wellington did not protest when the Prussian army arrived, although that army could only arrive in violation of a treaty'.
[121] DBFP ibid.

What Britain sought was an eastern arrangement encompassing: (1) Non-aggression; (2) Consultation; and (3) Mutual assistance.[122] Hitler said that Germany was the country most interested in the preservation of peace in light of Germany being 95 per cent more vulnerable than other European countries because of its densely populated industrial areas vulnerable to bombing.[123] What is also interesting are the references Hitler made to the prospects of war between eastern European states, as the Minutes of the meeting record:[124]

> Here the question arose as to the possible parties to any war in Eastern Europe. Such a war, for example, might be between-
>
> Germany and Poland.
>
> Russia and Germany.
>
> Russia and the Baltic States.
>
> Poland and the Baltic States.
>
> Germany and the Baltic States.
>
> Poland and Czechoslovakia.
>
> Germany and Czechoslovakia.
>
> As regards the practical probability of war between any of these groups of Powers. Herr Hitler wished to observe that Germany and Russia had no common frontier and therefore there would be no war; there would be no war between Germany and Poland because of the non-aggression pact between the two Powers; again, Russia and Poland had a non-aggression pact which was still good for eight or nine years; war between the Baltic States and Russia could, Herr Hitler thought, be excluded because there were to a large degree non-aggression pacts;[125] war between Germany and Czechoslovakia could be excluded because there was an arbitration agreement.[126] Therefore the real possibilities of conflict in those regions of Europe were limited. But there was another question as to which Powers might declare war on other Powers in those regions. It was impossible to suppose that the Baltic States would declare war on Russia, or that Poland would declare war on Russia. Further, Herr Hitler could give the British Ministers the assurance that Germany would never declare war on Russia … Herr Hitler repeated that because of the combination of Bolshevist doctrines with the political aims of Russia and because of the strength of the Russian military and economic organisation, it seemed to him that from Russia there was greater probability of war than from other countries.[127]

The British interest was to secure a European eastern settlement as useful as Locarno, but be confident that there could be no general settlement without it. Thus, Eden asked Hitler if he would be willing to include his bilateral pacts in a multilateral settlement? Russia, Hitler said, saw in Germany the champion of Europe against the Asiatic and Bolshevik menace, as Germany saw in Poland the bulwark against that menace.[128]

[122] ibid.

[123] ibid.

[124] ibid.

[125] See BFSP, vol 125, 890–3; vol 135, 478–80 and 638–40 respectively for the Treaties of Non-Aggression between the Soviet Union and (a) Lithuania, of 28 September 1926, renewed 6 May 1931; (b) Estonia, of 4 May 1932; (c) Latvia, of 5 February 1932.

[126] Signed at Locarno on 16 October 1925; see BFSP, vol 122, 288–9.

[127] DBFP Ser. 2. Vol 12, No. 651. *Notes of Anglo-German Conversations on March 25 and 26, 1935.*

[128] ibid.

Hitler had difficulty accepting the mutual assistance aspects which, in his view, 'merely serve[d] to organise war'.[129] Hitler concluded that Germany would not fight for the Bolsheviks, but he might be prepared to take negative measures and to say that no party to the proposed pact should give assistance to an aggressor.[130] The German government thought the best course would be to conclude a general pact containing obligations of non-aggression and consultation and an undertaking not to afford assistance to an aggressor. This would be sufficient if the parties had confidence in the signatures to the pact.[131] The German government would accept arbitration as already in force between Germany and other countries.[132] Hitler did not want an alliance with Russia and France.

ii. Hitler's View on Austria

As to Austria, Hitler said that until 1866 both countries were a single political unit and that their inhabitants had the same national origin and if a free vote were possible, the population of Austria would vote for closer relations, if not complete union, with Germany.[133] That may have been the case in 1919 but not in 1935. Hitler ruled out annexation. and '[n]ot for one minute did Germany think of violating Austrian territory or disregarding the treaty or imposing any regime upon Austria'. Later he said:[134]

> The Austrian problem did not interest the German Government or concern them … Germany did not intend to threaten the independence of Austria … In the Austrian question the German Government were not interested …. The German Government were indifferent to the Austrian question, which did not necessitate sacrifice or concessions by them. Why could not the question be settled by a non-aggression pact? The German Government feared by the suggestions which were put to them to complicate a troubled situation. They preferred clear-cut solutions, a nonaggression pact, for example. They did not see the utility of a guarantee of non-interference.

Hitler could not have been more explicit, and yet he most likely wanted to annex Austria, so he would not give any guarantee on non-interference despite his aim of a multilateral pact of non-aggression.

iii. Hitler's View on League of Nations

Simon opened the discussion by stressing the benefits of the League, where it provided an essential meeting place for discussion of difficulties and opportunity for constructive talks to reach adjustments about many dangerous matters. Britain wanted to facilitate Germany's return to the League.[135] Hitler, in reply, said that Germany had

[129] ibid.
[130] ibid.
[131] But later Hitler questioned excluding external non-interference in Austria in respect of any Central European Pact. Simon thought von Neurath could consider this further.
[132] DBFP Ser. 2. Vol 12. No. 651. *Notes of Anglo-German Conversations on March 25 and 26, 1935.*
[133] ibid.
[134] ibid.
[135] ibid.

suffered 'a great disillusionment' owing to the coupling of the Covenant with the Treaty of Versailles. The Treaty of Versailles had imposed inferiority on Germans, which they had never recognised. The imposition of that inferiority was the greatest mistake in the treaty. Eden countered that by arguing that ever since Germany had joined the League after Locarno, it was an equal.[136] Hitler was not taken with this argument, and 'what remained over and beyond that was the actual fact of Germany's position of inferiority on all those points which she had not rectified for herself'.[137] Again, there was a clear division between Hitler's and Simon's views on the League, with Britain convinced that some such organisation was indispensable in the modern world and Hitler expressing concerns as to inferiority.

Hitler said that his government wanted agreement with Britain and also with France, but in the case of the latter, it was very difficult to dissipate certain misunderstandings, and an understanding with Britain would be a valuable asset. The British government wished to have the closest association with Germany, but they wanted that without prejudice to their relations with France.[138] Again, there was an impasse, as Britain could not have such a relationship with Germany, nor could it do anything as to colonies.

iv. Naval Armaments

It was agreed that naval discussions would take place in London to discuss building programmes rather than ratios. Simon made it clear that Britain would not accept that the German fleet would equate to 35 per cent of the British fleet.[139] This led to the Anglo-German Naval Agreement which alarmed Churchill and his colleagues but pleased Hitler.

v. Military Armaments

Eden said that in the post-war years British armaments were reduced and Britain had tried to find a basis of international agreement. He enquired whether the German government wanted an arms limitation agreement. It was difficult when the recent announcement about the German Army having 36 divisions seemed to make agreement impossible. In all previous discussions, parity between the western European Powers had been accepted as the basis. This was an estimate that other western European Powers could never attain. It would make parity impossible and give Germany superiority. Eden wanted to know if it was correct that the proposed German strength in effectives was 500,000 men; what their length of service was (this was one year) and the role of the paramilitary formations (there were none according to Hitler[140]) and the police troops (these would be part of the army); whether Labour Service would be maintained; and what training reservists would receive in the future.[141] Hitler then produced a diagram

[136] ibid.
[137] ibid.
[138] ibid.
[139] ibid.
[140] ibid.
[141] ibid.

which showed the strengths in divisions of Germany and the neighbouring Powers as follows:

Germany: 36 divisions.

France: 34 divisions, plus 10 divisions in North Africa.

Italy: 34 divisions.

Czechoslovakia: 17 divisions.

Belgium: 8 divisions.

Poland: 34 divisions.

Russia: 101 divisions.

Hitler maintained that Germany was vulnerable to attack and that her iron and steel industries were in an unfortified region, the demilitarised zone; so were a large part of the coal mines.[142]

vi. Air Armaments

On this subject Hitler produced another diagram showing:

Britain-

August 1934, first line, 1,045 machines; including reserves, 1,847 machines.

April 1935, including reserves, 2,100 machines.

France-

August 1934, first line, 1,986 machines; including reserves, 3,800 machines.

April 1935, including reserves, 6,000 machines.

Italy-

August 1934, first line, 1,059 machines; including reserves, 1,600 machines.

April 1935, including reserves, 2,100 machines.

Czechoslovakia-

August 1934, first line, 570 machines; including reserves, 960 machines.

April 1935, including reserves, 1,200 machines.

Russia-

August 1934, first line, 1,979 machines; including reserves, 2,918 machines.

April 1935, including reserves, 4,300 machines.

Poland-

August 1934, first line, 695 machines; including reserves, 1,430 machines.

April 1935, including reserves, 1,500 machines.

Belgium-

August 1934, first line, 246 machines; including reserves, 400 machines.

April 1935, including reserves, 450 machines.

[142] ibid.

Simon said he did not recognise the figure attributed by the diagram to Britain. He thought we had 690 first-line machines.[143] Hitler said that if Britain would bring her air strength for the UK up to the French strength, ie, to parity with France, then it would be that parity which Germany would demand. If Britain persuaded France to come down to the British level, the German government would be delighted because they would have to spend less on their Air Force. But even if Britain did not consider herself threatened by France and preferred to have a smaller force than France, Germany could not help it because of the necessity of protecting herself. Hitler added that there could be no question of German hegemony over Europe. What was in question was the hegemony of Russia or the hegemony of a combination of smaller states with France. Hitler replied that Germany had reached parity with Great Britain.[144] No doubt this came as a surprise.

As to any Air Pact this would operate, according to Simon, in the event of unprovoked aggression by air attack; it would oblige the signatories to come immediately to the aid of the attacked party. There would not be a discussion at Geneva first.[145] Action would be required immediately. What was not envisaged by Britain was any such consequences of appearing to recognise as legitimate indiscriminate attacks from the air upon the civil population and industrial areas. The Air Pact could not contain the figures for air strengths; it was merely a promise that the signatories would use their air forces for the purposes and in the manner described. Other complex agreements would be required to secure the ultimate peaceful future of Europe.[146] Hitler supported this Pact and particularly liked the idea of the prohibition of indiscriminate bombing of densely populated regions. Hitler regretted that the order of priority was first an international agreement on the limitation of air forces and then the conclusion of an Air Pact.[147] He wanted the Pact to come first with an agreement on: (1) the prohibition of the use of gas and incendiary bombs; (2) the limitation of bombing to the fighting zones; and (3) possibly the complete prohibition of all bombardment from the air.

At the conclusion of the meetings, Simon felt disappointed that it had not been possible in two days to get a larger measure of agreement. It showed that these things were more difficult and complicated. Eden said he would report to the British government, who would continue to use their utmost efforts in the spirit of friendly cooperation. Hitler thanked the ministers for 'the loyal efforts they had made in the matter of the Saar vote', and for their 'loyal and generous attitude to Germany which hoped to co-operate'. On the other hand, he hoped the British ministers would see the difficulty of the German government's position who 'were struggling to lift up a country which had lived during 16 years under moral depression'. They were trying to lift her to that level of equality in a community of nations.[148]

In conclusion, Hitler said that:[149]

[143] ibid.
[144] ibid. There appears to be a misprint in the digital copy of the Notes with reference to a 'Herr Hider'.
[145] DBFP ibid.
[146] ibid.
[147] ibid.
[148] ibid.
[149] ibid.

> The British Ministers should be convinced that many of the German objections arose out of the feeling that if the present German Reich gave an undertaking, and freely gave it, it would be necessary for the Reich more strictly to observe such an undertaking than any other State in order to restore the reputation which had been lost in the last 16 years.

Hitler said he would not sign anything which he thought he could not accept, but if he gave an undertaking, he would never break it. A communiqué was then drafted to confirm that discussions had taken place on the London Communique of 3 February 1935 for the purpose of strengthening the peace of Europe by promoting international co-operation.[150]

> **Eastern Pact**
>
> Handed to the British Ministers the note on the Eastern Pact contained in Annex I.[151]
>
> Annex 1 to Third Meeting
>
> Eastern Pact[152]
>
> In the opinion of the German Government the Powers interested in East European questions might, following up the fundamental ideas of the Kellogg Pact, conclude a pact on the following basis:-
>
> 1. The contracting Powers agree not to resort to aggression or to force in any form against one another.
> 2. The contracting Powers agree to conclude among themselves, as far as they have not yet done so, treaties of arbitration and conciliation providing for an obligatory procedure of arbitration in the case of disputes of a legal nature, and for a procedure of conciliation with a view to arriving at an amicable settlement in matters of political conflicts.
> 3. If, nevertheless, one of the contracting Powers believes itself to be threatened with aggression or with the employment of force on the part of another contracting Power, then, on the demand of the Power in question, a conference of representatives of the Governments of all contracting Powers will immediately be convened, in order to deliberate on the situation and, if necessary, on the steps to be taken for the maintenance of peace.
> 4. If, in spite of the above agreement, hostilities should break out between any two contracting Powers, the other contracting Powers engage not to support the aggressor in any way, neither economically nor financially nor in the military way.
> 5. The pact is to be concluded for a period of ten years, with the possibility of extension for a further period.

B. Stresa Conference and Denouement of Anglo-German Naval Treaty

On 11 April 1935, Prime Minister McDonald and Simon attended a conference at Stresa with Mussolini and Flandin, the French Premier. They issued a resolution censuring the German repudiation of the Versailles Treaty disarmament provisions supported by

[150] Annex 1, *Notes of Anglo-German Conversations on March 25 and 26, 1935*. Nat. Arch. CAB/24.254. Secret C.P. 69(35).
[151] *Notes of Anglo-German Conversations on March 25 and 26, 1935* 27.
[152] Cmd. 5143 of 1936.

the League Council. In Patterson's cable to Baldwin from Geneva on 18 April 1935, he reported that an accommodation would not have been possible without the concurrence of France. The German reaction was against any question of rejoining the League and a continued effort to rearm with increased speed and expand the air force. So within less than a month, Hitler had reneged on his comments to Simon and Eden.

i. Revival of Pan-Germanism

On 21 May 1935 Hitler declared that Germany wanted peace and needed it and that Germany did not have the means to threaten anybody. This was intended to mislead whilst Germany continued its rapid rearmament programme.

As far as Austria was concerned he said:

> Germany neither intends, nor wishes to interfere in the internal. affairs of Austria, to annex Austria, or to conclude an Anschluss
>
> … The German government are ready on principle to conclude packs of non-aggression with their various neighbouring states.[153]

Lithuania was excluded.

He then disingenuously promised to fulfil all Germany's obligations under the Treaty of Locarno and that: 'The German Government considers its action as a contribution to the appeasement of Europe'. He also suggested, under his 13-Point Plan to complete the international outlawing of all aerial bombing. To the appeaser, all his points would seem attractive, and to the naïve, very reasonable.[154] Indeed he was granted a prize when Britain under Prime Minister Baldwin on 18 June 1935, signed the Anglo-German Naval Agreement The treaty limited the Kriegsmarine to 35 per cent of the size of Great Britain's Royal Navy based on tonnage. Whilst that may seem to benefit the British navy, Germany's U-boat tonnage would equal Britain's, jeopardising Britain's sea lanes.[155]

This complacency and isolationist tendency was not just found amongst British politicians and their hacks in the press but also across the Atlantic. When CBS reporter William Shirer went home on leave, he found New Yorkers 'too optimistic about European affairs'.[156] American isolationism was based on Washington's parting warning against European entanglements, especially on behalf of Britain and France, but not against intervention per se anywhere in the world. Americans, by their nature, objected to anyone who would limit their independence or sovereignty and thus had opposed membership in the League of Nations and the Treaty of Versailles.[157] Hodgson argued in his biography of Henry Stimson that American refusal to accept the Treaty of Versailles and membership of the League made war inevitable.[158] Indeed, the French had sought guarantees from Britain and America for that very reason, fearing a militaristic revival in Germany. France had earlier failed to reach agreement on naval rearmament with Japan

[153] BDFP Ser, 2. Vol XVI. No. 48. 60 [C 2361/4/18] 61, 62. See also BDFP Ser. 2. Vol XIII. No. 222.
[154] WL Shirer, *Berlin Diary* (London, Hamish Hamilton, 1941) 39, 40.
[155] ibid 41.
[156] ibid 43.
[157] G Hodgson, *The Colonel, The Life and Times of Henry Stimson 1867–1950* (New York, Alfred A Knopf, 1990) 176.
[158] ibid 180.

when agreement was reached between Japan, the US and Britain in 1930. Britain gave up supremacy of the seas, and Churchill maintained that 'British naval requirements ought to be fixed by ourselves alone'.[159]

Hitler lied about Germany's intentions, saying that they had no 'expansionist character' and he would never contemplate war against Czechoslovakia or Russia.[160] He refused to guarantee Europe's eastern borders but offered Britain an alliance to help protect the British Empire whilst exaggerating the strength of his air force. Simon said Britain could not do this at the expense of France and wanted to be 'loyal friends of all'. Eden saw this as a revival of the 'Old Prussian Spirit'.[161] Hitler used bluff, a tactic he was to use many times.

ii. Anglo-German Naval Agreement

These meetings were followed by an Anglo-German Naval Agreement, which in effect was a breach of the Versailles Treaty. This was seen by Mussolini as British acquiescence in German bullying, and he concluded that Britain was no friend of collective security. It may well have encouraged his dreams of Imperial Rome or an East African empire.[162] It was indeed a pivotal moment in British foreign policy as interpreted by Churchill when, on the 11 July 1935, he spoke of a 'scene that was gravely changed':[163]

> We have condoned, and even praised, the German treaty breaking in fleet building. I see that Lord Beatty, speaking somewhere else, said that we ought to be grateful to Germany for not having demanded 50 per cent. On that basis we ought to be more grateful that they did not demand 100 per cent. We have condoned this unilateral violation of the Treaty, and we have become a party to it without agreement with any of the other countries concerned. We have, however unintentionally, nullified and stultified the League of Nations' condemnation of treaty breaking in respect of armaments, in which we were ourselves concerned, in which, indeed, we took a leading part. We have, it seems to me, revealed, again quite unintentionally, a very considerable measure of indifference to the interests of other Powers, particularly Powers in the Baltic, who were encouraged by our example to join with us in the League of Nations in condemning treaty breaking …
>
> … For the moment, I only refer to them to bring to the notice of the Committee that we have in this matter, in the name of what is called practical realism, seemed to depart from the principle of collective security in a very notable fashion.
>
> We have seemed to depart from – although I hope we may return again to – the comradeship agreed upon at Stresa and from the League of Nations resolution against Treaty-breaking, and we have done it in order to make a side deal with Germany which we thought to be in our interests, and not contrary to other interests in Europe. We cannot have done this without affecting prejudicially – although, again, I hope only for the time being – the confidence which exists between us and France, which is so vitally necessary for us at all times, but never more vitally necessary for us than during these years upon which we are now entering, when our air defence will be so woefully inferior to that of Germany. It is not a very good tale

[159] RAC Parker, *Churchill and Appeasement* (London, Macmillan, 2000) 16–17.
[160] T Bouverie, *Appeasing Hitler* (London, Bodley Head, 2019) 65.
[161] ibid 65–68.
[162] ibid 71.
[163] *Hansard*, House of Commons Debates, 11 July 1935, Vol 304. cols 543, 544.

> which I have had to tell of what has happened since we last had a full dress debate on foreign affairs. But it is only one part of the story. At the same time that we have been diverging from the League of Nations in one direction for our particular and legitimate national interest, real or supposed, Italy has made it plain that she means to invade and conquer Abyssinia. I hope that the optimism of the right hon. Gentleman the Leader of the Liberal party may be borne out.

C. Occupation of the Rhineland

Before the Rhineland crisis erupted in March 1936, Vansittart wrote a memorandum pointing out the deterioration in relations between the Great Powers since Hitler became Chancellor.[164]

The Franco-Soviet Pact was signed on 27 February 1936, which Hitler used as an excuse to occupy the Rhineland. Hitler alleged a breach of the Treaty of Locarno. Under Locarno, Britain had pledged to defend the demilitarised zone.[165] Eden had just become Foreign Secretary and was considering what to offer Hitler when Hitler took the initiative and occupied the Rhineland in violation of the Versailles and Locarno Treaties and contrary to international law. The point to consider is why Eden would even have contemplated breaking the Treaty of Locarno and acquiescing by not defending the zone.[166] The Stresa Front of Italy, Britain, and France condemned German conscription and rearmament as contrary to the Treaty of Versailles. They pledged to resist further repudiations by Nazi Germany, but this was somewhat hollow in the light of Mussolini's support of the remilitarisation of the Rhineland, the Anglo-German naval treaty, and the Italian invasion of Abyssinia.[167]

In a question to the Foreign Secretary on Monday, 9 March 1936, Mr Atlee asked Mr Eden whether he had any statement to make on the action of the German government in sending troops into the Rhineland.[168] According to Nicolson, this was a moment of 'great excitement' about Hitler's coup and what he detected as a mood of fear. 'Anything to keep us out of war'.[169] Mr Eden, in answer, explained that on 6 March, he asked the German Ambassador to see him at the Foreign Office concerning a proposal of 13 December 1935 as to the prospects for an Air Pact between France, Britain and Germany as signatories of the Treaty of Lucarno – this would be a stabilising element in relations. On 7 March, the ambassador returned and gave Eden a Memorandum stating that the German government objected to the Franco-Soviet Pact and why the pact meant that the Locarno system 'ceased in practice to exist'.[170] The German government declared its sovereignty in the Rhineland and suggested

[164] Memorandum by Sir R Vansittart on 'Britain, France and Germany' [769/6] Foreign Office, 3 February 1936.

[165] T Bouverie, *Appeasing Hitler* (London, Bodley Head, 2019) 83.

[166] This was at a time when according to Harold Nicolson certain 'ex-cabinet ministers were trotting across to Germany' and others such as Lady Maureen Stanley were 'hobnobbing with Hitler'. H Nicolson, *Harold Nicolson Diaries and Letters 1930-1964* (London, Penguin Books, 1985) 93.

[167] See ch 3. The Wal Wal Arbitration.

[168] *Hansard* Vol 309, 9 March 1936.

[169] H Nicolson, *Harold Nicolson Diaries and Letters 1930-1964* (London, Penguin Books, 1985) 95.

[170] *Hansard* Vol 309, 9 March 1936.

proposals; first for a demilitarised zone on both sides of the Franco-German and Belgian-German frontiers; second, that non-aggression pacts for 25 years should be concluded between Germany, France and Belgium, and that Britain and Italy should guarantee these pacts; third, that the Netherlands might be invited to join this treaty system; fourth, that these security arrangements should be supplemented by an air pact; fifth, that non-aggression pacts should be concluded between Germany and the states bordering Germany on the East similar to the agreement between Germany and Poland (the exception previously made in regard to Lithuania being conditionally withdrawn). Finally, Germany was willing to re-enter the League of Nations once that equality of rights and the restoration of her full sovereignty over the entire German territory were attained.

Eden told Von Hoesch,[171] the German Ambassador, that this amounted to a unilateral repudiation of the Locarno Treaty. Germany's view on the effect of the Franco-Soviet Pact was not shared by the other signatories. There was a clear difference of opinion between the signatories to the Locarno Treaty, which could be referred to arbitration under Article V of the Final Protocol of the Locarno Conference 1925. Von Hoesch said that his government was willing to share in a policy of collective security and membership of the League of Nations unconditionally. He said that if Germany returned to the League, it was keen on having rights of colonial equality. Hitler raised this with Sir John Simon and Eden a year earlier.[172]

In a debate in the House, Eden's view was that Germany unilaterally repudiated its international obligations in renouncing the Locarno Treaty and struck a severe blow at the sanctity of treaties, which undermined the whole structure of international relations.[173] He cautioned that if Germany attacked France or Belgium, it would constitute a violation of Article II of that Treaty and Britain would support the country attacked.[174] On 7 March 1936, Hitler's Reichswehr occupied the Rhineland, repudiating the Locarno Treaty. On 8 March 1936, Eden sent a Memorandum on the Locarno Treaty to the Cabinet.[175] In that memorandum the Italian and Belgian governments were referred to as expressing agreement with the French view that there was no incompatibility between the Locarno Treaty and the Franco-Soviet Pact. Any differences should have been settled under Article 3 of the Locarno Treaty and the Franco-German Arbitration Convention. Hitler took advantage of the military unpreparedness of Britain and France and Italy's differences with her Locarno partners.[176] Eden would have preferred to negotiate with Germany and agree on terms for reoccupation to protect Anglo-French rights in the zone.[177] He pointed to the danger of making treaties with Hitler, who was unreliable, especially regarding any quid pro quo for colonial concessions. France, he said, should be dissuaded from any military action

[171] German diplomat in London 1932–1936 who warned the German government that the occupation of the Rhineland could provoke Britain and France. He distrusted Ribbentrop who succeeded him on 30 October 1936.

[172] DBFP 1919–1939 Ser. 2. Vol 12. *Meeting held at the Chancellors Palace Berlin, 25 and 26 March 1935*: European affairs 5 August 1934–18 April 1935, 703–746.

[173] *Hansard* Vol 309, 9 March 1936.

[174] ibid col 1812.

[175] BDFP Ser. 2. Vol. 16 No. 48. [C 2361/4/18], Nos. 51 and 54.

[176] ibid [C 2361/4/18].

[177] ibid 60 [C 2361/4/18].

to retake the Saar. Britain was bound by Articles 42 and 43 of the Versailles Treaty[178] and the Treaty of Locarno.[179]

Hitler's repudiation demonstrated his disregard for the Versailles Settlement and the League of Nations. Yet despite this flagrant renunciation of Locarno and occupation of the Rhineland, neither France nor Britain opposed it.[180] As with his earlier 13 Points, this time Hitler played another game to obfuscate his breaches of international law by suggesting a seven-point programme of so-called 'peace'. At his rally in Nuremberg, he referred to a 25-year non-aggression pact with Belgium and France to be guaranteed by Britain and Italy, demilitarisation of the Belgian and French frontiers, and Germany's return to the League of Nations.[181] This would hardly be acceptable to France with its Maginot Line and presumably intended to appeal to those naïve politicians in Britain and France who supported appeasement.[182] Hitler repeated his big lie 'We have no territorial demands to make in Europe … Germany will never break the peace.'[183] Hitler also promised Poland that it would be unreasonable for her not to have access to the sea. Upon hearing Hitler's speech, Shirer considered that the main pillar of the European peace structure, Locarno, was destroyed.[184] Hitler repeated an offer to conclude non-aggression pacts with states bordering Germany in the East, with Poland to include Lithuania: 'On condition that the guaranteed autonomy of the Statute of Memel is effectively developed.'

Whether it was the Manchurian debacle or the Rhineland crisis, the League's credibility and its effectiveness had certainly been reduced. From this point on, Hitler discounted the League. From the point of view of Britain and France, failure to take the initiative had serious consequences. From Germany's point of view, it gained in confidence and prestige. Its forces could have been defeated if France had stood firm. Its underequipped troops had orders to retreat if opposed. French hesitation was fatal, as was Britain's pathetic effort to restrain French action. Garvin's *Observer* and Rothermere's *Sunday Despatch* were 'delighted' at Hitler's move. Thus, Bloomberg could boast: 'We do not want an offensive war, but we do not fear a defensive war.'[185]

In December 1936, Vansittart warned of:[186]

> It is a thousand pities, for Germany presents the human animal at its most efficient and therefore-despite the envious self-pity of the Prussian character-at its most attractive for those who naturally prefer this quality to its shoddy opposites …

[178] Articles 42–43. Section III. Left Bank of the Rhine. Article 42. Germany is forbidden to maintain or construct any fortifications either on the left bank of the Rhine or on the right bank to the west of a line drawn 50 kilometres to the East of the Rhine. Article 43. In the area defined above, the maintenance and the assembly of armed forces, either permanently or temporarily, and military manoeuvres of any kind, 'as well as the upkeep of all permanent works for mobilization, are in the same way forbidden'.

[179] Parliamentary Debates, House of Commons. Vol 309. 9 March 1936. Cols. 1808–1813.

[180] BDFP Ser. 2. Vol. 16, No. 61. [C 1614/4/18]. Sir G Clerk, British Ambassador to France 1934–37 informed the Foreign Office on 10 March 1936 that Belgium would join in any action that Britain and France would take.

[181] WL Shirer, *Berlin Diary* (London, Hamish Hamilton, 1941) 48–49; BDFP Ser. 2. Vol. 16, No. 48. 61. [C 2361/4/18].

[182] Shirer believed that Hitler deliberately aimed his speech to the Reichstag that day to the Astors, Lords Londonderry, Lothian, and Rothermere.

[183] WL Shirer, *Berlin Diary* (London, Hamish Hamilton, 1941) 51.

[184] ibid 52, 53.

[185] ibid 54, 55.

[186] Appendix II Memorandum by Sir R Vansittart 'The World Situation and British Rearmament' [C 8998/8998/18] Most Secret [775/1].

Sir Orme Sargent[187] considered that Hitler's refusal to discuss revision of the Locarno Treaty was designed to divide France and Britain by a bilateral agreement with Britain.[188] The abandonment of Locarno meant that the other signatories could no longer rely on its provisions in relation to Germany and switched from reliance on mutual guarantees to appeasement.[189]

D. The Sino-Japanese War

i. British Policy

In 1933, Japan left the League of Nations, signalling her renunciation of collective security. In 1934, the Japanese made overtures to Britain and America for non-aggression pacts following the Manchurian crisis in China.[190] The moment was not opportune, as the 1935 Naval Conference was pending, and there would be difficulty in agreeing on naval limitations on existing ratios.[191] However, in order to reduce the risk of a further world war America, Britain, France and Japan convened a conference in London to agree on a limitation of naval armaments. Britain and America found it difficult to agree on the type and number of cruisers that each should build. At that time, Britain had the largest fleet to protect its trade routes and guard the Empire. America also had its empire in the Pacific but few foreign bases and therefore required heavy cruisers. These were of 10,000 tonnes or more with eight-inch guns rather than the lighter cruisers, which had six-inch guns. Britain had far more cruisers at that time.[192] Negotiations were protracted between 1922 and 1927. Due to the good personal relationship between Stimson, the US Secretary for War, and Prime Minister MacDonald, a compromise was reached in that the Americans could build heavy cruisers with six-inch guns, which could be adapted later if necessary.[193] This arrangement improved Anglo-American understanding, but it meant the end of British supremacy at sea by 1929. The French would not agree without a guarantee of American support if attacked.[194] Stimson rejected this, as Congress would not agree to any European entanglements,[195] even though McDonald told Simpson that France contemplated a war with Germany and Italy in the future.[196]

In November 1936, Germany and Japan signed the Anti-Comintern Pact to contain Russia, giving a freer hand to Japan in China and Southeast Asia. According to Vansittart, it brought 'Japan into the European orbit at a particularly delicate and dangerous phase

[187] Deputy Under Secretary at the Foreign Office.

[188] P Neville, 'The Foreign Office and Britain's Ambassadors to Berlin, 1933-39' (2004) 18(3) *Contemporary British History* 114.

[189] J Wright, 'Locarno: A Democratic Peace?' (2010) 36 *Review of International Studies* 409.

[190] BJC McKercher, 'The Foreign Office and British Diplomacy' (2004) 18(2) *Contemporary British History* 97.

[191] FO 371/17599/7695/1938 minute by Orde 28 Aug 1934 as cited in McKercher ibid 98.

[192] G Hodgson, *The Colonel, The Life and Times of Henry Stimson1867–1950* (New York, Alfred A Knopf, 1990) 181.

[193] ibid 191.

[194] ibid.

[195] A view that President George Washington had engrained in the American psyche.

[196] G. Hodgson, *The Colonel, The Life and Times of Henry Stimson1867–1950* (New York, Alfred A Knopf, 1990) 190.

[as] Japan was spending 45% of her entire national budget on national defence'.[197] As Vansittart wrote in a Memorandum of 31 December 1936:[198]

> Time was when Japan was thought to be our chief danger. Foreshadowed events 'have changed all that' only too quickly, and, while Japan is now generally considered likely to await a war in Europe, Germany has become the recognised storm-centre of the earth.

He also wrote that:

> Japan still aims at hegemony, on which it is as overtly set in Asia as Germany in Europe.

In the order of priorities, the balance of power in Europe took precedence so that British interests in Southeast Asia were secondary, although of concern in the early 1930s.[199] When Chamberlain's foreign policy ideas failed to improve Anglo-Japanese relations, he sought to replace Vansittart and change policy towards bilateral settlements with Britain's potential enemies through appeasement.[200] He therefore pursued some accommodation with Japan as with others until Hitler occupied the rest of Czechoslovakia.

Chamberlain found it tempting to agree to Japanese 'equality in status', which would alter the status quo, and on the other hand, a bilateral non-aggression pact would provide the Japanese with 'a free hand in China'.[201] Vansittart advised Simon to dampen Cabinet support for a non-aggression pact, but Chamberlain ignored the advice and pursued the pact, appeasing Japan on naval matters as well as taking a softer approach in naval discussions with Germany. Simon prevented Chamberlain from presenting this view to the cabinet. The Japanese suggested either a naval treaty or a non-aggression agreement,[202] which never transpired. Fortunately for Britain, Russia never concluded an alliance with Japan, and Japan sought territorial expansion in China. The movements of the Imperial Japanese Army (IJA) and the Imperial Japanese Navy (IJN) southward constituted a threat to British interests. Vansittart's strategic approach was to find common ground in East Asia with the Russians to offset a power imbalance in Europe.[203] Vansittart believed that peace in Europe could only be maintained by a balance of power in Europe. According to McKercher, he faced three choices suggested by colleagues: Alan Leeper, head of the Western Department, advised that following the collapse of the Disarmament Conference, France would align with Russia to contain Germany, but Mussolini would never join an alliance with communists. This could lead to an Italo-German alliance. Britain might have to choose between the two, recreating the old rival alliances pre-1914. The Assistant Under-Secretary of the Foreign Office, Craigie, suggested that Britain should join neither. Britain could just declare that it would oppose any attack on the Low Countries.[204] Wigram, in the Central Department, was in favour of deterrent strength, which would avert German aggression, dissuade

[197] Appendix II Memorandum by Sir R Vansittart 'The World Situation and British Rearmament' [C 8998/8998/18] Most Secret [775/1].

[198] ibid.

[199] BJC McKercher, 'The Foreign Office and British Diplomacy' (2004) 18(2) *Contemporary British History* 95, as to views of Vansittart and Warren Fisher who covered the Far East in the FO.

[200] ibid 104.

[201] ibid 98.

[202] ibid 98–99.

[203] ibid 99.

[204] FO 371/18527/5693/1 minute by Craigie, 24 May 1934 as cited in McKercher ibid 100.

Italy from allying with Germany, and incline the French to work with Britain.[205] If Britain established a Field Force, this could provide the necessary deterrent, but without it, things would be difficult.[206] This was cancelled after the Defence Review of 1937–38 just before Eden resigned over Italy.[207]

E. Mussolini's Imperial Dreams

In 1934 there were clashes at Wal Wal in Abyssinia,[208] and in 1935 Mussolini invaded. During this crisis, Britain's policy changed. Between mid-December 1934 and mid-June 1935, Britain was anxious to avoid any commitment to either Italy or Ethiopia, so it did nothing. On 8 June 1935, Vansittart sent a minute to Hoare[209] and Eden about his concern over the position of Italy and Abyssinia. In brief, he considered that Abyssinia would eventually perish and:

> That might itself matter less, if it did not mean that the League would also perish (and that Italy would simultaneously perform *anothe*r volte face into the arms of Germany, a combination of haute politique that we can ill afford just now.).

Between mid-June 1935 and the end of September 1935, Britain proposed certain plans for settlement, advocating strong League action. There was some discussion as to the cession of Zeila to Ethiopia from British Somaliland, a triangle of territory in the Ogaden province with its base on the existing frontier with British Somaliland and its apex at Wal Wal.[210] At this time an Anglo-Ethiopian Boundary Commission headed by Colonel E Clifford was in the process of completing a survey of the grazing areas used by the British Somaliland tribes. The British were unaware before 1934 of any occupation by Italian troops at Wal Wal and Wardair. Hence the events described in the Wal Wal arbitration on 5 December 1934.[211]

Britain and France were reluctant to intervene or censure Mussolini at this time since the presence of Italian troops on the Brenner Pass in July 1934 had discouraged Hitler's designs on his native Austria. Also, in April 1935, there was a meeting at Stresa[212] between France, Britain, and Italy, but little was resolved when Anglo-French differences prevented any restraint on Hitler's ambitions.[213] Hoare agreed with Vansittart that a war in Abyssinia could upset the balance of power in Europe and British interests elsewhere. This led to a British plan, which was adopted in the Hoare-Laval Pact, which gave seven-eighths of Abyssinia to Italy and the remainder to Emperor Haile Selassie. This met with public disapproval, and both Laval and Hoare were dismissed. Eden succeeded

[205] FO 371/18527/5693/1 minute by Wigram, 24 May 1934 as cited in McKercher ibid.
[206] FO 371/18524/4153/1 minute by Vansittart, 2 May 1934 as cited in McKercher ibid 98.
[207] CAB 24/273, CP(37)316, Inskip 'Interim Report on Defence Expenditure in Future Years', 15 Dec 1937; CAB 24/274, CP(38)24, Inskip 'Report on Defence Expenditure in Future Years', 8 Feb 1938; CAB 23/92, CC5(38)9, 16 Feb 1938. Cited in McKercher ibid 104.
[208] See: ch 3 The Wal Wal Arbitration.
[209] Then Foreign Secretary.
[210] BDFP 1919–1939 Ser. 2 Vol 16. vi.
[211] ibid vii. And see ch 3.
[212] Z Steiner, *The Triumph of the Dark* (Oxford, Oxford University Press, 2011) 88–90, 103.
[213] A Sharp, *Versailles. A Centennial Perspective* (Chicago, Haus Publishing, 2018) 65.

Hoare, and following the Italian victory in Abyssinia, the Stresa Front disappeared.[214] Eden wanted to reach an agreement with Germany, but Vansittart did not think that possible. Instead, Britain needed to rearm to meet the inevitable threat.[215]

Emperor Haile Selassie applied to the League of Nations under Articles 10 and 16. Under Article 10, which aimed at preserving the territorial integrity and existing political independence of all members of the League. The Council was to advise on action to be taken. Under Article 16 if any member of the League resorted to war in disregard of its covenants under Articles 12, 13 or 15, it would be deemed to have committed an act of war. All other members of the League undertook immediately to subject it to the severance of all trade or financial relations, etc. The duty of the Council would be to recommend to the several governments concerned what effective military, naval or air force the members of the League would each contribute to the forces to be used according to the covenants of the League. League members were to mutually support one another in these sanctions and any special measures and afford passage through their territory to the forces of any of the members which were cooperating to protect League covenants. Any member that violated any covenant could be excluded from the League by a vote of the Council concurred in by all other members.

Emperor Haile Selassie's justifiable appeal was ignored, and consequently the League lost credibility. The Manchurian and Rhineland crises confirmed its impotence, encouraging the dictators who felt that they could ignore its deliberations. On 4 October 1935, Mussolini began his attack on Abyssinia. From Berlin, Shearer commented: 'The League has provided a sorry spectacle, but its failure now, after the Manchurian debacle, certainly kills it.'[216] On 25 February 1936, Lord Londonderry visited Berlin. On 28 February the French and the Soviets signed the Franco-Soviet Treaty of Mutual Assistance and on 2 May 1936 Addis Ababa fell. On 18 July 1936, civil war broke out in Spain. There was little restraint. To all intents and purposes the organisation of peace was frustrated. British public opinion appeared to support the League contrary to the actions of its government. It proved ineffective, and the division between British and French interests gave further perceptions of weakness in the absence of a balance of power and collective security. British and French political ineptitude, as well as American isolationism, gave confidence to the dictators, enabled Hitler to remilitarise the Rhineland, enabled Japan to invade China, and Italy to conquer Abyssinia. The position of Italy was important because unless it could be detached from its alliance with Germany, an imbalance would remain.[217]

F. The Spanish Civil War

This lasted from 16 July 1936 until 31 March 1939. The war took over 400,000 lives. It presented an opportunity for Hitler to support the nationalists and divert attention from

[214] BJC McKercher, 'The Foreign Office and British Diplomacy' (2004) 18(2) *Contemporary British History* 101.

[215] ibid 103.

[216] W Shirer, *Berlin Diary* (London, Hamish Hamilton, 1941) 43, 44.

[217] BJC McKercher, 'The Foreign Office and British Diplomacy' (2004) 18(2) *Contemporary British History* 103.

his ambitions in Central Europe as well as obtain iron ore. Although Germany, France, Britain, and Russia signed a non-intervention pact, they all supplied assistance: 7,000 Germans, 14,000 Italians, and 24,000 volunteers from France took part in the war.[218] Italy sent 15,000 reinforcements to the nationalists who were defeated at Guadalajara on 18 March 1937. Following that, Germany offered to assist with reconstruction in consideration of Spain sending raw materials. Italy increased its support by 60,000 men. So far as Hitler was concerned, the Spanish Civil War was an excellent smokescreen for his Lebensraum ambitions. It also served his purpose by creating tension between France and Italy as well as between Britain and Italy so that Italy came ever closer to Germany. Gradually the Nationalists defeated the Republicans, and the foreign forces finally withdrew in May 1939.[219]

G. German Rearmament

On 13 November 1935, Sir Eric Phipps, Ambassador in Berlin, sent a dispatch to Hoare recording his observations of the German militarisation. It stated that:[220]

> it [was] difficult to drive along any road in this country without seeing striking evidence of the truth of this statement. On every side giant military establishments are springing up. There are few towns of any importance where barracks or military schools are not being built, some of them still far from completion. Enormous aerodromes, either finished or under construction march, sometimes for miles, with the main road … The streets of provincial towns are gay with uniforms; military cars and lorries painted in camouflage colours, mix with civilian traffic. In the air, the ceaseless hum of aeroplanes bears witness to the expansion of the German air force.
>
> …
>
> 6. Except that battles are not being fought, Germany may be said without exaggeration to be living in a state of war. Everything is subordinated to the needs of the defence forces. The government controls the distribution of raw materials and the output of the factories. The military chiefs are in complete control of the armed forces; there is no parliamentary or civilian interference. A high degree of secrecy is still preserved.

Ambassador Phipps ended his dispatch with an ominous warning:

> … that the present Ethiopian imbroglio is merely child's play compared to the problem that will in some not very distant future confront His Majesty's Government.[221]

The obvious conclusion from this is that of Eden in his Very Confidential Memorandum dated 17 January 1936.[222] He concluded that Hitler's foreign policy aimed at the destruction of the peace settlement and re-establishment of Germany as the dominant power in Europe. The means by which this was to be effected were twofold:

> (a) Internally, through the militarization of the whole nation in all its respects:

[218] J de Launay, *Major Controversies of Contemporary History* (Oxford, Pergamon Press, 1965) 164.
[219] ibid 165.
[220] BDFP Ser. 2 Vol 15. No. 231. 264, 266.
[221] BDFP, Ser. 2. Vol 15. Nos. 231, 268.
[222] ibid Nos. 460, 569. [C454/4/18].

(b) Externally, by economic and territorial expansion, so as to absorb as far as possible all those of German race who are present citizens of neighbouring states, to acquire new markets for German industry and new fields for German emigration, and to obtain control of some of the sources of those raw materials at present lacking to Germany.

Eden warned that the country had to be ready for all eventualities and that it was 'vital to hasten and complete our own rearmament'. Whilst pursuing rearmament, he told the cabinet that it would be well to consider: 'whether it is still possible to come to some *modus vivendi* with Germany'.[223] Phipps's view of the Nazi regime did not find favour with Chamberlain.[224] He was posted to Paris, and a more pro-German diplomat, Neville Henderson, replaced him.

Whilst the cabinet discussed the possible effects of German rearmament and Hitler's intentions, the City of London appeared unaware of the threat, which was expressed in a letter dated 9 March 1936 from Nigel Law[225] to Sargent in the Foreign Office saying that:[226]

> The sentiment in the City of London is overwhelmingly pro-German. … I confess I had never realised before the depth of anti-French feeling which forms the background of all foreign political judgments here … The most extreme are the *Daily Mail* readers, who, though they completely disregard Lord Rothermere's advice in the Hoare-Laval crisis, are now content to repeat the parrot cry of 'You can't keep down forever a nation of 67 million.' These people know nothing of the Locarno Treaty or of Hitler's previous acceptance of it, and confuse it in their minds with the 'unjust' Treaty of Versailles. Next come those who disregard the denunciation of Locarno and affirm the right of Germany to re-occupy the demilitarised zone. They look hopefully towards a new era in Europe based on acceptance of Hitler's offer. Lastly, there are those who, when dislodged by argument from the contention that it is any good making a new treaty with a country which has just repudiated obligations, freely entered into and confirmed quite recently by the Führer himself, declare that it is really no use making treaties with anyone and that heavily armed isolation is the only policy which can give any hope of security. Hardly anyone seems to give a thought for the future, and to the implication of Hitler's remarks on the colonial question.

H. Roosevelt's Intervention

i. Quarantine Speech

On 5 October 1937, President Roosevelt made a speech of dramatic international importance contrasting the prosperity and peace in America with the threats to

[223] ibid Nos. 460, 569. n 3. Eden endorsed the memorandum, with a note that there had been serious leakages of information from the British embassy in Berlin and if this Memorandum and its annexures were leaked this could prejudice Phipps's position and sources of his information. Eden's Memorandum to the Cabinet quoted here and its annexures came into the hands of Signor Grandi who sent them to Mussolini on 3 September 1936 and discussed by Count Ciano with Hitler in Berchtesgaden on 24 October 1936.

[224] P Neville, 'The Foreign Office and Britain's Ambassadors to Berlin, 1933-39' (2004) 18(3) *Contemporary British History* 115. Phipps told William Bullitt, the US Ambassador to France, that Hitler wanted Nazi 'domination of Europe' and that the only thing that impressed Hitler was 'military force.'

[225] Mr Law was a former First Secretary in the Foreign Office and then working as a Stockbroker in the City of London.

[226] BDFP Ser. 2. Vol 16. No. 55. [C 1643/4/18].

peace and democracy and the threats of war. He recalled how 15 years before, in the Briand-Kellogg Peace Pact, there were high peaceful aspirations when 'more than sixty nations solemnly pledged themselves not to resort to arms in furtherance of their national aims and policies'.[227] He referred to a 'present reign of terror and international lawlessness'. This, he said, began through unjustified interference in the internal affairs of other nations or the invasion of alien territory in violation of treaties and had then reached a stage where the very foundations of civilisation were seriously threatened.

He warned that the:

> landmarks and traditions which have marked the progress of civilization toward a condition of law, order and justice are being wiped away. Without a declaration of war and without warning or justification of any kind, civilians, including vast numbers of women and children, were being ruthlessly murdered with bombs from the air. In times of so-called peace, ships are being attacked and sunk by submarines without cause or notice. Nations are fomenting and taking sides in civil warfare in nations that have never done them any harm. Nations claiming freedom for themselves deny it to others. Innocent peoples, innocent nations, are being cruelly sacrificed to a greed for power and supremacy which is devoid of all sense of justice and humane considerations.

Roosevelt cautioned that America was not inviolable and that peace-loving nations should make a concerted effort to oppose violations of treaties, which were creating a state of international anarchy and instability, as to which isolationism and neutrality were no defence against attack.[228] He continued:

> There can be no stability or peace either within nations or between nations except under laws and moral standards adhered to by all. International anarchy destroys every foundation for peace. It jeopardizes either the immediate or the future security of every nation, large or small. It is, therefore, a matter of vital interest and concern to the people of the United States that the sanctity of international treaties and the maintenance of international morality be restored.[229]

It was a threat to 'all international order and law'.[230]

The questions involved related not merely to violations of specific provisions of particular treaties; they were questions of war and of peace, of international law and especially of principles of humanity. They involved definite violations of agreements, especially of the Covenant of the League of Nations, the Briand-Kellogg Pact and the Nine Power Treaty. But they also involved problems of world economy, world security and world humanity. It was unfortunately true 'that the epidemic of world lawlessness is spreading'.[231]

Roosevelt was determined to pursue a policy of peace despite all the challenges to the world order and to minimise the risk of America's involvement. On the other hand, it was clear that in making the speech he was educating the American public to the risk of war.

[227] F Roosevelt, 'The Constitution Prevails' in *The Public Papers and Addresses of Franklin D Roosevelt*. Vol 3 (London, Macmillan, 1941) Nos. 128, 407.
[228] ibid 128, 408.
[229] ibid 128, 409.
[230] ibid 128, 410.
[231] ibid.

ii. Roosevelt's Peace Plan

Discussions took place between Lord Halifax and Hitler in late 1937 when Hitler continued to make demands for colonies, which Halifax rejected. Whether Belgium, France or Portugal could give up colonies was a question for them.[232] Halifax may have given Hitler the wrong impression that Britain had little interest in Central Europe; at least that was the view of Chautemps to Ambassador Bullitt.[233] Chautemps and Bonnet were in favour of French retreat from Central European affairs and supported appeasement.[234]

On 11 January 1938, Sumner Welles[235] delivered a message from President Roosevelt to the British Ambassador in Washington, Sir Ronald Lindsay, for Neville Chamberlain. The President, impressed by 'the danger of general conflagration with all its disastrous results' and by the tendency of smaller states to gravitate towards the dictatorships, had devised a scheme designed to lay 'the practical foundations for peace'. This followed from his Quarantine Speech on 5 October 1937. He proposed, if the British response were favourable, to 'warn confidentially' the French, German and Italian governments of this scheme on 20 January and to summon the entire diplomatic corps to the White House on 22 January to announce the details. He wanted an assurance of the 'cordial approval and whole-hearted support' of the British government by 17 January, within five days of the receipt of his message in the Foreign Office.[236]

On 12 January Cadogan sent a minute to Chamberlain.[237] In it he noted:

> … I should have thought we ought to be favourable. It involves risks for us-cf. his point about access to raw materials and the hint about reversal of settlements reached at the end of the war (telegram No. 39). But if we can keep in touch with the President we may be able to mitigate his worst ideas on these points.

Behind this initiative was the advice of Ambassador Bullitt on 21 December 1937 that Europe was ready for peace negotiations. Roosevelt therefore revised what was called the Welles Plan to convene a meeting at the White House with diplomatic representatives of all governments regarding international conduct and reduction of armaments.[238] On 13 January 1938, he also indicated that he would send several US cruisers to Singapore to support Britain and to accelerate the date for the transfer of the US Pacific Fleet to Hawaii. Roosevelt's offer was rejected by Chamberlain because he felt he could better negotiate without American help.[239] According to Bullitt, Roosevelt took this as a sign that Britain was not willing to cooperate with

[232] *US Foreign Relations 1937* Vol 1, 186. *Ambassador Bullitt to Secretary of State* 4 December 1937.
[233] ibid.
[234] Z Steiner, *The Triumph of the Dark* (Oxford, Oxford University Press, 2011) 405.
[235] US Under-Secretary of State.
[236] G Bennett, FCO Historical Branch, Occasional Papers. No.1. November 1987 'The Roosevelt Peace Plan of January 1938' 27.
[237] DBFP 1919–1939 Ser. 2. Vol 19. No. 428 *Minute by Sir A. Cadogan for Mr. Chamberlain* 12 January 1938.
[238] R Dallek, *Franklin Delano Roosevelt and American Foreign Policy 1932 1945* (New York, OUP, 1979) 155.
[239] He thought presumably that he was better placed than FDR or Eden to do this. A view that was to have disastrous results.

the US. This increased American suspicions about British intentions. Recognition of Italian occupation of Ethiopia would reinforce the feeling in the US that this would be a corrupt bargain at the expense of the Far East.[240] Roosevelt found recognition distasteful but was compelled to say that British action was 'proof of the value of peaceful negotiations'.[241] Chamberlain did not appreciate the political risk Roosevelt was taking in trying to facilitate Britain's peace initiatives, and when the invitation to Chamberlain failed, Roosevelt asked Congress to increase the defence budget.[242] Chamberlain's recognition of Italy's conquest of Ethiopia surrendered the principle of non-recognition. This, another demonstration of appeasement, and Chamberlain's private foreign policy encouraged Japanese aggression in the Far East and soured Anglo-American relations.[243]

No doubt Roosevelt had the best of intentions, but Chamberlain was concerned about the President's statement that spoke of a world where people 'live in constant fear and where physical and economic security for the individual are lacking'. Chamberlain underlined this part of the message, commenting: 'Germans & Italians will laugh at this.'[244] Roosevelt wanted all governments to strive to reach unanimous agreement upon four points. First, on the 'essential and fundamental principles which should be observed in international relations', second, on ways of limiting and reducing armaments; third, 'equal and effective access to raw materials'; and fourth, the rights and obligations of governments on land and sea in time of war.[245]

The President acknowledged that agreement on the four principles might not alone be sufficient to ensure the maintenance of peace: certain 'international adjustments' must be found 'through pacification of the universe' in order to remove inequities which may have been caused by the settlements reached after the First World War. He also referred to the well-known 'traditional policy of freedom from political involvement which U.S. Government has maintained and will maintain'. If he received support for his plan, the President, while disclaiming the intention of a world peace conference, proposed to invite certain governments, listed as Sweden, the Netherlands, Belgium, Switzerland, Hungary, Yugoslavia, Turkey and three Latin American governments, to negotiate in Washington on the four principles.[246] This was all proposed in the utmost secrecy for the Prime Minister, although Chamberlain shared this with certain members of the cabinet. Cadogan noted that Chamberlain's adviser, Sir Horace Wilson, was 'very anti-Roosevelt' and Chamberlain 'hates Roosevelt's idea'.[247] Churchill commented that Roosevelt's initiative was 'the last real chance to save the world from tyranny otherwise than by war'.

[240] R Dallek, *Franklin Delano Roosevelt and American Foreign Policy 1932 1945* (New York, OUP, 1979) 156.
[241] ibid 158.
[242] C Hull, *The Memoirs of Cordell Hull*, Vol 1 (London, Hodder & Stoughton, 1948) 573, 574.
[243] R Dallek, *Franklin Delano Roosevelt and American Foreign Policy 1932 1945* (New York, OUP, 1979) 157.
[244] DBFP 1919–1939 Ser. 2. Vol 19. No. 423. n 3. *European affairs July 1937–August 1938*. R Lindsay to Foreign Office. Rec'd 12 January, 9.30 am. 727.
[245] G Bennett, FCO Historical Branch, Occasional Papers. No. 1. November 1987 'The Roosevelt Peace Plan of January 1938' 27–28, and DBFP 1919–1939 Ser. 2. Vol 19. No. 424. 728.
[246] G Bennett, FCO Historical Branch, Occasional Papers. No. 1. November 1987 'The Roosevelt Peace Plan of January 1938' p. 28 and DBFP 1919–1939 Ser. 2. Vol XIX. No. 423. 729 and No. 424. 729–730.
[247] DBFP 1919–1939 Ser. 2. Vol 19. No 428. n. 734/4.

I. The Price of Appeasement

i. Eden's Resignation and Vansittart's Demotion

Lady Chamberlain (Ivy)[248] spent the autumn of 1937 on an extended holiday in Rome. She took the opportunity of visiting Count Ciano and reading a letter to him from Chamberlain.[249] Although she had no official diplomatic status, she was presumably assumed to be an unofficial agent of Prime Minister Chamberlain. It appears he was conducting his own amateur, unofficial form of diplomacy through her with Mussolini without reference to the Foreign Office. Upon returning from a short holiday in France Eden discovered this and wrote to Chamberlain on 8 February 1938, expressing his concerns and the difficulties, nay embarrassment, that such connections posed.[250] Another cause of mischief was certain press reports leaked by the Conservative Central Office illustrating differences between Chamberlain and Eden.

Relations with Italy had deteriorated because Britain would not recognise the Italian conquest of Abyssinia. In September 1937, Mussolini visited Hitler in Berlin, and they agreed that Germany would not impede Italy in the Mediterranean and the special German interests in Austria would be respected by Italy. Germany and Italy signed an anti-Comintern pact with Japan. Chamberlain clearly disagreed with Eden's approach and that of the Foreign Office. He felt he knew better than them and how to deal with tensions between the League and Italy. He was against Eden's proposal for a joint declaration giving de jure recognition to Abyssinia.[251] Chamberlain applied his policy of general appeasement. He rejected Eden's support for a declaration by President Roosevelt. Roosevelt had intended to issue a world appeal to end international tension by general agreement, to abide by international law and order reducing armaments and securing access to raw materials.

Roosevelt was not overtly dismayed, as the dispatches from Washington confirm:[252]

No. 462 Sir R. Lindsay (Washington) to Mr. Eden (Received January 23, 9.30 a.m.)

No. 78 Telegraphic [A 2127/64/45]

Immediate Very Secret

Washington, January 22, 1938, 8.25 p.m.

My immediately preceding telegram.

Again, after reading Prime Minister's message about de jure recognition the Under Secretary, of State expressed approval and the view that it would make a good impression on the President …

I think it was a relief to him to find that His Majesty's Government only contemplate grant of recognition as part of general settlement with Italy and therefore not in the immediate future …

[248] Chamberlain's sister-in-law.

[249] A Eden, *Facing the Dictators* (London, Cassell, 1962) 573.

[250] ibid 574.

[251] Extract from Mr Neville Chamberlain's Diary 19 and 27 February 1938. DBFP 1919–1939 Ser. 2. Vol 19. 1138–1144.

[252] ibid 775, 776. This episode demonstrates an example of Chamberlain's lack of foresight as to consequences in other places where the British interest would be compromised.

> I also said that if we reached the point where we had general settlement with Italy within our grasp we should probably by then have made marked progress in negotiations with Germany and something approaching a world settlement would be in view …
>
> Under Secretary of State said that as regards the Far East it was not only the recognition of Manchukuo that was giving concern but also that of other puppet governments which Japan might set up in any part of China.

and,[253]

> **No. 463** Sir R. Lindsay (Washington) to Mr. Eden (Received January 25, 9.40 a.m.)
>
> No. 84 Telegraphic [A 2127/64/45]
>
> Very Secret
>
> Washington, January 24, 1938, 5.45 p.m.
>
> My telegrams Nos. 77 and 78.
>
> Under Secretary of State for Foreign Affairs telephoned to me today to say that the President had been 'deeply gratified by contents of Prime Minister's two messages'. In the course of the next few days Under Secretary of State for Foreign Affairs would have conversations with me about further procedure and probably there would be a further message in writing from the President.

Chamberlain thought 'it would excite the derision of Germany and Italy',[254] since conversations were about to commence with Italy and Germany. Instead of discussing this with his Foreign Secretary, he consulted Horace Wilson[255] and Cadogan before sending his reply in Eden's absence.[256] On the following Sunday, when Eden returned from his holiday in France, he was shocked by Chamberlain's rejection of Roosevelt's initiative. Eden informed the British Ambassador in Washington that the Prime Minister did not say what he meant exactly. But the damage was done. It was obvious Chamberlain did not want to cooperate with the US. Roosevelt told Chamberlain that the surrender of the principle of non-recognition would encourage Japanese aggression in the Far East.[257] It would also damage public opinion in America and be detrimental to US interests in the Far East.[258]

The break with Eden came over Chamberlain's meeting with Grandi in Downing Street on 17 February 1938. Eden wanted to meet with him alone before the meeting with Chamberlain.[259] Chamberlain felt there would be either a rupture with Italy or with Eden. He concluded that if he followed Eden's approach, it would mean that Austria would lose her independence, the Balkan countries would turn towards their powerful neighbours, Czechoslovakia would be incorporated in the Reich, and France

[253] DBFP ibid 776.

[254] Extract from Mr Neville Chamberlain's Diary 19 and 27 February 1938. DBFP 1919–1939 Ser. 2. Vol 19. 1138–1144.

[255] Chamberlain's Chief Adviser with no particular expertise in foreign affairs.

[256] A Eden, *Facing the Dictators* (London, Cassell, 1962) 575–577 where Eden suggests that Chamberlain was taking over Foreign Policy removing Vansittart and relying on his own defeatist coterie of advisers. Eden's speech to the Junior Imperialist League on 12 February 1938 gives the clue to Chamberlain's 'political pessimism'.

[257] R Dallek, *Franklin D. Roosevelt and American Foreign Policy 1932-1945* (Oxford, OUP, 1979) 156.

[258] ibid 157.

[259] Extract from Mr Neville Chamberlain's Diary 19 and 27 February 1938. DBFP 1919–1939 Ser. 2. Vol 191138–1144.

would either submit to German domination or fight, in which case Britain would be drawn in.

ii. Chamberlain's Private Foreign Policy

Eden gave an account of his meeting on 18 February 1938 with Chamberlain and Count Grandi (an account approved by Chamberlain himself)[260] to discuss the European situation and especially the Anglo-Italian conversations. Chamberlain asked Grandi if there was some agreement between Germany and Italy. Grandi denied this. Grandi said that Mussolini had been able to preserve 'the integrity of events in Austria'.[261] Grandi said that Italy had two great potential enemies: Germany and Britain. In his account of the Anglo-Italian relationship after the sanctions period, matters deteriorated until the July 1937 exchange of letters between Mussolini and Chamberlain was marred by events in the Mediterranean.[262] Chamberlain mentioned that Lady Chamberlain had reported her conversation with Count Ciano in Rome, indicating early discussions.[263] Grandi said that if it was impossible to improve relations with Britain, Italy would draw closer to Germany. A decision would be final, and there was very little time left. This was contrary to the Anti-Comintern Pact, which Italy had already signed with Japan and Germany. If no final decision had been taken, Chamberlain suggested talks between Eden and Grandi in London, with Ciano joining in despite Grandi saying talks must be held in Rome.[264] The key point asked of Grandi in relation to Austria was whether his government would exchange views with other Stresa signatories. Grandi said he had no instructions regarding Austria. Italy would not effect any such exchange. Thus, Chamberlain's overtures to Italy through his private communications proved futile. Eden concluded that there was nothing to be gained by this, but Chamberlain seemed either to ignore it or expect it, which was odd.[265] Any discussion on the withdrawal of Italian forces from Spain would be subject to other countries agreeing to withdraw their volunteers.[266] Grandi was then asked to return to Downing Street at 3 pm. After that meeting, Chamberlain told Eden that he would open discussions at once and recall the British Ambassador from Rome, Lord Perth.[267] Eden was rightly suspicious of Grandi's 'now or never' approach. Chamberlain then became very vehement and told Eden: 'Anthony you have missed chance after chance. You simply cannot go on like this.'[268] The impasse had to be discussed with the cabinet and Eden had to consider his position, which had become untenable. When Grandi returned at 3 pm he was told that Chamberlain would have to consult colleagues but would see him again on 21 February.

[260] A Eden, *Facing the Dictators* (London, Cassell, 1962) Appendix C. 616–618.
[261] ibid Appendix C. 616.
[262] When Italian submarines turned to piracy. Eden ibid.
[263] H Macmillan, *Winds of Change* (London, Macmillan, 1966) 527. Macmillan was concerned that Lady Chamberlain (Ivy) indiscretions in talks with Ciano were 'embarrassing and dangerous'.
[264] A Eden, *Facing the Dictators* (London, Cassell, 1962) Appendix C. 617.
[265] ibid 518. Eden did not know what underhanded intentions Chamberlain had at that time, but Grandi's dispatch of 18 February 1938 to Ciano revealed it as in Appendix C. 617.
[266] Eden ibid 618.
[267] James Eric Drummond, 7th Earl of Perth, GCMG, CB, PC, DL (17 August 1876–15 December 1951), was the first Secretary-General of the League of Nations (1920–1933). British Ambassador to Italy (1933–1939.
[268] A Eden, *Facing the Dictators* (London, Cassell, 1962) 582.

On Spain, Grandi agreed to consult his government as to whether the British plan for withdrawal of forces from Spain could be agreed.[269]

What is very troubling about this meeting and calls into question the action of Chamberlain was a dispatch from Count Grandi to the Italian Foreign Minister dated 19 February 1938. In that dispatch Grandi wrote:

> Chamberlain … expected from me this was obvious-nothing more nor less than those details and definite answers which were useful to him as ammunition against Eden. This I at once realised and naturally tried to supply Chamberlain with all the ammunition which I considered might be useful to him to this end. There is no doubt that in this connection, the contacts previous established between myself and Chamberlain through his confidential agent proved to be very valuable.[270]

This extraordinary document demonstrates the extent to which Chamberlain undermined Eden's position. It discloses evidence of duplicity damaging the British interest as understood by Eden and the Foreign Office. That interest required that there should be no secrets between the Prime Minister and his Foreign Secretary.[271]

Chamberlain felt he had to stand firm, and consequently he decided to dismiss Eden, not so much as a matter of principle, but because Eden was more cautious in approaching Italy at that time.[272] Eden distrusted the Italians for good reason, as Italy had close relations with Germany. Grandi's assurances were questionable. In his view, Britain 'running after' the Italian government would be seen in Berlin as enhancing Mussolini's prestige.[273] Chamberlain felt that Eden had missed one chance after another for advancing towards peace. Despite many representations from cabinet members to convince Eden not to resign, he stuck to his position and resigned.[274] There was perhaps also another reason why Eden had to resign, as he wrote: 'Ever since the discussions on Roosevelt's offer, I had realised how deep was the difference in outlook and opinion between the Prime Minister and myself.'[275] They also differed over the position of Italy because Eden wanted a proportionate Italian withdrawal from Spain[276] and over rearmament and alliance with the US[277] or Russia. So far as that was concerned, Chamberlain was 'by temperament, contemptuous of the one and suspicious of the other'.[278]

iii. Opposition to Chamberlain's Policy

The loss of Eden and Vansittart undoubtedly weakened Britain's position and could not have occurred at a more precarious time.[279] As Mussolini observed: 'The trouble is

[269] ibid 618.
[270] *Ciano's Diplomatic Papers*: Odhams Press, 1948; Eden ibid Appendix D. 619.
[271] H Macmillan, *Winds of Change* (London, Macmillan, 1966) 526.
[272] What's the context? The resignation of Anthony Eden, 20 February 1938 – History of government (blog.gov.uk) accessed 19 April 2024.
[273] A Eden, *Facing the Dictators* (London, Cassell, 1962) 589.
[274] DBFP 1919–1939 Ser. 2. Vol 19. 1138–1144. *Extract from Mr Neville Chamberlain's Diary February 19 and 27 1938.*
[275] A Eden, *Facing the Dictators* (London, Cassell, 1962) 591.
[276] A Eden, *Foreign Affairs* (London, Faber & Faber, 1939) 261.
[277] ibid 264.
[278] H Macmillan, *Winds of Change* (London, Macmillan, 1966) 529.
[279] ibid 522.

that there are now more gangsters than policeman.'[280] Thus, on the 20 February, Hitler declared that Germany would protect herself and the 10 million Germans living outside the Reich's borders. This obviously meant the seven million in Austria and the three million Sudeten Germans in Czechoslovakia, in his words, 'racial self-determination'.[281] Eden's fall caused a vigorous debate in the House of Commons with criticism by Churchill, Lloyd George and Harold Nicolson. Churchill led the onslaught. It was 'an irreparable loss to the Government'.[282] Eden had caused the Italians to cease their unrestricted submarine attacks in the Mediterranean after the Nyon Conference. Eden had importantly fostered a good relationship with the Americans, and it was an inopportune time for negotiations with Italy. In the first place, he said:[283]

> all these acts of bad faith which have been described to the House are fresh in everyone's mind. In the second place, the dictator Powers of Europe are striding on from strength to strength and from stroke to stroke, and the parliamentary democracies are retreating abashed and confused.

In a debate on 21 February 1938, Churchill said that Eden had been removed at the behest of the Italian government on the authority of Signor Farinacci, that: 'Our opinion will not change until London's foreign policy ceases to be directed by Mr. Eden'.[284] Chamberlain then decided to take over the conduct of the matter. There was little hope of any alteration in the Berlin-Rome Axis as a result and no evidence that Italy would oppose any Nazi annexation of Austria.[285] The resignation played havoc in Anglo-American relations.[286] What Churchill detected here was a 'new diplomacy'. The old policy was 'an effort to establish the rule of law in Europe and build up through the League of Nations, or by regional pacts under the League of Nations, effective deterrents against the aggressor'.[287] This amounted to coming to terms with the dictators 'by great and far-reaching acts of submission' so peace could be maintained.[288]

A more pointed attack came from Churchill's old friend Lloyd George. He accused Chamberlain of being disingenuous in not revealing what he described as: 'the crowning piece of evidence with which to crush the late Foreign Secretary, the production of a telegram that was handed to him by Count Grandi'.[289] Chamberlain said that Grandi simply communicated the contents of the telegram on Sunday. He did not give him the telegram. Chamberlain reported it to the Cabinet on the Sunday evening when Eden resigned.[290] Although this made no difference to Eden's decision to resign, the telegram was withheld by Grandi until the Monday when Eden was no longer Foreign Secretary. Lloyd George charged that there was: 'no doubt at all that the dictators were determined to drive the late Foreign Secretary out because he was the only man in this

[280] ibid 528.
[281] WL Shirer, *Berlin Diary* (London, Hamish Hamilton, 1941) 80.
[282] *Hansard* Vol 332, 21 Feb 1938. col. 237.
[283] 238.
[284] ibid 239.
[285] ibid 242.
[286] ibid 243.
[287] ibid 245.
[288] ibid.
[289] ibid 257.
[290] ibid.

Government who would stand up to them'.[291] Brigadier General Speirs MP, questioned why Count Grandi went to see Chamberlain on Monday morning prepared to discuss with him the withdrawal of volunteers from Spain. Grandi said that he had received his orders not on the Monday, but on the Sunday morning, when the ex-Foreign Secretary was still in office. He noted that Hitler spoke after Grandi had received his orders from Rome earlier, and Hitler confirmed that both countries would stay in Spain until the Nationalists won. Somebody was being tricked. In Speirs's view, Hitler was giving Italy a free hand in the Mediterranean, and Britain would gain nothing.[292] Another friend of Churchill and Eden, Harold Nicolson, spoke of the resignations being 'a fundamental issue. It is the issue whether our foreign policy is to be conducted on a basis of expediency or on a basis of principle.'[293]

As a corollary to this story, Mr Mander MP raised the question of the other difference between Chamberlain and Eden.[294] He asked why certain American and Canadian newspapers published a story about another reason for Eden's resignation involving America. Chamberlain refused to elaborate. However, it may not be coincidental that on the night of 22 February 1938, two days after Eden's resignation, Harold Ickes, American Secretary of the Interior, made an address on the BBC via a linkup with CBS.[295] He attacked the Nazi regime in harmony with Roosevelt's Chicago Speech attacking totalitarianism 'either to the right or to the left'. Roosevelt approved the speech, as did Cordell Hull, his Secretary of State.[296] The question raised by Mr Mander and Churchill's serious concern for the effect on Anglo-American relations makes the resignation of greater significance, supporting the reaction of Sumner Welles to the British Ambassador in Washington and the mortification Americans felt 'because it strikes at the fundamental doctrine of non-recognition of territories acquired by force'.[297] Lord Robert Cecil was also reported as saying:

> … I deprecate running after dictators, and most of all any ground for saying that we are ready to sacrifice British Ministers in order to please despots.

Both Chamberlain and Eden exaggerated their points of view at the time, as Gilian Bennett's paper[298] suggests quoting Cadogan when he said: 'I think [Eden] exaggerates as much one way as PM does on the other'[299] as far as Anglo-American relations were concerned. It did not appear to do serious damage, save that it was likely that the views expressed by Roosevelt in his October 1937 Quarantine Speech were quite distinct from Chamberlain's and far closer to those of Churchill, Macmillan, Amory, Nicolson, Duff Cooper and others who opposed appeasement. More than that, Oliver Harvey, Principal

[291] ibid 260.
[292] ibid (??) 10.02 pm.
[293] ibid 100.
[294] *Hansard* Vol 337, 20 June 1938. 11.14 pm.
[295] MJ Harmon, 'Some Contributions of Harold L Ickes' (1954) 7(2) *The Western Political Quarterly* 238–252, 244.
[296] H Ickes, *The Secret Diaries of Harold L Ickes Volume II The Inside Struggle 1936-1939* (London, Weidenfeld and Nicolson, 1955) 321–325.
[297] As reported in the *Londonderry Sentinel* 22 February 1938. British Newspaper Archive.
[298] G Bennett, FCO Historical Branch Occasional Papers, No. 1. November 1987. (Foreign Commonwealth Office).
[299] *The Diaries of Sir Alexander Cadogan 1938–1945* (ed. D Dilks, London, 1971) 37.

Private Secretary to Eden when he was Foreign Secretary, wrote that 'the PM is temperamentally anti-American'.[300]

Writing in his diary on 19 February 1938, Chamberlain noted that 'the United States has drawn closer to us, but the isolationists there are so strong and so vocal that she cannot be depended on for help if we should get into trouble'.[301] To appease Germany, Chamberlain considered handing over Tanganyika. This was at a time when Italy was threatening to leave the League of Nations and when, at the beginning of February 1938, Hitler assumed personal command of all German armed forces. Chamberlain had continued to pursue appeasement, whilst since 1937[302] Eden had strongly advocated arousing support in the US, the League of Nations, and the Dominions with a programme for rapid and large-scale rearmament.[303] Chamberlain clung to the belief that he could use Mussolini against Hitler, whereas Eden could not trust the 'gangster', knowing he had already sold out to Austria.[304] When Britain signed the 'Easter Accords' with Italy on 16 April 1938, it gave recognition to Italy's Ethiopian Empire (subject to League acceptance).[305] Italy agreed to withdraw troops from Spain and reduce the Libyan garrison. This was, as Lloyd George suggested, no benefit to British interests in the Mediterranean.[306]

J. The Anschluss

Diplomatically, this was opposed by France, Britain and Italy. Foreseeing the threats from Germany, Louis Barthou, the French Foreign Minister, visited eastern Europe seeking support from the Little Entente[307] and Poland. On 25 July 1934 the Austrian Nazis, in league with the SS (*Schutzstaffeln*) attacked the Ballhausplatz and murdered Chancellor Dollfuss. The SS attack was repelled by Austrian troops, and the murderers were arrested. Mussolini reacted by sending five divisions to the Brenner pass,[308] although Hitler had warned him at their meeting on 15–16 June 1934 that Dollfuss should be replaced.[309] Mussolini wanted Austria to remain independent and was assured by Hitler's Reichstag speech on 21 May 1935 that Germany would not interfere in Austria's internal affairs and had no intention of annexing Austria.[310] On 11 July 1936, Von Papen, the Nazi Ambassador to Vienna, met Schuschnigg, whereby the Nazis recognised Austria as

[300] O Harvey, *The Diplomatic Diaries of Oliver Harvey 1937-40*. (Collins, London, 1970) 71.

[301] Extract from Mr Neville Chamberlain's Diary 19 and 27 February 1938. DBFP 1919–1939 Ser. 2. Vol 19. 1138–1144.

[302] Following the Japanese attacks on Shanghai and Nanking, the incursion in the Yangtze Valley and the Italian submarine attacks in the Mediterranean.

[303] H Macmillan, *Winds of Change* (London, Macmillan, 1966) 524.

[304] Z Steiner, *The Triumph of the Dark. European International History 19331939* (Oxford, Oxford University Press, 2011) 562.

[305] O Harvey, *The Diplomatic Diaries of Oliver Harvey 1937-40* (Collins, London 1970) 73.

[306] Z Steiner, *The Triumph of the Dark. European International History 19331939* (Oxford, Oxford University Press, 2011) 562.

[307] Czechoslovakia, Romania and Yugoslavia.

[308] J de Launay, *Major Controversies of Contemporary History* (Oxford, Pergamon Press, 1965) 140.

[309] Z Steiner, *The Triumph of the Dark. European International History 1933-1939* (Oxford, Oxford University Press, 2011) 75.

[310] ibid 104.

sovereign, and Austria acknowledged that it was 'a German state'.[311] Later that year, on 1 November 1936, Mussolini proclaimed the Rome-Berlin Axis, not an alliance but an understanding of mutual interests indicating disinterest in Austria as with the Nazi relationship.[312] On 20 February 1937, disturbed by the deepening crisis, Ambassador Bullitt in Paris informed Cordell Hull that Delbos, French Minister for Foreign Affairs, said that France would not support Austria if France itself was not attacked, and in any event, it had no obligation to protect Austria.[313] Later, on 30 April 1937, Bullitt reported a conversation with Phipps, the British Ambassador in Paris, in which Phipps confirmed that the only chance of preserving the peace was for Britain to rearm as quickly as possible. Only if Britain and France acted in unison with a benevolently neutral America could the risk of war be averted.[314] Phipps also confirmed that it would be impossible for Britain to promise support to Czechoslovakia if she should be attacked by Germany. He also said that Germany could take Austria at any time.[315] As it happened, neither Czechoslovakia nor Hungary was prepared to support Austria. Schuschnigg was isolated and undermined continually by Seyss-Inquart.[316] Hitler manipulated not only the gullible Mussolini but also the Sudetendeutsche with the rallying cry of self-determination denied them at Versailles and implacable support for Nazification.[317] As further evidence of Mussolini's submission to the will of the Fuhrer, in September 1937 he agreed with Hitler that he would urge Austria to abide by its agreement with Germany and that Italy would leave the League of Nations.[318] Italy would accept German annexation of Austria. If only Chamberlain had known what Eden anticipated. What is alarming is that his sister-in-law was meeting with Mussolini as his envoy in the autumn of 1937.[319] Subsequently, contrary to Hitler's Reichstag speech on 25 May 1935, Shirer, who was then reporting from Vienna, wrote in his diary on 7 February 1938 that the Austrian police had raided the Nazi headquarters in the Teinfaltstrasse and found a plan initialled by Rudolf Hess for a new putsch. Shirer noted that the plot envisaged a riot in front of the German embassy in the Metternichgasse, Von Papen and the German Military Attaché were to be assassinated. This would give Hitler a *casus belli* to invade Austria.[320]

On 15 February 1938, Hitler summoned Schuschnigg to Berchtesgaden and demanded that Seyss-Inquart become Minister of the Interior and that the economies of Germany and Austria be integrated.[321] Schuschnigg was affronted by these demands and secretly planned a plebiscite for 13 March, which infuriated Hitler, who demanded

[311] ibid 156.
[312] ibid 157.
[313] The Foreign Relations of the United States, Diplomatic Papers 1937 vol. I. General (Washington, 1954) *The Ambassador in France (Bullitt) to The Secretary of State, 20 April 1937*, Paris.
[314] ibid 85.
[315] ibid 86.
[316] Z Steiner, *The Triumph of the Dark. European International History 1933-1939* (Oxford, Oxford University Press, 2011) 363. Seyss-Inquart became Chancellor of Austria two days before the Anschluss. He was Deputy Governor of Occupied Poland and Reich Commissioner in Holland. He was hanged for war crimes in 1946.
[317] Z Steiner, *The Triumph of the Dark. European International History 1933–1939* (Oxford, Oxford University Press, 2011) 264.
[318] ibid 314–315.
[319] A Eden, *Facing the Dictators* (London, Cassell, 1962) 573.
[320] WL Shirer, *Berlin Diary* (London, Hamish Hamilton, 1941) 79.
[321] Z Steiner, *The Triumph of the Dark. European International History 1933-1939* (Oxford, Oxford University Press, 2011) 552.

that Schuschnigg resign. He refused but postponed the plebiscite. In desperation Schuschnigg appealed to Britain, but his appeal was rejected.[322] So Hitler by subterfuge, propaganda and a fifth column organised by Seyss-Inquart, took over a sovereign state, benefiting the Nazi Treasury by 782 million Reichsmarks.[323] On the other hand, Austria could not feed itself, nor did it have raw materials following its imperial dissolution in 1919.[324] Hitler was quite aware that Britain would not act, maybe because Halifax had suggested Britain had no interest in Central Europe.[325] Chamberlain was surprised that after all his efforts to appease Mussolini. they came to nothing. He had ignored the warnings of Vansittart, Churchill, Eden and others. It is quite likely that the *Forschungsamt* part of the Nazi intelligence network had intercepted and deciphered all diplomatic signals and tapped the phone calls from the British embassy in Berlin so that the Nazis were fully aware of the British position.

At 5.30 am on 11 March 1938, the Wehrmacht overran Austria. Schuschnigg was removed from office, and the Nazis had effective control. In Berlin, Hitler's propaganda machine was in full swing. His newspaper *Völkische Beobachter* proclaimed: DEUTSCHÖSTERREICH VOR DEM CHAOS GERETTET,[326] describing alleged violent Red disorders in the streets of Vienna. There were no socialists or communists in Vienna on the night of 11 March, as William Shirer attested.[327]

K. The Sudetenland Crisis

The next major Central European crisis was in the Sudetenland, a part of the polyglot state of Czechoslovakia created by the Versailles Treaty and characterised by its majority Sudetendeutsche population excluded from the Kaiserreich under the Versailles Treaty. The crisis instigated by the Nazi regime was met with Chamberlain's efforts to appease Hitler through duplicitous diplomacy. Hinting to Hitler that Britain would support France but telling the French that Britain would not support France if it met its treaty obligations to Czechoslovakia and then telling the Czechs that Britain would not support them if Hitler invaded. This episode ranks as probably the most disreputable episode in modern British diplomatic history in terms of the excessive pressure placed on the Czechs by its so-called ally and the Runciman Mission.

i. The Illusion of Appeasement

On 14 March 1938, after Hitler's occupation of Austria, Churchill said that Britain should adhere to the League of Nations covenant and 'resolve to procure by international action the reign of law in Europe'. He proposed a Grand Alliance of small states in Europe bound by a defence treaty. This, he said, might be the last chance to prevent

322 ibid 553.
323 ibid 556.
324 ibid.
325 ibid 526. See above as to the visit that concerned Eden.
326 GERMAN AUSTRIA SAVED FROM CHAOS.
327 WL Shirer, *Berlin Diary* (London, Hamish Hamilton, 1941) 88.

the approaching war.[328] Such foresight demonstrates another example of Churchill's perception and intelligence of Nazi intentions. France would not fight for Austria and was in the middle of a change of government.[329] Also on 14 March, Paul-Boncour,[330] who was in office for less than three weeks, had assured the Czech minister in Paris, M Osusky, that France would fulfil its obligations to Czechoslovakia.[331] Daladier denied that France would give any military assistance to the Czechs. General Gamelin agreed.[332] Russian Foreign Minister Litvinov warned Britain that it was 'perhaps, our last call for co-operation in Europe'.[333] On 18 March, Chamberlain told his sister that he had abandoned any idea of giving guarantees to Czechoslovakia or to France in connection with French obligations to Czechoslovakia.[334] A full cabinet met on 22 March to consider a pessimistic report from the Chiefs of Staff (COS) on the military threat posed by Germany to Czechoslovakia.[335] Chamberlain and Halifax used this as a pretext for appeasing Germany, as it would be difficult for Britain and France to remove Germany from Czechoslovakia. Halifax and Chamberlain considered the question of giving a guarantee to the Czechs or a guarantee of support to France if France honoured her treaty obligations.[336] They decided not to call for a halt to German aggression but to work for a peaceful settlement. They agreed to announce publicly speedier rearmament. Duff Cooper said that if France went to war, Britain should follow them.[337]

The Czechs placed reliance on the Little Entente, Yugoslavia and Romania. President Beneš had confidence in Czechoslovakia's treaty of mutual assistance with France signed in 1925, and with the Soviet Union signed in 1935, dependent on France taking action first. In turn, the French had a treaty with Russia for mutual assistance and guarantee made in 1935, and Britain had pledged support to France in 1936 if France became the victim of unprovoked German aggression. Beneš and his government at this stage appeared to have, as Sir John Wheeler Bennett[338] famously said, 'a naïve belief in the good faith of their allies'.[339] Beneš also told Wheeler-Bennet: 'I have France, and if I have France I have Russia, and you have given your pledge to France.'[340] The problem was that Britain had no obligation to support France if France acted according to its guarantee with Czechoslovakia.

[328] RAC Parker, *Chamberlain and Appeasement* (London Macmillan, 2000) 142–144.

[329] Z Steiner, *The Triumph of the Dark. European International History 1933–1939* (Oxford, Oxford University Press, 2011) 557.

[330] French Foreign Minister from 13 March 1938–8 April 1938.

[331] DBFP 1919–1939 Ser 3. Vol 1. No. 84. *Sir E Phipps to Viscount Halifax* 15 March 1938.

[332] Z Steiner, *The Triumph of the Dark. European International History 1933–1939* (Oxford, Oxford University Press, 2011) 558.

[333] Z Steiner, 'The Soviet Commissariat of Foreign Affairs and the Czechoslovak Crisis in 1938' (1999) 42(3) *Historical Journal* 755.

[334] G Gorodetsky, *The Maisky Diaries* (New Haven, Yale University Press, 2016) 105.

[335] W Wark, *The Ultimate Enemy* (Oxford, OUP, 1986) 235–236. The March COS Report contrasts with the more optimistic intelligence data of September 1938 but not assessed for Chamberlain's benefit.

[336] RAC Parker, *Chamberlain and Appeasement* (London, Macmillan, 2000) 137.

[337] ibid 138.

[338] GCVO, CMG, OBE, FBA. Historian and unofficial government adviser on international affairs, lecturer at University of Virginia and at St Antony's College and New College Oxford, Assistant Director, Publicity Department Foreign Office, assisted Sir Maxwell Fyfe KC at the Nuremberg Trial with his knowledge of the accused Nazi leaders.

[339] J Wheeler-Bennett, *Knaves, Fools and Heroes* (London, Macmillan, 1974) 136.

[340] ibid 136.

Contrary to Churchill's view Chamberlain ignored Russia, although Russia and France had the same treaty obligations to defend Czechoslovakia. Chamberlain did the opposite of what Churchill advised: he deliberately put pressure on Beneš, the Czech President; Hodza, the Prime Minister; and Krofta, the Foreign Minister, to concede to Henlein of the Sudeten German Party (SDP) Nazi demands. Britain pressured the French government to do the same.[341] What was questionable was Henderson's relationship with Ribbentrop in Berlin to ascertain Germany's demands, although Britain did entreat them and the SDP to be patient.[342] Hitler had no intention of acceding to any intervention and instructed Henlein to increase his demands.[343]

Britain made it clear that any agreement by the Czechs with the Sudetendeutsche was conditional on their support for Czech independence, which seems a contradiction in terms. Chamberlain's policy becomes very clear at this point: to appease the dictators to keep the peace and to reach a general settlement, including arms limitation, with the Nazis. He felt he could persuade them, but in effect this appeared as collaboration enabling their objective. His approach was contrary to international law, to British foreign policy aims since 1688,[344] and to the Locarno and Versailles Treaties. This would inevitably strengthen the dictator's prestige and increase the risks of war. On 24 March 1938, Chamberlain rejected Churchill's pleas for a reform of the defence departments. Churchill warned Chamberlain that this was a last chance to rouse the country to prevent war.[345]

Hitler began to harass Czechoslovakia with his propaganda machine and military threats, sending 10 divisions of the Wehrmacht to the Czech frontier on 21 May 1938. Halifax warned Ribbentrop that if conflict arose, Britain might be forced to become involved. He followed that up later that night of 21 May, instructing Henderson in Berlin to warn Ribbentrop, who was threatening action after two Sudetendeutsche were killed allegedly by a Czech officer, that Britain would not stand aside if such a threat was carried out. Halifax warned that if conflict arose, he could not guarantee that Britain would not be forced by circumstances to become involved also.[346] Halifax also reminded Ribbentrop of Chamberlain's speech of 24 March 1938, when he referred to the common ideals of France and Britain: democratic liberty and determination to uphold them.[347]

On 22 May, contrary to what he suggested the day before, Halifax instructed Phipps, the British Ambassador in Paris, to tell Bonnet, the French Foreign Minister, that France should not assume Britain would help France to defend Czechoslovakia. Halifax's advice is highly significant and gives the reason why the Sudeten question was so dangerous, as Halifax stated:[348]

[341] RAC Parker, *Chamberlain and Appeasement* (London, Macmillan, 2000) 146.

[342] ibid.

[343] ibid 147.

[344] A Toynbee, *Survey of International Affairs 1938,* Vol II (Oxford, OUP, 1951) 8. As Toynbee remarked Britain gave up continental acquisitions in 1558 after the loss of Calais and after 1688 ensured that no one country dominated the continent.

[345] RAC Parker, *Chamberlain and Appeasement* (London, Macmillan, 2000) 158–149.

[346] ibid 148.

[347] ibid 139.

[348] DBFP 1919–1939 Ser. 3. Vol 1. No. 271. *Viscount Halifax to Sir E. Phipps (Paris)* 22 May 1938, 4.30 pm.

1. It is of utmost importance that French Government should not be under any illusion as to attitude of His Majesty's Government, so far as it can be forecast at the moment, in the event of failure to bring about peaceful settlement in Czechoslovak question.
2. His Majesty's Government have given the most serious warnings to Berlin, and these should have prospects of success in deterring German Government from any extreme courses. But it might be highly dangerous if the French Government were to read more into those warnings than is justified by their terms.
3. His Majesty's Government would of course always honour their pledge to come to the assistance of France if she were the victim of unprovoked aggression by Germany. In that event they would be bound to employ all the forces at their command.
4. If, however, the French Government were to assume that His Majesty's Government would at once take joint military action with them to preserve Czechoslovakia against German aggression, it is only fair to warn them that our statements do not warrant any such assumption.
5. In the view of His Majesty's Government the military situation is such that France and England, even with such assistance as might be expected from Russia, would not be in a position to prevent Germany over-running Czechoslovakia. The only result would be a European war, the outcome of which, so far as can be foreseen at this moment, would be at least doubtful.

What seems clear is that Britain would support France if she were attacked by Germany but could not venture to support France in joint military action to save Czechoslovakia, although Britain appreciated French treaty obligations, which were a matter for France, not Britain. The negative British military appreciation[349] was that a combination of France, Britain and Russia would not have driven Germany out of Czechoslovakia.[350] Halifax told Jan Masaryk, the Czech minister in London, that at most Czechoslovakia could be autonomous on the Swiss model, but this was wishful thinking.[351]

ii. Living in a Fool's Paradise[352]

On 25 May 1938, Hugh Dalton[353] opened a debate on the government's conduct of air defences and the demand for a public enquiry.[354] He noted that the three principal politicians had been moved, which strengthened the case for an enquiry. This was an admission that all was not well at the Air Ministry, but removing those with experience and replacing them with people less experienced was questionable. Churchill made the same point. The new Secretary of State had practically no knowledge of the department. Dalton charged that since 1931 the foreign policy of Britain was continually mishandled, with the consequence that international law and order and national security had

[349] One wonders what the Russian miliary appreciation was bearing in mind their last-minute support for the Czechs on 30 September 1938. See below evidence of Sir John Wheeler-Bennett in J Wheeler-Bennett, *Knaves, Fools and Heroes* (London, Macmillan, 1974) 153.

[350] This was the subject of fierce debate in the House of Commons on 25 May 1938 especially regarding the lack of air defence.

[351] RAC Parker, *Churchill and Appeasement* (London, Macmillan, 2000) 148.

[352] Churchills conclusion in his attack on the inadequacy of air defence in his letter to Major Percy Davies cited in M Gilbert, *The Prophet of Truth* (Minerva, 1990) 945.

[353] Dalton later served in Churchill's cabinet and became Minister of Economic Warfare, and established the Special Operations Executive responsible for clandestine operations in occupied Europe.

[354] *Hansard*, House of Commons 25 May 1938 Vol 336. Cols. 1233–1253.

been seriously compromised. For nearly seven years, 'a policy of fumbling fingers and faltering feet'. Baldwin proposed parity with Germany, but that disappeared. Germany's new production was at least 200 to 300 aircraft a month ahead of Britain. He questioned the quality of the replacement ministers. The principal permanent official of the Air Ministry was from the Post Office, and the second man was from the Ministry of Agriculture, both of whom had no practical knowledge of air problems and aircraft.

Supporting Churchill's idea, a ministry of supply was essential because of the extraordinarily complex, antiquated process of procurement through various committees and referrals. There were grave shortages of supplies of navigational instruments, gun turrets, blind flying equipment, blind landing gear, night flying instruments, anti-aircraft guns and barrage balloons. A balloon barrage for London would not be ready until Christmas, 1938, and there were no plans for other cities. The air defence of London was grossly neglected; there were no 3.7-inch guns, only some 3-inch guns with barely half the vertical range of the 3.7-inch. In defence, the Dominions had been ignored in assisting Britain in getting supplies or in meeting Dominion requirements.

Chamberlain[355] denied the charges made by Dalton on the basis that his critics had an insufficient appreciation of the magnitude and difficulties in the task of aircraft manufacture. His procurement regime depended on persuasion to make an enormous expansion of the industry that, in his view, had 'never been dreamed of'. He admitted that there had been delays, disappointments and checks in the programme, caused by the development of the all-metal monoplane, the design of new engines of unprecedented efficiency and the invention of the variable-pitch airscrew.[356] He explained that in such aircraft there were upwards of 70,000 separate parts for which between 6,000 and 8,000 separate drawings were required.[357] He rejected calls for a Ministry of Supply, saying that the existing process was sufficient.[358] Sir Archibald Sinclair, leader of the Liberal Party, rejected Chamberlain's suggestions.[359] The debate, he said, was not a motion of no confidence. It was simply about the widening gap in the disparity in armaments between Germany and Britain. False assurances had been given over the years, but governments had not performed. It was the 34th month since Lord Baldwin decided that the Air Force must be tripled.[360] Replying further to these charges, the new Secretary for Air, Sir Kingsley Wood, said that the RAF would require during the next two years 4,700 pilots, 33,000 airmen, and 6,000 others to be trained for a special trade.[361] There was no need for an enquiry which would 'rather hinder than help', but he promised to carefully review the points made.[362]

The debate exposed the acute anxiety regarding Britain's defence capabilities, which fostered the case for appeasement as a temporary expedient to delay any war whilst Britain increased rearmament. Chamberlain may have thought that the longer the delay,

[355] ibid 1254–1267.
[356] ibid 1257.
[357] ibid 1261.
[358] ibid 1264.
[359] ibid 1268–1280.
[360] ibid 1281–1294, 1293.
[361] ibid 1346.
[362] ibid 1349.

the less risk of war and less money spent on rearmament. Such thinking, in Churchill's view, was simply living in a fool's paradise.[363]

iii. Dealing with the Nazis

It was against this background that discussions took place between Vansittart, former Under-Secretary at the Foreign Office, and Henlein, the leader of the Sudetendeutsche, whom he knew. Henlein at first appeared to accept the British proposals. Halifax pressured Beneš because Hitler had suggested that any agreement between Henlein and the Czechs would be respected.[364] Henderson wanted to assure Hitler of Britain's belief in his 'good faith'.[365] Vansittart warned Chamberlain that a Nazi attack would come between the end of September and mid-October and urged that Runciman, who was to mediate, should support a plebiscite and that Britain should warn it would aid France. As a result, Halifax warned Hitler about anti-British sentiment in the German press and the German mobilisation, which would make Runciman's task of investigation and mediation more difficult.[366]

Vansittart had a meeting with Ewald von Kleist-Schmanzin, one of his informants, who warned of a German invasion at the end of September. Von Kleist-Schmanzin said that in Germany: 'There is only one real extremist and that is Hitler himself. He is the great danger, and he is doing this entirely on his own.'[367]

A *Times* editorial on 3 June 1938 suggested that the Czechs should hold a plebiscite for the Sudetendeutsche and ask whether they wanted to join the Third Reich. On 18 July, Hitler sent his former trusted World War I senior officer, Captain Wiedemann, to London to persuade Halifax as to the merits of the German case. Wiedemann suggested that Goering might come to London to discuss Anglo-German relations. He gave Halifax and Chamberlain a binding assurance that the German government was not planning to resort to force 'limited to a definite period'. When Halifax returned from a state visit with the King and Queen to Paris, he suggested to Chamberlain that Lord Runciman be sent to Prague to resolve the impasse between the Czechs and the Sudetendeutsche. The Czechs had requested this, not knowing that the intention was to use Runciman to tell Beneš what to concede to the Sudetendeutsche.[368]

L. The Runciman Mission: Forlorn Hope or Sell Out

Notwithstanding the existence of an arbitration agreement in the Locarno Treaty of 1925 between Germany and Czechoslovakia, Chamberlain decided to send Runciman as a mediator to Prague as the Czechs had requested to resolve growing anxieties and tensions between the Sudetendeutsche Partei (SdP Sudeten German Party)

[363] M Gilbert, *The Prophet of Truth* (Minerva, 1990) 945.
[364] RAC Parker, *Chamberlain and Appeasement* (London, Macmillan, 2000) 150.
[365] ibid 152.
[366] ibid.
[367] ibid 153.
[368] ibid 151.

and the Czechoslovakian government. Chamberlain's aim was to prevent a general war involving Britain.[369] Thus, on 15 July 1938, Halifax wrote to Henderson regarding the appointment of 'an investigator and mediator'[370] to act independently to elaborate the views that might harmonise relations between the SdP and the Czechs.[371] On 26 July, Halifax announced the appointment of Runciman in the House of Commons.[372]

i. Questionable Status

He defined the role as that of:

> … an investigator and mediator would, of course, be independent of His Majesty's Government – in fact, he would be independent of all Governments. He would act only in his personal capacity, and it would be necessary, of course, that he should have all the facilities and all the information placed at his disposal in order to enable him to carry through his task … He is characterised by fearlessness, freedom from prejudice, integrity and impartiality, and I am quite certain that everyone here will wish him all success.

In Newton's[373] dispatch to Halifax on the same date, he confirmed Runciman's role as:[374]

> … to investigate problem and grounds for differences of opinion at the same time in detail and if necessary, act as a mediator with advice and influence. It would be very important that the person concerned should receive every help and that different points of view and the various difficulties should be frankly and fully explained to him by all competent and well-informed authorities. He would be completely independent of the British Government and of every other Government.

The characteristics described as freedom from prejudice and his impartiality by Chamberlain would not pass that test in terms of Runciman's befriending Sudeten aristocrats most weekends on their estates, nor his instructions/advice from Halifax via Ambassador Newton in Prague, nor the fact that Foreign Office officials constituted his staff. He was, in effect, a British agent in receipt of instructions from the Foreign Secretary via Ambassador Newton. It is evident that Runciman, an isolationist, was supporting the principle of self-determination as were Chamberlain and Halifax for the Sudetendeutsche. On 12 September 1938. Hitler at Nuremberg adopted the same principle and used the partition of Ireland in 1922 as an argument in his favour.[375] In order to achieve his goal of dismantling the Czechoslovakian state, Hitler mobilised his army

[369] The newspaper headlines in Prague on 14 September 1938 summed up the reaction of the Czech's: 'How the Mighty Head of the British Empire Goes Begging to Hitler.' WL Shirer, *Berlin Diary* (London, Hamish Hamilton, 1941) 110.

[370] The terms of reference given to Lord Runciman a Liberal Peer and former member of the government were vague. The idea of a mediator being an investigator is odd. Runciman was given an impossible task with little likelihood of success, albeit he very nearly succeeded but for the duplicity of Henlein the SGP leader and the overwhelming undue influence of Hitler.

[371] DBFP 1919–1939, Ser. 3. Vol 2. No. 541.

[372] Chamberlain Speech Parliamentary Debates 3rd Ser. House of Commons 26 July 1938 Vol 338. Cols. 2957–2958.

[373] British ambassador in Prague.

[374] DBFP 1919–1939, Ser. 3. Vol 2. No. 547.

[375] See: ibid No. 919. Suggested by Hitler's entourage on 18 September 1938 as confirmed in Newton's despatch of that date.

to threaten and intimidate. Whether he would invade Czechoslovakia was a moot point because Hitler remained undecided during the Runciman mission.

Before Runciman arrived at Prague, Halifax told Newton on 29 July 1938 that, on information received from 'persons in contact with Henlein',[376] he should pressurise Beneš to agree immediately to the following German demands and synchronise these with Runciman's arrival:

(a) a beginning of the exchange of Sudeten and Czech officials, with the object of gradually transferring them to their respective racial territories;
(b) the introduction into the Czechoslovak press, especially the newspapers of the frontier areas, of a spirit of conciliation;
(c) disarmament of the various Czech political organisations;
(d) the gradual withdrawal of the much increased number of state and secret police from the Sudeten districts and their replacement in towns and open districts by the old Stadtpolizei (uniformed municipal police);
(e) government approval of the mayors elected some weeks ago in the Sudeten areas.

Newton reported that the impression in Czechoslovakia was that the western Powers would save themselves at the expense of the Czechs.[377] Meanwhile, the German army was bringing seven to eight divisions up to war strength. Beneš informed Newton that Runciman would be given every facility, and he would be glad to see him. Contrary to this, Runciman tended to spend far less time with Czechoslovakian delegates than with the SdP. On 3 August, Chamberlain wrote to Dr von Dirksen, the German Ambassador in London, informing him that Runciman was to act as a mediator and conciliator in the hope that this would relieve anxieties. He hoped that von Dirksen would speak to Hitler, relaying Chamberlain's anticipation of settling the Sudeten question and then developing an understanding with the Reich.[378] This followed a letter from Halifax to Ribbentrop of 28 July urging that tension be reduced.[379] Ribbentrop gave filtered information to Hitler that would please him and not an objective assessment. On 4 August the Czechs responded to the SdP with their Nationality Act and Language Bill, seeking the SdP's cooperation on proposals for reform. The Czechs would continue the negotiations with a group of six representatives from the coalition parties in the Czech Parliament.[380] As anticipated, Runciman found the mediation process 'very hard going' with the parties who were far apart on first principles. All Runciman could hope for would be 'a little accommodation on some practical problems'.[381]

When Halifax wrote to Henderson on 5 August 1938, he developed his bifurcated policy of telling Beneš 'what we might not do in the event of trouble and tactfully remind the Germans of what we might do'.[382] He was under no illusion as to the consequences of Runciman making no settlement, suggesting a solution unacceptable to the

[376] Halifax, Chamberlain and Ashton-Gwatkin a Foreign Office official on Runciman's staff seemed blissfully unaware that Henlein was a leading Nazi agent.
[377] DBFP 1919–1939, Ser. 3. Vol 2. No. 567. 2 August 1938.
[378] ibid No. 574. *Letter Neville Chamberlain to Dr von Dirksen.*
[379] ibid No. 555. *Letter from Viscount Halifax to Herr von Ribbentrop* 28 July 1938.
[380] ibid No. 582. *Newton to Halifax* 4 August 1938.
[381] ibid No. 583. *Runciman to Halifax* (undated).
[382] ibid No. 587. *Halifax to Henderson.*

SdP or unacceptable to the Czechs, or suggesting a clean cut by way of plebiscite. Halifax had no intention of 'doing over' the Czechs if he could help it. He also suggested that Henderson should send Newton an appreciation from time to time that would show Runciman and tell him Halifax had told him to do so. Halifax caveated that by writing: 'I think it is very important that Runciman should have the aspect of things as you see them for the present to his mind.'[383] Halifax was giving mixed messages to both sides in the attempt to encourage some peaceful outcome.

The question arises as to the degree to which Runciman was independent of the British government, given they were not a party to the dispute. It is arguable that it was a dispute between Czechoslovakia and Germany not Czechoslovakia and the SdP. The amount of pressure Beneš was subjected to by Runciman in favour of the SdP and Germany by the intervention of Halifax, Newton, and Henderson was surprising, as Britain was not a party to the dispute and had no locus standi.

On 10 August Runciman reported to Halifax that he had received the demands of the SdP and the Czech government's Statement of Proposals. The parties were far apart, but he was trying to induce both sides to agree on some common ground. He had met with the Czechoslovakian government leaders and the SdP, but it all depended on Hitler.[384] Runciman was under no illusion about that although he, Halifax, and Ashton-Gwatkin[385] were taken in by Henlein, perhaps not realising that he was acting under instructions from Berlin. The SdP delegation refused to meet the Czech coalition parliamentary committee, although the Czechs were prepared to make some concessions employing Germans in government services.[386] That same day Halifax sent a Memorandum via Henderson to Hitler urging an amicable and peaceful outcome and stating that any mobilisation, such as had been reported by the British Military Attaché, would result in countermeasures by Czechoslovakia. That would destroy Runciman's mission.[387] The following day the SdP agreed to meet the Czech committee, and Runciman agreed to meet Henlein in northern Bohemia.[388] Runciman met Herr Franke[389] Henlein's deputy.[390] Runciman reported this to Halifax. Meanwhile Henderson, an ardent appeaser, was pressing Halifax not to ignore the principle of self-determination and that Runciman could recommend 'a plan which approximates to Hitler's present views'.[391] However, according to General Goering,[392] if the Runciman mission endured, the Nazis would not attack.[393] The attitude of Henderson is questionable in pressing the Nazi case, knowing the totalitarian nature of the regime.

[383] ibid No. 587. *Runciman to Halifax* 5 August 1938.

[384] ibid No. 602. *Runciman to Halifax* 10 August 1938.

[385] Head of the Economic Relations Department Foreign Office 1934–1939.

[386] DBFP 1919–1939, Ser, 3, Vol 2. No. 603. *Newton to Halifax*11 August 1938.

[387] ibid No. 603. *Halifax to Henderson* 11 August 1938. encl. Memorandum for Hitler. French not immediately informed of the demarche. Henderson advised Halifax not to tell the French. No. 647. *Henderson to Halifax* 19 August 1938.

[388] DBFP 1919–1939, Ser. 3. Vol 2. No. 609. *Newton to Halifax* 12 August 1938.

[389] Herr Franke was a ruthless Nazi agent who took instructions from Hitler to extend the campaign of sabotage and unrest in the Sudetenland. He later became Obergrupenfuhrer in command of the Nazi police, Gestapo, SD and the Kripo. He was executed as a war criminal at Nuremberg in 1946.

[390] DBFP 1919–1939, Ser. 3. Vol 2. No. 611. *Runciman to Halifax* 12 August 1938.

[391] ibid No 613. *Henderson to Halifax* 12 August 1938.

[392] Second in command to Hitler. Found guilty of war crimes and committed suicide at Nuremberg in 1946.

[393] DBFP 1919–1939, Ser. 3. Vol 2. No. 626. *RI Campbell (Paris) to O Sargent* 13 August 1938.

ii. Another Warning from Roosevelt

Whilst the Runciman mission was obstructed across the Atlantic, Cordell Hull, Roosevelt's Secretary of State, made a radio address following warnings from Ambassadors Bullitt in Paris and Kennedy in London regarding the deteriorating situation in Central Europe. This could not have been broadcast without the President's approval. Unlike Chamberlain, Hull adopted a quite different tone, saying:

> The invasion of territory of foreign states, destruction of lawfully constituted governments and forcible seizure of hitherto independent political entities, interference in the internal affairs of other nations, wholesale violation of established treaty obligations, growing disregard of universally accepted principles of international law, attempts to adjust international differences by armed force rather than by methods of pacific settlement, contemptuous brushing aside of rules of morality -all these appalling manifestations of disintegration seriously threaten the very foundations of our civilisation.[394]

In his memoirs, Hull explained that he had two thoughts in mind when making his broadcast. First to show Americans that an isolationist position would not protect them from the effects of a major war and second, to tell the Axis nations, as emphatically as he could, that contrary to the isolationist sentiment in the US they could not ignore America in pursuing their plans for conquest.[395]

iii. Nazi Intimidation and Deadlock

On 17 August there was a meeting where neither side was prepared to accept the other's proposals. In view of the increasing military threat to Czechoslovakia, Halifax advised Runciman on 18 August as the military threat increased. This was a guide for Runciman to consider pronouncing on those points that the parties had agreed rather than providing his own scheme. Points of disagreement might be reserved for the Powers.[396] The 'Powers' were not identified. Runciman was told that he 'must strain every nerve to produce a result of some sort within this time limit'. This meant before Hitler spoke at Nuremberg. The Nazi *Parteitag* was due to commence on 5 September 1938. The same day Runciman reported to Halifax that he had a practical difficulty in dealing with seven parties and five races. In some matters the Czech government followed his suggestions. He described himself as 'something less than a dictator and more than an adviser'.[397] He met Henlein, who rejected the government posts offered by Beneš whilst accepting reorganisation within the Czech territory but with Germans and Czechs segregated and the withdrawal of the gendarmerie.[398]

The 18 August was also the day, ignored by the Nazis, on which Roosevelt issued a warning (contrary to the impression given by Ambassador Kennedy in London) that if Canada was threatened, the US would not stand idly by. The US was not ignored by foreign Powers, and it did not ignore them.

[394] C Hull, *The Memoirs of Cordell Hull* (London, Hodder and Stoughton,1948) 587.
[395] ibid.
[396] DBFP 1919–1939, Ser, 3, Vol 2. No. 603. *Halifax to Runciman* 18 August 1938.
[397] ibid No. 644. *Letter from Runciman to Halifax* 18 August 1938.
[398] ibid No. 652. *Newton to Halifax* 19 August 1938.

On 21 August a new basis for negotiation was prepared under Beneš' instructions and considered favourably by SdP. Henderson warned Halifax that Hitler intended to attack Czechoslovakia 'towards the end of September', confirming Vansittart's information. The anticipated main attack would come through Austria.[399] Halifax then received a telegram from Ribbentrop saying that the Runciman mission was the initiative of the British and French governments without any consultation with the Reich. His government would not collaborate nor take any responsibility for the mission. Ribbentrop complained about British negative press reports and that the British had fortified the Czech's intransigence and aggressiveness.[400] Henderson wrote again the next day to press the German case and suggest that Britain should back Henlein more.[401] Henderson's dispatches from Berlin infer a persistent preference for the SdP and the Nazis' case.

On 23 August Runciman saw President Beneš and Prime Minister M Hodza[402] of Czechoslovakia and also Herr Kundt (SdP).[403] The two Czechs agreed to negotiate, although there was some doubt about Kundt. Henlein agreed. On 24 August, Beneš, Hodza, Kundt and Sebekowsky, who some days later led an attempted coup in Sudetenland, met to discuss the three local autonomous districts in the Sudeten German lands; the exchange of officials ie, Czech officials in German lands to be removed and German officials in Czech lands to be restored to German lands, to begin at once; an independent budget for the three districts; a loan from central government to the three districts; a Commission to meet within one to three months to decide on necessary changes in the Constitution, Propaganda and Press Armistice and the withdrawal of state police from German districts if all goes quietly. This was a favourable meeting, as was the meeting the following day.

The political side of the problem concerned the question of the integrity and security of the Czechoslovak Republic. This depended on German policy and on relations between Germany and Czechoslovakia. Runciman was not dealing directly with the Reich, but essentially with Beneš and Henlein. Henlein had instructions from Berlin of which Halifax, Runciman and Gwatkin were unaware.

Kundt told Runciman on 23 August that at the meeting between Beneš and Hodza on 24 August, not only internal questions would be discussed but also matters of foreign policy, eg, the Soviet Treaty and relations between Germany and Czechoslovakia. This deviated from Henlein's assurance given in London that external problems should not be considered in connection with internal problems. Runciman was aware of the distress and unemployment in the Sudetenland, heightened by the Sudetendeutsche question, which was entirely racial and incapable of being solved by economic remedies.[404]

On 25 August, Henderson speculated that Hitler might give three alternatives at the Nuremberg *Parteitag*.[405]

[399] ibid No. 658. *Henderson to Halifax* 21 August 1938.
[400] ibid No. 661. *Ribbentrop to Halifax* 21 August 1938.
[401] ibid Nos. 665 and 666. *Letters from Henderson to Halifax* 22 August 1938.
[402] Prime Minister from 9 November 1935 until 22 September 1938.
[403] Kundt was more moderate than Henlein.
[404] DBFP 1919–1939, Ser. 3. Vol 2. No. 696. *Halifax to Henderson* 26 August 1938.
[405] ibid No. 689. *Henderson to Halifax* 25 August 1938.

(a) that he will still be prepared to recognise integrity of a neutralised Czechoslovakia if complete home rule is accorded to Sudetendeutsche, or
(b) that a plebiscite based on the right of self-determination is the only solution which he will accept, or
(c) that the British having failed to bring Beneš to reason, Germany claims her inalienable right to secure herself in her own way the lives and interests of her German brethren across the frontier.

It appears that Henderson had some very close informants in Berlin to make these points, stressing again that it was imperative that Britain and France persuade Beneš as above or be left to his fate. Meanwhile, contrary to the defeatist pessimism in Downing Street and the Quai d'Orsay, Newton reported that Romania and Yugoslavia would regard Hungary as an accomplice if Hungary allowed German troops passage through its territory to attack Czechoslovakia.[406]

The same day, Halifax told Henderson[407] that Gwatkin had informed him of Runciman's progress on questions of constitutional, political and economic importance. The first question concerned the constitutional question, viz. the provision of some degree of home rule for the Sudetendeutsche within the Czechoslovak Republic. His first task was to make himself acquainted with the history of the question, with the principal persons concerned, and with the suggestions for its solution proposed by the two sides, viz. by the SdP in their 'Sketches' submitted to the Czech government on 7 June, and by the Czech government in their draft nationality statute, language bill and administrative reform bill. This enquiry was pursued by Lord Runciman's staff[408] making summaries of these proposals and submitting them in draft to the respective sides to obtain agreed documents which would adequately represent the point of view of each side.

iv. Excessive Pressure on the Czechs

A further report was given to Halifax on 27 August after Runciman saw Beneš and urged him to 'the limit of concessions and even beyond'.[409] Halifax had been informed by Henderson that day that Hitler would only be satisfied with autonomy for Sudetenland.[410] Sir John Simon, the Chancellor of the Exchequer, spoke at Lanark that afternoon, extolling the benefits of appeasement to reduce tensions and remove the causes that promoted war.[411] He referred to Czechoslovakia and Runciman's mission, who was 'not an arbitrator nor a judge-he is a mediator and a friend'. He was not the representative of the British government but 'the representative of all men everywhere who desire justice and who love peace'. It was, he said, 'the duty not only of us but of all others-and all are concerned in world peace-to do nothing to imperil a satisfactory solution'.[412] Contrary

[406] ibid No. 658. *Henderson to Halifax* 27 August 1938.
[407] ibid No. 696. *Halifax to Henderson* 26 August 1938.
[408] Foreign Office staff.
[409] DBFP 1919–1939, Ser. 3. Vol 2. No. 702. *Troutbeck (Prague) to Halifax* 27 August 1938.
[410] ibid No. 701. *Halifax to Henderson* 27 August 1938.
[411] ibid No. 704. *Halifax to Newton* 27 August 1938.
[412] ibid. This speech followed an earlier radio address by Secretary of State Cordell Hull on 16 August following warnings of Hitler's threats to invade Czechoslovakia from Ambassadors Kennedy and Bullitt (see above).

to the views being expressed *The New Statesman* that day stated: 'the strategical value of the Bohemian frontier should not be made the occasion of a world war'.[413] No doubt this emboldened the *Sudetendeutsche Partei* and their Nazi adherents in Berlin. Meanwhile, Hitler kept pressing for a quick solution. Ashton-Gwatkin saw Frank and then Henlein, who had a recent meeting with Hitler. Henlein intimated that if Runciman's solution was based on the Karlsbad Eight Points[414] this might also facilitate an Anglo-German agreement. If Britain pressed the Czechs to adopt Henlein's Karlsbad Points outlined in his speech, then he was ready to go to Berlin to put this to Hitler.[415] Halifax told Runciman through Newton on 29 August that this was out of the question, but Henlein could inform Hitler that he believed Britain desired an Anglo-German agreement and that a settlement of the Czechoslovak question might lead to such an agreement. Halifax understood that Gwatkin's idea of sending Henlein to see Hitler was to assure Hitler that the new proposals by Beneš revived the prospect of an agreed settlement so that negotiations could continue. Hitler's proposal, as reported by Frank, suggested that the Czechoslovak government should abandon Beneš' proposals and accept the Karlsbad programme.[416] What Runciman had to say was:

> … that you propose to assist both parties to reach a settlement on the basis both of the Karlsbad eight points and of Benes' seven new proposals

It seems that both Ashton-Gwatkin and Runciman were in danger of going beyond their remit. Runciman may be excused because he was under enormous pressure to produce a settlement and make some pronouncement. Beneš failed to appreciate the dire urgency and amplify his seven proposals, and thus Runciman could not make any pronouncement.[417] He told Halifax on 30 August[418] that the position was most difficult. Beneš made his contribution in an unpublishable memorandum. What he requested was a concise synthesis of the Karlsbad Points and Beneš' new proposals. He feared that Hitler would find some excuse for invading, not realising that such disturbances were instigated and planned in Berlin. Runciman suggested if the Karlsbad Programme was agreed 'The Mission's end would then be in sight and a tranquil future assured for at least a few months.' In reply, Halifax said that Beneš should respond by publishing his seven proposals at once. If not, Runciman should publish his own recommendations and comments as a basis for continued mediation.[419]

At this point Campbell reported from Paris that if there was no settlement, the French would support British arbitration. If Britain considered the proposals fair and these were rejected by Beneš, then '*tont pis pour eux*'.[420] In reply, Halifax stressed that it would be deplorable if Beneš were to resile from his seven proposals and that Campbell should tell Bonnet to ensure the French minister in Prague supported Newton in influencing

[413] *The New Statesman* 27 August 1938 as cited in J Wheeler-Bennet, *Munich Prologue to Tragedy* (London, Macmillan, 1963) 95.
[414] Based on Helein's speech.
[415] DBFP 1919–1939, Ser. 3. Vol 2. No. 706. *Troutbeck (Prague) to Halifax* 29 August 1938.
[416] ibid No. 710. *Halifax to Newton* 29 August 1938.
[417] ibid No. 717. *Newton to Halifax* 30 August 1938.
[418] ibid No. 723 *Letter Runciman to Halifax* 30 August 1938.
[419] ibid No. 724. *Halifax to Newton* 31 August 1938.
[420] ibid No. 725. *Campbell to Halifax* 31 August 1938.

Beneš.[421] Halifax had urged that Beneš publish his proposals in view of the increasing military threat, but Runciman told him that would be disastrous.[422] Runciman must be credited here for not panicking under intolerable threats of war. Instead of publishing his proposals Beneš withdrew them and produced a Memorandum since the SdP simply regarded his proposals as a 'bridge to restart negotiations'. Kundt of the SdP would see Beneš again, but in the meantime, Runciman would tell Beneš to go to the 'utmost limits'.[423] The position was grave because the Wehrmacht was ready for occupation of the Sudetenland, as reported to the Chief of Staff by Colonel Gauche of the Deuxième Bureau.[424]

v. *Beyond the Limits of Diplomatic Norms*

Whilst urging Beneš to go to such limits, it is questionable as to what limits the British government was encouraging Runciman and the Foreign Office staff supporting him to go beyond mediation. Despite Halifax's unease at Henlein acting as a messenger for Britain, Ashton-Gwatkin reported that Henlein would carry two messages to Hitler as to the necessity for continuance of the negotiations and the possibility of wider discussions on Anglo-German relations.[425]

These messages to Hitler bear analysis and are repeated here in full as being at the crux of the negotiation – a quid pro quo-peace in Czechoslovakia in consideration of an Anglo-German Treaty. Whilst the primary objective may have been the peaceful resolution of the Sudeten question a secondary objective emerges:[426]

> (Very confidential).
>
> In order to convince Herr Henlein and Herr Hitler that Lord Runciman and also His Majesty's Government are sincere in their determination to promote a quick as well as a comprehensive settlement Lord Runciman desires to inform Herr Henlein very confidentially of his readiness to produce a scheme by some given date (say September 15) should the two parties have failed to reach an agreement on present basis.
>
> (Second message begins.)
>
> As regards general question of Anglo-Czech [*sic*][427] relations Lord Runciman would be glad if Herr Henlein would tell Herr Hitler that he (Herr Henlein) believes Great Britain desires an Anglo-German agreement and that he further believes that a settlement of the Sudeten question might well open the way to such an agreement. Lord Runciman is not in a position to give any list of subjects which His Majesty's Government would be prepared to discuss; the actual initiation and programme of such discussions would presumably have to be arranged between the two Governments through their own channels.

These secret messages were questionable in terms of a mediator consulting a third party without the Czech's consent or knowledge. Runciman was there to mediate the dispute

[421] ibid No. 726. *Halifax to Campbell* 31 August 1938.
[422] ibid No. 728. *Newton to Halifax* 31 August 1938.
[423] ibid No. 730. *Newton to Halifax* 1 September 1938.
[424] K Strong, *Men of Intelligence* (London, Cassell, 1970) 47.
[425] DBFP 1919–1939, Ser. 3. Vol 2. No. 731. *Newton to Halifax* 1 September 1938.
[426] ibid No. 732. *Newton to Halifax* 1 September 1938.
[427] Error should be Anglo-German. See: ibid ft.1 201.

between the Czechs and the Sudetendeutsche, not to negotiate an Anglo-German understanding. Halifax, who had informed Henderson on 5 August[428] that he had no intention of 'doing over' Czechoslovakia if he could avoid it, links the fate of an Anglo-German understanding to settlement of the Sudetenland question. If Hitler believed the British warning of intervention, these messages gave him support for his view that neither France nor Britain would intervene. These messages may have undermined any advantage Chamberlain's 24 March speech would have given. Furthermore, to trust a diehard Nazi like Henlein was a gross error of judgement. No doubt the purpose was to ensure Hitler did not act precipitously so that Runciman could break the impasse or publish his own proposals. Halifax was playing for time for the parties to reach agreement but also acting in the British interest for an Anglo-German understanding. That same day, Halifax told Runciman to see Dr Kundt, a more moderate member of the SdP, and encourage him to proceed with the negotiations.[429]

vi. So Near Yet So Far

Ashton-Gwatkin informed Mr Strang[430] that Henlein was conscious of his personal responsibility for war or peace, although convinced the friendship between Britain and Germany was the true basis for peace. No doubt Henlein and Hitler appeared to use that to their advantage in the negotiations, and a matter of which Runciman was aware. When Henderson met with State Secretary Ernst von Weizsäcker,[431] he told Weizsäcker that nobody in Britain wished to fight for either Czechs or Sudetendeutsche, but if Germany took precipitate action, then Britain would support France if France felt obliged to honour her obligations. Weizsäcker said France would not fight if she lacked British support, and Britain could stop her. Henderson was quite firm with Weizsäcker and told him that it seemed inconceivable that Britain would do so. He said that the German government should not miss this opportunity, as Beneš was now definitely considering big concessions.[432] This was one of Henderson's better ripostes, together with another to Ribbentrop the same day.[433] Ribbentrop said that it was France's ambition for hegemony of Europe (another example of reverse logic by Nazi totalitarians when it was Hitler who wanted to dominate the continent). Ribbentrop protested the British *démarche* on 21 May and threatened consequences if repeated. Henderson told Ribbentrop that Britain was avoiding any misunderstanding as may have occurred in July 1914.[434] Ribbentrop reiterated Germany's distrust of Beneš and the need for some impartial tribunal as a guarantee for the implementation of any scheme. Henderson was optimistic that more time would be given to Runciman.[435]

[428] DBFP 1919–1939, Ser. 3. Vol 2. No. 587. *Halifax to Henderson* 5 August 1938.
[429] ibid No. 735. *Halifax to Newton* 1 September 1938.
[430] ibid No. 734. *Newton to Halifax* 1 September 1938.
[431] ibid No. 736. *Henderson to Halifax*. 1 September 1938. Weizsäcker served as Sate Secretary from 1938–1943. Weizsäcker later defended himself at the Nuremberg trials as an anti-Nazi who had opposed the attack on Czechoslovakia.
[432] DBFP 1919–1939, Ser. 3. Vol 2. No. 736. *Henderson to Halifax* 1 September 1938.
[433] ibid No. 738. *Henderson to Halifax* 1 September 1938.
[434] See: MP Reynolds, *Instruments of Peacemaking 1870–1914* (Oxford, Hart Publishing, 2021).
[435] DBFP 1919–1939, Ser. 3. Vol 2. No. 738. *Henderson to Halifax* 1 September 1938.

Mindful of Hitler's pending address to the *Parteitag* in a few days' time, Runciman told Beneš that nothing less than the Karlsbad Points would provide a settlement.[436] Beneš was to see Dr Kundt (SdP) that day. If Beneš accepted the Karlsbad Points he would lose support. If he published his own proposals, the Sudetendeutsche would reject them.

Dr Hodza dined with Newton and Lord and Lady Runciman that evening. Newton told Hodza that his government must 'go to the limit of concession immediately and unreservedly'. Newton reported to Halifax:[437]

> If situation resulting from Herr Henlein's visit to Berchtesgaden should thus make more formal action on my part desirable I would propose to intervene with President or in other quarters at once as authorised in your telegram and without seeking further instructions.

In other words, Newton would go beyond what he had already been told to do to force Beneš to a settlement. So, the British government was using Runciman to harass Beneš whilst disturbances were being orchestrated by Henlein to undermine Beneš in the Sudetenland.[438]

a. American Concern

Whilst this was happening, President Roosevelt was not oblivious to the predicament. He was restrained by the Congress and the Neutrality Act; he could only warn of the danger of war. Despite Chamberlain's resentment of American interference, he appreciated Roosevelt's recent speech which he said was 'of great value'.[439] More than that, in discussions with Joseph P Kennedy, the US Ambassador, Chamberlain said that Britain was not able to stop Hitler, and in the circumstances, it would be unwise to utter threats. Kennedy agreed. Chamberlain said that war was not inevitable, and he was considering what more his government might do if Runciman failed. Chamberlain also said that he did not accept that if Germany took Czechoslovakia the Nazis would dominate Europe. Such an admission revealed Chamberlain's gross misjudgement and miscalculation of the threat as well as Kennedy's acquiescence. However, Kennedy did suggest that:

> if France went in and we had to go in too, the United States would follow before long.

An interesting view, bearing in mind his subsequent defeatist attitude and reports to Washington. Kennedy said he was convinced that President Roosevelt had decided 'to go in with Chamberlain; whatever course Chamberlain desires to adopt he would think right'. What authority Kennedy had for that must be questioned, as Roosevelt had little influence over Chamberlain. Secretary Hull was concerned that Kennedy was pursuing his own private foreign policies, giving the wrong impression of America's position.[440]

[436] ibid No. 740. *Newton to Halifax* 2 September 1938.
[437] ibid.
[438] D Faber, *Munich* (New York, Pocket Books, 2008) 244.
[439] DBFP 1919–1939, Ser. 3. Vol 2. No. 744. *Halifax to Lindsay (Washington)* 2 September 1938.
[440] *Morgenthau Diary* I September 1938. 138–135.

Roosevelt's subsequent warning to Hitler may have had some effect in convincing Hitler to set up the Munich meeting, or possibly it was because his generals were sceptical about risking a general war. Halifax himself met with Kennedy on 31 August, and his impression is also interesting.[441] Kennedy felt that the German government was bluffing and intimidating but that no final decisions had been taken, a view shared by US ambassadors in Paris and Berlin. Halifax reported:[442]

> The Ambassador thought that while American opinion would be much shocked by any German aggression, it would not feel it necessary or justifiable to plunge Europe into a general war on such an issue.

b. Settlement Proposals

On 2 September, Herr Kundt (SdP) explained to Newton[443] the outcome of his discussion with President Beneš that morning.

> He had accepted with certain additional suggestions of no vital importance the President's proposals relating to:
>
> A. State officials;
> B. Proportionality in public municipal appointments (budgetary grants, allocation of State orders and public works);
> C. Loan (with additions);
> D. Language;
> E. Police (but with immediate action in withdrawing State police).
>
> He has asked for consideration of additional suggestions under the following headings:
>
> A. New elections for Social Insurance Organisations also for mayors of certain communes and fresh nominees of Social Commissions in accordance with results of the 1935 Elections.
> B. Reparations: Commission to study the removal of disabilities suffered by the Germans for the last twenty years, e.g. those resulting from land reform;
> C. Governmental instructions to officials that members of Sudeten German Party should not be penalised and finally:
> D. Self-government Proposals

Everything of course turned on this last point-self-government. The other points can be agreed upon without great difficulty. Dr. Kundt considered that the President's present proposal is the same in principle as nationalities statute only with 'Gau' substituted for 'province'.

> He saw the same objection that this proposal leaves Germans living in Gaus other than the three German Gaus at the mercy of a Czech majority; further he thought that the creation of 20 Gaus would be cumbrous and very expensive since a large number of additional officials would have to be taken on.
>
> He said that no compromise is possible between the demands of Sudeten German party (eight Karlsbad points) and the proposals hitherto made by Czechoslovak Government; but

[441] DBFP 1919–1939, Ser. 3. Vol 2. No. 744. *Halifax to Lindsay (Washington)* 2 September 1938.
[442] ibid.
[443] ibid No. 755 *Newton to Halifax* 3 September 1938.

a compromise is possible between the principles represented in the President's position *viz.* united sovereignty and integrity of the State-and principles of eight Karlsbad points.[444]

This marked the high point of Runciman's mission and gave hope of a peaceful transition. Following this, Runciman produced his scheme the next day thus:

Following for Secretary of State from Lord Runciman.

Following is a summary of the proposals which I am preparing, though they are of course subject to alteration in the light of developments here.

1. Recognition of equality of 'Volks' and 'Volksgruppe' and of principle of their 'Rechtspersönlichkeit' in the State. The 'Rechtspersönlichkeit' will be expressed through National organs in provinces and districts as described below.
2. Recognition of principle of language equality.
3. Proportionate allocation of officials' posts. Exchange of officials on population basis to begin at once and be completed over an agreed period.
4. Provinces to be administered by an elected Governor, and an executive responsible to a Diet which is elected on the basis of proportional representation. In any province where a fifteen per cent. national minority exists, a separate administration to be established for that national minority. Provision to be made for all such National Diets in a province to meet periodically in joint session to deal with matters of common concern to the whole province. National Executives would similarly meet in joint session.
5. Commission composed of representatives of Nationalities in equal numbers to be appointed forthwith, and report within four months on division of subjects between Central and Provincial Government on the basis of granting as full powers as possible to provinces. It will also report on division between subjects within sole competence of national Diets in provinces and those which are matters of common concern.
6. Central Government to remain unchanged but all bills affecting one or more Nationalities to be referred to Racial Curiae composed of all members of each of the Nationalities concerned. The Curiae would report and have power to propose amendments for consideration of Parliament.

   An Advisory State Council (to advise the President) would be appointed consisting of representatives of the Cabinet and also two or three representatives of each Nationality.

   Advisory Committees would also be appointed of members of National Executives concerned with a particular subject (e.g. finance) which would meet periodically under the chairmanship of the Central Minister concerned for the purpose of securing uniformity in legislation between Provinces.
7. Districts to be organized on the same basis as provinces and under control of provincial authorities concerned.

   Minorities under fifteen per cent. in districts to have individual Minority Treaty protection, and to be allowed to establish committees for protecting their position with the right of appeal by individual or committee to Supreme Administration Court.
8. Secondly. Proportionate grants-in-aid from State Budget to Provincial or National Provincial authorities. Separate Budgets for Provincial or National Provincial Governments with the right of taxation.

   Loan of 'x' million kronen of which large proportion for German areas.
9. State police in so far as they have recently been introduced into frontier and other regions where they had not previously been stationed should be progressively withdrawn-their

[444] ibid.

> functions being taken on by gendarmerie and communal police who had previously exercised them. The stages and dates of progress of the withdrawals to be fixed forthwith and the first stages appropriately put into action at once.
>
> Repeated to Berlin.

The two approaches were quite different. Runciman providing a more definitive solution to breaking the deadlock in the negotiations. Apart from submitting this to Halifax and Henderson, it was not given further publicity as external events overtook his further involvement. Newton continued to pursue Beneš on the Karlsbad points. Beneš felt this was a trap and that he would be giving Hitler a 'blank cheque'.[445] Despite this, Newton and Runciman continued to bully Beneš telling him that Britain preferred Karlsbad to war. Beneš was considerably shaken by Newton's warnings and Runciman urged Beneš 'to make all sacrifices necessary to preserve existence of his country'.[446] The French were affronted by Britain's attitude towards their ally, forcing Czechoslovakia into an impossible position.[447] The French subsequently resiled from their position under British pressure, dishonouring their alliance with Czechoslovakia. Contrary to the British position on 5 September 1938, Soviet Foreign Minister Litvinov informed the German Ambassador in Moscow that the USSR was prepared to fight for Czechoslovakia.[448]

Runciman was all for appeasement and wrote to Halifax that 'anything is better than war'.[449] The next day, 6 September, Henderson added his contribution to warn against French mobilisation which would encourage Beneš to further delay.[450] Newton reported that Dr Hodza had now replaced Beneš in discussions with Herr Kundt. Herr Kundt had expressed his idea of compromise by which unity, sovereignty and integrity of state would be preserved while the furthest compatible degree of self-government, which the Sudetendeutsche appear to have accepted.[451] This was further confirmed in a report from Runciman that Hodza explained the new proposals were a basis for further developments and could accommodate a national area of three German Gaus,[452] which would be given self-government for over two million Germans, which Hodza believed was within the scope of the Karlsbad Points.[453] Just as this negotiation was making some progress, two events disrupted the negotiations and Runciman's mission. First, Émile Roche, a close collaborator of Bonnet, wrote in *La République* that the two races in the Sudetenland should be separated.[454] This was taken up by *The Times* the following day when Dawson, Editor of *The Times* and friend of Halifax, published a leading article

[445] ibid No. 758. *Newton to Halifax* 4 September 1938.
[446] ibid No. 759. *Newton to Halifax* 4 September 1938.
[447] ibid No. 658. *Halifax to Phipps* 5 September 1938.
[448] *Bulletin of International News*, B.I.N. XV The Royal Institute of International Affairs 794.
[449] DBFP 1919–1939, Ser. 3. Vol 2. No. 783. *Letter Runciman to Halifax* 5 September 1938.
[450] ibid No. 785 *Henderson to Halifax* 6 September 1938.
[451] ibid No. 788. *Newton to Halifax* 6 September 1938.
[452] A Gau was an administrative division of Nazi Germany which replaced the Länder and Prussian provinces from 1934 to 1945.
[453] DBFP 1919–1939, Ser. 3. Vol 2. No. 789. *Newton to Halifax* 6 September 1938.
[454] 6 September 1938. Cited in J Wheeler-Bennet, *Munich Prologue to Tragedy* (London, Macmillan, 1963) 95.

suggesting that the Sudetenland, with its alien population, be united with Germany. The article suggested:[455]

> … the advantages Czechoslovakia becoming a homogeneous state might conceivably outway the obvious disadvantages of losing the Sudeten German districts of the borderland.

The Dawson-edited article based on Leo Kennedy's draft[456] was prepared hastily. It went beyond any proposal of the Sudetendeutsche Partei or the German government. It came at the worst time for Runciman and the Czechs and caused embarrassment in Britain and internationally. It undermined Runciman's position and any influence the British government might have had with Hitler in discouraging expansionist intentions in Central and Southeastern Europe.[457] Worse it was published on the day the Nazis engineered an incident in Mährisch-Ostrau. They alleged that a riot took place in the Sudeten German districts of the borderland and that a Sudetendeutsche Deputy was beaten by a Czech policeman. That was false, as verified by Major Sutton-Pratt, a British Military Attaché.[458] Ashton-Gwatkin was able to confirm later that the negotiations would be resumed. In a further effort to resolve matters, on 8 September there was a joint meeting of the political directorate of SdP and representatives of the Slovak People's Party, United Hungarian Parties and Polish Committee of Understanding. A communiqué was issued after the meeting stating that agreement had been reached on the fundamental question of reconstruction of the state and solution of the nationalities problem.[459]

c. Worsening Tensions

On 9 September, Britain informed Germany that it would fight if Czechoslovakia was invaded. Three days before that, *The Times* leader had invited the Czechs to become a more 'homogeneous state' by handing the Sudetendeutsche over to the Nazis.[460] Reporting on the League Council and meeting of the Assembly of the League, Shirer noted that the war-threatening situation in Czechoslovakia was not even on the agenda.[461]

Halifax told Chamberlain that if Hitler attacked Czechoslovakia, then France would be involved and Britain 'could not stand aside'.[462] This he had communicated to Henderson in Berlin but Henderson advised that it would 'drive Hitler straight off the deep end'.[463] Churchill, anxious that a strong stand should be made against Nazi aggression, went to

[455] *The Times* 7 September 1938. 'Nuremberg and Aussig'. 13. See also J Wheeler-Bennet, *Munich Prologue to Tragedy* (London, Macmillan, 1963) 251 and RGD Laffan rev. V Toynbee and P Baker, *Survey of International Affairs 1938* (Oxford, OUP, 1951) 251, fn 2; G Martel, *The Times and Appeasement, The Journals of A.L. Kennedy* (Cambridge CUP, 2000) 276, fn 480.

[456] Journalist on *The Times*. Dawson asked Kennedy at 10pm on September to alter the final part. Whilst in more erudite language the meaning was clear.

[457] Although *The Times* had advocated self-determination and frontier revision earlier in the year.

[458] DBFP 1919–1939, Ser. 3. Vol 2. No. 801. *Newton to Halifax* 8 September 1938.

[459] ibid No. 817. *Newton to Halifax* 9 September 1938.

[460] WL Shirer, *Berlin Diary* (London, Hamish Hamilton, 1941) 104.

[461] ibid 105.

[462] RAC Parker, *Churchill and Appeasement* (London, Macmillan, 2000) 174.

[463] DBFP 1919–1939, Ser. 3. Vol 2. No. 815. *Viscount Halifax to Mr Kirkpatrick (Berlin)* 9 September 1938. See also: No. 819. *Sir G Ogilvie-Forbes (Berlin) to Viscount Halifax* 10 September 1938.

Downing Street to impress this upon Chamberlain, but supported by Hoare and Simon, Chamberlain overruled Halifax.[464] Coincidentally Churchill's views coincided with American opinion as conveyed to Halifax by Lindsay in Washington a few days later.[465]

On 10 September, Kennedy called on Halifax to ascertain the latest position. Halifax informed Kennedy of instructions sent to Henderson warning Hitler of the likely consequences of aggressive action. They discussed public feeling in Britain and America. Kennedy said that American opinion was much more excited against Germany now than he had ever known it; in his own words, 'twenty times as excited as in 1914', and if London was bombed, America was more likely to intervene.[466] The following day Kennedy confirmed the visit of two US Navy cruisers to England and suggested to Halifax he visit Chamberlain that evening to encourage German speculation.[467] In such actions, Kennedy may well have gone beyond his authority, albeit he had a contradictory role of supporting appeasement for Britain and maintaining American isolation.[468]

On 11 September, Litvinov told Bonnet that the USSR would not take military action until the League Council persuaded Romania to permit the passage of Soviet forces.[469] Following Hitler's vociferous and rancorous speech at the *Parteitag* on 12 September and an upsurge in violence, the Czechoslovakian government declared martial law in the Sudeten border region and partial mobilisation of 500,000 men.[470] The same day, Litvinov received Romania's consent for passage of Soviet forces, but this was only if France was also fighting for Czechoslovakia in accordance with her treaty obligations.[471]

On 13 September, Henderson warned Halifax that only immediate action by the Czechoslovak government could prevent the use of force by Germany. He recommended that the strongest pressure be put by the British and French governments on Beneš to make immediate concessions. If the French government would not agree, he suggested that the British should act alone, making it clear that if Czechs did not accept Runciman's last word, Britain could not be responsible for the consequences.[472] He also cautioned:

> If after all this Germany deliberately and maliciously attacks Czechoslovakia and His Majesty's Government do no more than express their disapproval we shall be regarded in Germany with universal contempt.

His statement demonstrates the difficulty that appeasement caused, as Henderson had been warning the Nazis at Nuremberg and in Berlin that Britain would support France if she was attacked. Bonnet, according to Phipps, had lost his nerve and was willing to agree to anything to avoid war.[473] To make matters worse, unrest was prevalent in

[464] RAC Parker, *Churchill and Appeasement* (London, Macmillan, 2000) 174.
[465] DBFP 1919–1939, Ser. 3. Vol 2. No. 841. *Sir R Lindsay (Washington) to Viscount Halifax* 12 September 1938.
[466] ibid No. 824. *Halifax to Lindsay* 10 September 1938.
[467] ibid No. 836. *Halifax to Lindsay* 10 September 1938.
[468] DF Schmitz and RD Challener, *Appeasement in Europe: Reassessment of U.S. Policies* (New York, Greenwood Press, 1990) 57.
[469] M Beloff, *The Foreign Policy of Soviet Russia 1936-41,* Vol 2. RIIA (Oxford, OUP, 1949) 146.
[470] Z Steiner, *The Triumph of the Dark. European International History 1933-1939* (Oxford, Oxford University Press, 2011) 593–594.
[471] M Beloff, *The Foreign Policy of Soviet Russia 1936-41,* Vol 2. RIIA (Oxford, OUP, 1949) 146, n 3.
[472] DBFP 1919–1939, Ser. 3. Vol 2. No. 849. *Henderson to Halifax* 13 September 1938.
[473] ibid No. 852. *Phipps to Halifax* 13 September 1938.

the Sudetenland, and Runciman was opposed to any publication of his plan in such circumstances.[474] The same day Oliver Harvey wrote that Chamberlain proposed that if Hitler was amenable, he would propose Runciman becoming arbitrator between the Czechs and the Sudetendeutsche. Chamberlain ignored the fact that Runciman would be conflicted by the nature of his existing role and that it was for the parties to agree to such a process, not the British Prime Minister nor the Chancellor of Germany since neither Britain nor Germany were parties to the dispute. As regards a plebiscite, Chamberlain thought it would be impossible for a democracy to resist, but he would seek to establish reasonable conditions and a delay to cool tensions.[475] It seemed to Harvey that Chamberlain had a self-compliant conviction to trust Hitler.

To intimidate the Czechs, Hitler amassed an army of 200,000 men on the Austro-Czech border[476] even though by 14 September the Czech police and forces were able to control the disturbances. It was then announced that Chamberlain would meet Hitler. The French army was partially mobilised. In Prague, Shirer heard a boy shouting: 'EXTRA! EXTRA! READ ALL ABOUT HOW THE MIGHTY HEAD OF THE BRITISH EMPIRE GOES BEGGING TO HITLER!'.[477] That day, Oliver Harvey noted in his diary '[Chamberlain] felt it might be necessary to neutralise it [the rest of Czechoslovakia excluding Sudetenland] under guarantee to Great Britain, France, Russia and Germany'.[478] It will be noted that Chamberlain referred to Russia as a guarantor, whereas in November 1938, at the meeting with the French government, he referred to Italy not Russia as a guarantor.[479] Churchill was of the view that a specific guarantee by Britain, France and Russia after the *Anschluss* might have moderated German opinion.[480]

On 15 September, Henlein told Hodza that in view of the unrest, he was withdrawing his delegation.[481] Despite the impasse, Gwatkin saw Frank, Henlein's Deputy, and was told Henlein insisted on four conditions for the continuation of discussions:[482]

1. The withdrawal of military law.
2. The withdrawal of all Staatspolizei from districts with a German majority.
3. The gendarmerie and the local police force to be restricted to normal functions.
4. The military to be restricted to purely military posts and tasks.

If these demands were accepted, the SdP would appeal for peace. Meanwhile, M Bonnet was saying that France would not sacrifice 10 million men for three and a half million Sudetendeutsche joining the Reich.[483] Following Henlein's earlier termination of negotiations and withdrawal of his delegation, he confirmed in a communiqué issued

[474] ibid No. 857. *Newton to Halifax* 13 September 1938.
[475] O Harvey, *The Diplomatic Diaries of Oliver Harvey 1937-1940* (London, Collins, 1970) 180.
[476] In an account of the crisis, GJ George wrote that reports that the Wehrmacht would attack the next day at 6 pm were falsely fed to British Intelligence and that this bluff induced Chamberlain to seek a meeting with Hitler. See: GJ George, *They Betrayed Czechoslovakia* (London, Penguin Books, 1938) 41–44.
[477] WL Shirer, *Berlin Diary* (London, Hamish Hamilton, 1941) 110.
[478] M Gilbert, *Profit of Truth Winston Spencer Churchill 1922–1939* (Minerva, 1976) 973.
[479] DBFP 1919–1939, Ser. 3. Vol 3. No. 306.
[480] M Gilbert, *Profit of Truth Winston Spencer Churchill 1922-1939* (Minerva, 1976) 997.
[481] DBFP 1919–1939, Ser. 3. Vol 2. No. 869. *Newton to Halifax* 14 September 1938.
[482] ibid No. 871. *Newton to Halifax* 14 September 1938.
[483] ibid No. 789. *Phipps to Halifax* 14 September 1938.

on 14 September 1938 (subject to an immediate realisation of SdP's demands) that he might still negotiate, but the Karlsbad Points would no longer suffice. On Hitler's instructions, he made the German right of self-determination the key point. Henlein thanked members of the Runciman mission for their work to settle relations between the nationalities and then placed the blame on the Czech government.[484] As a result, Runciman reported to the cabinet that his mission was over. Halifax confirmed that Chamberlain would see Hitler the following day. The day after that, Runciman left Prague.

Chamberlain's government used continuing undue pressure on Czechoslovakia to surrender the Sudetenland and used a bluff on Germany by suggesting that Britain would go to war to defend Czechoslovakia, which the Nazi regime doubted. On the other hand, the Wehrmacht was not prepared for a general war, although Hitler was prepared to risk it. Whilst Roosevelt watched from afar, monitoring the ever-deteriorating situation and the trend of British appeasement, Kennedy was told that: 'any compromise with Berlin would disappoint the President'.[485] Yet Kennedy, like Chamberlain, thought he could take personal initiatives as he became more supportive of Chamberlain and appeasement, undermining the policy of American isolationism.[486] Chamberlain met Hitler at Berchtesgaden on 15 September. The feeling in Prague was that Chamberlain sold Czechoslovakia down the river.[487]

d. Sell Out

Thanks to sluggish rearmament and appeasement in 1938, Britain and France were in a weak position strategically and militarily compared with Germany. Britain's diplomatic and negotiation position was weak as against an armed Germany now enhanced with the absorption of Austria. The statistics regarding fighter and bomber aircraft illustrate this starkly:

	Fighters	**Bombers**
Germany	3,500	
Britain	700	620
France	1,250	
Russia	4,000	
Czechoslovakia	300	300

No doubt Chamberlain was worried by the inequality in terms of fighter aircraft, but considering that a combination of France, Russia, and Czechoslovakia could have amounted to 5,850 fighters, which alone would have outgunned Germany, or even a

[484] ibid No. 880. *Newton to Halifax* 14 September 1938.
[485] MR Bechloss, *Kennedy and Roosevelt, The Uneasy Alliance* (New York, NW Norton & Co, 1980).
[486] DF Schmitz and RD Challener, *Appeasement in Europe: Reassessment of U.S. Policies* (New York, Greenwood Press, 1990) 53.
[487] WL Shirer, *Berlin Diary* (London, Hamish Hamilton, 1941) 111. Diary 16 September 1938.

combination of France, Britain and Czechoslovakia would have amounted to 3,170 aircraft as against 3,500 of Germany.[488]

On 18 September 1938 Daladier and Bonnet came to London. Daladier told Chamberlain that Hitler wanted more than Sudetenland and urged Chamberlain to give 'an international guarantee to Czechoslovakia against aggression'. Chamberlain refused.[489] Chamberlain did not think guarantees were practical and although the cabinet wished him to raise the point with Hitler Chamberlain and to bring Russia as a party into such guarantee, Chamberlain did not raise the question.[490] On the 19 September, Roosevelt was so concerned he invited Lindsey, the British Ambassador, to a private meeting. Roosevelt was under no illusions that the situation could easily lead to war, and he thought that the Czechs would fight and the western Powers find themselves at war with Germany and Italy.[491] He suggested that a blockade and a defensive war would be of advantage in terms of American assistance. He thought munitions could be supplied through Canada. If the democracies avoided declaring war on Germany and called it simply 'defensive measures', it could be argued that they were not at war. In this way the prohibition of exports of arms under the Neutrality Act need not be applied to them. The US could assist any blockade. If the Czechs capitulated, then there would be further Nazi demands elsewhere in Europe.[492]

On 20 September 1938, Chamberlain and Daladier pressed Benes to agree to the surrender of the Sudetenland to the Reich. France was in no position for a war and demoralised. Also, that day Chamberlain told Runciman to alter his draft letter confirming his views. He rewrote the letter, but it was further altered by Ashton-Gwatkin as part of it was typed (the Runciman amended version) and part in Gwatkin's handwriting. What was inserted criticised the Czechs' approach. Runciman rejected Chamberlain's view that districts with a German majority should be ceded to the Nazis. Chamberlain misleadingly stated that Runciman agreed with him.

On 21 September 1938 Churchill and his colleague, Brigadier-General Spears MP, were in Paris dining at the Ritz with Paul Reynaud, Mandel, and Champetier de Ribes, just as Harold Nicolson recorded in his diary that the Poles and Hungarians were demanding cessions of Czechoslovakia.[493] The three French ministers were prepared to resign, but after offering their resignations on 22 September, they retracted them, as Daladier said it amounted to desertion.[494] That same day the German army occupied Asch as the Czech army withdrew from the Sudeten areas. On 23 September, Reuters reported the *Freikorps* began the invasion.[495]

Russia suspected a plot by Chamberlain, who had privately met with Hitler, even though Russia was prepared to support Czechoslovakia and France to make every effort to ward off armed conflict. When President Roosevelt suggested an international conference to settle the matter, Russia welcomed this, but Chamberlain did not wish to

[488] J de Launay, *Major Controversies of Contemporary History* (Oxford, Pergamon Press, 1965) 169.
[489] M Gilbert, *Profit of Truth Winston Spencer Churchill 1922–1939* (Minerva, 1976) 976.
[490] J Bruegel, *Czechoslovakia before Munich* (Cambridge, CUP, 1973) 272.
[491] B Farnham, *Roosevelt and the Munich Crisis* (Princeton, Princeton University Press, 1997) 106.
[492] ibid 107.
[493] H Nicolson, *Harold Nicolson Diaries and Letters 1930-1964* (London, Penguin Books, 1985) 134.
[494] J de Launay, *Major Controversies of Contemporary History* (Oxford, Pergamon Press, 1965) 172.
[495] H Nicolson, *Harold Nicolson Diaries and Letters 1930-1964* (London, Penguin Books, 1985) 134–135.

engage in a conference with the Russians and the Poles. Instead, he asked Mussolini to intervene. Russia therefore took no part in the discussions and sensed a German movement eastward. Undoubtedly, Litvinov, the Russian Foreign Minister, was right in saying that Czechoslovakia was buried by a rare example of political stupidity.[496] Ambassador Maisky wrote that Sudetenland was handed to Hitler 'on a plate'.[497]

vii. *The Sacrifice of Honour*[498]

Many historians have criticised Neville Chamberlain for his handling of the Munich crisis, which led to the dismemberment of Czechoslovakia. On the one hand, he succeeded in stopping a war and gave more time to rearm,[499] hailed as a hero in Paris and London, but on the other hand, he instigated a betrayal of a democracy, induced France to betray its ally, and then played into Hitler's hands as the diplomatic documents may infer. He was a 'good man', as Roosevelt suggested in saving the peace, but was it peace in our time, or peace at any price, or perhaps peace now and war later, only much worse?

In his autobiography. Sir John Simon, former Foreign Secretary and later Lord Chancellor defended Chamberlain and his approach to Munich, referring to him as a 'high minded and courageous man' who acted in circumstances that fully justified attempting to avoid war. Simon regarded the settlement at Munich as invaluable, giving '12 months in which to strengthen our preparations to wage it'[500] In defence of his colleague Simon quoted Churchill who compared the Sudetendeutsche with Ulster Unionists and pointed out that:[501]

> … To exclude the German speaking population from the new state of Czechoslovakia, was deeply and perhaps fatally to weaken the new state: to include them was to affront the principle of self-determination.[502]

Czechoslovakia, a polyglot state, was problematic, as was the breakup of Austria-Hungary, especially when the people were of diverse ethnicity and did not freely consent to the settlement. The Teutonic fringe incorporated in that state had been the subject of much debate at Versailles. They were promised that they would have in Bohemia the same rights as the Czechs and that no irritating measures would be employed against the German population.[503] Despite this, when Runciman was sent to Czechoslovakia to enquire into the problem, he reported back that:[504]

[496] M Litvinov, *Notes from a Journal (1926-1945)* (London, 1955).
[497] G Gorodetsky, *The Maisky Diaries* (New Haven, Yale University Press, 2016) 133.
[498] Ascribed to Churchill's description in M Gilbert, *Profit of Truth Winston Spencer Churchill 1922–1939* (Minerva, 1976). 989.
[499] In terms of rearmament in 1938 the British army had two regular divisions; by 1939 it had 16. But the Wehrmacht had 81 in 1938 and 120–130 in 1939. France had 100 divisions in 1938 and 1939.
[500] J Simon, *Retrospect* (London, Hutchinson, 1952) 238.
[501] bid 239–240.
[502] Albeit Churchill might also have applied the analogy to the Irish Nationalists in Ulster who felt like the Sudetendeutsche excluded from their countrymen in the Free State.
[503] J Simon, *Retrospect* (London, Hutchinson, 1952) 240.
[504] ibid 241.

> … rise of Nazi Germany gave them hope, and I regard their turning for help towards their kinsmen and their eventual desire to join the Reich as a natural development in the circumstances.

Chamberlain's approach to the oncoming crisis was to search for means of conciliation for a peaceful adjustment of German claims if justified. On the other hand, Chamberlain also sought to rearm, as he was aware that without adequate force behind it, attempts to resolve differences were pointless when dealing with a dictator, or so Simon suggests.[505] There was every reason to suspect that if the Wehrmacht marched into Czechoslovakia there would be a European war which Simon referred to as: 'The beginning of a fire in a high wind.'[506] Whereas France and Russia had obligations to defend Czechoslovakia, Britain had not. Britain's legal obligation under the League Covenant did not amount to an automatic obligation to take any military action, but if France became involved, then Britain might follow, as in 1914. The position of the Soviet Union was uncertain, but Litvinov said that the Soviet's obligation would only be triggered if France was involved first.[507]

Chamberlain's meeting with Hitler at Godesberg ended in deadlock. Hitler proposed to march on 1 October. But Chamberlain wrote to him. As follows:[508]

> I cannot believe that you will take the responsibility of starting a World War, which may end civilization, for the sake of a few days delay in settling this longstanding problem.

At the same time, due possibly to the renewal of Anglo-Italian conversations, Mussolini told Hitler that he hoped Hitler would further postpone his action pending re-examination of the situation.[509] What may have accelerated Chamberlain's idea with plans to visit Hitler was certain faulty intelligence that Operation Green, Hitler's planned invasion of Czechoslovakia, would start on 19 or 20 September; in fact, Hitler was planning for 1 October. On 15 September, Chamberlain made his flight to Munich to parley with Hitler in his mountain retreat at Berchtesgaden.[510] However whilst Chamberlain and Halifax succeeded in averting another world war and indeed received the grateful thanks of the country, the King and President Roosevelt, behind that relief was the underlying sense of betrayal of a democratic state and submission to the threat of a dictator. What was perhaps more distressing was Chamberlain's remark to Jan Masaryk after Godesberg: 'My dear Jan, some people trust Dr Beneš; I prefer to trust Herr Hitler.'[511]

Churchill was highly critical of the betrayal, and behind the scenes in America a potential great ally had other views. Harold Ickes, a fierce critic of appeasement, saw the French approach of a plebiscite as a fraud because it was a foregone conclusion how the Sudetendeutsche would vote.[512] France might just as well have supported

[505] ibid 242.
[506] Sir John Simon, Speech at Lanark, 28 August 1938.
[507] G Gorodetsky, *The Maisky Diaries* (New Haven, Yale University Press, 2016) 135.
[508] J Simon, *Retrospect* (London, Hutchinson, 1952) 247.
[509] ibid.
[510] C Andrew, *Secret Service: The Making of the British Intelligence Community* (London, Heineman, 1985) 396.
[511] J Wheeler-Bennett, *Knaves, Fools and Heroes* (London, Macmillan, 1974) 139.
[512] H Ickes, *The Secret Diaries of Harold L Ickes Volume II The Inside Struggle 1936–1939* (London, Weidenfeld and Nicolson, 1955) 466–467.

Hitler's aim. In another context as to the diplomacy of Britain, the greater charge might be that Henderson, Chamberlain and Ashton-Gwatkin, via Henlein, were achieving the Fuhrer's wishes and saving him a war. As discussions progressed and Beneš made proposals, Hitler simply increased demands through the agency of Henlein. Hitler did this at Godesberg with Chamberlain. According to Ickes, Roosevelt believed that Chamberlain was for peace at any price and the betrayal of an international obligation, and in graphical terms 'England and France will "wash their Judas Iscariot hands"'.[513] But despite this, Roosevelt intervened with two messages to Hitler.[514] In the first of these messages, the President reminded countries of their obligations under the Kellogg-Briand Pact of 1928, and in the second, he emphasised not the past legacy of Versailles, but the futility of war and the fact that agreement in principle had already been reached. On 28 September Lipski, the Polish Ambassador in Berlin, reported that Mussolini telephoned Hitler and this broke the 'Gordian Knot' to initiate the Munich meeting.[515] Lipski reported that this followed constant attempts made by President Roosevelt to intercede in Berlin.[516] This may have been the reason, but there were others: the British fleet was mobilised, France was mobilising, certain diplomats and generals in Germany were encouraged by Britain's moderation, and there was a lack of popular support amongst Germany's working class. In effect, little enthusiasm for war in Germany.[517]

viii. Munich Agreement – 'The Dark Night of the Soul'[518]

On 29 September, Chamberlain flew to Munich and gave Hitler everything he wanted, having destroyed the structure of European defence against Germany.[519] The terms of secession of the Sudetenland were agreed at the Führebau in Munich. It was conducted in an unconventional manner: there was no agenda, there was no seating plan, or any of the accoutrements you would expect from such meetings.[520] Neither Czechoslovakia nor Russia was represented at the meeting. When Jan Masaryk was told about these exclusions, he told Halifax and Chamberlain:[521]

> If you have sacrificed my nation to preserve the peace of the world I will be the first to applaud you, but if not, gentlemen, God help your souls.

[513] ibid 468.

[514] See: 'The President's Message to Czechoslovakia, Germany, Great Britain and France Seeking A Peaceful Solution Of The Threat Of War, September 26, 1938, And Hitler's Replies thereto September 27, 1938 and The President Again Seeks Peace September 27, 1938' in *The Public Papers Of Franklin D. Roosevelt 1938 Vol. The Continuing Struggle For Liberalism* (London, Macmillan, 1941).

[515] W Jędrzejewicz (ed) *Diplomat in Berlin 1933–1939* (New York, Columbia University Press, 1968) 432. *Lipski to Beck* 28 September 1938 No. 113.

[516] Documents on German Foreign Policy Series D, Vol 11. No. 655.

[517] O Harvey, *The Diplomatic Diaries of Oliver Harvey 1937–1940* (London, Collins, 1970) 201.

[518] Sir John Wheeler Bennett's description of that week in September 1938. J Wheeler-Bennett, *Knaves, Fools and Heroes* (London, Macmillan, 1974) 139.

[519] CL Mowatt, *Britain Between the Wars 1918–1940* (London, Methuen, 1955) 609. Cited in B Pinlott, *Hugh Dalton* (London, Papermac, 1986) 286.

[520] Z Steiner, *The Triumph of the Dark* (Oxford, Oxford University Press, 2011) 639.

[521] J Wheeler-Bennett, *Knaves, Fools and Heroes.* (London, Macmillan, 1974) 140.

The terms agreed by Germany, the UK, France and Italy in summary were as follows:[522]

1. That the evacuation will begin on 1 October,
2. Britain, France, and Italy agreed that the evacuation of the territory was to be completed by 10 October without any existing installations having been destroyed, and that the Czechoslovak government would be held responsible for carrying out the evacuation and for any damage to installations.
3. The conditions for such evacuation would be given by an international commission composed of representatives of Germany, Britain, France Italy and Czechoslovakia.
4. The occupation by German troops would begin on 1 October by reference to the map appended to the agreement in various stages as between 1 and 10 October.
5. The International Commission would determine the territories where a plebiscite was to be held. This would follow the conditions for the Saar plebiscite, and the Commission would fix a date not later than the end of November for the holding of a plebiscite.
6. The final determination of the frontier would be carried out by the Commission which would be entitled to suggest to the Four Powers[523] in exceptional cases minor modifications in a strictly ethnographical determination of the zones transferred without a plebiscite.
7. There would be a right of option into and out of the transferred territories. Such an option was to be exercised within six months from the date of the agreement. A German-Czechoslovak Commission would determine the details of the option and consider ways of facilitating the transfer of the population and settle questions of principle arising out of the transfer.
8. The Czechoslovakian government was given a period of four weeks from the date of the agreement to release from their military and police forces any Sudeten Germans who wished to be released and, within the same period, release German prisoners who were serving terms of imprisonment for political offenses.

    The agreement was dated 29 September 1938 signed by Adolf Hitler, Neville Chamberlain, Edouard Daladier and Benito Mussolini.

In the Annex to the agreement Britain and France declared that they had entered into agreement on the basis of their offer in paragraph 6 of the Anglo-French proposals dated 19 September to give an international guarantee of new boundaries for the Czech state against unprovoked aggression.[524] Germany and Italy declared that as soon as the Polish and Hungarian minorities' position in Czechoslovakia had been settled, they would give a guarantee to Czechoslovakia.[525] If the matter of the Polish and Hungarian minorities in Czechoslovakia had not been settled within three months by agreement between the respective governments, then there would be another meeting of the heads of government of the four Powers.[526] The Supplementary Declaration to the Agreement

[522] DBFP 1919–1939 Ser. 3. Vol. 2. No. 1224. United *Kingdom Delegation (Munich) to Viscount Halifax* 30 September 1938. 627–629.

[523] Germany Britain France and Italy.

[524] DBFP 1919–1939 Ser. 3. Vol. 2. No. 1224. *United Kingdom Delegation (Munich) to Viscount Halifax* 30 September 1938. 628 Annex.

[525] ibid 629 Annex.

[526] ibid.

stated that any questions arising out of the transfer of the territory would be considered as coming within the terms of reference of the International Commission.[527] It further declared that the four heads of governments present agreed that the International Commission would consist of the Secretary of State in the German Foreign Office, the British, French and Italian Ambassadors accredited in Berlin and a representative to be nominated by the government of Czechoslovakia.[528]

It is significant that the reference to paragraph 6 of the Anglo-French proposals agreed between the British and French governments at their meeting on 18 September 1938[529] stated that the British government, as a contribution to the pacification of Europe, was prepared to join in an international guarantee of the new boundaries of the Czechoslovak state against unprovoked aggression. One of the principal conditions of such a guarantee was the safeguarding of the independence of Czechoslovakia by the substitution of a general guarantee against unprovoked aggression in place of the existing treaties, which involved reciprocal obligations of a military character.[530] It is clear that what was intended was a general guarantee and not a limited one. This was later a matter of misunderstanding by Daladier at the Anglo-French meeting on 24 November 1938.[531] Chamberlain was not committing Britain to joint and several liability, but to joint only: it was not a specific guarantee like the Treaty of Locarno.

France was placed in a humiliating position, having pledged to defend Czechoslovakia's sovereignty but now concurring in its dismemberment 'for guaranteeing surrender of a fifth of its territory and 800,000 Czechs'.[532] This information was given to two Czech statesmen Hubert Masařík and Vojtěch Mastný by Chamberlain's Private Secretary, Horace Wilson and Ashton-Gwatkin, who appear to have simply relayed what Hitler wanted.[533]

On 30 September 1938 Chamberlain met Hitler and asked him to sign a declaration that a mutual constant consultation should be undertaken to deal with any questions that may concern the two countries. The declaration was somewhat vague and rather meaningless, and Hitler had no trouble in signing it – a single piece of paper of no legal importance.[534] This piece of paper never amounted to a promise or undertaking or guarantee never to go to war. It might have expressed Chamberlain's hope, but that was all. According to Simon,[535] the Munich Agreement reached with Hitler was a programme for the orderly transfer of the state and territory under international supervision, with a delineation of a final boundary line by a properly constituted commission, which was at once set up. If there had been no agreement, it is very likely there would have been war because even Runciman suggested there was little alternative to cession or war.

[527] ibid 629. Supplementary Declaration.
[528] ibid.
[529] DBFP 1919–1939 Ser. 3. Vol. 2. No. 928. *Record of Anglo-French Conversations Held At No. 10 Downing Street* 18 September 1938. 373.
[530] *ibid* No. 937. *Viscount Halifax to Mr. Newton (Prague)* 19 September 1938. 405.
[531] DBFP 1919–1939 Ser. 3. Vol. 3. No. 325. *Record Of Anglo-French Conversation Was Held At The Quai D'Orsay* 24 November 24, 1938. 285.
[532] T Bouverie, in *Appeasing Hitler* (London, Bodley Head, 2019) 284.
[533] ibid 285.
[534] J de Launay, *Major Controversies of Contemporary History* (Oxford, Pergamon Press, 1965) 178.
[535] J Simon, *Retrospect* (London, Hutchinson, 1952) 248.

Chamberlain was triumphant on his return to Westminster and received congratulations from the Dominions and Roosevelt who wrote:[536]

> We in the United States rejoice with you, and the world at large, that the outbreak of war was averted. To me, the most heartening aspect of the situation is the fact that this feeling of relief has been so spontaneous and has been expressed with such obvious sincerity throughout the world … those who work for the peaceful solution of international problems have the overwhelming support of their fellow men.

ix. Peace in Our Time?

As JM Bruegel opines in his study of the Sudeten crisis,[537] between 15 and 28 September 1938, three states decided that a fourth, which was not consulted, had to give up part of its territory. No such precedent existed in modern diplomacy, which was contrary to the Covenant of the League of Nations and the German-Czech Arbitration Treaty. Upon Chamberlain's return from Berchtesgaden, he met with Hugh Dalton and other politicians who had had reservations about supporting Czechoslovakia because of the disparity in British and German forces. Dalton told him that he did not believe that this would be Hitler's last demand and that Hitler would simply continue his onslaught dominating Central and Southeastern Europe, then the rest of Europe, then the world.[538] Outside that meeting people in Westminster, in the country and around the world rejoiced at Chamberlain's achievement. Crowds lined the streets for his homecoming, and he was invited to meet the King and Queen.

Underlying all this, the problem was that it may have been based on false information. The Chiefs of Staff had told the cabinet in March 1938 that nothing the Allies could do, either by sea, land or air, would prevent Germany from invading and overrunning Bohemia and from inflicting a decisive defeat on the Czechoslovakian army.[539] No one in the cabinet appears to have challenged that sweeping assertion based on questionable intelligence.[540] The mistake of the Chiefs and the cabinet was to ignore the Czech's armaments industry and productive capacity, which undoubtedly facilitated the success of *blitzkrieg* in 1940.[541] Thus, Chamberlain and Halifax made it the basis of their policy. They therefore put pressure on Czechoslovakia, as did France, to make concessions to Hitler.[542] What Simon did not point out in his biography was that appeasement flew in the face of much of the intelligence available. The War Office's own battle order intelligence showed that the German army was badly outnumbered on the French frontier

[536] J Simon, *Retrospect* (London, Hutchinson, 1952) 248–249.

[537] J Bruegel, *Czechoslovakia before Munich* (Cambridge, CUP, 1973) 291.

[538] B Pinlott, *Hugh Dalton* (London, Papermac, 1986) 286.

[539] C Andrew, *Secret Service The Making of the British Intelligence Community* (London, Heineman, 1985) 397.

[540] The information available to the General Staff was subject to the shortcomings of and fragmented way in which intelligence reports were evaluated. For detailed analysis see: W Wark, *The Ultimate Enemy* (Oxford, OUP, 1986).

[541] D Porch, *The French Secret Services* (London, Macmillan, 1996) 146.

[542] C Andrew, *Secret Service The Making of the British Intelligence Community* (London, Heineman, 1985) 397.

and possessed only a limited numerical advantage over the Czechs.[543] In a subsequent report of the COS dated 14 September 1938, it was concluded that the French armies could not attack the Siegfried Line and that the Allied air forces were inferior to the *Luftwaffe* so that Czechoslovakia would be easily overrun.[544] In a further intelligence report of 24 September, it was stated that Germany had 9 divisions on the western front and 34 on the Czech front. The French had 23 divisions, and the Czechs had 25 regular divisions and some of the 21 divisions held in reserve. In other words, the combined forces of France and Czechoslovakia outnumbered the Germans by five or more divisions, depending on the Czech reserves.[545] Brigadier Stronge, the British military attaché in Prague, was convinced that the Czech forces could defend the frontiers and were willing to do so at any cost.[546] The Russians may have agreed because, according to Sir John Wheeler-Bennett, Soviet minister Alexandrovsky repeated Stalin's and Litvinov's assurances that Russia would stand by Czechoslovakia. Such assurances were reiterated more insistently during that September. On the morning of 30 September 1938, after the Munich Agreement had been signed, Alexandrovsky gave a telephone message to Beneš stating that if Czechoslovakia chose to reject or ignore the terms of the agreement and to resist the Nazi invasion, she could count on the military support of the Soviet Union, *whether the French fulfilled their treaty pledges or not.*[547] Thus, it may be that despite Chamberlain's reservation, if Hitler had marched, Czechoslovakia could have held out until the Russians or French came to the rescue. Whether the Russians would have acted we do not know, but maybe, as Wheeler-Bennett suggests, it may have influenced Beneš in his attitude to Russia after the war. According to Wollenberg, the Red Army made no preparations for supporting Czechoslovakia.[548]

So far as Britain was concerned, the sober assessment of SIS was[549]

> … Platitudinous though it may be, our only chance to preserving peace is to be ready for war on any scale, without relying too much on outside support.

An obvious point in the context of the woeful pace of rearmament and obstructionism of Chamberlain over organising British industry and having a Ministry of Supply.

On the evening of 30 September, Edward R Murrow broadcast to America:[550]

> The international experts in London agree that Herr Hitler has scored one of the greatest triumphs in modern history. The average Englishman, who really received his first official information concerning the crisis from Mr. Chamberlain's speech in the House of Commons on Wednesday, is relieved and grateful. Men who predicted the crisis and the lines it would

[543] W Wark, *British Military and Economic Intelligence: Assessments of Nazi Germany* (Ithaca, Cornell University Press, 2018) 89, and Andrew ibid.

[544] W Wark, *The Ultimate Enemy* (Oxford, OUP, 1986) 207.

[545] ibid 209. Table 9. Intelligence on army dispositions, 24 September 1938.

[546] K Strong, *The Czechoslovak Army* 171–172. C Andrew, *Secret Service The Making of the British Intelligence Community* (London, Heineman, 1985) 397.

[547] J Wheeler-Bennett, *Knaves, Fools and Heroes* (London, Macmillan, 1974) 153.

[548] E Wollenberg, *The Red Army* (New York, Hyperion Press, 1973) 283–285. Cited in M Beloff, *Foreign Policy of Soviet Russia 1936-41*, Vol 2. RIIA (Oxford, OUP, 1949) 154, n 1.

[549] C Andrew, *Secret Service The Making of the British Intelligence Community* (London, Heineman, 1985) 398.

[550] E Bliss Jnr (ed) *In Search of the Light The Broadcasts of Edard R Murrow 1938-1961* (New York, Da Capo Press, 1997) 10–11.

> follow long before it arrived did not entirely share that optimism and relief. One afternoon paper carried this headline: WORLD SHOWS RELIEF – BUT WITH RESERVATIONS.

On 1 October Poland gave an ultimatum to Czechoslovakia, which was discussed with Henderson and Ribbentrop, who both advised against hostilities. Ribbentrop and Goring suggested that if Poland was in conflict with Russia, Germany would support Poland.[551] In his diary entry on 1 October 1938, Oliver Harvey wrote that Chamberlain's piece of paper was causing serious concern in that he was implicitly trusting Hitler and would give up rearmament.[552] The aim of Hitler was to gain the advantage by preventing any alliances so they could pick off rivals one at a time using the Sudeten crisis as a model, but on 2 October 1938, the Polish forces occupied Teschen in Silesia with Hitler's consent.[553] Hitler further allowed Hungary to take parts of Slovakia and Ruthenia, but in the latter case only three days before he occupied Prague.[554]

On 3 October 1938, in a debate on the Munich Agreement, Hugh Dalton (Shadow Foreign Secretary) raised some very serious questions on the efficacy of the agreement.[555] First, he questioned the position of Russia as an ally. Was Britain prepared to sacrifice the British Empire with Russia being neutral or hold it with Russia as an ally? Second, he questioned the guarantee, which was very vague, and asked whether it was intended that the Soviet Union should be a party to the guarantee. Russia had been a contingent guarantor for old Czechoslovakia, but to please Hitler, the old treaties had been ignored. Such a guarantee was futile as Czechoslovakia was stripped of her natural defences and of any material means of her defence.[556] He warned that the best heavy artillery and other war material taken by the Nazis would be used against Britain in any war.[557] He made a telling point about pre-war Austro-Hungarian debts: who would pay Czechoslovakia's share, and would Czechoslovakia be compensated for the loss of state or private property?[558] None of this was agreed at Munich. As for the plebiscites to be held in areas where the German population was less than 50 per cent these were questionable, as was the question of whether there were to be any counterbalancing plebiscite arrangements where there were more than 50 per cent Germans. None of this was clear, but the inference was obvious. Also, the plebiscites were to be based on a 20-year-old register – another fraud on the Czech population – despite the Czech delegates having taken to Munich the 1930 census, which was ignored, as were the Czech delegates themselves. Finally, Dalton referred to the lack of anti-aircraft defence and air-raid precautions placing the country's great cities in immediate peril.[559] Dalton was in no doubt that Hitler was following the German edition of *Mein Kampf* to the letter. He referred to Colonel White, a minister of the Australian Commonwealth government who said: 'The Czechs' fate to-day will be

[551] W Jędrzejewicz (ed) *Diplomat in Berlin 1933-1939* (New York, Columbia University Press, 1968). *Lipski to Beck* 1 October 1938. No. 115.
[552] O Harvey, *The Diplomatic Diaries of Oliver Harvey 1937–40* (London, Collins 1970) 207–208.
[553] F Buttin, 'The Polish-Czechoslovak Conflict over Teschen Silesia (1918–1920): A Case Study' (2005/2006) 25 *Perspectives* 76.
[554] Z Steiner, *The Triumph of the Dark* (Oxford, Oxford University Press, 2011) 687, 690.
[555] *Hansard* House of Commons Debates, 3 October 1938. Cols 144–150.
[556] ibid Col 144.
[557] ibid Col 145.
[558] ibid Col 146.
[559] ibid Col 148.

ours to-morrow.'[560] After making the speech Dalton was invited by Macmillan to meet with Churchill, Eden, Brendan Bracken and others to discuss the opposition amendment and possible co-operation if Chamberlain called an election.[561]

Gradually it was realised that ceding Sudetenland to Germany left the dismembered Czechoslovakia at the mercy of the Nazis. It deprived the western Allies of the support of the Czech army, which was half as large as the Wehrmacht, and of a population less than half that of Greater Germany. France could not have hoped for a better opportunity in the future to fight Germany on even terms. It is arguable that in 1939 Britain and France were strategically in a worse position than before 30 September 1938.[562] Churchill perceptively described the unendurable predicament of Britain falling into the power, orbit and influence of Nazi Germany so that existence depended on the whims of a dictator.[563] More than that, his indictment of Munich was 'a total and unmitigated defeat'. Daladier was in no doubt as to Hitler's intentions and from 4 October put France in a state of 'permanent mobilisation'.[564] On 8 October Harvey wrote that the western democracies had bought peace by sacrificing a small nation to the dictators because they were afraid or unprepared to fight.[565] On 10 October he opined that Chamberlain had reduced the government to that of the 'businessman'; he was obstinate, unimaginative, and narrow-minded with his head stuck in the Victorian class system.[566] On 21 October 1938, Hitler directed the liquidation of the Czech state and occupation of Memel in central Lithuania. He decided that *Lebensraum* would be accomplished by a triple alliance of Germany, Italy and Japan. France would be defeated first, then Britain's lifelines cut.[567] Two days later, when Chamberlain visited Paris, he was greeted outside the Gare du Nord with cries of *Á bas Munich* and *Vive Eden*. French morale was defeatist, and pacifists were disillusioned because of Munich.[568]

On 24 November 1938, Chamberlain met Daladier at the Quai d'Orsay,[569] unknown to the two premiers that day General Keitel, Head of OKW,[570] issued his order for the occupation of Danzig and for a surprise attack on Poland. At the meeting, Daladier had the opportunity of informing Chamberlain of the Franco-German Agreement, similar to the Anglo-German Declaration.[571] The former simply affirmed good neighbourly relations; recognition of the Franco-German border confirmed that no further territorial questions remained and that the parties would consult if there should be any international difficulties. Chamberlain congratulated M Bonnet,[572] although the

[560] ibid Col 148.
[561] H Macmillan, *Winds of Change* (London, Macmillan, 1966) 569.
[562] M Hauner, 'Czechoslovakia as a Military Factor in British Considerations of 1938' (1978) 1 *Journal of Strategic Studies*. C Andrew, *Secret Service The Making of the British Intelligence Community* (London, Heineman, 1985) 400.
[563] RAC Parker, *Churchill and Appeasement* (London, Macmillan, 2000) 188.
[564] Z Steiner, *The Triumph of the Dark* (Oxford, Oxford University Press, 2011) 686.
[565] O Harvey, *The Diplomatic Diaries of Oliver Harvey 1937–40*. (London, Collins, 1970) 210.
[566] ibid 214, 221.
[567] Z Steiner, *The Triumph of the Dark* (Oxford, Oxford University Press, 2011) 682.
[568] O Harvey, *The Diplomatic Diaries of Oliver Harvey 1937–40* (London, Collins, 1970) 223.
[569] DBFP 1919–1939 Ser. 3. Vol 3. *Record of Anglo-French Conversations Held At The Quai d'Orsay* 24 November 1938. 285–311.
[570] High Command of the German Armed Forces.
[571] DBFP 1919–1939 Ser. 3. Vol 3. No. 285.
[572] Minister for Foreign Affairs.

Franco-German Agreement had not been ratified.[573] Following the Munich Agreement, Bonnet had sought a pact with Hitler, much to Hitler's advantage, undermining all the work of Briand and Barthou. The Franco-German Declaration of December 1938 proved equally meaningless as the Anglo-German Declaration, as Germany continued to assert its interest in eastern Europe as a 'sphere of interest'.[574]

Despite such agreements Daladier and Chamberlain had no illusions that Munich was final; it was a question of where Hitler would strike first. They discussed the Anglo-French defence measures and agreed to further defence cooperation. Belgium was a problem because it prevented direct action between France and Germany.[575] Chamberlain and Daladier discussed the question of what would happen if France or Britain were attacked by Germany. They agreed that each would defend the other.[576] Whilst they were discussing matters, Hitler offered Poland membership in the Anti-Comintern Pact and collaboration in commercial and colonial matters.[577]

The disparities in armaments due to defence cuts and disarmament policies had placed Britain and France at a serious disadvantage to the war economy of the Third Reich: France with regard to aircraft and Britain with regard to her army. Both countries had productivity issues but gave the following figures.

	France	**Great Britain**
Aircraft	2,600. Modern planes: 80	1938 production 300 aircraft per month
Army	100 Divisions. 2,000 tanks.	2 Divisions
Budget	20 billion fr/1940	

Source: Documents On British Foreign Policy 1919–1939 Ser 3 Vol 3. 289–291.

The balance had changed in Germany's favour because of the threat of aerial bombardment. London, according to Chamberlain, was 'the most vulnerable capital in the world'.[578] Britain was giving priority to antiaircraft defences, to fighters, and to bombers but was deficient in anti-aircraft defences and in tanks. Antiaircraft guns were being produced at the expense of field artillery.[579] This alarmed Daladier and accounted, in his view, for the inadequacy of the British army.[580]

573 DBFP 1919–1939 Ser. 3. Vol 3. No. 286.

574 Yellow Book, Item 163 and see: J de Launay, *Major Controversies of Contemporary History* (Oxford, Pergamon Press, 1965) 178.

575 On 24 April 1937, the British and French governments issued a joint declaration releasing Belgium from her obligations under the Treaty of Locarno and the arrangements of March 1936 on the understanding that Belgium would defend her independence and remain faithful to the Covenant of the League of Nations. The German government, on 13 October 1937, noted Belgium's position and reaffirmed its obligations towards Belgium provided she did not take part in military action directed against Germany.

576 DBFP 1919–1939 Ser. 3. Vol 3. No. 288.

577 WJędrzejewicz (ed) *Diplomat in Berlin 1933-1939* (New York, Columbia University Press, 1968) 509–510.

578 DBFP 1919–1939 Ser. 3. Vol 3. No. 291.

579 At that time Germany was producing three times the number of bombers to fighters. DBFP 1919–1939 Ser. 3. Vol 3. No. 294.

580 DBFP 1919–1939 Ser. 3. Vol 3. No. 292.

Bonnet questioned when the guarantee regarding the Czechoslovakian border would come into effect.[581] Daladier reminded everyone that there was a Russo-Czechoslovakia Treaty which was subordinate to the Franco-Czechoslovakian Treaty that obliged France to consult with Czechoslovakia if there should be any danger of infraction of the political principles contained in Article 88 of the Treaty of St Germain-en-Laye 1919 and the Geneva Protocols of 1922.[582] France and Britain had offered a guarantee to Czechoslovakia observing her new frontiers, not a formal agreement but only a 'moral obligation'.[583] Bonnet argued that the Czechs had been misled because when the Anglo-French Plan was presented to them, they had been led to believe that, while up until then, there were only French and Russian guarantees, in the future they would have the British guarantee as well.[584] Chamberlain admitted this, but the British government was contemplating a general guarantee which would be more effective than a limited one. Britain had no intention of taking sole liability. Bonnet argued that under the Locarno Treaty liability was joint and several.[585] Daladier thought that France would be going back on her guarantee to the Czechs. He admitted that 'France had offered to guarantee the new frontier in order to make it easier for the Czechs to accept the new frontier.'[586] Chamberlain contemplated that after negotiations the situation in Czechoslovakia would be 'one of almost complete safety'.[587] Despite such concerns, Chamberlain resisted calls for a major rearmaments programme for fear of provoking an arms race.[588] He capped defence spending and, in effect, increased the risk of greater losses in the event of war.[589] In the event Britain could only field four divisions and two mobile divisions as against Germany's 103 divisions on the outbreak of war.[590]

Halifax admitted that Britain and France were in a worse position because the Czechoslovakian army had been eliminated and the Nazis had a road through Czechoslovakia.[591] Halifax appears to have seen the danger more clearly than Chamberlain, and who, although very loyal to Chamberlain, gradually diverged from a policy so obviously distasteful to public opinion. As he wrote to Phipps in Paris: 'it would be fatal to us to be caught with insufficient strength'.[592]

Meanwhile, Eden visited President Roosevelt on a holiday in America. He spoke to the Annual Congress of American Industry and was careful to remind his audience of the 1914–18 war to defeat the power of arrogant militarism forever. He referred to the Kellogg Pact which renounced war, but contrary to that, rival ideologies had not made the world safe for democracy. 'A false complacency', he said, was 'the worst calamity that can befall any nation in critical times'. He assured his audience that appeasement was not a British habit … 'we all want to preserve our liberties, we all want freedom and security …

[581] ibid 300.
[582] ibid 301.
[583] ibid 303.
[584] ibid 304.
[585] ibid.
[586] ibid 305.
[587] ibid.
[588] Z Steiner, *The Triumph of the Dark* (Oxford, Oxford University Press, 2011) 698.
[589] ibid 724 and 725.
[590] W Wark, *The Ultimate Enemy* (Oxford, OUP, 1986) 111.
[591] DBFP 1919–1939 Ser. 3. Vol 3. No. 306.
[592] ibid No. 285. *Halifax to Phipps* 1 November 1938.

we all want peace ...'. Britain did not ask any other country to pull their chestnuts out of the fire but would fight to defend it.[593] As Harvey recorded Ambassador Kennedy had telegraphed that 'AE's visit had done more for Anglo-American relations than any other visit within memory'.[594] On 4 January 1939, President Roosevelt addressed the Congress and warned that the world was not assured of peace, contrary to Chamberlain's boast:[595]

> All about us rage undeclared wars – military and economic. All about us grow more deadly armaments – military and economic. All about us are threats of new aggression military and economic.

x. Annexation of Czechoslovakia 1939

In March, events moved at a rapid pace. Hitler was determined to enforce his will. On 12 March he told the Hungarians to take Ruthenia. On 16 March he seized the remainder of Czechoslovakia, and on 20 March he summoned the Foreign Minister of Lithuania and forced him to cede Memel to the Reich.[596] In order to guarantee vital oil supplies for his war on Poland, Germany signed a trade treaty with Romania on 23 March. Hitler so distracted the Poles with his promises that they eagerly assisted the Hungarians in taking Ruthenia, paying little attention to Memel. Had they been less greedy and more discerning, they would have been alarmed by the ruthless disregard for international law and the status of Memel, which was an autonomous territory guaranteed by international statute[597] detached from the German Empire under Article 99 of the Treaty of Versailles and given a government independent of Lithuania and Germany.[598] Polish diplomats like Ambassador Lipski in Berlin were already aware of the precedent Memel created in relation to Danzig. His Foreign Secretary would see Danzig as a casus belli.

By this time, fortunately, under Paul Reynaud's management of the economy, France attracted 26 billion francs in investment between November 1938 and September 1939 and a rise in aircraft production from 37 per month in 1938 to 100 in March 1939.[599] This contrasts with the impression that Sir W Seeds (Moscow) received from M Litvinov on 23 March 1939. Litvinov believed that France was finished, full of Nazi agents, disaffected and disunited at the mercy of certain leading politicians whom he profoundly distrusted.[600] Undoubtedly an exaggeration, but nevertheless, France had a serious shortage of aircraft and tried to purchase aircraft from America, offering the

[593] A Eden, *Foreign Affairs* (London, Faber and Faber, 1939) 321–327.

[594] O Harvey, *The Diplomatic Diaries of Oliver Harvey 1937–40* (London, Collins, 1970) 230.

[595] F Roosevelt, *The Public Papers and Addresses of Franklin D Roosevelt*, 1939 Volume. War and Neutrality (London, Macmillan, 1941) 1–12.

[596] Z Steiner, *The Triumph of the Dark* (Oxford, Oxford University Press, 2011) 727–728.

[597] ibid 732.

[598] *Origins of the Memel Question, Diplomatic and Other Documents from the Versailles Peace Conference Reference of the Question by the Conference of Ambassadors to The Council Of The League Of Nations (1919–1923) Including Historical Sketches Of The Memel Region and other Introductory Statements.* (Lithuanian Information Bureau, London December 1923).

[599] Z Steiner, *The Triumph of the Dark* (Oxford, Oxford University Press, 2011) 716, 718.

[600] DBFP 1919–1939 Ser. 3. Vol 4. No 658. *Sir W Seeds to Halifax* 3 April 1939. See also No. 593. *Sir W Seeds to Halifax* 31 March 1939.

Americans 10 billion gold francs, 10 per cent of the French gold holdings. Roosevelt refused.[601]

Ribbentrop imagined that after the Nazis occupied Prague, the Poles would be willing to concede Danzig and would not fight. As part of this objective, on 2 January 1939, Ribbentrop attempted to entice the British into an agreement and at the same time planned to tighten the Axis against her.[602] Suspecting something of this on 19 January 1939, Gladwyn Jebb, who was the Private Secretary to both Vansittart and Cadogan wrote:

> The extremist leaders are advocating a course which is likely to lead to a general war and … this is opposed not only by important people in the Army, the industrial world, and so on, but even the moderates in the ranks of the party itself'.[603]

It was clear as Neville concluded that the British government did not realise even at this late stage that Hitler had absolute control over policy.[604] It is therefore hard to understand, as Duff Cooper wrote, that the government was authorising commercial negotiations with Germany. On 15 March 1939, the Germans marched into Czechoslovakia, and yet the President of the Board of Trade was about to depart on a friendly visit to Berlin.[605] Despite the Nazi occupation of Prague and the remainder of Czechoslovakia, the Federation of British Industry and the German RI entered into a trade agreement on 16 March 1939, a day after the occupation. This provoked serious criticism on both sides of the Atlantic, suggesting that business interests came before security – another serious misjudgement by Chamberlain. The day after the occupation of Prague the British government made a complete reversal of foreign and domestic policy. It committed Britain to act in every quarter of Europe and then proceeded to draw up a compulsory register to conscript the whole youth of the country.[606] Having taken Czechoslovakia Hitler turned his attention to the East. Either Poland remained neutral, or it would be crushed before he turned his armies on the western democracies.

M. The Danzig Crisis

i. Assurance to Poland

Planning for the Nazis' next acquisition Ribbentrop had a meeting with Beck, the Polish Foreign Minister, on 26 January 1939 to discuss Polish-German relations. Ribbentrop tried to induce Beck to collaborate against Russia. Hitler wanted to pacify Poland to attack the West as favoured by Ribbentrop and Himmler.[607] Conversely, an attack on

[601] Z Steiner, *The Triumph of the Dark* (Oxford, Oxford University Press, 2011) 816.
[602] W Jędrzejewicz (ed) *Diplomat in Berlin 1933-1939* (New York, Columbia University Press, 1968) 519–522.
[603] Cited in P Neville, 'The Foreign Office and Britain's Ambassadors to Berlin, 1933-39' (2004) 18(3) *Contemporary British History* 125 from CAB 27/627, FP (36), Memorandum by Jebb, 'Summary of Information from Secret Sources', 19 Jan 1936. See: *Memoirs of Lord Gladwyn* (London, Weidenfeld & Nicolson, 1972) 23, 106.
[604] ibid.
[605] D Cooper, *The Second World War* (London, Jonathan Cape, 1939) 167.
[606] ibid.
[607] W Jędrzejewicz (ed), *Diplomat in Berlin 1933-1939* (New York, Columbia University Press, 1968) 512–513.

Poland by Germany (which Beck considered more likely) might be deterred by an alliance of Poland and Russia and by the revision of the US Neutrality Act 1935.[608] Fearing Nazi aggression and Hitler's ambitions regarding Danzig and Memel, where he could use the same propaganda and threats of force as he did against Czechoslovakia, Beck sought to reaffirm the Polish-Soviet Non-Aggression Pact of 1932. The fear was well founded because Lipski,[609] at a meeting with Coulendre the French Ambassador in Berlin, was told that the next blow would be against Romania and Poland.[610]

Ribbentrop was demanding a superhighway, a new railway link, and access to Danzig as well as Pomerania. At the same time, General Keitel knew that Hitler did not want to take Danzig by force notwithstanding the order Keitel had issued on 24 November 1938.[611] Hitler wanted to obliterate Poland and have an extended eastern border to East Prussia and Eastern Silesia. On 25 March 1939, Lipski received instructions from Beck that whilst Poland was prepared to facilitate railway travel between the Reich and Danzig, it could not consider any extraterritorial status for communications. He suggested a joint Polish-German guarantee to the Free City of Danzig to meet the aspirations of the German population and safeguard Polish interests.[612] That day Lipski met with Ribbentrop, who demanded that Danzig be incorporated into the Reich and a superhighway be constructed in consideration for a 25-year non-aggression pact and a guaranteed frontier with the Reich.[613] In England, attention was focused on a Four Power Pact comprising Poland, Russia, France and Britain, but this was rejected by Poland and Chamberlain was against any alignment with Russia.[614] Poland sought assurances from France. General Gamelin assured the Poles that offensive operations would commence against the Siegfried Line 15 days after mobilisation.[615] However, such assurance was conditional upon the Polish government not taking 'an uncompromising attitude or any provocative action in their dealings with Germany' and that the scheme could be put into effect.[616] This was to be regarded by the Poles as an interim measure designed to meet a possible danger pending consultations with Poland and Romania as to the contingency of a scheme which the guarantee depended on, as set out in Halifax's telegram of 27 March to Kennard, the British Ambassador in Warsaw. Thus, the continuance of the guarantee was dependent on effecting the scheme. This scheme was set out in Halifax's dispatch to Kennard on 27 March 1939 and provided:[617]

1. That it would not be possible to proceed without modification of the proposed Four-Power Declaration for while France and Russia accepted Poland did not.
2. Britain closely consulted Poland, but British attempts to consolidate the situation could be frustrated by Russian involvement because British missions abroad warned that

[608] Z Steiner, *The Triumph of the Dark* (Oxford, Oxford University Press, 2011) 783.
[609] The Polish Ambassador in Berlin.
[610] W Jędrzejewicz (ed), *Diplomat in Berlin 1933–1939* (New York, Columbia University Press, 1968) 501.
[611] ibid 522–523 and DGFP Ser. D. Vol VI. No. 99. 25 March 1939.
[612] Jędrzejewicz ibid 506. Doc No. 139. *Becks Instructions to Lipski.*
[613] Documents on German Foreign Policy Series D, Vol 11. No. 101.
[614] Z Steiner, *The Triumph of the Dark* (Oxford, Oxford University Press, 2011) 737.
[615] ibid 751.
[616] DBFP 1919–1939 Ser. 3. Vol 4. No. 584. *Halifax to Kennard (Warsaw)* 31 March 1939.
[617] ibid No. 538. *Halifax to Phipps (Paris) and Hoare (Bucharest)* 27 March 1939. This telegram is paraphrased by the author. Kennard and Hoare were instructed that 'No action should be taken on the present telegram pending further instructions'.

the inclusion of Russia would advantage the Anti-Comintern Pact and excite friendly Governments.

3. An alternative method had to be sought by the inclusion of Poland and Romania since Romania might be menaced by Germany's plans for Eastern expansion.
4. Britain and France decided to make an approach to the Polish and Romanian Governments as follows:
   (a) Whether Poland and Romania were prepared to actively respectively resist if their own independence was threatened by Germany either directly attacking Poland or Romania, or undermining either country's independence, whether by economic penetration or national disintegration, (e.g. Czechoslovakia) or by indirect military pressure, which, in the case of Romania, might take the form of Hungarian troop concentrations
   (b) If so, Britain and France would be prepared to aid the threatened State provided it promptly informed of any developments threatening independence.
   (c) The assurance offered in (b) was dependent upon Poland coming to the help of Romania, the question was whether Romania would help Poland if she were threatened.
   (d) (Communicated only to Poland) The undertaking given by Britain and France under (b) would be given on condition that if Britain or France were attacked by Germany, or if they went to war with Germany to resist German aggression anywhere in Western Europe or Yugoslavia, Poland would come to their help.
5. If the position of Poland and Romania can be consolidated, Turkey and Greece would be more likely to be able to make an effective contribution.
6. That Poland and Romania were to be made aware of the necessity of explaining to the Russians why if Poland or Romania were attacked there would be good reasons to secure some measure of Soviet participation in providing war material or being neutral. Halifax was keen on seeking Russian assistance in this respect.
7. This was to be kept secret as well as any negotiations until a public pronouncement could be made on the assurances which they had given to the Polish and Romanian Governments.

Kennard was told that his French colleague would receive similar instructions, and he should, after consulting him, speak to Beck on these points. Kennard was not to leave Beck with any written statement. Daladier confirmed similar undertakings by France on 13 April as to the British and Polish undertakings in the event of an attack and reaffirmed the Franco-Polish Alliance.[618]

It must be said that the declaration about Poland was an improvisation.[619] According to Strang, head of the Central Department of the Foreign Office, it was drafted on the afternoon of 30 March by Chamberlain with Halifax and Cadogan as a reply to a parliamentary question. Reports of an imminent attack on Poland no doubt stirred public opinion in demanding that Poland should not go the same way as Czechoslovakia.[620]

On 31 March 1939, the British government gave an assurance to Poland regarding their independence. This was confirmed by Chamberlain in the House of Commons

[618] French Yellow Book (1938–1939) No. 99. *Extract of a Declaration by Daladier 13 April 1939* (Hutchinson and Co Ltd) 114.

[619] Lord Strang, *Home and Abroad* (London, 1956) 161.

[620] ibid.

that afternoon and by Halifax in his dispatch to Phipps in Paris, which stated, inter alia:[621]

> … I now have to inform the House that during that period in the event of any action which clearly threatened Polish independence, and which the Polish Government accordingly considered it vital to resist with their national forces, His Majesty's Government would feel themselves bound at once to lend the Polish Government all support in their power. They have given the Polish Government an assurance to this effect. 'I may add that the French Government have authorised me to make it plain that they stand in the same position in this matter as do His Majesty's Government'.

ii. Prelude to War

Nazi propaganda was gradually increased to pressurise Poland as it had pressurised Czechoslovakia. Beck stressed the mutual obligations in the Polish-German Agreement of 1934 but also agreed to a British-Polish Communique on 6 April published in London confirming a bilateral pact of mutual aid if either country was attacked by a third power.[622] As a result, the Reich increased its propaganda campaign, spreading all kinds of false rumours and allegations contrary to the evidence of the French Ambassador in Warsaw who reported that: 'Polish public opinion could long endure its calm'.[623]

On 13 April 1939, similar unilateral guarantees were given to Greece and Romania.[624]

On 14 April President Roosevelt wrote in similar terms to Hitler and Mussolini, suggesting an international peace conference and requesting assurance that Germany would not attack European and Middle Eastern countries.[625] This was met with vitriolic abuse by Hitler, clearly intent on war with Poland, and unilaterally renounced the non-aggression pact (Polish-German Declaration 1934). Beck would not accept the cession of Danzig and stated, 'We in Poland do not recognise the conception of peace at any price.' He also denied that the British assurance was in any way contrary to the Polish-German Declaration of 26 January 1934.[626] On 6 May, an Anglo-Turkish Agreement was signed providing for mutual assistance in case of war although Britain and France were slow in seeking further Balkan security arrangements.[627] In seeking to ascertain Russian views by sending Robert Hudson, a member of the Ministry for Overseas Trade to Moscow, Litvinov was sceptical about Hudson's mission and advised Stalin it was for Britain to make suggestions.[628] Maiski, the Russian Ambassador in London, suggested talks

[621] Parliamentary Debates, 5th Ser. Vol 345, col. 2415 and DBFP 1919–1939 Ser. 3. Vol 4. No. 582. *Halifax to Phipps (Paris) and Lampson (Cairo)* 31 March 1939.

[622] W Jędrzejewicz (ed), *Diplomat in Berlin 1933-1939* (New York, Columbia University Press, 1968). Doc No. 141. *Lipski to Beck* 4 April 1939.

[623] W Jędrzejewicz (ed), *Diplomat in Berlin 1933-1939* (New York, Columbia University Press, 1968) 643–647. Affidavit of Józef Lipski, 23 September 1948, Nuremberg War Crimes Tribunal. Allegations also investigated by British Ambassador Kennard of beatings with chains and barbed wire found to be gross distortions of the truth. (Despatches Nos. 52 and 55, 24 and 27 August 1939.)

[624] Z Steiner, *The Triumph of the Dark* (Oxford, Oxford University Press, 2011) 746.

[625] F Roosevelt, *The Public Papers and Addresses of Franklin D Roosevelt* 1939 Volume. War and Neutrality (London, Macmillan, 1941) 209–217.

[626] W Jędrzejewicz (ed), *Diplomat in Berlin 1933-1939* (New York, Columbia University Press, 1968) 533–536.

[627] Z Steiner, *The Triumph of the Dark* (Oxford, Oxford University Press, 2011) 748.

[628] ibid 750 and Documents on Foreign Policy USSR, Vol XXII, No. 157 *Litvinov to Stalin* 20 March 1939.

with Litvinov in London, but Chamberlain and Halifax dithered even when Litvinov suggested a tripartite agreement and military alliance against Germany. As a result of the surrender of Czechoslovakia, the Little Entente, depleted by the German occupation of Czechoslovakia, turned to Germany, unable to rely on vague assurances from London and Paris.[629] France and Britain sought to make an agreement with Romania and Greece and on the 12 May, Britain signed a mutual assistance pact with Turkey. Relations with Russia became difficult. Russia required her traditional sphere of influence: the Baltic states, Bessarabia and the Straits. Churchill described Britain's attitude to Russia as 'the worst folly'.[630] David Lloyd George said: 'If we are going in without the help of Russia we are walking into a trap.' Chamberlain wanted to avoid war but had no thought to winning it. Russian support over Danzig was required. Chamberlain singularly failed to understand Russia's position as well as the traditional 'aims and spirit of Russian diplomacy'.[631] Negotiations for an understanding with Russia were dilatory and conducted in an offhand manner, possibly due to Beck's warning.[632] On 14 June 1939, the Soviet Ambassador to Poland told Beck that no one needed to anticipate an armed conflict in Europe. Up to 24 June 1939, Molotov had been open to discussion with France and Britain as well as Germany without making any commitments.[633] On that date, however, Anglo-French discussions ended with the military discussions to follow on. Schulenburg in Moscow told Stalin that Russia was likely to make an agreement with Britain and France. What changed was the dilatoriness and hesitancy of Britain and France and the lack of instructions regarding Poland.[634] On 22 July, the British signed the Cragie-Arita agreement with Japan, surrendering to Japanese demands to refrain from all acts and measures that would interfere with the Japanese forces in attaining their objectives.[635] President Roosevelt commented that in so doing Britain lacked 'not only the desire to save civilisation but the continued belief that they can do it'.[636] Public opinion in America was in favour of sanctions against Japan, and for this reason Roosevelt abrogated the Treaty of Commerce and Navigation of 1911 on 26 July 1939.[637] Roosevelt had to walk a very thin line in domestic politics between aiding the Allies and avoiding direct involvement in any European war. Many Americans were isolationist, and he had to educate the American people about the danger to the democracies.[638] Chamberlain, on the other hand, was wary of US competition, which he saw as a threat to imperial trade. It must have been obvious that Britain was incapable of defending the whole of its empire when through disarmament, slow rearmament and appeasement, it found it difficult to defend itself. Incredibly, Chamberlain was still trusting in Hitler's

[629] J de Launay, *Major Controversies of Contemporary History* (Oxford, Pergamon Press, 1965) 182.
[630] ibid and see: AJP Taylor, *The Origins of the Second World War* (London, Penguin Books, 1991) 225.
[631] J de Launay, *Major Controversies of Contemporary History* (Oxford, Pergamon Press, 1965) 183.
[632] ibid 184.
[633] ibid 188.
[634] ibid 188.
[635] C Hosoya, 'Miscalculations in Deterrent Policy: Japanese – U.S. Relations 1938-1941' (1968) 5(2) *Journal of Peace Research* 100.
[636] D Reynolds, *The Creation of The Anglo-American Alliance 1937–1941 A Study in Competitive Co-operation* (London, Europa, 1981) 43–44.
[637] C Hosoya, 'Miscalculations in Deterrent Policy: Japanese – U.S. Relations 1938-1941' (1986) 5(2) *Journal of Peace Research* 100.
[638] Z Steiner, *The Triumph of the Dark* (Oxford, Oxford University Press, 2011) 813–815.

word with his self-belief in his skill in foreign policy and told the Poles to restrain from any action against Germany and repeated the same protracted, unnecessary negotiations with Hitler over Danzig as he had over the Sudetenland. Hitler had been so frustrated by Chamberlain's interference that he was determined never to permit such interference again.[639]

Meanwhile, in Berlin, the Polish Embassy was reporting 600 cases of persecution of Polish nationals in Germany with deportations, religious persecution, and destruction of property. Tensions along the Pomeranian Corridor and in Danzig deteriorated rapidly with the Nazis training Germans for the SA[640] (*Sturmabteilung*) and SS (*Schutzstaffeln*) to be used for infiltration and sabotage.[641] Tourists from East Prussia were recruited, and tensions increased at the Customs Posts.[642] A *Freikorps* of one division was formed, and on 4 August 1939, the Danzig Chief of Customs ceased to recognise the Polish inspectors. This was repeated on the East Prussian frontier.[643]

Back in France, Bonnet proposed an agreement to the effect that in the event of France and Britain being at war with Nazi Germany, Russia would come to the aid of Poland or Romania if the victim of unprovoked aggression. If Russia was attacked by Nazi Germany in assisting Poland, France and Britain would come to her aid.[644] This may have been a constructive proposal, but there were concerns about transiting a Russian army through Poland. Negotiations with Russia were carried out by the British representative, Admiral Plunkett, without any clear instructions, whereas General Doumenc, the French government representative, had precise instructions. These discussions started on 11 August 1939. The breaking point was that Russia required passage through Poland, which Poland refused.[645] Reynaud instructed Doumenc to sign the agreement. Marshal Voroshilov said that Russia had been fully prepared to help Czechoslovakia, but Britain and France, as on this occasion, allowed talks to drag on; his government therefore required confirmation from Poland by 22 August 1939. The talks essentially failed because Chamberlain distrusted Russia, and he did not want an alliance with the Soviets.[646]

On 12 August 1939, Berlin was informed of Russia's willingness to negotiate. Russia was in no hurry, but Hitler was anxious as he planned to attack Poland on 1 September 1939. Molotov delayed and used the delay to his advantage so that on the 18 August he suggested a nonaggression pact. On 22 August, Hitler addressed his commanders admitting that he wanted to attack the West first but decided to attack Poland instead.[647]

[639] ibid 1006.

[640] Assault Section of the NSDAP – Nationalsozialzstische Deutsche Arbeiterpartei Nationalsozialistische German Workers Party.

[641] French Yellow Book (1938–1939) No. 161. *Coulondre* (Berlin) *to Bonnet* 11 July 1939 (Hutchinson and Co Ltd) 186–187.

[642] French Yellow Book (1938–1939) No. 160. *Leon Noel (Warsaw) to Bonnet* 10 July 1939 (Hutchinson and Co Ltd) 114.

[643] W Jędrzejewicz (ed), *Diplomat in Berlin 1933-1939* (New York, Columbia University Press, 1968) 648–650.

[644] J de Launay, *Major Controversies of Contemporary History* (Oxford, Pergamon Press, 1965) 184.

[645] ibid 185.

[646] ibid 186.

[647] *Trial of the Major War Criminals*, Vol. XXVI, No. PS-798.

On 23 August Ribbentrop arrived in Moscow and signed the Pact with secret protocols settling spheres of influence between the two countries.[648] It may be that from Russia's point of view in Britain and France abandoning Czechoslovakia, Stalin slowly turned to Hitler and deflected Hitler's attention from the East to the West.[649] The same day, Henderson delivered a letter personally to Hitler from Chamberlain. This informed Hitler that the government was determined to fulfil its obligations to Poland, that they were prepared, provided a peace atmosphere was created, to discuss all problems affecting Anglo-German relations, and that during a period of truce, direct discussions between Poland and Germany regarding minorities would be welcomed.[650] Hitler blamed Britain for giving Poland a 'blank cheque'. In his formal reply,[651] he argued that Britain had encouraged Poland and that the German population in Poland had been subjected to persecution. He told Chamberlain:

> … in your own letter, [you] can only refer to a contemplated act of menace directed against the Reich. *I therefore inform Your Excellency that in the event of these military announcements being carried into effect I shall order immediate mobilisation of the German forces.* (Emphasis in original).

Hitler ended his reply:

> 8. The question of the treatment of European problems on a peaceful basis is not a decision which rests with Germany but formerly on those who since the crime committed by the Versailles dictate[652] have stubbornly and consistently opposed any peaceful revision. Only after a change of spirit on the part of the responsible Powers can there be any real solidarity in the relationship between England and Germany. I have all my life fought for Anglo-German friendship; the attitude adopted by British diplomacy-at any rate up to the present-has however convinced me of the futility of such an attempt. Should there be any change in this respect in the future nobody could be happier than I.

He also proposed an Anglo-German alliance after he had dealt with Poland. This antagonised Mussolini, as Hitler was, in effect, protecting the British Empire from Italian attack. He also displeased Japan with his Nazi-Soviet Pact and then Italy declared that she would remain neutral in any war.[653] The proposed alliance was another ruse simply to separate Britain from Poland, which the British Cabinet rejected, with Henderson conveying the response to Hitler on 28 August.[654]

Hitler had already decided to attack Poland the morning after his meeting with Henderson.[655] This he postponed for a few days, as again Roosevelt's initiative may have given him pause for thought. On 24 August Roosevelt asked Poland and Germany to refrain from hostilities, and on 25 August sent another message to Hitler containing the President of Poland's (Moszicki) reply to Roosevelt's earlier request. President Moszicki stated that he had always considered direct negotiations between governments the most

[648] J de Launay, *Major Controversies of Contemporary History* (Oxford, Pergamon Press, 1965) 189.
[649] ibid 190.
[650] DBFP 1919–1939 Ser. 3. Vol 7. No 658. *Henderson to Halifax* 23 August 1938. 161–163.
[651] ibid No. 211. *Henderson to Halifax* 24 August 1938. 177–179.
[652] There may be some discrepancy in translation as Hitler may have meant 'dictat'.
[653] G Weinberg, *The Foreign Policy of Hitler's Germany* (Chicago, University of Chicago Press, 1980) 640, 641.
[654] ibid 643. DBFP 1919–1939 Ser. 3. Vol 7. No 431. *Henderson to Halifax* 21 August 1938.
[655] Weinberg ibid 632–633.

appropriate method of solving difficulties. This was why Poland concluded pacts of non-aggression with Germany and Russia. Poland favoured conciliation to resolve this matter and would refrain from hostilities so long as Germany agreed to do so. Roosevelt ended the message by saying that countless lives could be saved if the Reich would agree to negotiate or conciliate, as Poland was willing to do.[656] Mr Berle, Assistant Secretary of State, commented that such action had 'the same effect as sending a Valentine to somebody's mother-in-law out of season'.[657] Chamberlain's message to Hitler in reply was to confirm that if the disputes between Germany and Poland were settled by peaceful means, then discussions could be undertaken as soon as possible.[658]

Behind the scenes, Henderson, yet again, as he did with the Czechs, was urging that the Poles make concessions, which was rejected.[659] He met Hitler again on 29 August and told him bluntly that it lay with him as to whether he preferred a unilateral solution, which would mean war as regards Poland, or British friendship.[660] Replying to the British note, Hitler demanded a response from Poland by 12 noon on 31 August, which was based on 16 Articles which had been rapidly read out by Ribbentrop in German to Henderson, who refused to give Henderson a written copy.[661] Henderson explained his heated meeting with Ribbentrop, who adopted the vituperation of Hitler.[662] Henderson had finally discovered how disingenuous Dahlerus[663] was when he told Göring that Henderson agreed with the German proposals. Hitler had postponed the invasion of Poland pending discussions with Britain and Mussolini's suggestion.[664] All this was a simple ruse to keep Britain neutral in any war with Poland. After that meeting, Henderson called Lipski at 2 am to request a meeting.[665] Lipski could not go but sent a colleague who returned with Sir Ogilvie-Forbes and Dahlerus, an amateur peace broker between the Nazis and Britain who demanded that Lipski see Göring.[666] Lipski was understandably suspicious of Dahlerus and affronted by this peremptory demand, that Poland agree to the 16 Articles. Hitler was demanding a plebiscite in Pomerania and demilitarisation of Danzig. Henderson and Ogilvie-Forbes pressed Lipski to get authority to see Ribbentrop to discuss this.[667] Henderson told Halifax that the terms sounded moderate to him because of Germany's desire for good relations with Britain.[668]

Despite the riposte from Lipski, Dahlerus continued his interventions with the British government by directly telephoning the Foreign Office to speak to Sir Horace Wilson, Chamberlain's adviser. Dahlerus said that he was telephoning from the British

[656] F Roosevelt, *The Public Papers and Addresses of Franklin D Roosevelt* 1939 Volume. War and Neutrality (London, Macmillan 1941) 449–450.
[657] W Langer and SE Gleeson, *The Challenge of Isolation 1937–1940* (New York, Harper and Brothers, 1952) 188–190; A Krock, *New York Times* 25 August 1939.
[658] DBFP 1919–1939 Ser. 3. Vol 7. No. 447. *Henderson to Halifax* 28 August 1938.
[659] G Weinberg, *The Foreign Policy of Hitler's Germany* (Chicago, University of Chicago Press, 1980) 644, 645. *Lipski Papers* 569–570.
[660] DBFP 1919–1939 Ser. 3. Vol 7. No. 455. *Henderson to Halifax* 29 August 1939.
[661] ibid No. 568. *Henderson to Halifax* 31 August 1939. Reported to Halifax in Nos. 574 and 575. *Henderson to Halifax*. 31 August 1939. Sent 5.15 am.
[662] DBFP 1919–1939 Ser. 3. Vol 3. No. 628. *Henderson to Halifax*. 31 August 1939.
[663] Swedish engineer and amateur diplomat friend of Hermann Göring, President of the German Parliament.
[664] DBFP 1919–1939 Ser. 3. Vol 3. No. 628. *Henderson to Halifax* 31 August 1939.
[665] W Jędrzejewicz (ed), *Diplomat in Berlin 1933–1939* (New York, Columbia University Press, 1968) 606.
[666] ibid 609.
[667] DBFP 1919–1939 Ser. 3. Vol 7. No. 575. *Henderson to Halifax* 31 August 1939.
[668] ibid No. 587. *Henderson to Halifax* 31 August 1939.

embassy in Berlin and that Henderson and Ogilvie-Forbes were in the room.[669] Without any regard whatsoever for secrecy, Dahlerus told Wilson that the Polish government would not give way and blamed the Poles for being obstructive.[670] Wilson was aware that the Germans would be listening in and indeed heard a German voice on the line. Dahlerus would not stop, so Wilson put down the phone. Dahlerus was probably a stooge for the Nazis used to undermine the Poles as they had undermined the Czechs by using Henlein.[671] It would be tempting for Chamberlain and Halifax to put their trust in Dahlerus as they had in Henlein to prevent war. What they, unlike Churchill, did not understand was that appeasement was seen as weakness, so much so that Hitler was told by Ribbentrop that Britain and France would not fight over Poland. Thus, they offered a supposed Anglo-German Agreement in consideration for the destruction of Poland. In addition to Dahlerus, the Nazis were aided by Mussolini who offered a Peace Conference on 5 September to revise the Treaty of Versailles.[672] Loraine, the British Ambassador in Rome, was warned by Halifax not to take any action.[673] Count Ciano, the Italian Foreign Minister, was in the room with Loraine when Loraine spoke to Halifax.[674] All these interventions were pointless since the Wehrmacht was easily overwhelming the ill-prepared Polish forces. Daladier who obviously felt guilt over Munich and the betrayal of France's treaty obligations to Czechoslovakia told Phipps that he had instructed his ambassador in Rome to tell Mussolini that his invitation 'to a second 'Munich' in Italy was rejected'.[675] That afternoon Henderson was invited to see Göring with Ogilvie-Forbes; Dahlerus was also present. Henderson requested that Lipski be given the 16 Articles so he could take instructions.[676]

Kennard told Halifax that Beck refused to go to Berlin to be treated like Beneš, but Lipski would seek a meeting with Weizsäcker or Ribbentrop.[677] At 7.41 pm Kennard reported that his Military Attaché was informed that 40 German Divisions were now deployed on the Polish border and that railway and telegraphic communications had been sabotaged.[678] At 10.25 pm in a further report, Kennard took exception to Henderson's views on the 16 Articles. He reminded Halifax of Britain's obligations to Poland and that the current demands were peremptory and humiliating, by which

[669] ibid No. 592. *Halifax to Henderson* 31 August 1939. Henderson cautioned by Halifax about this.

[670] ibid No. 591. *Halifax to Henderson* 31 August 1939 1 pm.

[671] Dahlerus was later proved to be such as when Dahlerus was subjected to cross-examination at the Nuremberg Trials by Sir David Maxwell Fyfe QC Dahlerus had to admit that he lied about the meeting that night with Lipski. Dahlerus had reported that Lipski told him that the Polish army would march on Berlin:

> Sir David Maxwell Fyfe: And did not Sir David Ogilvie-Forbes tell you that Lipski made his opinion quite clear, that the German offer was a breach of Polish sovereignty, and in his view Poland and France and England must stand firm and show a united front, and that Poland, if left alone, would fight and die alone?
>
> Dahlerus: Yes.
>
> And see: W Jędrzejewicz (ed), *Diplomat in Berlin 1933–1939* (New York, Columbia University Press, 1968) 609.

[672] DBFP 1919–1939 Ser. 3. Vol 7. No. 590. *Minute by Viscount Halifax* 31 August 1939.

[673] ibid No. 594. *Halifax to Lorraine* 31 August 1939. 1.15 pm. Loraine had suggested that the Danzig Question be decided by Britain.

[674] ibid No. 595. *Loraine to Halifax* 31 August 1939. 1.30 pm.

[675] ibid No. 604. *Phipps to Halifax* 31 August 1939. Received 4.40 pm.

[676] DBFP 1919–1939 Ser. 3. Vol 3. No. 613. *Henderson to Halifax* 31 August 1939.

[677] ibid No. 608. *Kennard to Halifax* 31 August 1939.

[678] ibid 612. *Kennard to Halifax* 31 August 1939.

Poland would have surrendered the principle that discussions must be 'free and equal'. Britain was pledged to sustain Polish independence. He inferred that if that obligation was ignored then there would be catastrophic repercussions.[679] By that time. however. the Nazis had occupied Danzig railway station and arrested the staff.[680] On 31 August at 9.15 pm Henderson received the German reply to the British note of 28 August requiring the Polish envoy to meet and conclude negotiations on the German demand for Danzig, a plebiscite on the Corridor, and Polish access to Gdansk.[681] Meanwhile Halifax telephoned Ciano explaining that Chamberlain could not put pressure on the Poles to surrender Danzig.[682]

Lipski was not able to see Ribbentrop until 6.30 pm on 31 August,[683] the same time as the Wehrmacht received the order to attack Poland without any declaration of war and the guns of the *Schleswig Holstein* fired its salvos on the Westerplatte in Danzig. That evening the British Consul in Danzig reported on the arrest of several Polish officials by the Gestapo.[684] The diplomatic and consular Corps were given safe conduct and a Gestapo escort out of Danzig to go to Lithuania.[685]

In Washington, Lord Lothian presented his ambassadorial credentials to President Roosevelt. In his report to Halifax that day, he wrote that American public opinion would be seriously upset if it was perceived that Britain was putting pressure on Poland and France to abandon their vital interests.[686]

iii. The Attack on Poland

At 8.20 am on Friday 1 September, the French Ambassador in Warsaw, Leon Noel, reported that German forces had crossed the Corridor and had enveloped Danzig. At 8.30 am he reported that the German armies were attacking on all fronts and the Luftwaffe was bombing indiscriminately.[687] At 8.30 am Kennard reported to Halifax that Cracow, Katowice and other cities were bombed at 6 am that morning.[688] When the German armies attacked Poland, they had 3,000 tanks and 103 army divisions.[689] The Joint Planning Committee of the Chief of Staff (JPC) had warned Chamberlain's government of a *blitzkrieg* war and that Britain would be susceptible to aerial attack, so Chamberlain was well aware of the risks.[690]

[679] ibid No. 618. *Kennard to Halifax* 31 August 1939.

[680] French Yellow Book. No. 316. *Noel to Bonnet* 31 August 1939, 9.55 pm.

[681] DBFP 1919–1939 Ser. 3. Vol 3. No. 662. *Henderson to Halifax* 31 August 1939. (R. 11.55pm) and No. 619. *Henderson to Halifax* 31 August 1939. (R. 10.45pm).

[682] DBFP 1919–1939 Ser. 3. Vol 3. No. 627. *Minute by Viscount Halifax* 31 August 1939.

[683] G Weinberg, *The Foreign Policy of Hitler's Germany* (Chicago, University of Chicago Press, 1980) 645 and W Jędrzejewicz (ed), *Diplomat in Berlin 1933–1939* (New York, Columbia University Press, 1968) 609. Lipski could not communicate with Warsaw as all communications were cut. See: DBFP 1919–1939 Ser. 3. Vol 3. No. 639.

[684] Geheime Staatspolizei-Reich Secret Police.

[685] DBFP 1919–1939 Ser. 3. Vol 3. No. 607. *Shepherd to Halifax* 31 August 1939. 9.30pm.

[686] DBFP 1919–1939 Ser. 3. Vol 7. No. 568. *Lothian to Halifax* 31 August 1939.

[687] French Yellow Book. Nos. 322 and 323. *Noel to Bonnet* 1 September 1939.

[688] DBFP 1919–1939 Ser. 3. Vol 3. No. 638. *Kennard to Halifax* 1 September 1939.

[689] W Wark, *The Ultimate Enemy* (Oxford, OUP, 1986) 111. Hitler called the invasion a 'police operation'. Reichstag Speech 1 September 1939.

[690] Warkibid 195–197.

Amid all this, Dahlerus telephoned the Foreign Office. He said he arranged a meeting for 10 am between Henderson and Hitler and that Ogilvie-Forbes and Dahlerus should come to London to give proof of Polish intransigence. He suggested they take back an intermediary, General Ironside, with Ogilvie-Forbes and a French representative to negotiate between the Poles and the Reich on the condition the Polish representative was in the Polish Embassy in Berlin. The Polish representative would deal through the British and French representatives.[691] This resembled a reinvention of the Runciman Mission, but why were the Nazis so keen on this? Halifax confirmed to M Corbin that there was no doubt as to the application of the British Guarantee.[692] Dahlerus again telephoned Sir Alexander Cadogan at the Foreign Office at 12.20 pm to say that no doubt Halifax knew the fighting was begun by the Polish forces. He said he had seen Göring and Hitler, and Hitler did not want a world war but wished to discuss matters with Britain and to know whether Britain would act as a mediator. Dahlerus again offered to fly over with Ogilvie-Forbes. Cadogan saw no point in this. Dahlerus said it was his last-minute attempt to avert a catastrophe. Cadogan said it was not Britain's fault that possibilities for discussion had come to an end.[693] Here again we see the Nazi tactic of trying to isolate the war on Poland and then draw Britain into another Munich-type debacle. This time Hitler and Ribbentrop were mistaken and underestimated the strength of public disgust in Britain against another Munich, yet Dahlerus persisted and telephoned again at 1.25 pm.[694]

> Mr. Dahlerus rang up at 1.25, and I gave him the following message: -
>
> Nothing to be done on lines indicated: matter has been taken out of our hands.
>
> Any idea of mediation while German troops are invading Poland is quite out of the question.
>
> The only way in which a world war can be stopped is (1) that hostilities be suspended and (2) German troops should be immediately withdrawn from Polish territory.

In Berlin, Henderson said that he could do no more and that: 'Last hope lies in inflexible determination on our part to resist force by force.'[695] Roosevelt addressed an appeal to the belligerents and to Britain, France and Italy to refrain from bombing civilian targets.[696] At 4.45 pm Dahlerus again telephoned the Foreign Office. He spoke on behalf of Göring and said that if England did not bomb open cities, the Germans would not do so. Luftwaffe attacks would be confined to aerodromes and fortifications and not civilian populations despite the Germans' indiscriminate bombing of cities in Poland. He anticipated a solution in a few days. He could come to London at any time. He was offered an official decoration, but he refused the offer.[697] At the same time, Halifax sent Henderson instructions to expect a warning note to Ribbentrop. He then sent Henderson the warning at 5.45 pm not an ultimatum, which ended:[698]

[691] DBFP 1919–1939 Ser. 3. Vol 3. No. 639. *Record of Conversation (Mr Spencer)* 1 September 1939.
[692] French Yellow Book. No. 329. *Corbin (London) to Bonnet* 1 September 1939 12.15 pm.
[693] DBFP 1919–1939 Ser. 3. Vol 3. No. 651 *Minute by Sir A Cadogan* 1 September 1939.
[694] ibid No. 652. *Minute by Sir A Cadogan* 1 September 1939.
[695] ibid No. 658. *Henderson to Halifax* 1 September 1939.
[696] French Yellow Book. No. 325. *Appeal of President Roosevelt to Great Britain, France, Italy Germany and Poland* 1 September 1939.
[697] DBFP 1919–1939 Ser. 3. Vol 3. No. 663. *Record of a message from Mr. Dahlerus* 1 September 1939.
[698] ibid Nos. 664 and 669. *Halifax to Henderson* 1 September 1939.

> I am accordingly to inform Your Excellency that unless the German Government are prepared to give His Majesty's Government satisfactory assurances that the German Government has suspended all aggressive action against Poland and are prepared promptly to withdraw their forces from Polish territory, His Majesty's Government in the United Kingdom will without hesitation fulfil their obligations to Poland.

Henderson was instructed that if the German reply was unsatisfactory, the next stage would be either an ultimatum with a time limit order or an immediate declaration of war.

At 2.47 am on 2 September, Kennard sent a request to Halifax on behalf of the Polish government requesting support under the guarantee.[699] The French were delaying announcement of a declaration of war as it required the approval of Parliament. Halifax told Corbin that the ambassadors could deliver the declaration.[700] At 12.30 pm Halifax then informed Phipps that he had no intention of waiting, but Phipps said the French General Staff required 48 hours after the declaration of war to be ready for operations.[701] The Italian government's proposals for a suspension of hostilities and a conference were being given further consideration by the French, but Britain's position was clear: no further discussions unless the German forces were withdrawn from Poland.[702] At 4 pm Kennard sent a request that the Poles urgently required military aid, especially the aircraft they had purchased.[703] At 5 pm Bonnet telephoned Cadogan and said that the French would have to consider Britain's condition for a conference subject to the withdrawal of German forces. Cadogan pressed him for a decision on the ultimatum. Bonnet denied that the Poles had requested French assistance.[704] Halifax telephoned Phipps in Paris at 6 pm and told him that a 48-hour delay was unacceptable. Phipps should persuade Daladier that the ultimatum should expire at midnight that night because further delay would inhibit naval dispositions. Phipps explained that evacuations were in process and that, according to Bonnet, the Poles would accept a 24-hour time limit.[705] At 6.38 pm Halifax rang Count Ciano stating Britain's conditions for a conference namely the withdrawal of German troops from Poland and the reversion of Danzig to the status quo.[706] At 8 pm Kennard reported on a meeting with Beck and the French Ambassador. Poland urgently required some diversion on the western front to relieve pressure on the Polish forces that lacked air cover. He pressed Halifax about a declaration of war.[707] At 9.30 pm Halifax was informed that Mussolini was not prepared to press Hitler regarding the withdrawal of German forces.[708] Facing a divided cabinet and an outraged House of Commons, Chamberlain telephoned Daladier at 9.50 pm and told him that if the French government were to insist on a time-limit of 48 hours to run

[699] ibid No 693. *Kennard to Halifax* 2 September 1939.

[700] ibid No 693. *Kennard to Halifax* 2 September 1939 and French Yellow Book. No. 354. *Corbin to Bonnet* 2 September 1939.

[701] DBFP 1919–1939 Ser. 3. Vol 3. No. 700. *Halifax to Phipps* 2 September 1939 and No. 708. *Phipps to Halifax* 2 September 1939.

[702] French Yellow Book. No. 354. *Corbin to Bonnet* 2 September 1939.

[703] DBFP 1919–1939 Ser. 3. Vol 3. No. 705. *Kennard to Halifax*. 2 September 1939.

[704] ibid No. 718. *Telephone Record: Bonnet to Cadogan* 2 September 1939.

[705] ibid No. 727. *Minute by Sir A Cadogan* 2 September 1939.

[706] ibid No. 728. *Minute by Mr Jebb* 2 September 1939.

[707] ibid No. 735. *Kennard to Halifax* 2 September 1939.

[708] ibid No. 693. *Loraine to Halifax* 2 September 1939.

from midday on 3 September, it would be impossible for his government to hold the situation: he proposed as a compromise that he should announce that ambassadors had been instructed to present an ultimatum at 8 am on 3 September with time to expire at 12 noon.[709] At 10 pm Halifax saw the Polish Ambassador, but could not confirm a time for the declaration, and at 10.30 pm Halifax telephoned M Bonnet about the announcement to be made in the House of Commons and the time limit to be inserted in the ultimatum. It was agreed that Henderson should present the British ultimatum at 8 am on 3 September, to expire at 12 noon, and the French Ambassador should present the French ultimatum at midday to expire at whatever time French government liked.[710]

Kennard made further reports as to the deteriorating conditions in Poland and at 3.26 am on 3 September, he reported very heavy civilian casualties, with 27 Polish towns bombed. He reminded Halifax of support required under the Anglo-Polish Treaty.[711] This report was not received until 12.30 pm by which time Britain was at war with Germany. At 12.25 am that morning Halifax directed Henderson to see Ribbentrop at 9 am.[712] At 5 am, Halifax directed Henderson as follows:[713]

> Please seek interview with Minister for Foreign Affairs at 9.0 a.m. today, Sunday or, if he cannot see you then, arrange to convey at that time to representative of German Government the communication contained in my telegram No. 320.
>
> If the assurance referred to in that communication is received, you should inform me by any means at your disposal before 11.0 a.m. today, September 3. If no such assurance is received here by 11.0 a.m., we shall inform the German Representative that a state of war exists as from that hour, and you shall at that time act in accordance with the war instructions under the telegrams.

At 9.45 am Halifax received confirmation from Henderson that he had presented the British ultimatum to Dr Schmidt, who was acting on behalf of Ribbentrop.[714] Dahlerus telephoned the Foreign Office 10.50 am. As a last resort he suggested that Göring fly to London to discuss matters. Halifax saw no point in further discussions. Dahlerus said the German reply was on its way.[715] At 11.20 am Coulondre, the French Ambassador in Berlin, was given the German reply refusing to withdraw from Poland.[716] Consequently, Britain was at war with Germany at 11 am on Sunday 3 September 1939 and France at war with Germany at 5 pm that day.

iv. Chamberlain: Wrong Man at the Wrong Time

Chamberlain has been much criticised by historians writing after the events. Toynbee considered that Chamberlain believed he could stop the armaments race by settling German grievances. Chamberlain had no experience in settling disputes between states

[709] ibid No. 740. *Minute by Sir A Cadogan* 2 September 1939.
[710] ibid No. 741. *Minute by Sir A Cadogan* 2 September 1939.
[711] ibid No. 755. *Kennard to Halifax* 3 September 1939.
[712] ibid No. 752. *Halifax to Henderson* 3 September 1939.
[713] ibid No. 756. *Halifax to Henderson* 3 September 1939.
[714] ibid No. 760. *Henderson to Halifax* 3 September 1939.
[715] ibid No. 762. *Minute by Sir A Cadogan* 2 September 1939.
[716] ibid No. 763. *Minute by Mr Jebb* 2 September 1939.

as a Birmingham businessman who was used to negotiation between those who would honour their agreements. But here he faced a genocidal dictator on matters of war or peace. No doubt Chamberlain sincerely believed that it was morally right to avoid another Armageddon like the war to end all wars. Clearly, the masses supported his many attempts to stop war in Central Europe in 1938, and although some argue that Britain lost an ally in Czechoslovakia with a strong army and good defence, and France and Russia guaranteed Czechoslovakian independence, others argue to the contrary.[717] Russia was not trusted by Chamberlain, but then they could not trust him as he kept Maisky in London in the dark. By the time Russia considered helping Czechoslovakia, as Litvinov remarked, Czechoslovakia had already been sold down the river. Chamberlain even told Jan Masaryk he trusted Hitler more than Benes. Whilst Chamberlain may have believed in mediation and conciliation, these approaches could only work between willing, equal states. He mistakenly trusted Hitler and thought he could do business with him and strike a bargain for peace at any price without regard to the consequences for the people betrayed into Nazi captivity. Little did Chamberlain realise the misery and suffering his betrayal of the Sudetenland would cause. Many Czechs fled their homes and businesses in Sudetenland to Prague only to be turned back at Hitler's demand, returning to concentration camps and worse.[718] Chamberlain completely misinterpreted the deviousness of Hitler's strategy. He thought Hitler had 'put Danzig in cold storage', and as late as 23 July 1939, he wrote his sister that: '… the time is not ripe for the major war' and[719]

> what you need are defensive forces sufficiently strong enough to make it impossible for the other side to win except at such a cost to make it not worthwhile.

Chamberlain misjudged Hitler even after the disavowal of the Munich Agreement and Hitler's promises of no further demands and numerous transgressions of the Versailles and Locarno Treaties, and worse, he knew the necessity of deterrence and yet failed time and again to hasten rearmament, knowing the strength of the Nazi forces. It is sobering to reflect on those times, and it is easy in hindsight to second-guess decision-makers. Despite all the warnings from Rumbold, Phipps, Vansittart, Churchill and his colleagues Harold Nicolson, Julian Amory, Harold Macmillan, and Ronald Tree, Chamberlain failed to understand Hitler and what he was trying to do. They accepted assurances instead of reading his book *Mein Kampf*.[720] Chamberlain's rejection of experienced professional advice and failure to heed warnings from many sources begs the question as to whether earlier rearmament might have lessened the effects of blitzkrieg. Above all, as Kercher remarks:[721]

> The generation of British diplomats that achieved maturity before the Great War understood that Britain had to work with powers that shared its interests. Such cooperation permitted the maintenance of the balances of power in the world vital to British security. But as Chamberlain

[717] J Simon, *Retrospect the Memoirs of the Rt Hon Viscount Simon* (London, Hutchinson, 1952).
[718] J Wheeler-Bennett, *Knaves, Fools and Heroes* (London, Macmillan, 1974) 143.
[719] Z Steiner, *The Triumph of the Dark* (Oxford, Oxford University Press, 2011) 819–820.
[720] D Cooper, *The Second World War* (London, Jonathan Cape, 1939) 333.
[721] BJC McKercher, 'The Foreign Office and British Diplomacy' (2004) 18(2) *Contemporary British History* 104.

> showed after mid-1937, and as Lloyd George showed before late 1922, 'old diplomacy' worked only if there was political will to utilise it. In the 1930s, only Vansittart and the Foreign Office produced realistic policies able to protect British interests.

It must also be remembered that at that time, as Paul Kennedy wrote in *Strategy and Diplomacy*, Britain's approach changed because Britain was steadily losing her dominant role in world affairs, becoming democratised and recognising that a conciliatory approach was a great advantage rather than the use or threat of force. The Empire was becoming more of a burden than a benefit economically. In the context of the interwar years, appeasement may have been the legacy of 'Old Diplomacy' in terms of respect for international law and fair play as well as the national interest.[722] Similarly, Zara Steiner concluded that Britain adopted an approaching war settlement of international disputes 'through rational negotiation and compromise'.[723] Such is not possible. as this episode teaches us, when you are dealing with a genocidal despot and a fanatical militaristic race who ignore and despise the international rule of law and prefer war as a means of dispute settlement.

The final indictment of Chamberlain's policy in military terms and his failure to prepare the country for an inevitable war may be left to someone qualified to make that charge. In his *War Diaries*, Field Marshal Lord Alanbrooke commented on his return from France in July 1940 that:[724]

> 1 July 1940
>
> … It is now 10 months and yet the shortage of trained men and of equipment is appalling! At present I fail to see how we can make this country safe against attack.
>
> 2 July 1940
>
> Touring round southern command for which he was then responsible he commented:
>
> The more I see the nakedness of our defences the more appalled I am! Untrained men, no arms, no transport, and no equipment. And yet there are masses of men in uniform in this country but they are mostly untrained, why I cannot think after 10 months of war.

A second indictment of the British government's failure to provide adequate defence after 1932 can be made in respect of the unpreparedness for war when it was clear to many that war was inevitable. Whilst some mitigation can be raised for reliance on the strength of the French armies, British sea power and emphasis rightly on increased aircraft construction, the fact remains that French strategy was defensive rather than aggressive and their forces relied too much on the Maginot Line, completely disregarding the lessons of Captain Liddell Hart[725] on rapid armoured deployment supported by coordinated infantry and attack aircraft. Owing to the overwhelming onslaught through the Ardennes and then the rapid Wehrmacht advance to the channel ports, the BEF was cut off from the southern French armies. It was forced back from its defensive line on the River Doyle so that when the Belgian army surrendered and the French failed to break through from the south, the BEF had no choice but to retreat to the

[722] P Kennedy, *Strategy and Diplomacy 1870–1945* (London, George Allen and Unwin, 1983) 30.
[723] Z Steiner, *The Triumph of the Dark* (Oxford, Oxford University Press, 2011) 647.
[724] A Danchev and D Todman (eds), *War Diaries 1939–1945 Field Marshal Lord Alanbrooke* (London, Weidenfeld & Nicolson, 2001) 90.
[725] BH Liddell Hart, *The Memoirs of Captain Liddell Hart*, Vols I and II (London, Cassell, 1965).

channel ports and try to escape. In doing so and saving 360,000 men, it lost 2,472 guns, 63,879 vehicles, 20,548 motorcycles, 76,697 tonnes of ammunition, 415,940 tonnes of supplies and stores, and 164,929 tonnes of petrol, and the RAF lost 430 fighter aircraft. The figures speak for themselves.[726] Whilst the BEF was so equipped, it was totally outmanoeuvred and outgunned by the overwhelming Nazi *blitzkrieg*. Even between September 1939 and April 1940, Chamberlain hesitated to increase armament production and even failed to counter Nazi propaganda.[727] There can be little doubt as to the consequences of his appeasement policies and those of his government, enabled by an atmosphere of complacency and illusory isolationism or more accurately described by Lord Dannatt and Robert Lyman as a failure of strategic vision as much as it was of profound ignorance of the dynamics of power in Europe and its implications for British security.[728]

[726] P Goodhart, *Fifty Ships that Saved the World* (Portsmouth, Heinemann, 1965).

[727] J Wheeler-Bennett, *Special Relationships* (London, Macmillan 1975) 152. See also: Sir C Stuart, *Secrets of Crewe House*.

[728] R Dannatt and R Lyman, *Victory to Defeat, The British Army 1918–40* (Oxford, Osprey Publishing, 2023) 192.

5

American and Japanese Relations

I. American Foreign Policy

In December 1862, during the American Civil War, President Lincoln wisely declared that: 'this nation cannot escape history'. If the history of American foreign policy had been appreciated as Walter Lippmann suggested, it would have been better prepared for its entry into the Second World War.

When Walter Lippmann worked under Colonel House's direction on President Wilson's peace terms, he did not foresee that the transfer of the German possessions in the Pacific to Japan would threaten US security. In his view, US foreign policy had never had clear direction: it failed to determine its true interest. The US was unable to prepare adequately for war to safeguard the peace. The US had extended its commitments as a consequence of the Spanish-American War, acquiring territories in the far Pacific 7,000 miles from California.[1] The country was unable to prepare for war and consolidate the victory. Writing as he did in 1943, Lippmann warned, echoing the words of Alexander Hamilton, that if there was no settled foreign policy 'the course of foreign policy depended not on reflection and choice but on accident and force'.[2] The US was vulnerable to attack in the Pacific region in the Philippines, Guam, Midway, Wake and the Hawaiian Islands. These were not sufficiently protected against surprise attack, although the defences at Pearl Harbor and in the Philippines were formidable. In 1941 the forces were on a peacetime footing and, despite warnings, unprepared for attacks. The US was weak insofar as it did not have any military alliances, unlike the Tripartite Pact of Japan, Italy and Nazi Germany.[3] It did not have the force necessary to deter, prevent, or win a war.

Lippmann opined that statesmanship is about achieving the balance. If the country's ends and means are not brought into balance, it will end in disaster.[4] He recalled how it was Benjamin Franklin who negotiated a treaty with France to support the English colonies until independence and that in 1779 Spain had used New Orleans as a base to attack the British in West Florida and seize their posts. In 1780 the Netherlands declared war on Britain. Russia formed a League of Neutrality against

[1] W Lippmann, *US Foreign Policy* (London, Hamish Hamilton, 1943) 1.
[2] ibid 2.
[3] ibid 4. The Anti-Comintern Pact between Germany and Japan was signed on 25 November 1937 which was aimed at Russia.
[4] W Lippmann, *US Foreign Policy* (London, Hamish Hamilton, 1943) 5.

Britain, so deflecting British naval forces.[5] In context, the colonies achieved independence through a world war. Yorktown surrendered on 17 October 1781, but the general war was not concluded until 3 September 1783.[6] The US took possession of Louisiana on 30 April 1803. In 1819 it took Spanish possessions east of the Mississippi and Oregon. In 1846, Texas joined the Union. In 1848 California, Nevada, Arizona, and Utah were ceded by Mexico to the US. France and Spain were excluded from the Western Hemisphere. President Monroe declared that the US would resist the creation of any new European empires in the Western Hemisphere.[7] This was directed against France, Spain, Russia and Austria. This could not have been achieved without the support of the British navy. Madison and Jefferson approved of this secret undertaking by Britain's Foreign Secretary George Canning.[8] During the Civil War, Britain supplied arms to both belligerents.[9] Thomas Jefferson had warned that if a European Power 'came out of Europe' to attack Russia or Britain, then this would concern the US national interest.[10] The US was concerned with 'world affairs' in this context, not necessarily 'European affairs.'[11]

A. Extending Westwards Beyond the Limits of the Monroe Doctrine

In 1844 Caleb Cushing negotiated a treaty with China giving the US trade access to the treaty ports. In 1853 a naval squadron procured trading rights from the Japanese. Midway was acquired in 1859. In 1867 Seward purchased Alaska from Russia.[12] In 1878, the US established a coaling station in Samoa, and in 1885, by the Treaty of Paris, the Philippines were taken,[13] and in 1888, Guam. In 1893–98 the Hawaiian Islands were acquired. In 1899 the US opposed any dismemberment of China – 'Open Door Policy.'

The US had committed its defences from Greenland to Brazil, from Canada to Argentina, and from Alaska to Luzon. Her interests could not be properly defended. Thus, Lippmann concluded:

> From the day when Admiral Dewey sailed into Manila Bay until the day when General Wainwright surrendered Corregidor the United States never made a tactical or prudent or remotely adequate effort to bring its obligations and its power into balance.[14]

Lippmann wrote that from 1823 to 1898, the US lived in: 'Illusory isolation', employing the Monroe Doctrine but practically dependent on the British navy.[15]

[5] ibid 7.
[6] ibid 8.
[7] ibid 9.
[8] ibid 11.
[9] M Reynolds, *Instruments of Peacemaking. 1870–1914* (Oxford, Hart Publishing, 2021) and W Lippmann, *US Foreign Policy* (London, Hamish Hamilton, 1943) 13.
[10] Lippmann ibid 99.
[11] ibid.
[12] ibid 14.
[13] ibid 15.
[14] ibid 17.
[15] ibid 19.

B. American Isolationism and Japanese Expansionism

i. Naval Limitations

After 1918 the US became more vulnerable to attack with the reduction of the British and American navies. The Treaty of Washington 1922 limited the number of battleships and aircraft carriers each nation could maintain. It placed no limitation upon cruisers, destroyers, submarines, or aeroplanes. According to Senator Walsh, the US scrapped approximately $300,000,000 worth of naval vessels: seven new battleships in the process of construction; four new battle cruisers in the process of construction; four dreadnoughts; and 15 pre-dreadnoughts; a total of 30 vessels were destroyed.

It was this treaty and subsequent treaties that provided for a 5-5-3 ratio in certain categories between Great Britain, America, and Japan. Importantly, the treaty also provided for the maintenance of the status quo of naval bases and fortifications in the Pacific area. The London Treaty of 1930 extended the limitation to cruisers, destroyers, and submarines and made other slight modifications to the 1922 Treaty.[16] This increased the risk to the US, as Japan had seized former German and Spanish possessions in the Pacific in 1914, which could threaten Hawaii and the Philippines. The bases in Manila and Guam were not developed. The British navy found it difficult to protect the Mediterranean and the Far East against the forces of Japan, Italy and Germany.[17]

a. Relations with Japan

By Resolution 166 of 18 July 1939, the US abrogated its commercial treaty with Japan[18] following a series of aggressive actions by the Tripartite Pact: the seizure of Manchuria in 1931, the Italian conquest of Abyssinia in 1935, the Nazis intervention in the Spanish Civil War, the Nazi reoccupation of the Rhineland, and the Anti-Comintern Pact of 1936[19] of Germany and Japan, followed by the invasion of China in 1937.[20] President Roosevelt sounded the alarm that year with his Quarantine Speech. There was an obvious need to reinforce Alaska, Guam, the Philippines and Panama and also to ally with Britain, France and China, but nothing happened.[21] It seemed to Walter Lippmann that the American people could not agree to protect their vital interests because they had no foreign policy.[22] Roosevelt found it difficult to persuade the people, and more particularly the Congress. He could do little until Japan had conquered the Chinese coast, had invaded the Philippines, and was ready to attack Singapore, Burma and the

[16] D Walsh, *The Decline and Renaissance of The Navy,1922–1944.* Prepared by Senator David I Walsh, Chairman of the Committee on Naval Affairs United States Senate 'Brief History of Naval Legislation from 1922 to 1944 Pointing Out the Policy of the Government During These Years and Steps Taken in Recent Years to Rebuild Our Navy to its Present Strength.' Presented by Mr Walsh of Massachusetts 7 June 1944 (Legislative Day, May 9). United States Government Printing Office Washington: 1944.

[17] W Lippmann, *US Foreign Policy* (London, Hamish Hamilton, 1943) 36.

[18] ibid 26.

[19] The Anti-Comintern Pact was concluded between Germany and Japan in November 1936 and then between Italy, Germany, and Japan a year later aimed at the Soviet Union.

[20] W Lippmann, *US Foreign Policy* (London, Hamish Hamilton, 1943) 27.

[21] ibid.

[22] ibid.

East Indies; France had fallen; and Britain was threatened with invasion. The Congress obstructed the repeal of the arms embargo, the Lend-Lease legislation, the transfer of destroyers for bases to Britain, and any movement towards conscription as well as the repeal of neutrality laws. People were still fixated on isolationism, oblivious to their commitments 7,000 miles off the West Coast[23] and any understanding of the need for allies to fight against the power of the totalitarian allies.[24] Whilst there was a potential threat in the East it was events in Europe that were of more concern.

b. Hitler's Rise

In Germany the success of the National Socialists in the 1932 Reichstag elections brought Hitler to power. In 1933 he became Chancellor, converting his country into a militaristic, ultranationalist dictatorship. Hitler became Chancellor of Germany the day after Roosevelt explained his foreign policy objectives to the British Ambassador.[25] Anticipating Hitler's belligerence, Roosevelt issued a letter to the heads of the 54 nations attending a disarmament conference in Geneva. He suggested that each nation pledge an intention to disarm, sign a non-aggression pact, and affirm that they would send no armed force across their frontiers.[26] In his speech to the Reichstag on 17 May 1933, Hitler declared that Germany was ready to join a solemn non-aggression pact and referred to the magnanimous proposal of the US as 'a guarantor of peace'. In the Geneva discussions, Ambassador Norman Davis declared that the US would be willing to consult with other states in case there were a threat to peace,[27] and if it concurred in the judgement that the nation was violating its international obligations, the US would do nothing to interfere with collective efforts to restore peace. Unfortunately, these promises were undermined by the Republicans in the Congress preventing Roosevelt from declaring an arms embargo against any aggressor.[28]

c. Isolationism

Domestic economic priorities prevented Roosevelt from developing his foreign policy at this time. Protectionism and isolationism were the order of the day in the 1920s and 1930s and any overt intervention in Europe was seen as reactionary, militaristic, and imperialistic.[29] Peace, disarmament, and non-intervention weighed against collective security. Disarmament meant the US was inadequately protected and armed.[30] Non-intervention and collective security inhibited it from making

[23] ibid 28.
[24] ibid 29.
[25] F Freidel, *Rendezvous With Destiny* (Boston, Little Brown and Company, 1990) 111.
[26] ibid 114.
[27] ibid. Davis was a Democrat and a strong internationalist supporting the League of Nations and the World Court and advocated the reduction of tariffs. In 1921 he helped organise the Council on Foreign Relations. He led a League commission in 1924 which settled a dispute over the Baltic port of Memel. He was a delegate to the Geneva Economic Conference of 1927 and at the second London Naval Conference (1935–36) and headed the delegation to the Nine-Power Treaty Conference of 1937 at Brussels.
[28] F Freidel, *Rendezvous with Destiny* (Boston, Little Brown and Company, 1990) 115.
[29] W Lippmann, *US Foreign Policy* (London, Hamish Hamilton, 1943) 30.
[30] ibid.

alliances. General Washington's warning as to 'entangling alliances' was contrary to the colonies' alliance with France, the question of the Louisiana purchase and the Monroe Doctrine.[31] He believed it should be directed by: 'the national interest guided by justice'.[32]

Roosevelt's options were limited, and his uncompromising message to London objecting to currency stabilisation, which would reduce gold reserves,[33] together with the diktat of Adolf Hitler wrecked the conference and further disappointed France and Britain.[34] Whilst in the first 100 days Roosevelt had restored public confidence at home, he was unable to reduce tensions abroad. In July 1934, fearing a fresh British devaluation, Roosevelt resorted to unilateral stabilisation. He told Morgenthau[35] that if the Nazis' inhuman aggressions should extend to England, the US would help.[36] He kept his word. It may be, as Lippmann said, that the pacifist nation can discern itself, but not its enemies. It was the pacifist ideal that ignored the invasion of Manchuria in 1931 and the invasion of Poland in 1939 and encouraged the ambitions of the aggressors and contributed to the war.[37] The same charge can be laid against Foreign Secretaries Simon, Hoare and Halifax, although the latter certainly appreciated the danger. Simon and Hoare had the opportunity to support the Little Entente and the Franco-Soviet Treaty but apparently let their political prejudice override the national security interest. The pacifists played into Hitler's hands regarding Sudetenland, Czechoslovakia, Austria, Indochina, the Rhineland, and the neutralisation of Russia in 1939, laying the ground for domination.

d. Strategic Interests

Henry Stimson observed that Europe suffered from a 'moral abdication' and 'extraordinary weakness and cowardice' juxtaposed by isolationism and disillusionment in what the US gained in World War I: people did not want any repeat. According to Stimpson, he has sailed 'the wave of ostrich-like isolationism which are swept over us'. Neutrality laws, he wrote, imposed a 'dead level of neutral conduct' on the country, giving it a policy of 'amoral drift'. When the war started in September 1939, he commented that at the end of 'hopeless years of concession appeasement', Europe's democracies were forced to come to grips with the consequences of their failure to recognise reality before it overwhelmed them with crushing force.[38] Until early 1940, continental defence of the US had been a priority, as confirmed by the Defence Plan Rainbow 1. By 1940 that changed when the subjugation of the continent became a reality when Hitler's blitzkrieg swept through the lowlands and northern France. General Marshall advised that 'we have to be prepared to meet the worst situation that may develop, that is, if we

[31] ibid 31.
[32] ibid 32.
[33] F Freidel, *Rendezvous With Destiny* (Boston, Little Brown and Company, 1990) 116.
[34] ibid 117. It was applauded by John Maynard Keynes and Winston Churchill.
[35] Henry Morgenthau was US Treasury Secretary (1934–45).
[36] F Freidel, *Rendezvous With Destiny* (Boston, Little Brown and Company, 1990) 118.
[37] W Lippmann, *US Foreign Policy* (London, Hamish Hamilton, 1943) 33.
[38] H Stimson, *Stimson Diaries* 17 April 1932. S Dunn, *A Blueprint for War: FDR and the Hundred Days that Mobilised America* (Yale University Press,2018) 36.

do not have the allied fleet in the Atlantic'. Marshall was impressed by Britain's strong resistance and concluded that 'as long as the British fleet remains undefeated and England holds out the Western Hemisphere is in little danger of direct attack'.[39] From the American point of view, the northern approaches to the US were related to the air and sea power of Britain. If Iceland and Greenland had fallen to the Nazis, then the US would be threatened.[40] Britain had the overriding control of strategic entrances to the Mediterranean, the Indian Ocean via Cape Town, and the South Atlantic and South Pacific via the Falkland Islands, and therefore, Britain must inevitably go to the defence of the US as Walter Lippmann opined, or the British Commonwealth would dissolve.[41] In June 1940, Stimpson was invited by Roosevelt to join the cabinet as Minister of War. In June 1940, Roosevelt also invited Frank Knox to join the cabinet as Secretary of the Navy. Frank Knox had been a Rough Rider with Theodore Roosevelt at the battle of San Juan Hill and served as an army Colonel in France in World War I. Knox was very much a realist who publicly demanded action against the 'alien dogs of war that snarl and fight in murdering packs'. He emphasised also that it was not 'what we say but what we do that counts'.[42]

e. Efforts to Contain Japanese Advances

It may be argued that if the US had been at war with Japan and Germany from June 1940, it could not have provided the support to Britain to defend itself against the Nazi onslaught. The same might also be argued about the onslaught on Russia. As it was, it might be argued that American diplomacy and statesmanship delayed the Japanese attack on America, giving America time to evaluate Japanese intentions. Unfortunately, its intelligence services had marginal success in interpreting Japanese intentions, let alone a surprise attack at Pearl Harbor. Japan's tendency towards belligerence was evident by its breach of the conditions of its League of Nations mandates regarding the dredging of harbours and construction of seaplane ramps in the Marianas, the Carolinas, and the Marshals. Fortifying these islands surrounding Guam and menacing Wake Island constituted a threat to America's Pacific lifeline.[43]

Trying to avoid war with a hostile and increasingly militaristic regime in Tokyo was difficult, but efforts were made after January 1940, when trade relations deteriorated. Roosevelt foresaw this from his first cabinet meeting when he referred to the possibility of a war with Japan. He adopted Hoover's 'Stimson Doctrine' that the US would not recognise Japan's conquest of Manchuria.[44] By 1940, Roosevelt would have liked to have gone further and issued embargoes against Japan, but America was still isolationist and did not want to sever commercial relations with Japan. The government would be

[39] S Dunn, *A Blueprint for War: FDR and the Hundred Days that Mobilised America* (New Haven, Yale University Press, 2018) 43.

[40] W Lippmann, *US Foreign Policy* (London, Hamish Hamilton, 1943) 75.

[41] ibid 76.

[42] S Dunn, *A Blueprint for War: FDR and the Hundred Days that Mobilised America* (New Haven, Yale University Press, 2018) 38.

[43] R Smith Thompson, *A Time of War: Franklin Roosevelt and the Path to Pearl Harbor* (New York, Prentice Hall Press, 1991) 309.

[44] F Friedel, *A Rendezvous with Destiny* (New York, Little, Brown and Company, 1990) 109.

accused of warmongering, and some wanted it both ways. The fact was, as Cordell Hull noted:

> that any half-informed person should have known that our Navy during those years of armament by the aggressor nations was not satisfactorily prepared to station itself for anytime in the far eastern waters.[45]

In October 1940, the US refused all licences for shipment of iron and steel scrap of any kind to Japan, having restricted other basic materials. The problem for Roosevelt was that he was inhibited in promoting substantial increases in defence expenditure by the isolationists until after the November 1940 election. He was aware of the shortcomings and the criticism of the navy in its vulnerability in the face of a two-front war with inadequate naval forces to guard both the Atlantic and the Pacific.[46] As with all politicians, Roosevelt was concerned about the election and sensitive to public opinion and the advice he received from colleagues. At this time, General George Marshall, the Army Chief of Staff, was concerned at the lack of planning and direction from his Commander in Chief.[47] Following the election, Frank Knox was able to spell out his response to the Nazi aggression. This was a hard-hitting speech and for many it was time that someone spoke out. He said:

1. We are going to give Great Britain every possible degree of aid we can-short of leaving ourselves defenceless.
2. We will have concern for the Chinese people.
3. We will pile up our armaments, whatever the cost.
4. We won't appease anybody on earth.
5. We won't talk about what we're going to do but do it.
6. We're going to move our muscle and our will because self-preservation is possible only by self-sacrifice.[48]

Anglophiles in the US were obviously weighing the chances of Britain winning the war against a military machine led by Nazi fanatics that had been well prepared with the latest weaponry and battle-hardened. It was thought that as against that brutal onslaught, the perceived British attitude was 'overly optimistic'. In their view, Britain's forces, apart from the navy, were 'very poorly prepared'.[49]

f. Countering Isolationists and Defeatists

At that time Roosevelt's focus was on deciding whether to run for an unprecedented third term and overriding that, his concern about the appropriate strategy to deal with a two-front war. Although his decision-making at this time may have seemed erratic or slow, his deliberations and the advice of his Cabinet, Stimson, Hull, and Knox and that of his defence chiefs, Admiral Stark and General Marshall eventually produced

[45] Cordell Hull, *The Memoirs of Cordell Hull*, Vol.2 (London, Hodder and Stoughton, 1948) 1103.
[46] S Dunn, *A Blueprint for War: FDR and the Hundred Days that Mobilised America* (New Haven, Yale University Press, 2018) 32–33.
[47] ibid 33.
[48] *New York Times*, 15 November 1940, Text of Address on National Defence by Secretary Knox.
[49] S Dunn, *A Blueprint for War: FDR and the Hundred Days that Mobilised America* (New Haven, Yale University Press, 2018) 45.

the most effective defence strategy and military expansion in history. Admiral Stark had been concerned about the imminence of war since October 1940, and naturally he had considered matters with his colleagues, in particular, General Marshall. He told Secretary Knox that 'if Britain wins decisively against Germany we could win everywhere; but if she loses, the problem confronting us would be very great; and while we might not lose everywhere, we might possibly not win anywhere'.[50] He concluded that if Britain fell 'we would find ourselves acting alone and at war with the world'.[51] Churchill found such an approach helpful simply because the US recognised that Britain was incapable of winning alone.[52] In order to mitigate the effect of isolationist propaganda, both Churchill and Roosevelt realised that their countries' relationship evolved from their common history and geographical position, which in the two world wars was determinative as to outcome. But Roosevelt had to educate his countrymen carefully, and so he pledged at a meeting on 30 October 1940 in Boston:

> I have said this before, but I shall say it again and again and again:
>
> Your boys are not going to be sent into any foreign wars.
>
> They're going to go into training to form a force so strong that, by its very existence, it will keep the threat of war far away from our shores.
>
> The purpose of our defence is defence.

During that week, Admiral Stark was considering American participation in a full-scale land offensive in Europe.[53] This was part of Plan Dog, which meant that the fate of the US was inextricably bound to that of Britain and that the US would do everything it could to meet Britain's 'vital needs' and that American soldiers might have to fight a land war in Europe. This was quite logical because the US Navy itself could not ensure victory; it would depend upon an American land offensive. Stark foresaw that America would have to intervene in Africa and Europe, General George C Marshall said

> I never had any idea that we could settle the question in Europe by purely air offensive. You've got to get down and hold things. You can't destroy plants. You can destroy cities … but that doesn't win.[54]

Marshall also had reservations about Plan Dog. Bearing in mind it required a strong offensive in the Atlantic, it was limited in defence in the Pacific. The Atlantic Fleet was reinforced by taking battleships from the Pacific Fleet in Hawaii namely, the Idaho, Mississippi, and New Mexico and two destroyer squadrons with cruisers Philadelphia, Brooklyn, Savannah and Nashville. This reduced the Pacific Fleet by 25 per cent.[55]

Roosevelt's domestic political challenge was to educate the American public on the threat to democracy and independence. His advocacy in support of Britain was

[50] ibid.

[51] D Kaiser, *No End Save Victory: How FDR Led the Nation into War* (New York, Basic Books, 2014) 140.

[52] FD Roosevelt, *The Public Papers and Addresses of Franklin D Roosevelt* 1940 Volume – War and Aid to Democracies (London, Macmillan, 1941) 517.

[53] *Washington Post*, 31 October 1940 Text of Roosevelt's Boston Speech.

[54] George C Marshall: interviews and reminiscences for Forest Pogue, tape 9, 290–291, marshallfoundation.org/library collection/george-c-marshall- interviews- reminiscences/#!collection=341.

[55] E Larabee, *Commander in Chief* (London, André Deutsch, 1987) 47–51.

essential to the defence of the US: marrying those objectives by skilful persuasion in his press conference on his return from a cruise in the Caribbean, his Fireside Chat on 29 December 1940 concerning America's independence, his Four Freedoms Speech in his State of the Union Speech on 6 January 1941, his Third Inaugural Address on 20 January 1941, and his Lend-Lease Speech on 15 March 1941, he awoke the American conscience and prepared Americans for war. In so doing, he declared what America and the democracies stood for: their fundamental principles of democracy, freedom and the rule of law forged by a common heritage of language, history, religion, and law. His inspiration no doubt came from the Founding Fathers, who, he inferred paradoxically perhaps, but in a way that appealed to all Americans, that Britain itself was then fighting its war for independence against Nazi tyranny.

One of the most effective statements of Roosevelt was perhaps that made in his press conference on 17 December 1940. He started by disarming his audience by saying: 'I don't think there is any particular news, except possibly one thing that I think is worth my talking about.' The 'one thing' turned out to be of the greatest importance in finding the policy of the US and its strategy to deal with the world crisis. He told them that the best way of defending the US was to help Great Britain defend itself. That was vital for the survival of democracy, but it was also very much in the interests of the US because in defending Britain, it would be defending itself. But it is arguable that it was not just strategic and economic interests that were considered but also a certain community of interest, as Lippmann called it: the Atlantic was not America's frontier but the inland sea between Europe and America.[56]

He said America needed slipways for more ships, factories and munitions plants – the more the stronger America's defence. He had considered lending money to Britain or gifting the amount. But the better view was that the US government would undertake the British orders and as the circumstances arose lease or sell them to Britain. Armaments were more useful to Britain than being stored in the US. The simple intention was 'to get rid of the dollar sign' as he put it.[57] In this press conference he introduced his famous garden hose example: that if your neighbour had a fire, you would help him extinguish it by lending him your hose. A fire that might well spread to your property. If it was damaged, he, the neighbour, would replace it. In the same way, America would lend munitions and armaments to Britain to be returned at the end of the war if intact. If damaged, then replaced. Supplying Britain with armaments would not place America in a state of war with the Axis Powers.[58] Another advantage to Britain was that British manufacturing factories could be moved to America out of the range of Luftwaffe bombers.

On 29 December 1940, he made a radio address that could reach 100 million listeners to talk about national security. His purpose was to preserve American independence and all things that American independence meant to Americans.[59] 'Never before since Jamestown and Plymouth Rock', he said, 'has our American civilisation

[56] W Lippmann, *US Foreign Policy* (London, Hamish Hamilton, 1943) 83.

[57] FD Roosevelt, *The Public Papers and Addresses of Franklin D Roosevelt* 1940 Volume – War and Aid to Democracies (London, Macmillan, 1941) 607.

[58] ibid 607–608.

[59] ibid 633–644. Fireside Chat on National Security.

been in such danger as now'.[60] He bluntly told his listeners that the Nazis intended not only to dominate all life and thought in their own country but also to enslave the whole of Europe and then to use the resources of Europe to dominate the rest of the world. He attacked the evil forces from fascist Europe, which was the enemy within the US: secret emissaries and troublemakers sent to destroy the nation's unity and shatter America's will to defend itself. He referred to many of 'those in high places' aiding and abetting the dictators. Industry in such circumstances could not afford strikes when it needed to operate continuously to arm itself as well as Britain, China and Greece. He concluded by saying that America must become 'the great arsenal of democracy'.[61] This broadcast was followed by his Annual Message to Congress on 6 January 1941. In that address he proclaimed what became famously known as the Four Freedoms. He recalled how America had avoided war in the nineteenth century and had enjoyed 99 years of peace without a single war in Europe or Asia constituting any real threat to the US. He proclaimed that those who would give up essential liberty to purchase a little temporary safety deserve neither liberty nor safety.[62] In concluding his address he said:

> the first is freedom of speech and expression-everywhere in the world.
>
> the second is freedom of every person to worship God in his own way-everywhere in the world.
>
> the third is freedom from want-which, translate it into world terms, means economic understandings which will secure to every nation a healthy peacetime life for its inhabitants-everywhere in the world.
>
> the fourth is freedom from fear-which, translated into world terms, means a worldwide reduction of armaments to such a point and in such a thorough fashion that no nation will be in a position to commit an act of physical aggression against any neighbour-anywhere in the world.

Whilst Roosevelt declared his guiding principles of freedom, his focus was more on the war in Europe not on the situation in the Far East. This was dangerous and becoming worse. Roosevelt's policy was to delay and deter the Japanese by sanctioning certain goods and materials, especially those used for war. Thus in 1938 and 1939, a series of 'moral embargoes' or commercial sanctions were applied to Japan by the US. During those two years there had been brought about a cessation of the US' export to Japan of aeroplanes, aeronautical equipment, and certain other materials. Exports to Japan of strategic materials declined, and in July 1940, under the Export Control Act, the President curtailed or prohibited the export of basic war materials. Licenses were refused for the export to Japan of aviation gasoline and most types of machine tools in September 1940.[63] Such sanctions were interpreted by the Japanese as insults and increased the likelihood of war. Ambassador Grew was aware of this as he testified to the Board:[64]

[60] ibid 634.
[61] ibid.
[62] ibid 664–665.
[63] *Report of the Army Pearl Harbor Board*. 39.
[64] ibid 40.

> It seemed to me at that time, whether we were fully prepared for war or not that we must in our own interests put those embargoes into effect; and shortly thereafter, those embargoes were put into effect.

That month the export of iron and steel scrap was prohibited. The effect of the US policy was to cut off from Japan by the winter of 1940–1941 the shipment of many strategic commodities, including arms, ammunition, implements of war, aviation gasoline and many other petroleum products, machine tools, scrap iron, pig iron and steel manufactures, copper, lead, zinc, aluminium, and a variety of other commodities important to a war effort.[65] On 27 September 1940, the German, Italian and Japanese governments signed the Tripartite Pact an alliance that was aimed at deterring the US. Subsequently the pact was joined by Hungary, Romania, Slovakia, Bulgaria, Slovakia and Croatia. In August 1941, Roosevelt and Churchill agreed on parallel action in a warning to Japan against new moves of aggression.[66] Ambassador Grew stated in his evidence to the APHB:

> we were up against what I would call a 'tidal wave' of military extremism in Japan; and I think the results as culminating in Pearl Harbor proved that fact.[67]

The ambassador's communications during 1941 are indicative of the progressive deterioration in relations and the contradictory policy of Washington. On 27 January 1941, Grew warned of an attack on Pearl Harbor by Japan:[68]

> There is a lot of talk around town to the effect that the Japanese, in case of a break with the United States, are planning to go all out in a surprise of mass attack on Pearl Harbor. I rather guess the boys in Hawaii are not precisely asleep.

On 1 February 1941, he reported that the outlook was 'never darker for peace'. On 25 of March 1941, Haan Kilsoo, a Korean, warned Secretary of State Hull that the Japanese would attack Hawaii, conquer the Philippines, and try to close the Panama Canal.[69] On 25 July 1941, the US froze Japanese assets in a move to dissuade Japan from pursuing its expansionist policy. This caused bitter Japanese resentment. Japanese credits were frozen so that trade with Japan virtually ceased. It was by this method that the US gained more time to prepare. Secretary Hull's view was that if Japan had attacked Pearl Harbor in June 1941, then Hitler might have abandoned Operation Barbarossa and might well have turned on Britain, which might have had its sea routes cut in the Pacific to New Zealand and Australia, but also threatening India and possibly South Africa.[70]

On 4 August 1941, the Japanese Prime Minister Prince Fumimaro Konoye suggested a meeting with President Roosevelt. He wanted to get recognition of the Greater East Asian Co-Prosperity Sphere before the German-Soviet War was decided.[71]

[65] ibid.

[66] ibid.

[67] ibid 41.

[68] R Smith Thompson, *A Time of War: Franklin Roosevelt and the Path to Pearl Harbor* (New York, Prentice Hall Press, 1991) 309 and also T Morgan, *FDR A Biography* (New York, Simon and Schuster, 1985) 575.

[69] Thompson ibid. Kilsoo, according to Thompson, was known to the US Army Intelligence as head of the Sino-Korean People's League.

[70] Cordell Hull, *The Memoirs of Cordell Hull,* Vol 2 (London, Hodder and Stoughton, 1948) 1104.

[71] TM Leonard, 'Stanley K. Hornbeck: Major Deterrent To America. Japanese Symmetry, 1941' (1974) 8 *Towson State Journal of International Affairs* 113.

On 18 August 1941, Grew reported Japanese protest at US economic sanctions. On 29 August 1941, the US applied its oil embargo. On 3 September, Roosevelt met Ambassador Nomura and stipulated that the precondition to any meeting between him and Kanoye was subject to four fundamental principles:

(1) respect for the territorial integrity and sovereignty of each and all nations,
(2) support of the principle of non-interference in the internal affairs of other countries
(3) support of the principle of equality, including the equality of commercial opportunity, and
(4) non-disturbance of the status quo in the Pacific, except as the status quo may be altered by peaceful means.

Following that, on 6 September, Grew reported the statement of the Japanese Premier that if the US continued economic sanctions, there would be no settlement for the next six months or a year. On 24 September 1941, a radio message in code was sent from Tokyo to Honolulu to the Japanese spy Nagao Kita and intercepted by US Army Intelligence. Colonel Rufus S Bratton, Chief of the Far Eastern Section of the US Army Intelligence, who reviewed the intercept, was so troubled that he wrote a memorandum to his superiors. He reported that the Japanese were seeking specific information on the disposition of the fleet in Pearl Harbor. That message was ignored.[72] On 29 September 1941, Grew reported that the Japanese action could only be halted by a show of force. In Japanese eyes, the US was only playing for time. On 30 September 1941, he protested at the secrecy over the conversations with Japan, as it was all common knowledge in Japan, but the American public was kept in ignorance. On 9 October he significantly reported that the frozen credit policy of the US was driving Japan to international bankruptcy, and she would be forced to act. As a result of Japanese reaction and increased support for militarism, Tojo became Prime Minister on 16 October 1941. He was a dominant military figure, and even the wish of the emperor not to make war on the US was ignored by the new regime. From then on the situation deteriorated. On 28 October, Haan Kilsoo gave a further warning from Korean sources in Japan that the Japanese were planning to bomb Pearl Harbor.[73] This prompted a note from Stanley K Hornbeck[74] to Secretary Stimpson saying that this information should not be dismissed.[75] On 3 November 1941, Grew warned that war was not only possible but probable, and Japan was preparing for hostilities 'with dangerous and dramatic suddenness'.[76] On 5 November 1941, Admiral Yamamoto received orders to prepare for the Pearl Harbor attack. This was to commence in the first 10 days of December.[77] On 7 November, Secretary Hull informed

[72] R Smith Thompson *A Time of War: Franklin Roosevelt and the Path to Pearl Harbor* (New York, Prentice Hall Press, 1991) 370.
[73] ibid 370–371.
[74] Stanley Kuhl Hornbeck was Chief of the State Department Division of Far Eastern Affairs (1928–1937), a special adviser to Secretary of State Cordell Hull (1937–1944), and ambassador to the Netherlands (1944–1947). Hornbeck had analysed the evidence of Japan's expansionist tendencies in August-September 1941 which were persuasive in the policy Roosevelt adopted. See: TM Leonard, 'Stanley K. Hornbeck: Major Deterrent to America. Japanese Symmetry, 1941' (1974) 8 *Towson State Journal of International Affairs* 115.
[75] R Smith Thompson *A Time of War: Franklin Roosevelt and the Path to Pearl Harbor* (New York, Prentice Hall Press, 1991) 371.
[76] ibid 369.
[77] ibid 369.

the Cabinet that relations between Japan and the US were 'extremely critical' and that there was an 'imminent possibility' that Japan might at any time start a new military movement of conquest by force.[78] This was followed by warnings of the impending seriousness of the situation in speeches made by Secretary of the Navy Knox and Under Secretary of State Welles on 11 November 1941. The White Papers stated:

> On November 17 Ambassador Grew cabled from Tokyo that we could expect a 'sudden Japanese Naval or military attack in regions not then involved'.

On 20 November 1941, the US rejected Japanese proposals because it meant discontinuing American aid to China.[79] On 25 and 28 November, Secretary Hull, at meetings of high officials of the government, stated:

> there was practically no possibility of agreement being achieved with Japan; that in his opinion the Japanese were likely to break out at any time with new acts of conquest by force; and that the matter of safeguarding our national security was in the hands of the Army and Navy. The Secretary expressed his judgment that any plans for our military defence should include an assumption that the Japanese might make the element of surprise a central point in their strategy and also might attack at various points simultaneously with a view to demoralizing efforts of defence and of coordination for the purpose thereof.[80]

The Board concluded that it did not appear that such a statement was sent by the Army and Navy to their field forces.[81]

On 25 November, the Japanese fleet sailed for Pearl Harbor, a day before a critical juncture was reached on 26 November 1941 when Mr Hull handed the President's Ten Points of Settlement to Ambassadors Nomura and Kurusu. These proposals were verbally rejected by the Japanese ambassadors at once, but they enquired as to any other basis of negotiation or a modus vivendi. The key point was that Roosevelt demanded that:[82]

> The Government of Japan will withdraw all military, naval, air and police forces from China and Indochina.

The following day, at the request of the Japanese ambassadors, the President received them and Secretary of State Hull, at which time the President reaffirmed with finality the 'Ten Points', stating the three primary considerations upon which the 'Ten Points' were based.[83] On the same day, General Marshall and Admiral Stark wrote a joint memorandum to the President requesting that no ultimatum be delivered to the Japanese as the Army and Navy were not ready to precipitate an issue with Japan, and notified him of the agreement reached with the British and the Dutch for reciprocal action in the case either one of them was attacked.[84] The Marshall-Stark Memorandum of 27 November to the President did not reach him until after the meeting with the Japanese Ambassador on 27 or possibly 28 November. Ambassador Grew testified that

[78] *Report of the Army Pearl Harbor Board*. 42 and (White Papers, 136).
[79] *Report of the Army Pearl Harbor Board*. 42 and (White Papers, 144).
[80] ibid.
[81] *Report of the Army Pearl Harbor Board*. 42.
[82] H Brands, *Traitor to His Class* (New York, Anchor Books, 2008) 623.
[83] *Report of the Army Pearl Harbor Board*. 42.
[84] ibid.

the Japanese so regarded it.[85] They acted upon it, as did Mr Hull, because he so informed the Secretary of War, Mr Stimson, on the morning of 27 November.[86] The latter testified, based on his diary of contemporaneous events, thus:

> The first thing in the morning I called up Hull to find out what his final decision had been with the Japanese – whether he had handed them the new proposal which we passed on two or three days ago or whether, as he suggested yesterday, he had broken the whole matter off. He told me now he had broken the whole matter off. As he put it, 'I have washed my hands of it, and it is now in the hands of you and Knox, the Army and Navy.'[87]

After all of Secretary Hull's efforts were obstructed by Japanese cunning and deception in negotiations and making no effort to halt their aggressive actions and encroachments in Southeast Asia, with troop movements continuing unabated, Hull concluded that he could do no more. The 'Ten Points of Settlement' were America's best available negotiating position. The public was unaware of the seriousness of the danger. Hull told the British ambassador that the Japanese would launch

> a desperate gamble and require the utmost boldness and risk.[88]

His foresight was confirmed when Ambassador Grew noted that:

> everything was over and I would soon be leaving Japan.[89]

Six weeks after the attack, Harry Hopkins wrote that Secretary Hull was willing to work at a deal with Japan.

> There was no question that up until the last ten days prior to the outbreak of war he was in hopes that some adjustment could be worked out.[90]

According to Sherwood, Hopkin's biographer, he says that the 10 days before Pearl Harbor from 27 November 1941 to 7 December 1941, 'a sort of paralysis set in at Oahu and in the Philippines … and perhaps worst of all in Washington.'[91] On 29 November just as President Roosevelt had started a break at Warm Springs in Georgia, he received warning from Hull that Tojo was declaring that the Japanese would 'Wipe out United States and British exploitation in the Far East.'[92]

Realising the increasing difficulties and threats from Japan, the idea of any preventive attack against the Japanese was entirely academic, as the US was in no position to take the offensive. The second course of action would have been to agree to Japan's demands. The US wanted a multilateral nonaggression pact among the governments principally concerned in the Pacific; an agreement among the principally interested governments to

[85] ibid (R. 4208, 4215, 4221, 4222).

[86] ibid 42. Hull previously consulted Stimpson on 8 August when Nomura was trying to arrange a meeting between Konoye and Roosevelt. Hull was against such a meeting and Stimpson thought it was merely a ruse. He knew that the Japanese already had their sights on Thailand. See also *Stimson Diary* Vol 35, August 1941, Yale University Library.

[87] *Report of the Army Pearl Harbor Board*. 42.

[88] ibid 43.

[89] ibid.

[90] R Sherwood, *Roosevelt and Hopkins An Intimate History*, Vol 1 (New York, Harper and Brothers, 1948) 517.

[91] ibid.

[92] D Kearns Goodwin, *No Ordinary Time* (New York, Simon and Schuster Paperbacks, 1994) 287.

respect the territorial integrity of Indochina and, equally, of the economic opportunity therein. It was fundamental that Japan would have to recognise the national government under Chiang Kai-shek and relinquish its extraterritorial rights in China. If that could be accomplished, then there could be a trade agreement between the US and Japan on liberal lines. In that respect, America would remove freezing measures and steps taken to stabilise the dollar with the yen. Another fundamental condition was that Japan would have to withdraw from the Tripartite Pact with Hitler. The one unilateral commitment was that Japan would withdraw her armed forces from China and Indochina.[93]

America's defence against attack from Japan were its advanced bases at Guam, Midway and Hawaii. Its decision to move its battleships to Hawaii whilst its cruisers were based on the East Coast to meet the Nazi threat was a strategic necessity whilst the country re-armed and supported Britain. In January 1941, Roosevelt was concerned that without American aid, Britain would not win, which was essential for ensuring American security.[94] He wanted to delay hostilities by diplomatic and economic means until the US could militarily deter Japan.

Roosevelt was aware that he was taking a gamble by dividing his naval forces between the Atlantic and the Pacific, but he and his advisers perceived the Atlantic as the greater threat to America. If Britain should fall, then America would come under attack. To avoid that, he would make America the arsenal of democracy. By supplying Britain with weapons they would be fighting America's war and it was in America's interest, therefore, to assist Britain. Thus, on his return from a short recuperation cruise in the Caribbean in January 1941, he gave another Fireside Chat followed by an interview with reporters, telling them of his ideas for lending military aid to Britain. The idea he worked on with his Treasury Secretary Morgenthau was that Britain would be lent the ships, tanks, guns, planes, etc and return them in kind or specie at the end of the war. In dividing his limited naval forces, Roosevelt had little choice given the isolationist movement and its influence on defence spending that had prevented rearmament to match the Axis Powers. Until the attack on Pearl Harbor, industry was not prepared to reduce its prices.[95]

Whilst the Americans had been fairly successful in intelligence gathering, cracking the Japanese Purple Code and using Magic to decipher and read diplomatic cables, they had difficulty in breaking variations of the Japanese military codes so that they were unaware of the sailing of the Japanese forces that attacked Pearl Harbor on 7 December 1941.

Relations between Japan and the US gradually deteriorated in the course of 1941 as the US became aware of Japan's imperial ambitions in Southeast Asia and its idea of a Co-Prosperity Sphere at the expense of the British Empire, the US, Vichy France and the Netherlands, although Nazi collaborators in France facilitated the Japanese occupation of Vietnam.

In a letter to Ambassador Grew on 21 January 1941, Roosevelt conceded that he was weighing the problem of Japanese aggression in the light of its possible effects on

[93] Cordell Hull, *The Memoirs of Cordell Hull*, Vol.2 (London, Hodder and Stoughton, 1948) 1083.
[94] L Farrago, *The Broken Seal* (New York, Random House, 1967) 178.
[95] D Kearns Goodwin, *No Ordinary Time* (New York, Simon and Schuster Paperbacks, 1994) 197.

'the chances of England's winning her struggle with Germany'.[96] Hull became the chief negotiator in relations with the Japanese, but was probably unaware of the particular foibles of the Japanese and how to interpret their approach. He was assisted by three officers of the State Department: Dr Stanley Hornbeck, Maxwell M Hamilton and Joseph W Ballantine.[97] These discussions between Hull and the Japanese ambassador to Washington, Mr Namura, were official and complemented other informal discussions which were set up through the Catholic bishop, Bishop Walsh in Tokyo, where the US was represented by Senator Walker and Japan by Mr Wikawa. It was the view of Dr Hornbeck that:

> The decision of Japanese Leaders whether to move or not to move southward will be made in the light of the physical situation in Europe as they view it and the physical situation in the Pacific as they view it.[98]

Hornbeck concluded his recommendation by saying that:

> … we should do all that we can toward giving them an impression that we are both prepared and expecting to oppose them by force any further moves southward if attempted by them.[99]

The deliberations that were going on between Mr Wikawa, Colonel Iwakuro and Postmaster General Walker were running in parallel to the diplomatic efforts of Cordell Hull and his staff. Wikawa and Walker were attempting to settle the differences between the US and Japan, covering the relationship between Japan and the US including mediation in the Sino-Japanese conflict, naval forces, merchant marine, trade, credits, oil and rubber as well as the status of the autonomous states in the Southwestern Pacific area, Far Eastern states, international conferences and airline communication between Japan and the US, developing a so-called Joint Far-Eastern Monroe Doctrine. This was a difficult exercise in diplomacy, with little chance of success, but intended to play for time giving the US more time to rearm and help Britain. Certainly, Dr Hornbeck would have been under no illusions.[100] Walker may have been naïve[101] so far as the Japanese were concerned, but he was of use in terms of delaying an immediate threat of a Japanese attack on America so long as he could delude Wikawa and Iwakuro. Walker was accused of being a pawn of the Japanese. Iwakuro was not quite what he seemed to be. He had been a representative of the War Ministry, working for General Tojo. He had a dubious record in Manchuria and China. He was no humanitarian and had recommended 'the radical eradication of the bandits' who opposed Japan's conquest of China as well as participating in the 'Rape of Nanking', where the Japanese committed atrocious war crimes, killing an estimated 300,000 people.[102] In December 1948, Lieutenant General Akira Mutō, Chief of Staff of the Japanese 14th Area Army and Iwakuro's senior officer, was sentenced to death by the International Military Tribunal for the

[96] L Farago, *The Broken Seal* (New York, Random House, 1967) 178.
[97] ibid 180.
[98] ibid 183.
[99] ibid 184.
[100] ibid 183 and 184.
[101] He was also carried away by the enthusiasm of Father Drought acting on behalf of Bishop Walsh. No doubt with the best humanitarian intentions but devoid of realpolitik.
[102] L Farago, *The Broken Seal* (New York, Random House, 1967) 187.

Far East. According to Farago, Walker had told Iwakuro that the American fleet in the Pacific would be capable of checking any southward move by the Japanese, which would threaten the overseas outposts of Japan.[103] This might well have influenced Japanese strategic imperial ambitions.

Another problem encountered was the leaking of a Magic intercept through Sumner Welles, who confided in the Russian representative Oumansky that there would be a German attack on the USSR within two months. Oumansky, a confirmed Stalinist, was on friendly terms with Dr Thomsen, the German ambassador in Moscow. He told Thomsen that the US had evidence of German plans to attack the Soviet Union and that it had been obtained from intercepts of Ambassador Oshima's telegrams to Tokyo.[104] Despite this untoward leak, American intelligence operations were not compromised.

Such a leak did not mean to say that this was a frequent occurrence; indeed Op. 20 G and SIS, the services responsible for this intelligence, restricted distribution of such intercepts to the White House,[105] so to an extent, President Roosevelt was kept in the dark save later in autumn 1941, when he insisted on seeing the raw intercepts.[106] Despite this, the American analysts concluded that Japan would not go to war against Russia but would intensify preparations for a southward move. This meant an all-out war against Britain and the US.[107] Such information justified all the warnings that President Roosevelt had given in his fireside chats and speeches, as well as the increased effort in arms production helping Britain, China and then Russia. Apart from this, Roosevelt received information from the British Security Co-ordination led in New York by William Stephenson, a former Canadian fighter pilot.[108] Stephenson's success was enhanced by his excellent working relationship with William Joseph Donovan, an ebullient Irish American New York lawyer and World War I hero who had access to the President and his Cabinet.[109] Whilst Japan was secretly undertaking these preparations for war against Britain and the US, it continued its duplicity in its negotiations with the US. The benefit of Magic intercepts was that on occasion American diplomats would be informed of the instructions sent to the Japanese ambassador in Washington, Mr Nomura, which gave Secretary Hull and Roosevelt some benefit. What they did not know was the exploits of Japan's principal agent in Hawaii, Yoshikawa, an officer in the Imperial Navy, who, by flying over the island, mixing with the sailors, reporting the movements of the Pacific Fleet, and photographing the area, was able to send invaluable reports to Tokyo in the weeks before the attack.[110] So far as the Dutch and the

[103] ibid 188.
[104] ibid 197.
[105] ibid 200.
[106] Whilst the Magic intercepts gave the Americans some indication of Japanese intentions to move south, the German and Russian espionage procured more detailed information from its agents in Japan. By July 1941 the Germans knew that Japan would attack the Dutch oilfields and Manila and blockade Singapore. Farago ibid 208.
[107] Farago ibid 212.
[108] Stephenson obtained invaluable intelligence from one of his agents who had obtained highly secret information from a member of the Kurusu Mission in Washington. Stephenson had correctly interpreted the purpose of that mission either demanding that the US accept Japanese hegemony in the Orient, or lulling the US into a false sense of security.
[109] It was Donovan who later headed the OSS the forerunner of the CIA.
[110] L Farago, *The Broken Seal* (New York, Random House, 1967) 234–247.

British were concerned, any incursion by the Japanese crossing the line of the 6° parallel north between Malaya and Borneo would be deemed an act of war. To counter this, the Americans cooperated in staff talks with a Joint Basic War plan, known as ABC-1, whereby it was agreed that the primary strategic objective would be the Nazi threat. To counter this, the US would increase its naval forces in the Atlantic and Mediterranean.[111]

g. Background

Before 1941 and the Pacific War, America was at peace and her forces were not on a wartime footing. The public were not immediately concerned with war and the President had fought his campaign in 1940 repeating the mantra that Americans are 'not going to be sent into any foreign wars'.[112] America was not ready for war. There existed a confusion of thinking and organisation of conflict, opinion and a diversity of views, as the Army Pearl Harbor Board opined.[113] There were conflicting plans and purposes. Public opinion blowing in all directions, isolationists and nationalists struggling for dominance, public opinion both against war and clamouring for reprisals against Japan at a time when negotiations were progressing, sanctions were being applied, and the American forces were under considerable pressure because much of their armament was being diverted to Britain in its war with Nazi Germany. Thus, the American forces stationed in Hawaii were inadequately prepared to meet any attack from Japan in the Pacific.[114] The War Department was acting on a peacetime basis; neither its management nor general staff had perfected an organisation for war. There was a lack of central command and directness, with decisions being made by conference and compromise rather than by command.[115]

Part of the problem in America's unreadiness for war at dawn on 7 December 1941 was the psychological condition of American public opinion and its government. As in all democracies, its policies and actions were dependent on public opinion, the state of the public mind. War can only be waged through a state of mind and a state of public readiness for war. For much of the time prior to war, America was reluctant even to consider war. There was a strong isolationist organisation; propaganda groups against war led by Charles Lindbergh, America First and other populists whose campaigns raised doubts in the minds of many, which restrained the government. Public opinion was slow to react, but later it went ahead of the leadership.[116] On the other hand, Japan had been at war for several years in China. The people in government were psychologically and physically geared toward war by a policy of cunning, hatred and patriotism; extreme nationalism; and oriental intrigue.[117] Japan, like Nazi Germany, was fixated on world conquest. In 1932, Henry Simpson, the Secretary of State opined that:

> The Japanese army has been built for war, it feels prepared for war, and it wants war.

[111] ibid 250.
[112] FDR Speech at Boston 30 October 1940.
[113] *Report of the Army Pearl Harbor Board*. 28.
[114] ibid 27, 34.
[115] *Report of the Army Pearl Harbor Board*. 28.
[116] ibid 29.
[117] ibid.

One of the problems in the interwar years in Japanese-American relations was a failure of America to challenge Japan on its fortifications of the mandated islands under a mandate dated 11 February 1922, whereby under Article 1, Japan's mandate extended to 'all the former German islands situated in the Pacific Ocean and lying north of the Equator'. The Report stated that the mandate also provided that there would not be any military or naval bases established or fortifications erected in the territory.[118] The Board concluded that had the US successfully insisted upon Japan living up to those treaty stipulations, the entire naval and military structure in the key Pacific Islands erected by the Japanese might have been made impossible. Japan, without any legal right and in violation of treaties and League mandates for nearly 20 years successfully and completely excluded other nationals from the mandated territories and, during this time, built up considerable army, navy and air installations. Consequently, Japan gained an enormous strategic advantage over a string of naval, air and army bases across America's lifeline to the Philippines and rendered Guam, Midway, Christmas, and Palmyra vulnerable.[119] It placed great danger on the Hawaiian Islands. Jaluit in the Mandated Islands was 1,000 miles closer to Hawaii than to the homeland of Japan. American policy after 1918 appears to have been based upon a combination of fear of the Japanese and an obsession not to give offence to the Japanese. This was seen as one of weakness rather than of strength; there was obvious mistrust on both sides.[120]

h. Japanese Infiltration of Hawaii

The Japanese consulate and its consular agents in Hawaii enjoyed diplomatic immunity. This gave them free rein in their spying activities and unrestricted communication by radio and cable with the mainland of Japan for reporting upon the movements of the Pacific Fleet and the status of defences in Hawaii. Neither the army, the navy, nor the FBI had authority to tap these lines and find out what was going on because of legal restrictions under the Communications Act 1934. The Board concluded that there was no better example of the failure to control consular agents than that of the Japanese Consul General in Honolulu. This man had about 200 consular agents in the islands. The Board found that he used the commercial telephone and telegraph for reporting on US defences and fleet movements with impunity. Such spying activities as took place in Pearl Harbor should have been detected. Together with the removal of artillery defences from the island of Guam, it gave the Japanese the impression of weakness.[121] The Board stated that a policy of compromise between economic sanctions

[118] This was not expressly stated in the Treaty Between The United States and Japan Regarding Rights of the Two Governments and Their Respective Nationals In Former German Islands in the Pacific Ocean North of the Equator, and in Particular the Island Of Yap. [Signed at Washington, 11 February 1922; ratification advised by the Senate, 1 March 1922; ratified by the President, 2 June 1922; ratified by Japan, 23 June 1922; ratifications exchanged at Washington, 13 July 1922; proclaimed, 13 July 1922].

[119] *Report of the Army Pearl Harbor Board*. 31.

[120] The Japanese were also excluded from the Aleutian and Pribilof islands after 1936. Their visits to the latter arose out of the Convention for the Preservation and Protection of Fur Seals 1911 which was the subject of the Bering Sea Arbitration discussed in *Instruments of Peacemaking 1870–1914*.

[121] *Report of the Army Pearl Harbor Board*. 33. Ambassador Grew stated that there were three lines of defence for a nation such as the US; the diplomatic line of defence, the navy, and the army.

and negotiations in turn influenced War Department action.[122] General Short was told by the War Department not to alarm the population nor to disclose intent. He chose to follow that policy although given a war warning on 27 November 1941.[123] The American counterproposals of 26 November to the Japanese government were considered an ultimatum by them. Hence the anticipatory war warning.

In Short's defence, his orders, taken together, appear contradictory: he was not to cause alarm in preparing defensive positions, he was focused on training, and he did not believe Pearl Harbor would be attacked. Indeed, it was a surprise to the Chief of Staff.[124] This misunderstanding was critical to unpreparedness and Japanese success. This was complicated by the fact that America needed time to rearm and supply Britain and was not ready for war, hence a need not to provoke Japan. On the other hand. America's policy towards Japan regarding the oil embargo and the abrogation of certain Japanese commercial treaty rights contradicted this policy. It is difficult to understand this bifurcated policy: appeasement through continued negotiations aimed to delay the inevitable on the one hand and sanctions on the other. In such a situation there was little choice because America was simply not ready for a war on two fronts. It is unlikely that the oil embargo had a significant impact on the attack on Pearl Harbor since the decision to attack Pearl Harbor was taken before the oil embargo was operational.[125] On the diplomatic front, Japan never made any concessions. It had been at war with China since 1937, and it had no intention of agreeing to America's proposals of 26 November 1941.[126] So clearly did Japan understand American national psychology that it selected Sunday morning, early, as the time for attack, well knowing this to be the best time to achieve surprise.[127]

i. The Attack on Pearl Harbor

In his last report to Tokyo, the Japanese agent, Yoshikawa, reported that there were nine battleships, three light cruisers, three submarine tenders, 19 destroyers, and four light cruisers lying at their docks in Pearl Harbor. There was no air reconnaissance. In fact, there were heavy cruisers in dock and another 10 destroyers as well as four minesweepers and eight minelayers.[128] A few days later, on 2 December, when the President had returned from Warm Springs at the urgent request of Secretary Hull, he read three intercepts: the first, which confirmed Japanese intelligence was moving its operatives to South America from the US; the second, a direction for the destruction of the codes and confidential papers in the Japanese missions; and the third, a dispatch from Foreign Minister Togo to Ambassador Oshima in Berlin to inform Hitler and Ribbentrop that war may suddenly break out with the Anglo-Saxon Nations. It is clear from the accounts given by the intelligence sources that the President did not know of the instructions to

[122] *Report of the Army Pearl Harbor Board.* 25, 33.

[123] The Japanese taskforce that attacked Hawaii moved out of its rendezvous at Tankan Bay on the 27 or 28 of November to launch the attack against Pearl Harbor on 7 December 1941.

[124] *Report of the Army Pearl Harbor Board.* 35, 38.

[125] E Larabee, *Commander in Chief* (London, André Deutsch, 1987) 92.

[126] *Report of the Army Pearl Harbor Board.* 30, 35.

[127] *Report of the Army Pearl Harbor Board.* 38.

[128] L Farago, *The Broken Seal* (New York, Random House, 1967) 311.

Nomura from Tokyo that such instructions had to be delivered to the American government by 1 pm Washington time, nor of their content. Neither he nor his intelligence services knew where any attack would come from, although there was speculation that the Japanese would attack the Philippines, Malaya, Thailand, and Hong Kong. Hawaii was not mentioned, although as will be discussed, a general alert had been sent to Hawaii earlier, although Ambassador Grew had warned of such an attack in February 1941 and an air attack was considered the greater threat to the fleet.

j. Billy Mitchell's Prophecy

In the autumn of 1923, Brigadier General William 'Billy' Mitchell, Assistant Chief of the Army Air Service, went on a tour of inspection in the Pacific region, including the Hawaiian Islands.[129] His prescient reports on a hypothetical attack by the Japanese on Pearl Harbor were revealing. If it had been in the contemplation of Admiral Kimmell, Commander in Chief, Pacific Fleet, and General Short, who commanded the Hawaiian Department of the US Army in Hawaii, between 27 November 1941 and 7 December 1941, they might, in hindsight, have made Pearl Harbor more defensible. In Mitchell's Report, he referred to the military importance of the island of Oahu. If there was a state of war, the Japanese knew that the defence of the islands was based on Oahu, with its military depots naval and land fortifications, airfields, and water supplies. The city of Honolulu, together with its wharves and supply points, was vulnerable to air attack. Mitchell rightly concluded that there was no defence against the air attack except by an Air Force. It could be supplemented by auxiliaries such as canon, machine guns, and barrage balloons. Without any air power, such an arrangement, he concluded, could only give a false sense of security. Regrettably, as we shall see, that was the case on 7 December 1941.

Mitchell had foreseen what the Japanese might do. They would attack with submarines loaded with six pursuit planes and two aeroplane transports, each loaded with 50 bomber planes. They would launch their attack from Midway and Niihau, the smallest of the Hawaiian Islands. Whilst he was wrong about the precise means of attack, he was correct in his view that it would be an air attack. He foresaw an attack on Ford Island aerodrome hangars, storehouses, and ammunition dumps; the navy fuel oil tanks; the water supply of Honolulu; the water supply of Schofield Barracks, airdrome and troop establishments; the naval submarine station; and the city and wharves of Honolulu. At that time the American navy had not sent battleships to Pearl Harbor. Had they done so, he would surely have considered that a greater risk.

His preliminary report is dated 10 December 1923 as a Preliminary Report of Inspection of Air Service Activities in the Hawaiian Department.[130] General Mitchell's report was very thorough. He also investigated the organisation of the Department of Hawaii, the air brigade, their telephone system and communications, anti-aircraft defence, the danger from aerial torpedoes and the use of aircraft carriers and submarines as means of defence, the question of anti-aircraft cannons, the policies of Japan and

[129] 'Billy Mitchell's Prophecy' (1962) 13(2) *American Heritage*.

[130] The author is grateful for the assistance of the Librarian at the Library of Congress Washington DC of the Congress of the United States in providing copies of the index and list of charts to the preliminary Report of Inspection of General Mitchell.

Britain, the level of defence against aircraft gliding bombs, and possible Japanese plans of attack and the targets. It was an extremely thorough report of 525 pages. In hindsight, if those in command had read this report, there might have been a more realistic assessment of the risks. No references were made to it in any of the subsequent enquiries. It is also remarkable in hindsight to refer to the warning given by Ambassador Grew, the American ambassador to Japan, in a telegram to the State Department:

> Tokyo, January 27, 1941–6 p. m.
>
> (Received January 27–6: 38 a. m.)
>
> A member of the Embassy was told by my … colleague that from many quarters, including a Japanese one, he had heard that a surprise mass attack on Pearl Harbor was planned by the Japanese Military forces, in case of 'trouble' between Japan and the United States; that the attack would involve the use of all the Japanese military facilities. My colleague said that he was prompted to pass this on because it had come to him from many sources, although the plan seemed fantastic.
>
> Grew.

C. The Pearl Harbor Enquiries

The history of this attack is well documented and studied by historians and others, so there is no purpose here in rehearsing the encyclopaedic analysis and vast literature on this topic since 1941. This study focuses on some of the key legal and military substantive and procedural aspects of the enquiries and investigations: the Roberts Commission, commissioned by President Franklin Roosevelt on 18 December 1941; the Army and Navy Board of Inquiry, which was appointed by the Secretary of State for War, Henry Stimson, in June 1944; and the Navy Inquiry convened in July 1944, as well as subsequent investigations carried out by Lt. Colonel Clausen at the request of Henry Stimson. In this chapter consideration is given to the findings of the Roberts Commission, some of the key evidence given to the Navy Court of Inquiry, the Report of the Navy Enquiry, and the findings of Lt. Colonel Clausen's investigations, which were incorporated into the Report of the Army Pearl Harbor Board by way of Memoranda and the Clausen Investigation. What we have is a contrast between the official formal Board of Inquiry of the Army and the Navy and the more informal investigation of Lt. Colonel Clausen which in many respects was more effective in getting to the truth of the matter so far as unpreparedness was concerned

i. The Attack

At 7.55 am Hawaiian time on Sunday, 7 December 1941, the Imperial Japanese Navy (IJN) launched a surprise air and submarine attack upon the US forces stationed on the island of Oahu. Although the submarine attack was ineffective, the carrier-based strike force destroyed most of the Pacific fleet. In his book *Day of Infamy* Walter Lord[131] states that there were 96 ships in Pearl Harbor on that day and 394 planes. The army had

[131] (Ware, Wordsworth Editions Limited, 1998) 221–222.

93 fighters, 35 bombers, and 11 observation planes. The navy had 15 fighters, 61 patrol planes, 36 scout planes and 45 miscellaneous. Many of these aircraft were obsolete or in a state of repair. The Japanese striking force comprised 31 ships: six aircraft carriers, two battleships, two heavy cruisers, one light cruiser, nine destroyers, three submarines, and eight tankers with an air strength of 432 planes: 39 for Combat Air Patrol, 44 in reserve and 353 for the attack on Pearl Harbor. There was an additional force of 28 submarines carrying 11 small aircraft and five midget submarines. None of the midget submarines survived the attack. According to Rear Admiral Wilkes B Farley, who witnessed the attack at 7.55 am, he saw low-flying planes over Ford Island, then an explosion. He ordered general quarters and signalled: 'All ships harbour sortie.' 40 torpedo bombers plus 27 dive bombers attacked in the first wave; 353 planes in all were involved in the attack; 18 ships were sunk; 188 planes destroyed; and 159 planes damaged.[132] According to the University of Hawaii War Records Depository, 2,403 people were killed, nearly half of them were on the USS Arizona. 18 ships were sunk or seriously damaged. The battleships destroyed were the USS Arizona and the USS Oklahoma and also the target ship, USS Utah, and destroyers USS Cassin and USS Downes. Although the battleships USS West Virginia, USS California and USS Nevada and the minelayer USS Oglala were sunk or beached, they were later salvaged. The battleships USS Tennessee, USS Maryland and USS Pennsylvania; the cruisers USS Helena, USS Honolulu and USS Rayleigh; the destroyer Shaw; the seaplane tender Curtiss; and the repair ship Vestal were damaged and later repaired.

Considering the forces arrayed against the US Pacific Fleet, the result was not surprising in terms of the state of alert on Oahu when peace then existed between the US and the Empire of Japan. The Pacific Fleet was on alert, and the army in Hawaii was on Alert No. 1 to counter sabotage. The forces were instructed not to alarm the residents but, at the same time, to take precautions. The US was then at peace with Japan, and intelligence was unaware of the location of the Japanese attack force. The thinking was that if Japan attacked, it was more likely in to be East Asia, Malaysia, and the Philippines and in any event, there was some feeling that the forces on Hawaii were impervious to any attack.[133]

ii. The Roberts Commission

This Commission was appointed in 1941 by Executive Order of the President 'to ascertain and report the facts relating to the attack made by Japanese armed forces upon the Territory of Hawaii on December 7th, 1941'.[134] In the event the Commission concluded that to ensure success in wartime the foreign and military policy of the nation must be coordinated as well as those of the army and the navy.[135] The Commission's conclusions were important insofar as they were critical of the senior officers based in

[132] E Larabee, *Commander in Chief* (London, André Deutsch, 1987) 168–169.

[133] Hearings before the Joint Committee on the investigations of the Pearl Harbor Attack, Congress of the United States, 79th Congress, First Session, Pursuant to S. Con Res. 27; Proceedings of the Navy Court of Enquiry. Part 32.

[134] ibid Part 39. Report of the Roberts Commission. 1.

[135] Report of the Roberts Commission. 19.

Hawaii and the measures they took to protect the base and the fleet. On the other hand, they exonerated the government, concluding that the Secretary of State, Mr Cordell Hull, fulfilled his obligations by keeping the army and navy departments in close touch with the international situation and fully advising them respecting the course and probable termination of negotiations with Japan.[136] So, on the diplomatic front and the intelligence gleaned presumably from the MAGIC intercepts, Secretary Hull was cleared of any criticism, as were Secretary Stimson, the Secretary for War, and the Secretary of the Navy, Frank Knox, who also fulfilled his obligations, keeping the Chief of Staff and the Chief of Naval Operations, Admiral Stark, informed of the course of negotiations with Japan and the significant implications thereof.[137] In the Navy Inquiry the question arose as to whether Admiral Stark kept the navy fully informed, making them clearly aware of the dangers facing American territories in the Pacific.[138]

The Roberts Commission was not critical of the Chief of Staff, General Marshall or the Chief of Naval Operations, Admiral Stark, as it was concluded that they had fulfilled their obligations by cooperating with each other and their superiors respecting the joint defence of the Hawaiian coastal frontier and that they concurred in the warnings and orders sent by the other to the responsible commanders with respect to such defence.[139] The Chief of Staff gave warning to his commanders as to possible hostile Japanese action and told them to undertake necessary reconnaissance and other measures.[140] Admiral Stark issued a specific warning in his dispatch of 27 November 1941 by way of a direct order to the Commander in Chief of the Pacific Fleet, Admiral Kimmel, to execute 'appropriate defensive deployment preparatory to carrying out the tasks assigned' in accordance with his warning.[141] That would have meant compliance as anticipated in the War Plan known as Rainbow 5. What was apparently understood in Washington was not necessarily understood in Hawaii. In Washington, the risk of war was clear to the President, Secretary Hull, Secretary Stimson, Secretary Knox and those who were aware that the Japanese government had instructed its embassies to destroy their codes and coding machines. This was not appreciated by Kimmel or Short, neither of whom believed that the IJN or the Imperial Japanese Army (IJA) posed a threat to Hawaii but more likely to Southeast Asia, the Philippines, Wake Island and Midway.[142]

Roberts concluded that the prepared plans were adequate to deal with the attack. It was their responsibility to enact them according to the joint defence plans.[143] They failed because Alert No. 1, issued by General Short, was inadequate; the state of readiness of the naval forces was not sufficient to meet the emergency in light of the warning messages, and had the orders of the Chief of Staff and Chief of Naval Operations been complied

[136] ibid.
[137] ibid.
[138] Hearings before the Joint Committee on the investigations of the Pearl Harbor Attack, Congress of the United States, 79th Congress, First Session, Pursuant to S. Con Res. 27; Proceedings of the Navy Court of Enquiry. Part 39. Joint Committee Exhibit No. 157. 297 et seq.
[139] Report of the Roberts Commission. 19.
[140] ibid.
[141] ibid.
[142] This was also the view of their intelligence staff (Ref: Hearing Navy Inquiry).
[143] Report of the Roberts Commission. 20, para 9.

with the aircraft warning system of the army would have been in operation.[144] This is a harsh judgement on the state of readiness in Pearl Harbor insofar as the resources and material available to the army and navy were insufficient and could only provide partial anti-aircraft cover. On the other hand, it is arguable that if the priority was not to focus so much on training then some of the aircraft would have been in the air at the time of the attack, and more mobile stations would have been manned.

The state of readiness of the fleet in Pearl Harbor was not sufficient to meet the emergency described in the warning messages.[145] A high state of readiness despite the deficiencies in personnel, weapons, equipment and facilities to maintain a war footing, the Commission concluded such a state could have been achieved. This again is a harsh judgement when the forces were in training and in peacetime; on the other hand, it is arguable that the war warning was quite sufficient to dispel any lack of alertness and to place the forces in a wartime mode. It was the responsibility of the commanders to ensure that the forces were in such a state of readiness.[146]

It was a serious misunderstanding on the part of the War Department to observe that General Short, in his reply of 27 November to the Chief of Staff's message of that date, had reported the measures taken by him. General Short was under the impression that Washington had approved his Alert No. 1 regarding sabotage and not alarming the civilian population. What Washington did not know was that General Short had altered the sequence of the army alert code, and it may be that Washington thought that Alert No. 1 was the old Alert No. 3 which was a full alert, not simply a sabotage alert that Short had ordered. Colonel Clausen later discovered that General Short had altered the alert sequence without informing Washington.[147] This could explain why the War Department did not question the army's state of alert on Oahu and may have assumed it had taken maximum defence positions when it had not.

Roberts also criticised the failure of the commanding general, General Short, Hawaiian Department, and Admiral Kimmel, the Commander in Chief of the Pacific Fleet, for not conferring and cooperating sufficiently on the warnings.[148] They were accused of having a 'sense of security prevalent in the diplomatic, military, and naval circles and in the public press that any immediate attack by Japan would be in the Far East'.[149] The Commission also found that it was a dereliction of duty that the system of coordination and cooperation was not effective in that they did not consult and confer with each other respecting the meaning of the intent of the warnings as to what appropriate measures of defence were required by the imminence of hostilities. The chiefs were heavily criticised for not appreciating their responsibilities as Commander in Chief of the Pacific fleet or as Commanding General of the Hawaiian Department.[150]

[144] There were six mobile radar units available, but the operatives were still being trained. This was fatal as the Japanese attack was detected at 7 am as a large blob on the screen, but the officer receiving the report from the operative thought it was a flight of US aircraft not an enemy force (Evidence of Lt Col. Tyler, Proceedings of the Navy Court of Enquiry. Part 39. 345–351.

[145] Report of the Roberts Commission. 20, para 11.

[146] ibid 21, para 17.

[147] H Clausen and B Lee, *Pearl Harbor: Final Judgment* (London, Leo Cooper, 1993) 87.

[148] Report of the Roberts Commission. 20, para 16.

[149] ibid 20, 21, para 16. It is fair to say that not all such circles had the same view. They knew war was imminent, but not where or when the enemy would strike.

[150] Report of the Roberts Commission. 21, para 17.

The conclusions of the Commission were widely reported in the US at the time, with most of the blame falling on Admiral Kimmel and General Short, with some blame being attached to General Marshall which was subsequently revised by the Report of the Army Pearl Harbor Board following investigations by Colonel Clausen. It will be obvious that the sending of the final warning message by General Marshall was delayed because the communications were disrupted and the information was transmitted by telegraph then via cable and radio, and in Oahu via RCA transmission delivered during the attack. Had that transmission gone through the usual channels, those in command might have been better prepared.

iii. Report of the Army Pearl Harbor Board

This Army Board was composed of six officers.[151] It heard evidence from 151 witnesses and held hearings in Washington San Francisco and Hawaii. Its terms of reference authorised the board to investigate the circumstances regarding the attack on Pearl Harbor on 7 December 1941 and to proceed against such persons as the facts may justify. Apart from the main hearing, the Board received evidence from extended investigations which had not been given to the Roberts Commission. The Board received an Interim Report of the Committee on Military Affairs of the House of Representatives. They were assisted by the FBI, the Department of Justice, and a Report from the Tenney Committee in California.[152] The Report consisted of 41 volumes and 70 exhibits. The Board considered the background to the Pearl Harbor attack, the events of 7 December story of the Pearl Harbor attack on the day of the attack, and subsequent events. They considered the actions of those in authority in Washington and at the defence of the harbour prior to the attack.

a. Proceedings of the Army Board

The Army Pearl Harbor Board convened 20 July 1944 and was in continuous session from 24 July 1944 to 20 October 1944. It held hearings twice in Washington, DC, twice in San Francisco, California; and in Hawaii. It heard a total of 151 witnesses.[153] Whilst the US had excluded Japanese nationals from immigration to the US to protect American labour it had admitted 160,000 Japanese nationals to Hawaii; all 160,000 of them claimed dual citizenship. General Shorts Alert No. 1 did not disturb this population. The intelligence he received from Washington and from other sources,[154] including the informative local press regarding increasing tensions with Japan, even as late as 6 December 1941, raises the question as to what precautions he ought reasonably to have taken.

[151] Lt. General George Grunert, Major General Henry Russell, Major General Walter Frank, Colonel Charles West, Colonel Harry Truman, and Major Henry Clausen. The last three officers being Recorder, Executive Officer and Assistant Recorder respectively had no vote.

[152] Hearings before the Joint Committee on the investigations of the Pearl Harbor Attack, Congress of the United States, 79th Congress, First Session, Pursuant to S. Con Res. 27. Part 39 Joint Committee Exhibit No. 157. *Report of the Army Pearl Harbor Board.* 25.

[153] *Report of the Army Pearl Harbor Board.* 24.

[154] ibid 43.

The newspaper headlines in question read as follows:[155]

'U. S. Waits Japan Reply' (29 Nov 41) Honolulu Star-Bulletin);

'Japanese May Strike Over Weekend'; 'Kurusu Bluntly Warned Nation Ready For Battle' (30 Nov 41) Honolulu Advertiser);

'Hull, Kurusu In Crucial Meeting Today' (1 Dec 41) Honolulu Advertiser);

'U. S. Army Alerted in Manila, Singapore Mobilizing as War Tension Grows'.

'Japan Envoys Resume Talks Amid Tension'; 'War Fears Grow in Philippines' (1 Dec 41) Honolulu Star-Bulletin);

'Japan Called Still Hopeful of Making Peace with U. S.'; 'Japan Gives Two Weeks More to Negotiations' (2 Dec 41) Honolulu Advertiser);

'Huge Pincer Attack on U. S. By Japan, France Predicted' (3 Dec 41) Honolulu Advertiser);

'Japan Spurns U. S. Program' (4 Dec 41) Honolulu Star-Bulletin);

'Pacific Zero Hour Near; Japan Answers U. S. Today' (4 Dec 41) Honolulu Advertiser): 'singapore on War Footing'; 'New Peace Effort Urged in Tokyo'; 'Civilians Urged to Leave Manila' (6 Dec 41) Honolulu Star-Bulletin.

'America Expected to Reject Japan's Reply on Indo-China'; 'Japanese Navy Moving South' 'Detailed Plans Completed for M-Day Setup' (6 Dec 41) Honolulu Advertiser);

'F. D. R. Will Send Message to Emperor on War Crisis' (7 Dec 41) Honolulu Advertiser).'

Despite all this common knowledge, General Short did not believe that Hawaii would be attacked. His feeling was that the attack would come somewhere in Southeast Asia, and this was also the view in Washington. He also had opposition to the deployment of his forces from certain business and commercial interests in Hawaii who employed Japanese labour and who did not want to offend the Japanese who were working in the fields and in the factories.[156] The Army Pearl Harbor Board considered that factors such as national pride, vanity and complacency, as well as a false sense of security, had their effect on the failure of the commanders in Hawaii to take effective defensive measures.[157]

The Board investigated the relationship between General Short and Admiral Kimmel, and it concluded that whilst there was a friendly and close personal relationship, the professional relationship was questionable. General Short deferred too much to the Admiral, whilst the Admiral withheld information that may have been valuable to Short. A prime example of how dangerous this became was Short's assumption that Kimmel's navy was conducting long-range reconnaissance. Short never checked this with Kimmel despite the seriousness of the diplomatic situation. There was no definitive intelligence on the Japanese fleet's disposition nor as to the timing of the attack[158] without the long-distance reconnaissance. This was supposed to be conducted by the navy. This is as explained by Admiral Delany, who was Assistant Chief of Staff for Operations on the staff of the Commander-in-Chief, United States Fleet, during this period. He testified that there was absolutely no protection or screen thrown out by the Navy on the morning of 7 December, and no attempt to obtain information about the launching

[155] ibid 46.
[156] ibid 44–45.
[157] ibid 46.
[158] ibid 47.

of an attack upon Oahu. He further testified that there were neither planes, pilots, nor other facilities available to conduct and maintain such a continuous reconnaissance to maintain a 360-degree reconnaissance around the island. They realised the danger, but there was nothing that could be done about it.[159]

In sum, the position on 7 December 1941 was:[160]

> No distant reconnaissance was being conducted by the Navy; the usual four or five PBYs were not out; the antiaircraft artillery was not out on its usual Sunday manoeuvres with the fleet air arm; the naval carriers with their planes were at a distance from Oahu on that Sunday; the aircraft were on the ground, were parked, both Army and Navy, closely adjacent to one another; the fleet was in the harbour with the exception of Task Forces included some cruisers, destroyers, and the two carriers LEXINGTON and ENTERPRISE. Ammunition for the Army was, with the exception of that near the fixed antiaircraft guns, in ordnance storehouses, and the two combat divisions as well as the antiaircraft artillery were in their permanent quarters and not in battle positions. Everything was concentrated in close confines by reason of the antisabotage alert No. 1. This made of them easy targets for an air attack. In short, everything that was done made the situation perfect tor an air attack and the Japanese took full advantage of it.

The Board commented that the commanders seemed oblivious to the warnings of 18 October 1941 regarding the deteriorating relationship with Japan. On 24 November 1941, the Chief of Naval Operations informed Kimmel of the outcome of negotiations with Japan and warned of the possibility of a surprise attack. Two days later, General Short was instructed to photograph Jaluit Island in the Carolina group while simultaneously making visual reconnaissance. The War Department sent Short three messages on 27 November, which were received.

The one signed 'Marshall' read as follows:[161]

> Negotiations with Japanese appear to be terminated to all practical purposes with only the barest possibilities that the Japanese Government might come back and offer to continue. Japanese future action unpredictable but hostile action possible at any moment. If hostilities cannot, repeat cannot, be avoided. United States desires that Japan commit the first overt act. This policy should not, repeat not, be construed as restricting you to a course of action that might jeopardize your defence. Prior to hostile Japanese action you are directed to undertake such reconnaissance and other measures as you deem necessary, but these measures should be carried out so as not, repeat not, to alarm the civil population or disclose intent. Report measures taken. Should hostilities occur you will carry out the tasks assigned in Rainbow 5 as far as they pertain to Japan. Limit dissemination of this highly secret information to minimum essential officers

On 27 November 1941, the Chief of Naval Operations gave Kimmel a warning, and that same day, Washington informed the Hawaii War Department that hostilities may begin. In response Short ordered an Alert No. 1, which was aimed at sabotage rather than a full alert. Further messages were received by the navy on 3, 4 and 6 December 1941. Altogether the messages represented a failure of considerable proportions.[162] Whilst

[159] ibid 119.
[160] ibid 120, 121.
[161] ibid 236.
[162] ibid 235–238.

there may be some question regarding some communications and a lack of clarity in the war warning, their reactions were questionable. It is easy in hindsight to draw such conclusions by reading the Reports of the Army Pearl Harbor Board and the Navy Court of Inquiry, the Congressional Hearings and the contributions made by Colonel Clawson's searching investigations for Secretary Stimson. In such cases it is better to err on the side of caution and to expect the unexpected. Interestingly, the judgement of Myron C Cramer, Major General, the Judge Advocate General of the Army Pearl Harbor Board, concluded that if General Short was guilty of errors of judgement for which he was properly removed from command that constituted 'sufficient disposition of the matter at this time'.[163]

In General Short's case, it appears that his failure was primarily a failure to follow instructions and orders from General Marshall, most notably the first instruction, which contained the following directives:[164]

> [66] …
>
> Admiral Stark said that Kimmel had written him at length about the deficiencies of Army materiel for the protection of Pearl Harbor. He referred specifically to planes and to antiaircraft guns …
>
> What Kimmel does not realize is that we are tragically lacking in this materiel throughout the Army and that Hawaii is on a far better basis than any other command in the Army. The fullest protection for the fleet is the rather than a major consideration for us, there can be little question about that; but the Navy itself makes demands on us for commands other than Hawaii, which make it difficult for us to meet the requirements of Hawaii …
>
> You should make clear to Admiral Kimmel that we are doing everything that is humanly possible to build up the Army's defences of the naval overseas installations, but we cannot perform a miracle …
>
> However, as I have already said, we are keeping clearly in mind that our first concern is to protect the Fleet.
>
> … The risk of sabotage and the risk involved in a surprise raid by air and by submarine, constitute the real perils of the situation …

If we contrast the conduct of General Short with that of the Commanding General of the Philippines Department, General Douglas MacArthur, who received the same General War Department information as General Short, General MacArthur testified before Colonel Clausen:[165]

> Dispatches from the War Department gave me ample and complete information and advice for the purpose of alerting the Army Command in the Philippines on a war basis, which was done prior to 7 December 1941.

One of the practical problems on that fateful morning of 7 December 1941 was that the army's access to ammunition was frustrated by safety precautions. Ammunition

[163] ibid 269. The Judge Advocate General also alluded to President Lincoln and how he refused to rebuke Secretary of War, Simpson Cameron for a gross error of judgement. The Judge Advocate considered that if there was a court martial it might simply result in a reprimand.

[164] *Report of the Army Pearl Harbor Board*. 56.

[165] ibid 290.

was loaded up in magazines dispersed over the island so that it could take from a few minutes to six hours to put the artillery in position and ready to fire.[166] The guns were not placed in the right position because of the difficulties in getting access to private land. On 7 December, there were fixed gun batteries in position, half of which were without ammunition.[167] This demonstrates the lack of preparedness despite the war warning and the peril described by General Marshall.[168]

b. The Navy Court of Inquiry

The Navy Court Inquiry was convened in July 1944 to determine whether any officers or serious blame could be attributed to any member of the naval forces and, if so, to recommend what further proceedings should be taken.[169] The Court concluded that a large number of vessels of the Pacific Fleet in Pearl Harbor on 7 December 1941 was necessary and that the information available to the Commander in Chief, Admiral Kimmel, did not require any departure from his operating and maintenance schedules.[170] The Court found that Kimmel was prevented from taking offensive action as a means of defence in the event of Japanese vessels or planes appearing. He had to be careful to avoid taking any action which might be construed as a hostile act prior to a declaration of war by the Congress. It also concluded that prior to a declaration of war by Congress, no blow could be struck until a hostile act has been delivered.[171]

The Court concluded that as the commanders were each cognisant of the measures taken by the other, the deficiencies in material had a direct adverse bearing upon the effective defence of Pearl Harbor. The defence of Pearl Harbor was the responsibility of the army, subject to some assistance from the 14th Naval District.[172] The Court found that the Naval Air Defence Participation Plans were ineffective as they relied on advance intelligence of enemy attack. Admiral Kimmel was right to implement a comprehensive plan for the security of the Pacific Fleet on operations at sea. They were adequate and effective so far as his instructions were concerned. It would not have been practical, in the Court's view, to place all naval planes in the air each day and man all anti-aircraft guns. The attack on Pearl Harbor was unpreventable. No one knew the Japanese force was en route to Hawaii. They found that Kimmel was right not to order routine long-range reconnaissance, although Short assumed that to be the case.[173] This somewhat contradicted the inquiry's finding as to the point of agreement on the measures and communications undertaken. The shore-based air warning system operated by the army was ineffective on the morning of 7 December. The tracking system had no provision for training or tracing planes near or over Oahu or distinguishing friendly from hostile

[166] ibid 114.
[167] ibid.
[168] ibid 56 and 115.
[169] Joint Committee on the Investigation of the Pearl Harbor Attack. 79th Congress, First Session Part 39. *Reports of the Naval the Navy Court of Inquiry.* 297.
[170] *Navy Court of Inquiry.* 318 *Opinion.*
[171] *Navy Court of Inquiry.* 318.
[172] ibid 319.
[173] ibid.

planes.[174] On the morning of the attack, confusion was caused by a flight of B-17s incoming from the US when the attack took place.[175] The greatest damage inflicted on the fleet was caused by specially adapted torpedoes. The inquiry found that such design was unknown in the US. Yet it may be said the attack from HMS Illustrious upon the Italian fleet at Taranto had used a similar type of torpedo. The precautions taken by Kimmel after receiving the dispatch of 24 November 1941 to continue preparations of the fleet for war were sound in the context of the information available to him.[176] Kimmel's interpretation of the 'war message' of 27 November 1941 was based on the same impression that prevailed in the State, War and Navy Departments, which was that hostilities would begin in the Far East.[177]

The Court, however, found that Admiral Stark, the Chief of Naval Operations, failed to display sound judgement in not giving a clear warning to Kimmel during the critical period of 27 November to 7 December 1941 of the information that he had on the Japanese threat.[178] He should have informed Kimmel of the breach of diplomatic relations with Japan implicit in the intelligence he had received and signalled that an early attack on Hawaii was imminent. In Admiral Stark's defence it might be said, as Colonel Clausen later ascertained, that Kimmel had other means of direct sources from his intelligence officers, but that did not excuse Short's responsibility to his men in Hawaii.[179] Despite all this, the naval Court advised that no further proceedings be taken nor serious blame be attributed to any member of the Naval Services. The findings of the Court were subject to a review, and certain addenda were later published. These drew upon further inferences from additional evidence relating to the criticisms levelled at Admirals Stark and Kimmel for lack of superior judgement resulting in errors which may have prevented some of the loss and damage.[180] Despite the review, the Secretary of the Navy, Mr Forrestal, was not satisfied with this and ordered a further investigation.

In December 1944, a further endorsement to the Navy Court of Inquiry report added the Roberts Commission Report, which was augmented by additional evidence and consideration. This concluded that Admirals Kimmel and Stark should have been retired and should never return to active duty.[181]

The final verdict on Pearl Harbor remains in the investigations carried out by Lieutenant Colonel Henry C Clausen, JAGD, on behalf of the Secretary of War, Mr Stimpson. Clausen undertook an extensive and comprehensive review of the evidence of the attack, travelling over 55,000 miles and interviewing 92 army, navy, and civilian personnel in 13 countries.[182] In *Pearl Harbor Final Judgement* Colonel Clausen

[174] ibid 320.
[175] ibid.
[176] ibid 321. Conrad Black states that Richardson (Kimmel's predecessor) had rejected torpedo nets despite Admiral Stark's advice to the contrary. *Franklin D Roosevelt, Champion of Freedom* (New York, Public Affairs, 2003) 688.
[177] *Navy Court of Inquiry.* 321.
[178] ibid.
[179] ibid.
[180] ibid 354, Second Endorsement.
[181] *Navy Court of Inquiry.* p 370.
[182] Pearl Harbor Attack. Part 35. Clausen Investigation. Joint Committee, Exhibit No. 148 (Top Secret).

and his co-author Bruce Lee[183] list the specific charges brought against Kimmel and Short that:[184]

1. they failed to discharge their responsibilities in the light of the warnings from Washington and elsewhere; that they failed to mutually cooperate;
2. they failed to integrate and coordinate their defences and the facilities for defence;
3. they failed to liaise and exchange fully all intelligence;
4. they failed to maintain effective reconnaissance;
5. they failed to maintain effective readiness capable of meeting all possible attacks;
6. they failed to employ the facilities in their possession to properly repel Japanese attacks;
7. they failed to appreciate intelligence and other information available to them.

The conclusion of the Senate Committee of Inquiry agreed that Kimmel and Short had failed to perform their responsibilities in Hawaii.

Many concluded at the time that this was a harsh judgement and that these commanders were scapegoated for political reasons: that the fleet was positioned to tempt Japan into an attack. President Roosevelt had a deep respect for his navy having been Secretary of the Navy under Woodrow Wilson in the First World War. The disposition of the fleet was to deter Japanese expansion, not to encourage it. Whilst the sinking of the ships was an unexpected shock, the damage was mitigated as most of them were salvaged.

Pearl Harbor taught the US a harsh lesson not to ignore the buildup of rival forces nor to neglect its own defence where its national interest was concerned. Importantly, Colonel Clawson concluded, so far as intelligence operations were concerned, that the intelligence services of the army and navy should be integrated. Intelligence should be shared between services without inter-service rivalry or short service periods. It should be staffed by dedicated professionals. What the intelligence services required was imagination and alertness, with the forces ever vigilant. It also required common sense and competence. He reflected that in peacetime, intelligence gathering was considered a chore, so it would not attract the best. The alternative to the best appointments was Pearl Harbor.[185]

The critical evidence against General Short was General Marshall's clear instructions to him on his appointment, and against Admiral Kimmel was the letter from the Chief of Naval Operations dated 24 January 1941 to the Secretary of War that the threats to Pearl Harbor were: (1) Air bombing attack; (2) Air torpedo plane attack; (3) Sabotage; (4) Submarine attacks; (5) Mining; (6) Bombardment by gunfire.[186] That appreciation of the risk was proved correct. The Japanese attack on Pearl Harbor was a setback for the US naval forces in the Pacific, and a day later the attack on the Philippines was a disaster for the defence forces. Of the 600 aircraft, 300 were destroyed by the invading forces.[187]

[183] London, Lee Cooper, 1993.
[184] H Clausen and B Lee *Pearl Harbor Final Judgement* (London, Lee Cooper, 1993) 290.
[185] ibid 297.
[186] *Report of the Army Pearl Harbor Board*. 56.
[187] T Morgan, *FDR A Biography* (New York, Simon and Schuster, 1985) 619.

On 10 December, the British battleships HMS Prince of Wales and Repulse were sunk by Japanese bombers.

Politically the attack united the American people in their resolve that, in President Roosevelt's words, no matter how long it would take they would win through to absolute victory.[188] The losses to the fleet were limited, but within two years America would have 23 battleships, four being of the Iowa class. Despite the losses at Pearl Harbor, the Allies still had three times the enemy strength in surface vessels. Historians may debate whether the Pacific War might have been avoided. It seems unlikely from the course of events described, considering the evidence as to the course of action pursued by the parties. Japan's guilt is clear from her violations of international law, her violation of the Root-Takahira Agreement, the Lansing Ishii Notes, her Twenty-One Demands against China, her violation of the League of Nations Charter, her dismissal of the Nine Power Treaty, and her continued aggression in China.[189]

In 33 minutes at a special meeting of the Congress on 8 December 1941, the Congress passed the War Resolution. It was suggested that even if the Japanese had not attacked the Philippines or Hawaii and the British had to fight over the Isthmus of Kara, then the US would also have fought.[190] Some reflection, possibly, of that old familial tie or common interest that had existed since Canning's secret agreement with President Monroe when Britain had undertaken to defend America in the Pacific and Atlantic against the imperial ambitions of Russia, Austria, France and Spain.[191] If the Japanese had just attacked Malaya, Singapore and Hong Kong, the US would not have been directly involved. A direct attack upon the United States Pacific Fleet base at Pearl Harbor proved to be an enormous strategic mistake for Japan and sealed its fate in what then became the Second World War.

Historians may attempt to predict the future by knowing what a state has previously done, but as Walter Lippmann suggested, the facts of geography are permanent, the movement of history is massive, but behaviour is usually modified: it is not transformed.[192]

[188] FD Roosevelt, *The Public Papers and Addresses of Franklin D Roosevelt* 1941 Volume–The Call to Battle Stations (London, Macmillan, 1941) 514.

[189] In an interview in September 1962 Dr Stanley K Hornbeck opined that there was no evidence to suggest that Konoye would have reversed this approach. See: TM Leonard, 'Stanley K. Hornbeck: Major Deterrent To America. Japanese Symmetry, 1941' (1974) 8 *Towson State Journal of International Affairs* 116.

[190] F Friedel, *A Rendezvous with Destiny* (London, Little, Brown and Company, 1990) 401, 406. Stimson Diary, 27 November 1941.

[191] W Lippmann, *US Foreign Policy* (London, Hamish Hamilton, 1943) 9.

[192] ibid 85.

INDEX

Introductory Note

References such as '178–79' indicate (not necessarily continuous) discussion of a topic across a range of pages. Wherever possible in the case of topics with many references, these have either been divided into subtopics or only the most significant discussions of the topic are listed. Because the entire work is about 'instruments of peace', the use of this term (and certain others which occur constantly throughout the book) as an entry point has been restricted. Information will be found under the corresponding detailed topics. Cross-references in a form such as 'see also *individual wars*' direct the reader to headings in a particular class (e.g. in this case 'World War I') rather than a specific '*individual wars*' entry.

www.ingramcontent.com/pod-product-compliance
Ingram Content Group UK Ltd.
Pitfield, Milton Keynes, MK11 3LW, UK
UKHW020240290926
15470UKWH00002B/653

9 781509 976287